TOWARD RESTORATION

The Center for Japanese and Korean Studies of the University of California is a unit of the Institute of International Studies. It is the unifying organization for faculty members and students interested in Japan and Korea, bringing together scholars from many disciplines.

The Center's major aims are the development and support of research and language study. As part of this program the Center sponsors a publication series of books concerned with Japan and Korea. Manuscripts are considered from all campuses of the University of California as well as from any other individuals and institutions doing research in these areas.

PUBLICATIONS OF THE CENTER FOR JAPANESE AND KOREAN STUDIES

CHONG-SIK LEE
The Politics of Korean Nationalism. 1963

SADAKO N. OGATA
Defiance in Manchuria: The Making of Japanese Foreign Policy, 1931–1932. 1964

R. P. DORE
Education in Tokugawa Japan. 1964

JAMES T. ARAKI
The Ballad-Drama of Medieval Japan. 1964

MASAKAZU IWATA
Okubo Toshimichi: The Bismarck of Japan. 1964

FRANK O. MILLER
Minobe Tatsukichi: Interpreter of Constitutionalism in Japan. 1965

MICHAEL COOPER, S.J.
They Came to Japan: An Anthology of European Reports on Japan, 1543–1640. 1965

GEORGE DE VOS AND HIROSHI WAGATSUMA
Japan's Invisible Race. 1966

RYUTARO KOMIYA, ed.
Translated from the Japanese by Robert S. Ozaki
Postwar Economic Growth in Japan. 1966

ROBERT A. SCALAPINO
The Japanese Communist Movement, 1920–1966. 1967

SOON SUNG CHO
Korea in World Politics, 1940–1950: An Evaluation of American Responsibility. 1967

KOZO YAMAMURA
Economic Policy in Postwar Japan: Growth versus Economic Democracy. 1967

C. I. EUGENE KIM AND HAN-KYO KIM
Korea and the Politics of Imperialism, 1876–1910. 1967

EARL MINER, Trans.
Japanese Poetic Diaries. 1969

DONALD C. HELLMANN
Japanese Foreign Policy and Domestic Politics. 1969

IRWIN SCHEINER
Christian Converts and Social Protest in Meiji Japan. 1970

TOWARD
RESTORATION *The Growth*
of Political Consciousness
in Tokugawa Japan

H. D. HAROOTUNIAN

UNIVERSITY OF CALIFORNIA PRESS
Berkeley Los Angeles London · 1970

University of California Press
Berkeley and Los Angeles, California
University of California Press, Ltd.
London, England
Copyright © 1970, by
The Regents of the University of California
Standard Book Number: 520-01566-5
Library of Congress Catalog Card Number: 79-94993
Printed in the United States of America

In Memory of My Mother,
VEHANUSH HAROOTUNIAN,

and to My Father,
JOHN HAROOTUNIAN

Acknowledgments

This book is largely a product of my years at the University of Rochester, where contact with an unusual group of historians taught me that Japanese historiography must be made comparable to other kinds of historical inquiry, and that it must be accessible to historians in every field. I am also indebted to colleagues and friends who provided me with familiar historical metaphors with which to interpret my new, unfamiliar, historical information. I think particularly of Professors Loren Baritz, Marvin Becker, R. J. Kaufmann, Sidney Monas, Hayden V. White, and my friend Bernard Silberman of Duke University.

On the Japanese side, my debts are equally large. First I must acknowledge how much I learned from the works of Professor Maruyama Masao, of Tokyo University; these works collectively attempt to provide the study of Japanese intellectual history with a structure and operational method. I owe as much to Professor Maruyama's former student Professor Matsumoto Sannosuke of Tokyo Kyōiku Daigaku, whose writings on Japanese social and political thought are models of clarity and imagination. I also wish to thank Professors Sakata Yoshio, Motoyama Yukihiko, and Minamoto Ryōen, whose conversations during a seminar on Meiji history, at the Kyoto University Institute of Humanistic

Sciences, were extremely fruitful for me. Special thanks to Professor Sakata, who directed the seminar and allowed me the privilege of attending.

The United States Educational Commission in Japan gave me time and funds to carry on research in 1963, and the University of Rochester generously provided summer grants and typing facilities. The staff of the University of California Press and Mr. John Pairman Brown, in particular, brought their experience to bear on an unruly manuscript. Finally, I owe much appreciation to my wife, Polly, who took all this in her stride and whose sensibilities taught me more about Japan than I ever learned from reading texts, and to Mrs. Florence Harada of Kyoto, who gave her time in the final stages of proofreading.

Preface

In the prewar debate over the nature of Japanese capitalism, historians tried to answer the question whether the Meiji Restoration of 1868 was a revolutionary event. Among the central combatants, the so-called Lecture Group (*kōza-ha*) saw nothing particularly revolutionary about the Restoration whereas the Labor-Agriculture Faction (*rōnō-ha*) saw in it the beginning of a bourgeois democratic revolution. The more extreme members of the *kōza-ha* condemned the act as a reinforcement of the trend toward political absolutism, and described the Meiji achievement as a refeudalization of Japan in modern dress; the moderate *rōnō-ha* viewed the event as the first stage in Japan's modernization and argued that it was Japan's closest approximation to a middle-class revolution. Both groups, as the voluminous proceedings of the debate reveal, plundered the Tokugawa period for material and evidence to support their views and to show, by appealing to prior historical development, that the results could not have been different.

Interestingly, the view of the Restoration held by historians of the *kōza-ha* resembled the interpretation proposed in the 1930s by writers of a more conservative stripe (*tenkoku shiken*, emperor-centered historiography). Hiraizumi Noboru, a vociferous patriot and a representative of prewar patriotic historiograhy, wrote in an article, "The Meiji Restoration Seen from Japanese History," that the Restoration was propelled by a combination of indigenous forces, which included nativism (*kokugakuron*), the later Mito persuasion (itself a syncretism of Neo-Confucianism and nativism), and a syncretic fusion of Shinto and Confucianism as expressed by Yamazaki Ansai's *kimon* school. The Restoration was also "a natural development by which the Japanese spirit was manifested." Hiraizumi was assured that "this great enterprise," as he called it, was not in any sense a revolution. Revolutions are events that occur in China and in the West but never in Japan. This argument seemed to suggest a common ground of agreement between ultranationalistic historians and Marxists. As embarrassing as it must have been to members of both camps, it raised a profoundly important question about the nature of the Restoration and its generating intellectual principles, which escaped the attention of the more moderate *rōnō-ha:* namely, how did an essentially reactionary and atavistic ideology, *sonnō jōi,* become the motive force of a revolution? The underlying assumption was the belief that, since revolutionary events are progressive and transforming, they must surely be generated by progressive and transforming forces.

From the standpoint of the ultranationalist historians, who saw the Restoration as a manifestation of a unique folk spirit, *sonnō jōi* was considered its most important motivating principle. From the view of the leftist *kōza-ha,* who saw the Restoration as a reorganization of the feudal system or as a new kind of feudal absolutism, the feudal and reactionary character of the *sonnō jōi* ideology was suitably reexpressed in the feudal and reactionary character of the Restoration. For both schools of historical thought, restoration and *sonnō jōi* fit nicely and served, strangely, to support different impulses, even though the ends seemed the same. Yet for those who saw the Restoration as basically revolutionary, there was the paradox, still unresolved, of defining the relationship between the reactionary ideology (*sonnō jōi*) and the revolutionary restoration (*ishin*).

The importance of this paradox was not disclosed either in the tortured dialectics of the prewar debate on capitalism (although the Canadian E. H. Norman hinted at it in his classic synthesis of the debate, *Japan's Emergence as a Modern State*), or in the opaque pronouncements of emperor-centered nationalists. Although they suggested a relationship between the Restoration and the growth of the *sonnō jōi* ideology, neither leftists nor ultranationalistic historians examined the actual relationship between an intellectual experience and a political movement. This failure resulted in a failure to see that a paradox in fact existed. Yet the question was raised.

Nearly twenty years ago the Japanese historian Tōyama Shigeki published two articles on the Restoration and its ideological origins: "The Character of the Mito Learning" (*Mitogaku no seikaku*), and "The Ideology of Emperorism, Expulsionism, and Nationalism" (*Sonnō jōi shisō to nashonarizumu*). The substance of these two articles was later incorporated into his masterful book *Meiji Ishin*. In these articles Tōyama identified this paradox between a reactionary ideology and a revolutionary political movement—but not directly. By taking up the question that prewar writers had ignored, the intellectual origins of the Meiji Restoration, Tōyama hoped to reveal something important about the character of the Restoration. More important than his conclusions, his studies showed, brilliantly I think, that no complete statement could hereafter be made about the Restoration without a consideration of the ideas that went into its making. Tōyama's two studies alerted historians to the historiographical significance of late Tokugawa intellectual discourse, especially the *sonnō jōi* current, and demonstrated its relevance to any effort to determine whether the Restoration was a revolutionary movement.

Tōyama located the origins of the Restoration in the rhetoric of the later Mito school as it was formulated by Fujita Yūkoku, Aizawa Seishisai, and Fujita Tōko. In explaining the reasons for Tōyama's interest in late Tokugawa intellectual history, some writers argued that in the environment of defeat and despair im-

mediately after the Second World War, the study of the Mito
school had been generally ignored even though study of the Restoration was flourishing. This neglect was all the more serious
since, it was believed, this late Tokugawa intellectual experience
was what linked the Restoration to Japan's recent and disastrous
road to ultranationalism, fascism, and imperialism. Just as Aizawa's *Shinron* served as an inspirational handbook for the loyalists
of the late Tokugawa period, it is not surprising that it was a
popular book among military groups in the 1930s. And the whole
rhetoric of Japanese jingoism—*kokutai-ron*—in the prewar period was little more than a restatement of the intellectual spirit of
the Restoration. Tōyama saw this connection between ideas and
spirit, and by labeling the Mito school the enemy in the drama of
restoration, he established not only how late Tokugawa intellectual life would be examined in the postwar historical world but,
and more important, the idea of a continuous tradition informing "modern Japan" and linking the restoration achievement
(political absolutism) to Japan's later development (the emperor
system, fascism, and imperialism).

Tōyama had no doubt that *sonnō jōi,* as a system of ideas
rather than a political movement, was the intellectual motor behind the Meiji Restoration. But he asked whether this ideology,
which led to the Restoration and to the creation, presumably, of
a new society, actually represented a rejection of the feudal system. To this question he argued: "The actual fact is that *sonnō
jōi* thought originally was not a theory which substantially rejected the *bakuhan* system; within its relationship to contemporary national life it revealed its essential feudal substance. This
was not limited solely to the Mito learning. It is possible to say
that this view was shared by nearly all late Tokugawa intellectuals and loyalists." Undoubtedly, Mito learning, which gave expression to the political theory of *sonnō jōi,* was an effort to rescue the flagging feudal effort; it was not a revolutionary ideology
proposing new alternatives. Tōyama put this claim even more
pointedly in his essay on *sonnō jōi* and nationalism where he
argued that the very substance of "emperorism" and "expulsion-

ism" was expended in the restructuring of the established political order. This endeavor was nationalistic in the strict sense of the word, since it sought to stem changes threatening the independence and integrity of the realm. But Japan paid a high price for this nationalistic surge. While *sonnō jōi* provided intellectual motivation for the Restoration, the Restoration itself failed to become a truly revolutionary event.

Tōyama's studies and his subsequent work left unanswered the questions whether the Restoration was a revolutionary event; and, since "emperorism" and "expulsionism" provided its major intellectual motive force (there is no disagreement on this), how an ethic designed to maintain a system yielded a destructive theory of action leading to profound political, social, and economic changes. Tōyama concluded his major study on the Meiji Restoration by arguing that the event and its achievement represented a new incarnation of feudalism in the establishment of an absolutist state. But surely such a view glosses over the profoundly revolutionary changes that in fact took place after 1868, regardless of the arrangement of power. And a vision, a set of ideas, a perception, a quest, must have generated this change.

In response to this problem, a number of writers over the last two decades have proposed the argument that the later Mito learning, despite its emphasis on *taigi meibun* ("duties and designations"), which Tōyama saw as "a rationalization of feudal relationships," gave expression to what Ueyama Shunpei has called "a logic of opposition." This view was notably articulated by Sakata Yoshio in his revisionist attack upon the Tōyama and Inoue (Kiyoshi) thesis in a series of articles which later were amalgamated into a book, *Meiji Ishinshi*. Sakata accepted the identification between the Mito celebration of a status order (*chūkō no michi*) and Tōyama's judgment that such an ethic was galvanized into a feudal theory of action (*sonnō-jōiron*). But he went further when he argued that Mito writers sought, in their criticism of the shogun-first policy, actually to reconstitute the sociopolitical system. In their celebration of the feudal order lay the possibility for restatement and, of course, criticism. This was the meaning of their call to *meibun* and their reminder to the shogun of his role in the ideal arrangement of authority. Responding to what they perceived as essentially a domestic crisis, which they described in moral terms, they made possible a discourse of critical opposition which finally culminated in the destruction of the *bakufu*. In welding moral, religious, and political ideals into a theory of political action, *sonnō jōi,* in creating the limits of a political theory for the first time, Mito writers gave to late Tokugawa Japan not only the idea of political criticism but also the means by which such criticism might be expressed.

The cultural critic Ueyama Shunpei, following Sakata's lead, has recently argued that not only did the Mito learning, in the guise of *sonnō jōi,* offer this tradition of opposition, but the opposition it inspired also gave expression to a bourgeois democratic revolution in Japan. His argument rests on a reading of Fujita Tōko's cryptic epic poem, *Seiki no uta (Song of the Correct Spirit),* which *bakumatsu* loyalists were fond of quoting. The poem, for Ueyama, reveals a spirit which could only lead to a destruction of the feudal order. It is Ueyama's contention that Tōko, in this poem, sought to provide moral and spiritual justification for criticism and opposition. In a passage in which Tōko summons an opaque quote from Mencius, the true meaning of the poem is disclosed. Tōko wrote in his preface that "the true spirit of heaven and earth is vitality and energy." Ueyama has argued that Tōko was trying to capture a sentiment which, echoing Mencius, enjoined men to opposition and criticism. In this interpretation, Ueyama cites the late Meiji political thinker Nakae Chōmin, who equated the Mencian notion of an "energetic spirit" (*kōzen no ki*) with "liberty, morale," which Nakae identified as the origin of freedom (*jiyū*). And freedom is the moving force behind all revolutionary movements. Nakae wrote, in the *Tōyō Jiyū Shimbun,* that ancient man subordinated the spirit of energy to the Way and principle. This is, Ueyama continued, what Mencius meant when he alluded to "the energetic spirit." Now, Tōko explained that the "correct spirit" really amounts to the Way and principle, to morality itself. When such a spirit has been lost, it is necessary to employ "energy and vitality" to reestablish it. In this context, Tōko stressed in his poem the necessity for loyal and principled men to offer their lives in order to realize correct principle, and Ueyama interprets this invitation to selfless heroism as the first step to the revolution which took place in 1868.

There is no straight line leading from the Mito rhetoric to the Meiji Restoration. Despite the claims for *sonnō jōi* and its relationship to the political events of 1868, it is my purpose to show in this study that the intellectual sources of the Restoration did not originate in Mito. While Tōyama is correct in arguing that the Mito statement, as it was expressed in the formulation of the *sonnō jōi* ideology, was an elaborate effort to shore up the *bakuhan* order, Sakata is equally correct in suggesting that this ideology did seek to alter the established arrangement of power in favor of the large domains. But an examination of the political rhetoric of activists in the last decades of the Tokugawa period suggests that though men received their initial intellectual indoctrination from Mito writers, they found it necessary to abandon the major premises of this statement. The final result of their efforts, which culminated in the Meiji Restoration, discloses in fact how far they were willing to go to break with this intellectual tradition. The Restoration was neither the reactionary resurgence envisaged by Tōyama, nor the bourgeois revolution imagined by Ueyama. Yet it was a revolutionary event insofar as writers and activists were able to liberate themselves from debilitating historical and moral associations. And the sources of this break were not in the original Mito formulation but rather in a recessive nativist tradition which writers discovered in the late years of the Tokugawa epoch.

But if the Mito statement on men and politics did not lead to the Restoration, what was its meaning to the late Tokugawa discourse? It is my view that Mito writers, in trying to come to grips with what they perceived as serious domestic moral failure, began a process of politicization that ended with and in the Meiji achievement. By politicizing the elements of an ethical tradition into a theory of action, they offered subsequent writers and activists not so much a workable theory as a method by which to deal with changing political reality. Although events repudiated the contents of the Mito solution by the late 1840s, writers went on to accommodate Japanese society to changes, new knowledge, and new problems. Aided by the precedent of Mito writers, *bakumatsu* ideologues were able to incorporate the datum of contemporary experience into their political formulations and into their attempts to find concrete solutions to the very real problems facing Japan in the 1850s and 1860s. It was this heritage of politicization, inadvertently set into motion by the writers of the later Mito school, which ultimately provided the intellectual motivation of the Meiji Restoration and the route Japan was to follow in modern times.

This book is essentially concerned with the growth of political consciousness in Japan from the late eighteenth down to the mid-nineteenth century. Specifically, its purpose is to show, by examining the political rhetoric of principal activists in these years, how the Japanese responded to new alternatives raised by what they believed to be a conspiracy consisting of progressive domestic social failure and the challenge of foreign assault. In this response Japanese intellectuals were forced to politicize an intellectual endowment that was essentially unpolitical and ethical. Since they saw the terms of this "conspiracy" as a threat to cultural and political independence, their responses were directed at showing how traditionalist ethical assumptions about the nature of political relationships might work under a new political dispensation. While the efforts of these intellectuals seemed to reach out in different directions, generally in response to immediate stimuli, all men shared a common purpose of finding a political solution to what they clearly saw as a unique instance of progressive political failure. This collective effort—if the Tokugawa discourse can be called a collective effort—ultimately yielded a political solution in the Meiji Restoration of 1868. Then, having gone this far, restorers became revolutionaries and went on to create a modern state and society. It is the pursuit of this revolutionary impulse, which undoubtedly informed their purpose and thought, that has directed my effort in writing this book.

Contents

xvii

I *Introduction*

Everything fell apart,
the pieces to pieces again, and
nothing could be comprehended any more with
the help of customary notions.

HUGO VON HOFMANNSTHAL

The twilight years (1840–1867) of the Tokugawa shogunate
were a time when traditional order was falling apart and its
meaning was being buried under the fragments. Elements once
tied together to make a world presented themselves to writers,
thinkers, and activists in monstrous separateness. There was a
classical Chinese formulation to describe such situations, *naiyū
gaikan:* "Internal dislocation leads to external catastrophe." And
this lapidary phrase was clearly seen by many in the thick of
events as naming the nemesis of the Tokugawa house and perhaps of Japanese civilization itself. Toward the end of the epoch,
only the most imperceptive could still believe that domestic
moral adjustments offered any resolution of the threat facing the
country. Few during those days, in their outpouring of rhetoric,
failed to suggest that traditional political institutions were giving
way to the uncertainty of new alternatives. Few could disagree
with the loyalist poet Yanagawa Seigan who, writing more than
a decade before the Restoration, defined the failure of nerve and
the hollow claims of that power (the shogun) which could claim
his life:

> You, whose ancestors in the mighty days
> Roared at the skies and swept across the earth,

Stand now helpless to drive off wrangling foreigners—
How empty your title, "Queller of the Barbarians!" [1]

Yanagawa was pointing at the double failure of the *bakufu*,
the shogunal bureaucracy, to deal with the increasing demands of
foreign powers and with domestic economic troubles. The Tokugawa arrangement of power was proving inadequate in the face
of internal and external problems; likewise, the symbolic framework by which action had been oriented was no longer yielding
norms of conduct. What had seemed to generations of Japanese
to be timeless principles of action and symbols of meaning now
appeared to be irrelevant diversions from appropriate action. Social crises generally occur in times when the center of gravity of
a civilization ceases to be attractive; that is, when the metaphors
governing choice and behavior are rendered obsolete by a new vision of reality. So Talcott Parsons sees a disequilibrium arising
from the inability of a collectivity to achieve consensus on non-
empirical ideas. If the demand for order is met by restating traditional assumptions—in Parsons' phrase, by the introduction of
"non-cognitive mechanisms in the enforcement of uniformity
and stability"—the old center of gravity will fail, overloaded by
the burden of holding too many things together. The end of the
Tokugawa *bakufu* was a time when, in the language of Yeats,
the falcon could not hear the falconer and the center could no
longer hold.

Those who sought to arrest institutional and intellectual frag-
mentation found themselves engaged in forging a new unity out
of the splinters of the sociopolitical tradition. Thus, for example,
while each of the writers of the later Mito school was trying to
resolve a somewhat different problem, their collective effort had
a clear unity of purpose: to locate a new center of gravity for Japanese political society. Although these thinkers rarely knew
where they were going, they knew where they had been. It is the
principal aim of this study to follow the response of these late

[1] Yanagawa Seigan (no title), trans. Burton Watson, in *Anthology of
Japanese Literature*, ed. D. Keene (New York, 1955), p. 489.

Tokugawa ideologue-activists to the demands of social and political order. What is important is not their final solutions (since few lived to see the application of their ideas) but the perceptions of reality which they brought to the task of restructuring values they were unwilling to abandon.

Late Tokugawa Japan, failing to understand itself, was haunted by a fear of the unknown which could not be exorcised even by heroic effort, for it arose from weaknesses built into the foundations of the *bakuhan* system. The first seventeenth-century shoguns, in an effort to enshrine their concept of good government for all time to come, worked out the classical ethics of a natural order in a series of political measures: the seclusion edicts, the hostage system, the arrangement of the domains, the hereditary monopoly of responsible political positions by loyal lords mutually related, countrywide espionage. All these testify to Tokugawa ingenuity in constructing a viable social order to rescue Japan from the uncertainties of the preceding period of civil war (*sengoku jidai*). But the innovations of the Tokugawa by their very efficacy became the system itself, indistinguishable from the ethic that had promised to insure its eternity.

THE BACKGROUND: NEO-CONFUCIANISM AND NATIVISM

The early Tokugawa leadership in the seventeenth century was concerned to save Japan from protracted civil disorder, unplanned social mobility, and material destruction; and thus to ensure a well-ordered and disciplined life. It believed that the turbulence and disorganization of the *sengoku* period ran counter to the orderly functioning of nature, and that, since society was constructed after the paradigm of nature, it was imperative to restore a "natural" order to society. Thus the Tokugawa system, although it rested on the consolidation of family power, was rationalized as a victory of order over chaos in a long struggle toward civilization. The Tokugawa were genuinely convinced that they were recreating an ideal unity amply supported by history. It is this conviction above all else which explains their sponsorship of Neo-Confucianism, with its central concept of a natural order.

Chinese Neo-Confucianists had usually identified the social order with the natural order, but had never fully articulated the metaphysical relationship between the two. The cosmic order was fixed, and the social order was an image or echo of it. The cosmos and society were governed by the same organizing principle: differentiation, or "discrimination." Just as the cosmos was ordered into levels, so society should be organized hierarchically. The capacity of each individual determined how closely he could approach the Way; if all could not be sages, each would seek, in his own manner, to achieve a measure of wisdom. High and low were realities. This discrimination was morally binding on all and was determined by proximity to the Way.

For Japanese Neo-Confucianists, the notion of social order was expressed in the morality of the Five Relationships: the relations between father and son, ruler and ruled, husband and wife, older and younger brother, friend and friend. These relations were the moral ligaments holding society together; they had the authority of a cosmic law because they revealed an absolute morality informed by "principle" (*ri*). Fujiwara Seika (1561–1619), a Japanese Neo-Confucianist, held that human character, because it is informed by *ri*—that is, because it knows the requirements of proper morality—unites the natural world to the human world in an organic whole. Seika argued that man's nature is disposed to goodness because he possesses the "heavenly principle." "If men follow in the path of principle, they will exist within the Great Way. If the heart of man is united to the heart of heaven and earth, the limits of the Way will be defined. If the heart of man passes into the mind of all things, there the Way will be materialized." [2] The heart of man, because it is constituted by the unity of *ri* with human character, knows that it must establish an order on earth that will reflect the moral perfection of the univer-

[2] Kokumin seishin bunka kenkyū-jo, *Fujiwara Seikashū*, 4 vols. (Tokyo, 1938–1939), I, 131–132. See also Bitō Masahide, "Hōken rinri," in *Nihon rekishi,* 23 vols. (Tokyo, 1963), X, 277–287.

sal principle. Men make society (Seika continued), but they do
so out of a moral imperative which is built into them. They are
endowed with the moral obligation to construct a social order
and with knowledge of the shape it must take—namely, one
which will reveal the essential "discrimination" found in all
things.

The process by which principle (*ri*) receives concrete embodiment is, in the thought of Seika, always the same. Man, as the
Great Learning (*Ta hsüeh*) advises, must first "illumine virtue"
because he is innately good. Next he must cleanse his heart and
mind to make it truthful and sincere. Then he must so regulate
his conduct that it will show a truthful and sincere mind. Finally, if man observes the Five Relationships on top of all this,
whatever his status, he can be unified with the Heavenly Way
and become like a sage.

Even though Fujiwara Seika was writing about family relationships, he believed they set a valid moral example for larger
collectivities. Normative behavior is learned first in the family.
And since the social order is an enlargement of the family, the
moral order which keeps the family as a cohesive unity will also
"tranquilize" the realm. The size of the collectivity is secondary
to observance of the proper morality of behavior. "King T'ang of
the Shang dynasty," Seika wrote, "transformed a small domain
into a large country. Possessing the virtue of benevolent rule, he
was able to hold the realm in equilibrium. . . . We will become
as Yao and Shun [the archetypal sages of pre-Confucian
antiquity], and the people will become the people of Yao and
Shun." [3] Politics is the Way of morally pure leaders who can harmonize the inner with the outer. Benevolence is possible if the
natural requirements of order are observed. This heavenly Way
of social order (Seika argued) implies authority. Proper morality
bestows authority on certain leaders to do, to act, and to adjust,
in order to achieve government. Seika was specifically interested
in the conditions of Tokugawa Japan and concerned to justify
contemporary practice by the precepts of Neo-Confucianism mor-

[3] *Fujiwara Seikashū,* I, 247.

alism. So the personal virtue of the ruler is not enough for him. "If the obligations of the lord [to his people] are forgotten, then the domain will tilt; sons will become unfilial to their parents. . . . When there are evil men in authority, then wisdom, power and bravery will disappear." [4] In accepting contemporary political procedure as a datum, Seika established a precedent for later writers; but he also indicated why political reality must reflect the requirements of a cosmic moral order, the Way of Heaven. The lord must possess inner morality, sincerity (*makoto*), and wisdom; and also an outer sagacity, which is found in his exercise of authority. This outer manifestation of authority, as expressing his inner morality, is what entitles him to rule. As for retainers, they are obliged to "exhaust [i.e., practice] loyalty to the lord day and night." There can be no conflict of loyalties; even though they have been taught to "cultivate their own family, they must obey first and foremost the commandment of the lord." [5]

Seika's thought was refined by his student Hayashi Razan (1583–1657). Although Razan was elevated by the Tokugawa later in his career as the official ideologue, his own interest in Neo-Confucianism, like that of his teacher, was always intellectual. But his definition of social and political order coincided with the policy of the Tokugawa; his partnership with them gave a political regime claim to lofty moral order. Assisted by the notion of a restoration of the domestic moral order, the Tokugawa in the seventeenth century would eventually explain their rise to power as the triumph of a universal ethic. Their achievement could be represented as the retrieval of civilization, since it promised the restoration of the normative society postulated by Neo-Confucianists.

Hayashi Razan also asserted that the Five Relationships embraced the entire range of civilized human intercourse; they were eternally fixed. This permanency was explained by the immanence in nature of *ri*, the principle of "discrimination." On the

[4] *Ibid.,* II, 397–412.
[5] *Ibid.*

basis of this assumption, Razan sought to deduce the contours of society from observation of the natural world. He saw nature as *providing the principle of reality*. Hierarchical relationships in a status society were the natural mode of organization, because they reflected the divisions found in nature itself.

Heaven is above by nature and earth is below. Since the statuses of upper and lower have been determined in advance, the superior is honorable, the inferior is despicable. Where the order of the principle of nature prevails, the distinction between high and low can always be observed. The mind of man should be likewise. When high and low are in harmony and the honorable and despicable are not confused, just human relationships will prevail. If human relationships within the domain and realm are just, the country will be in order. When the country is in order, the Kingly Way (*ōdō*) will be accomplished.[6]

Hayashi Razan's celebration of a natural order based on inequality had little to do with the actual Tokugawa arrangement of social and political power. It really reflected his belief in a natural order serving as the paradigm of human organization. Yet it was not a lifeless or abstract ideal. History showed that such perfection had occasionally been reached by sages and kings, but also that men had often departed from the true path into immorality. Razan was close enough to the *sengoku* period to remember its corrosive change and unchecked social mobility. And he saw change as counter to the rhythm of nature; it appeared where the principle of nature was no longer observed. Change represented a descent from perfection to uncertainty, from civilization to barbarism. Razan could confirm the contemporary political leadership in its authority. His celebration of eternally fixed relationships attributed to contemporary social arrangements—in particular to the inherited lord–vassal relationship—the authority of a cosmic framework.

As a Neo-Confucianist, Hayashi Razan believed that the purpose of writing history was to prove the value of social order. A central feature of Chinese Neo-Confucian intellectual activity was

[6] Quoted in Kuranami Shoji, *Edo jidaishi* (Tokyo, 1962), p. 76.

the compilation of histories, especially in the Sung school of the tenth to thirteenth centuries. Now the Sung writers made no qualitative distinction between past and present. If the past appeared different from the present, it was because certain relationships of the past had been abandoned in the present. It would then be the job of the present to reinstate those past relationships, which were regarded as eternally valid. But Sung historians would not have been interested in social conditions of a past believed to be qualitatively different from the present. Rather they looked upon the writing of history as an attempt to recapture the original vision underlying a particular past which they saw as applicable to all times and places. Behind their program for intellectual and political renewal (*fu-ku*, "restoration of antiquity") was the ironclad conviction that past and present were the same; ancient principles of authority could be restored in the present because they were timeless and universally valid. Certainly the immediate past represented a break in the continuity of institutions. The Sung writers saw those universal principles as the best or only means to restore the continuity between that distant past and their present. Ironically, Sung writers had resisted the historical consciousness which in the nineteenth century became emblematic of modernity. Japanese ideologues in the *bakumatsu* generation (the "end of the *bakuhan* system"), schooled in Sung thought, openly acknowledged the discontinuity dramatized by the coming of the West and accepted the uniqueness of their times as a datum of thought.

The usefulness of these Neo-Confucian principles is illustrated by the flurry of scholarly activity in the opening years of the new Tokugawa order. On the one hand, Japanese writers felt the Chinese experience to be irrelevant, being the past of another people. On the other hand, they found the Chinese historical effort to bridge the gap between past and present of inestimable service to the Tokugawa concept of order and authority. The new Japanese mode of writing history undergirds the Tokugawa style of masking their seizure of power with ethical embellishments by the Confucian power of providing political legitimation through the appeal to historical succession. All the histories hoped to show that the Tokugawa departure from the immediate past was not a totally new start, but rather a repudiation of disorder. While in actuality the *bakufu* and domainal lords brought about a fundamental revolution in political society, they proposed to show how revolutionary change had been overcome. The *Honchō tsugan,* compiled under the direction of Hayashi Razan, the *Butoku taiseiki* (a history relating the rise of military families to virtue), and later Arai Hakuseki's *Dokushi yoron* are all good examples of this compulsion to dignify the essentially military basis of Tokugawa power with its crowd of loyal retainers. Essential to this Confucian historicism was the normative ethic which separated civilization from barbarism. It was the purpose of historical writing to distribute praise and blame according to ethical principles upon the rise and fall of political leaders. Past relationships were not investigated; the historian used the past to make ethical judgments for the instruction of the present.

The histories compiled under Tokugawa or domainal patronage explained the rise of the military estate as the retrieval of civilization, the culmination of a long process in which the forces of evil (the Buddhist clergy and their creature, the imperial court, but not the emperor) were overcome. The Tokugawa family was the vehicle of this ethical mission, the last of a line of warriors who had struggled to suppress political illegality and immorality. They had restored "history" to its rightful course.

The military estate, in this instance the Tokugawa, is portrayed as the agent of an ethic and servant of civilization; its achievement has nothing to do with self-seeking power. Tokugawa Confucianism posited an ethical order managed by wise and virtuous ministers who were thereby not in need of political institutions. The Tokugawa apologists saw the meaning of the immediate past as replacement of moral leadership by immoral institutions. This is why many Japanese thinkers failed to present any specific program of political organization and structure, and why the Tokugawa referred to the power which they had seized through violence as an ethical realm. The new leadership

announced that it was its duty only to restore this natural principle to society, "to tranquilize and harmonize the realm." Finally,
the Tokugawa endorsement of an ethical polity (*jinsei*) explains
the attempts very early in the Tokugawa period to set up a permanent political arrangement in which all authority was centered on the emperor. It was important for the Tokugawa that
their victory be placed within the context of ethical legitimacy.
Because their achievement was consistently explained as the restoration of a particular set of principles, the notion of *restoration*
became an established metaphor with specific moral and political
associations.

Now when early Tokugawa writers spoke about a restoration,
they had an idea much different from that of later writers. In describing the rise of the military families and the triumph of the
Tokugawa as a "restoration" of virtue in politics and a return to
a perfect moral order, they used the word *chūkō* (Chinese
chung-hsing). This concept had great resonance in Chinese historical and moral writing, which saw in it a reassertion of talent,
ability, and moral responsibility in public affairs as a means of arresting domestic failure. For the Chinese, signs of collapse were
seen in rebellions which reflected a more basic failure in leadership. But decay could be averted, at least for a time, if the causes
of improper leadership were rooted out. As a resurgence of vigorous leadership, winning for the dynasty a new lease on life, was
called a "restoration" or a "regeneration" (*chung-hsing*). Virtue
was thereby returned to political society, and the promised harmony between the natural and human orders was restored. It was
in this sense that Japanese Confucianists explained the Tokugawa
achievement in the seventeenth century. They saw the final success of the Tokugawa house as the outcome of the long rise of
the military estate and its struggle to restore harmony to the
human order. They argued that the requirements of the moral
order were symbolized by the emperor; when they spoke of hon-
oring the emperor they meant maintaining the domestic social
order which the Tokugawa were commissioned to "tranquilize"
and "administer." This concept of restoration—*chūkō*—demanded

neither a radical overhaul of political institutions nor a repudiation of imperial leadership; it identified the reassertion of morality with the reemergence of talented and able men (*jinzai*) to positions of political responsibility. And thus the Tokugawa, in the hands of Neo-Confucian writers in the seventeenth century, were transformed from illiterate sword-fighters into refined and literate mandarins.

This notion of "talent and ability" bound up with the achievement of *chūkō* survived throughout the Tokugawa period, but was given new expression in the *bakumatsu,* when activists linked it to their theory of political change. The idea of regeneration (*chūkō*) was abandoned in favor of another concept of restoration which, while it also had Chinese origins, was immersed in native Japanese associations. This was the notion of *fukko,* literally "a return to antiquity," which acquired, as a result of Tokugawa nativists (*kokugakusha*), a more specific meaning. With them, *fukko* meant restoration of the political society of antiquity (which preceded both the coming of Chinese civilization to Japan and the rise of the military estate), and in particular, direct imperial rule. This notion stressed the sacral right of the emperor to rule directly, as he had in ancient Japan. A call for *fukko* did not mean regeneration of domestic society and its realignment with the natural moral order; it meant, as in the Meiji Restoration, reorganization around a new principle of political authority. This distinction is crucial to Tokugawa thought. The intellectual history of this period is a transition between these two metaphors of restoration. In calling for a regeneration of the human order, *chūkō* reminded men of the lessons of history; but a summons (*fukko*) to restore antiquity liberated men from history into the undemanding and flexible world of myth. A restoration of the latter kind could only mean a completely new political order, free from all of those historical associations which *chūkō* required as a condition of its success.

Seventeenth-century writers took for granted the concept of restoration as *chūkō*. At the same time they combined elements of the native experience, Japanese mytho-history, with Chinese

ethical theory, and felt no conflict. But this early intellectual encounter with nativism was the first step to a theory of restoration
(*fukko*) based on an appeal to ancient Japan and its political and
psychological associations. In citing examples of the native experience, writers believed they were only providing particular confir-
mation of universal Chinese truths; yet this early use of mytho-
history in the service of Chinese theory would later be elevated to
major importance by writers seeking an alternative to the
Chinese style of life. They simply accepted the shogun's procedure of relating his rule to the imperial house and justifying his
claims over the several daimyo (domainal lords) in the name of
the emperor. The Tokugawa had revived a long-abandoned principle of civilized social life, and their celebration of the emperor
announced this "restoration."

Neo-Confucianists had long argued that the emperor was the
carrier of political authority by virtue of the assumption that he
possessed perfect virtue. In this view, the emperor, although he
represented the principle of political authority, was imprisoned
in his role. Since his power depended on his virtue, he was forced
to play an impossible moral role that was not of his own making; and since failure in virtue resulted in a loss of political
power, inactivity was the only guarantee of survival. This concept of kingship, inspired by Chinese experience, created and justified a bureaucracy underneath it, and thus satisfied the Tokugawa arrangement of power. History showed that an emperor
was necessary, but also that he would not participate directly in
the political process. Japanese practice had come closer to this
ideal than Chinese. Tokugawa theory still had to admit the possibility that an emperor, through his power to confer titles, might
withdraw his ministers. But unlike the Chinese, few Japanese
writers seriously considered this problem. While most Japanese
writers in the seventeenth and eighteenth centuries removed the
emperor from the active world of political affairs, none that I
know of denied to his *role* an indispensable place. Just as the sun
and moon were essential to the cosmic order, so the emperor was
essential to the social order. Early Tokugawa ideologues thus

had to include the restoration (*chūkō*) of imperial authority (which meant return to the proper ethical basis of civilized life) in any statement about organized political society.

The emperor was of supreme importance to those aristocratic houses near enough to the top of the hierarchy to have their status defined in terms of court rank. Although power rested on military strength and on ownership of land, the social organization was a complex court society in which positions were determined by proximity to the emperor. The Tokugawa were seen as merely fulfilling the duties assigned to their office when they restored rank to society. But since only the emperor could confer titles, the principle of imperial rule had to be retained as a guarantee of eternal order, even though as a distinct personality he was removed (in the words of Maki Izumi, at a later date) "to an existence beyond the clouds." [7] When Tokugawa Neo-Confucianists took a divinely appointed imperial line from native mythohistory and combined it with a universal Confucian principle of ethicopolitical rule, they denied the emperor any personality or direct involvement in politics. Although the *bakufu* rescued the emperor and his court from their oblivion in the preceding *sengoku* period, it insulated him from politics and power. The Imperial Palace in Kyoto (Goshō) and the great villas, such as the Katsura and Shugakuin, show how far the Tokugawa underwrote imperial grandeur; at the same time these architectural masterpieces were prisons from which only fire or death offered escape.

In the early seventeenth century, Confucian ideologues put together a syncretic theory of restoration (*chūkō*) that would serve Japan until the opening of the country in 1854. This theory saw the Tokugawa restoration of the ethical principle of imperial rule as having arrested a decay in progress since the eighth century. A composite of several writers (Hayashi Razan, Kumazawa Banzan, Yamazaki Ansai) would go as follows: The Imperial Way which was the ideal of Confucianism was virtually identical

[7] Matsumoto Sannosuke, "Sōnjō undō ni kindaiteki seiji ishiki no keisei," in *Meiji ishinshi no mondaiten,* ed. Sakata Yoshio (Tokyo, 1962), pp. 134–135.

to the spiritual foundations of the Japanese state—namely, the descent of the first emperor from the national deities; the divine origin of the realm was a guarantee of righteousness. This Imperial Way, practiced in antiquity, had suffered progressive degeneration since the Nara and Heian periods of the eighth to twelfth centuries. This decay was caused by the spread of an alien religion, Buddhism, which eclipsed the national spirit (*kokusui*) and caused degeneration. The political consequences were spread across history: loss of imperial virtue, weakening of the imperial policy, takeover by the Fujiwara regents, the insidious superstitions promoted by the Buddhist clergy to acquire political influence, disruption of political tranquillity, hardships among the people. Good Confucians like Kumazawa and Yamazaki saw the destruction of a secular polity, which they called "benevolent government" (*jinsei*), by the wiles of religion, magic, and superstition. The triumph of a military polity (*buke seiji*), the theory continues, reminded Japanese of the true tradition. The establishment of the *bakufu* rescued the imperial way (*ōdō*) from the decaying court government and restored the legitimate principle of political authority. The military estate restored the only possible political organization, the *jinsei:* an ethical realm based on the righteousness of the imperial way. The political organization ultimately adopted by the Tokugawa—the *bakuhan* system, a balance of centralized and decentralized elements—became the concrete manifestation of this "benevolent polity" operating under imperial sovereignty. Tokugawa Confucianists explained the Tokugawa achievement as the last stage in the process of returning authority to the emperor begun by the first military families in the twelfth century.

Although Tokugawa writers wished to validate only a principle of political authority, even this acknowledgment compelled them to admit that the emperor was the hidden center of gravity in all political arrangements, and also that he never participated in actual decision making, but only authenticated. Despite the guarantee of eternity that this view of politics offered to Tokugawa Confucianists, it contained the potential for destroying the very system supporting it. In the declining years of the Tokugawa shogunate it was not the concept of an emperor that was discovered and subsequently restored by loyalists, for it had never really been lost. Rather, writers investigated possibilities involving his relationship to authority, in response to pressing political demands which the Tokugawa order was unable to meet. What resulted was an emperor liberated from his universal ethicopolitical moorings, a personality capable of participating directly in the making of history. Restoration of the emperor in this sense was no part of the program envisaged by early Tokugawa Confucianists. In fact it was not a very Confucian idea at all.

Tokugawa ideologues could not help but make a distinction between an emperor who *has* authority (as *principle* of politics) and one who *is* authority (as *principal* in politics). At the core of Confucian political thought was the idea of the king who by virtue of his morality possessed absolute authority. But he was a prisoner of his own morality since, as the Chinese proverb had it, heaven dispenses and heaven withdraws and would punish his dereliction by natural disaster or war. An emperor who *has* authority fitted the requirements of the "imperial way" (*ōdō*, Chinese *wang-tao*), the classical Confucian notion of kingship based on consensus. But the concept of an emperor who *is* authority raised the thorny problem of his divinity. Moreover, the notion of an emperor supported by Confucianists was required by the established political order, the *bakuhansei*: shogunate and domain. The alternative concept, which came to be called *sonnō-ron* ("reverence for the emperor") by restorationists in the 1860s, meant both return to direct imperial authority and dismantling of the Tokugawa *bakufu*.

Early Tokugawa writers went to scholastic extremes to show that the emperor was known only by his virtue. Some suggested that the notion of his divinity, forced on them by his special relationship to the national deities, was merely a label for superior virtue. Thus Hayashi Razan's equation (in his *Jimmu tennōron*) of the emperor's three virtues with the three items of the divine regalia was in effect a desacralization of the regalia. More explic-

itly, Kumazawa Banzan (in the *Shūgi washo*) claimed that the
military families, while continuing to recognize imperial preroga-
tives, had transferred their prior veneration for the emperor to
virtue itself. And among these thinkers none went as far as Satō
Naokata (1650–1719) in reducing the human proportions of emperorship to the more rational principle of virtue. Of all Tokugawa Confucianists, Satō was the most radical in his insistence
that the emperor played no effective role whatsoever in the administration of political society. "No other basis of politics exists," he wrote in his *Gakudan zatsuroku,* "than the resolution of
men who are the lords of the realm." [8]

Such writers argued relentlessly that ethics was the only rational principle of politics, and linked political procedure to what
they called the management of the Way. Acquiescence of the emperor in the demands of virtue was the criterion of proper political conduct for him. Virtue as regulative principle was prior and
superior to all leadership, including the emperor; failure to meet
the requirements of virtue diminished his political authority and
order in general. In this sense Confucianism is the highest expression of the bureaucratic ethic (as much Chinese political history
shows), and hence the Tokugawa were willing to transform
their role from military estate to administrative class. The rewards for accepting this transformation were high for the bureaucrats, since this ethic located authority outside the actual administrative system; if the system broke down it was the fault
not of the managers but of the emperor. When the Tokugawa
modestly announced that they were restoring virtue to politics,
they also reinstated the emperor to a position of showy eminence,
even though he was removed from active participation in political affairs. Through their retrieval of the emperor, who symbolized the moral order, the Tokugawa were saying that the emperor and virtue are one and the same thing.

Most Confucian writers in the early Tokugawa period agreed
with Fujiwara Seika on the essential elements of civilized life.

[8] Quoted in Matsumoto Sannosuke, *Kokugaku seijishisō no kenkyū*
(Osaka, 1957), p. 13.

He wrote in the *Chiyo motokusa* that "in the Way there are no marvels, no mysteries. There is only clear virtue, families and people, truth and sincerity, loyalty, the Five Elements, and the Five Relations. When the corrected heart [of the rulers] is extended to the people, then the realm will flourish." [9] Politics for such theorists, was at best a reflection of the "corrected heart." There could never be any conflict between morality and politics; and since morality was prior to all other considerations, politics must be the active exercise of moral tenets in the administration of human affairs. The Way was morality, and it established the task of any who sought to rule. The ruler would be known by his "corrected heart" and his perfect morality, and this in turn would be reflected among the people. His superior morality, springing from knowledge of the Way, is sufficient pledge for political order; and once the ruled are exposed to "clear virtue and sincerity," the "eternity of the realm" will be assured. Hayashi Razan was even more pointed. "How and where will politics be found?" he asked. "Keep it in your bosom and you will subject the whole realm (*tenka*)." [10] If politics is no more than laws and institutions, it proclaims failure of ethical example and decline from civilized life. Rather, politics is the subjugation of the ruled by the ruler, not through force or coercion, but through the exercise of virtue.

But how can this ruler who is at the top be followed naturally and voluntarily by those who are at the bottom? Satō Naokata answered this question by saying that politics does not exist apart from the ruler who possesses virtue. "There is no other basic principle of politics than the intention of the people who are the lords of the realm." [11] In order to follow the example of men whose heart and mind are corrected, "those who are below must exhaust their every effort." That is, the ruled must submit voluntarily to superiors (the shogun and the several daimyo) who

[9] *Fujiwara Seikashū*, II, 401.

[10] Quoted in Matsumoto, *Kokugaku seijishisō*, p. 13.

[11] Inoue Tetsujirō, ed., *Nihon rinri ihen*, 10 vols. (Tokyo, 1901–1903), VIII, 39.

through self-cultivation have achieved a superior normative morality which deserves to be obeyed. The morality achieved by the ruler, which constitutes his right to rule, becomes the basis of social organization and acquiescence. His morality is not a personal possession but an instrument of public discipline and control. The private morality of the sage, reached through cultivation and purification, becomes the public morality of the masses. By the acquisition of an inner (*nai*) moral perfection, some men are entitled to tranquilize the outer world (*gai*). And the masses submit voluntarily to the ruler, through reverence and respect (*kei*).

There is an old proverb which Japanese Confucians were fond of quoting: "If a ruler upholds righteousness, all of his subjects will pay homage to him just as the moon does to the sun." Politics is possible wherever the ruled willingly submit to superior morality. But paradoxically the result of this state of affairs is the annihilation of politics. If it is impossible to imagine a people's will independent of the ruler (as Neo-Confucianists never tired of arguing), it is also impossible to imagine the need for techniques of political control. In a polity so conceived, there is no need for specific forms of organization, which would just imply the loss of morality and example. Institutions, rules, instruments of control, reveal only a reliance on force and coercion.

In the absence of political organization, what guarantee did the virtuous ruler have that the ruled would willingly fall into line? The instrument at his disposal to achieve what the Chinese called a *chih-kuo p'ing t'ien-hsia* ("correction of the state by tranquilizing the world") was moral training and instruction, Japanese *shūshin*. The ruler was really a sage, whose purpose was to instruct those not naturally able to achieve virtue through meditation and purification. Just as it was natural to distinguish between the morally superior and the others, it was also natural to expect the differentiation of society into mutually exclusive social categories. Despite the functional nature of class organization, the crucial division within society was according to status groupings between ruler and ruled, since the basis of all relationships was morality itself. Long before the Tokugawa came to power,

Mencius had argued that those who work with their mind should rule, while those who work with their bodies should be ruled by others. Tokugawa ideologues modified this concept to state that all classes from peasant down to artisan and merchant had to be taught morality by those who are at the top. The trouble with such political theorizing is that it endowed nature with normative status and required human society to use these norms as the basis of all organization. It also required the ruled to internalize the public morality which the ruler had achieved privately. No provision was made for the culmination to which the theory itself pointed: a higher stage in the development of humanity when the ruled might themselves become rulers. Instead, Tokugawa Confucianists resorted to propriety and ritual as a substitute for the internalization of morality among the people.

Rather than avoid politics by an internal morality, the Neo-Confucianists created even stronger instruments of political control. And the most important questions to them were these: Must the private morality of the sage become the basis of the ruler's political behavior? Or could his behavior be its own justification? According to the answer, we see Japanese thinkers dividing into one school of political moralism and another of political realism. The first called for a political order steeped in morality; the second liberated politics from moral norms. The first sought to realize norms extracted from nature; the second made its norms from reality, whatever it might be. The first optimistically enjoined the ruler to be a sage first, who, in spreading morality, would not need political institutions; the second encouraged him to use any institutions or laws needed to preserve his order and himself in a position of leadership. The former stressed virtue, the latter power. A political order organized upon the moral principles of nature looked to natural achievement, while the latter celebrated the work of the ruler as an artificial construct (*sakui*) necessary to its concept of power. The first concentrated on the virtuous ruler and his role; Neo-Confucianism spoke much about rulers and little about the ruled. The second was concerned with means to keep the ruled, the ruled.

This contrast between opposing concepts of political organization and leadership was the subject of an interesting dialogue between the aging Ieyasu (1542–1616), the first Tokugawa shogun, and his chief ideologue, Hayashi Razan.[12] They speculated over the relationship between the mean (*chū,* Chinese *chung*) and authority (*ken,* Chinese *ch'uan*): Was it proper to exercise authority without recourse to the mean of morality? Ieyasu wanted to know if the mean and authority might become either good or bad, and cited the famous case of T'ang and Wu, out of China's legendary past, who overthrew their lord. While the act of a vassal overthrowing his lord is bad, its results were good. Ieyasu, perhaps mindful of his own stormy rise to power, argued that the mean was neither good or bad; it was rather the norm that is established once power is seized and political society consolidated. Razan argued that "men who possess the mean [morality] are good. With principle they relate all things to loyalty. When they employ this principle they are good; when they do not, they are evil." Finding himself in an intellectual corner, Razan argued that T'ang and Wu, knowing the requirements of loyalty, justified their actions by claiming they were obeying the will of heaven. Their act did not betray any private selfishness, even though disloyalty usually is an expression of such human weakness. "But then how did a bad act become good?" Razan asked rhetorically, and answered "T'ang and Wu possessed both virtue (*chū*) and authority." Razan was simply affirming the classical theory which sanctions the transfer of the heavenly mandate; but he was careful, like all Confucianists, not to invite others to employ the claims of *ken,* even though Ieyasu's military success was closer to the example of T'ang and Wu than to the ideal expectations associated with *chū.*

But the problems raised by Ieyasu (and his successor Hidetada) were irrelevant in the Tokugawa discourse of the seventeenth century. The example of Ieyasu's brilliant take-over was still fresh, and the echoes of power still audible to ideologues in these years. Seventeenth-century Neo-Confucianism sought to

[12] See Bitō, *op. cit.* (n. 2 above), pp. 288–293, for a very incisive discussion of this "dialogue."

provide Tokugawa society a guarantee of eternity while that society was still being constructed. The system most writers described was thought a natural one, informed by the reality-principle of nature itself; it showed none of the contradictions that
later writers were to expose. Yet even the work of such early
writers as Yamaga Sokō, Yamazaki Ansai, and Kumazawa Banzan reveal a disparity between aspirations to a virtuous and
benevolent natural polity and the harder reality of actual Tokugawa life. In time, the policies undertaken by the *bakufu* to diminish the strength of the lords and their retainers, and to exact as
much as it could from the peasantry, made this disparity more
evident. From the beginning of the *bakuhan* order, policies were
designed to fulfill not the expectations of ideology but the concept of continuous control. These policies resulted in changes that
never could have been anticipated by the ideologues who had
seen the policies as expressions of perfect morality and virtuous
polity: for example, the removal of the samurai from the land
and castles, the burdensome system of "alternate hostages" (*sankin kōtai*), the impoverishment of the daimyo and samurai class,
the estrangement of a depressed peasantry, and the growing affluence of a socially inferior merchant class.

Neo-Confucian writers in the seventeenth century had absorbed into their thinking only the moral assumptions underlying the Tokugawa arrangement of power. Since they accepted
the Tokugawa regime as the perfection for which society was designed, they could not admit the possibility of change or process.
They could not take into account the practical consequences of
Tokugawa policies. For example, as soon as chronic economic
change was an evident fact, they had no course but to reassert rational ideal norms that, in the eighteenth century, would keep
getting further and further from what was really happening.
They could only adjust to change by radically altering their
model of society to account for the widening breach between
ideal expectations and the actual consequences of Tokugawa policies. Such a revision in Neo-Confucianism could not be carried
out by the effort of writers such as Yamazaki and Asami Keisai

to show how the nativist tradition of Japanese mytho-history had conserved the classical ideals of China. The break from ortho-doxy only came when Ogyū Sorai (1666–1728), responding to the signs of social and economic failure in the eighteenth cen-tury, mounted an assault against the normative claims of official Neo-Confucianism and enunciated a powerful relativism which made possible a new kind of political leadership opening the way for a politics liberated from moralism. Paradoxically, Ogyū never explicitly articulated either a theory of imperial restoration or a new concept of political leadership.

Ogyū Sorai claimed that the Way (*tao*) was a fiction used by men to legitimize their acquisition of power. And his discovery of laws of historical change enabled him to develop a theory of political change; he saw history as a constant series of discontinu-ities. Ogyū also returned to the most ancient sources (*kogaku*) of China's past in his search for undistorted political and historical truths, and found the notion of creative leaders who, in each age, made their own moral codes. Once the sages of China's antiquity had done this for their own times, their norms were given the au-thority of a universal ethic; but this was not the intention of the sages, Ogyū held. "The Way," he believed, was merely the name that men had given to their political inventions. It was not a preexisting fixed pattern which men were obliged to follow in the same manner in all times and places, nor was it an inner mo-rality inducing the rulers to teach. Rather, it was simply the ex-ternal technique used to cover up the fact that *men made norms.* Only the spirit, not the letter, of antiquity could serve the pres-ent. "When antiquity is not known, neither will the present be. When the present is not grasped, neither will the past be." [13] The spirit of antiquity, Ogyū wrote, teaches men that they must destroy old norms to create new norms. Statesmen in any age must keep in mind the achievement of the sages, but they must also include the datum of contemporary experience in their for-mation of norms and policies.

Important to Ogyū's analysis is the notion of a creative leader:

[13] Quoted in Tahara Tsuguo, *Tokugawa Shishōshi kenkyū* (Tokyo, 1967), p. 256.

a political personality who, in imitation of the sages of China's antiquity, establishes laws and institutions without seeking legitimation for them either in nature or in heavenly principles (*tendō*). Such a creator, he believed, was a necessity for his times. He saw the early Tokugawa shoguns as creators of new norms, but he felt that this truth had been obscured by the changes of times and by Neo-Confucian rhetoric. "It was not the Way of Heaven," Ogyū stated, "that divided society into samurai, peasant, artisan, and merchant and established the Five Relations. Rather the Way is that which is made by the sages in order to tranquilize the people." [14] Tokugawa society was virtually created by a dominant personality, Ieyasu, who knew what had to be done. Ogyū knew that in certain times and places creative political leaders would emerge, "make an inventory of contemporary historical circumstances," incorporate their perceptions into the formation of polity, and then use a wide range of institutions to maintain political order. Ogyū was calling for a leader to erect a system of control embodying his own insights. And he had a specific candidate in mind, the eighth shogun, Yoshimune. There is little doubt that he was affirming contemporary leadership, yet he did deliver to later political discourse a powerfully discordant concept. In providing an alternative to the Neo-Confucian ideal of the moral sage who teaches rather than rules, Ogyū was preparing the ground for a new kind of leadership. Owing to his unshakable love for the Chinese classics and sages and his genuine devotion to the Tokugawa arrangement of power, Ogyū never went beyond raising speculative possibilities. He spoke only of the Chinese world and this made his writing oddly out of place in Tokugawa Japan. When the nativists (*kokugakusha*) replaced Ogyū's archetypal Chinese sages with a truly Japanese emperor, the real potentiality of his thought was realized. Without becoming a seditionist, Ogyū wrecked the Neo-Confucian paradigm; he transformed a moral ruler-teacher with innate political authority into a politician liberated from an impossible moral role to create norms and institutions suitable for his own times.

[14] Inoue, *Nihon rinri ihen*, VI, 22ff. This is the central argument of Ogyū's philosophic essay, "Discrimination of the Way" (*Bendō*).

Ogyū Sorai never adequately exploited his scholarly method of return to ancient texts which stripped restoration of historical associations. Nor did he fully develop his notions of change and creative political leadership. Rather, it was the *kokugakusha*, especially Motoori Norinaga, the most gifted of all, who creatively adapted Ogyū's vision to the material of native experience. Inspired by Ogyū's advice to return to ancient texts for unadorned truth, nativists rejected the rage for things Chinese and went back to the Japanese literary and cultural tradition. This enterprise had effects that were neither literary nor cultural. Besides rescuing the literature and aesthetic of Japan's remote antiquity, the nativist writers fashioned a theory of "return" linked to the reassertion of a Japanese-style emperor. Just as Ogyū had responded to contemporary problems by providing a more realistic attitude, so nativists, who were indebted to Ogyū both for an awareness of the contemporary political malaise and for an intellectual method, responded by a flight from the public world of politics to the private realm of beauty and feeling. The rediscovery of purely Japanese literature gave the eighteenth century an alternative to the public world of Confucian politics, decorum, and rite. The nativist affirmation of things Japanese was a kind of privatization. Ironically, it was Ogyū's philological method that permitted this flight; and while the nativists stressed the sovereignty of the private realm, they also reinforced the world of public discipline and behavior. Motoori Norinaga, for example, believed that a rediscovery of true feelings unencumbered by artificial codes of conduct (as revealed in the ancient Japanese experience by literature only) would dispose the ruled naturally to support the leadership and its policies. Since the leadership drew its authority from the emperor, the ruled would learn how to submit voluntarily to the authority of the emperor and the national gods. The emperor, he argued, is always a reminder of pure feeling and sentiment and of the need to give expression to them. Once these sentiments were liberated from Confucian public norms, then the feelings of people would naturally move toward the emperor. Motoori saw this rediscovery of a truly Japanese private life as a means of enforcing order: mass obedience to public authority. Unpolitical ideas converged onto a new concept of political authority. Somewhere in the process Ogyū's sage shed his Chinese dress and acquired a new set of clothes made in Japan.

Not only did the Chinese sages acquire a Japanese personality, but their age, the Three Dynasties, found a Japanese equivalent in the Age of the Gods (*shindai*). In their rejection of Confucian culture the nativists were bridging a gap in the formation of national personality, caused by the increased Confucianization of society in Tokugawa times, and the routinization of life by those alien norms. The nativists, although claiming to be nonpolitical, were responding to changes they perceived in the social structure. In adopting Ogyū's method, they had acquired a ready-made evaluation of the *bakuhan* system and a critique of the Neo-Confucian theory of Tokugawa society. Nativists continued the process begun by unorthodox Confucians like Ogyū; they differed in their understanding of change. Ogyū saw change as a cyclical affair of ups and downs, fortune and misfortune. The nativists saw change as linear, a departure or a descent from something. They presuppose a three-stage view of historical time. The first stage of pre-Chinese high antiquity is the ideal, because it marks the creation of the gods. The second stage is the descent since the beginning of the Middle Ages; the nativists traced it back to the Nara period of the eighth century. The third stage is the present, which can offer renewal in the achievement of a new life (*shinsei*) based on the ideals of the first age.

Under the authority of this view of history, nativists at first took refuge in the solitary pursuit of "national learning." But later they demanded a restoration in contemporary life by invoking past values now elevated to timeless norms: direct imperial rule and the basic psychological life of the Japanese people. This program, they believed, was of concern not only to a few disinterested scholars but to all members of society; hence their solitary pursuit became the basis of full-fledged political agitation and several religious movements in the nineteenth century. Na-

tivists found an unexpected contemporary use for the myth of origins recorded in the national chronicles which they thought they
were studying disinterestedly. They saw their present as essentially different from all pasts, except for the time, before the coming of Chinese civilization, when the Age of the Gods shaded
into the beginning of the Japanese state under the first "human"
emperor Jimmu Tennō. They saw discontinuity in life as a result
of their studies, which steeped them in a poetic tradition antedat-
ing the coming of Chinese civilization to Japan; and they noted
this break in the psychological sector.

In examining ancient Japanese poetry, nativists caught a
glimpse of a way of life not anchored in artificial and alien
norms of behavior. This way of life was in great contrast to that
of the eighteenth century, in which Japanese were exhorted to
live by customs that had not grown out of their own experience.
The first nativists turned to a study of Japanese poetry before it
was corrupted by Confucian didacticism, and there they found
true and unadorned sentiments which they called *magokoro,* the
"sincere heart." To be Japanese meant retrieving the *magokoro*
of that remote time, the age of the gods; and to be Japanese in
the eighteenth century was first and foremost a psychological
problem, since public Confucian morality threatened to destroy a
way of life more in keeping with their own experience. But any
return to the interior life of the Japanese ultimately raised political problems. Evocation of the society in which the pure heart
prevailed necessarily raised as a current possibility the government of ancient Japan which, nativists agreed, was indissolubly
linked with the psychological life of the Japanese.

This double concern with poetic studies and the true nature of
political authority matured under the greatest nativist thinker,
Motoori Norinaga (1730–1801). Like Ogyū Sorai, from whom
he learned a good deal, Motoori believed the sages of China to
have been mere men who ornamented their seizure of power by
calling it the Way and by asking humanity to accept its demands. In his most political work, the *Naobi no mitama,* Motoori made public his denunciation of Confucianism and the

Way. The sages of Ancient China were certainly men of great ability; but it would be wrong to believe they were like deities (*kami*) possessing miraculous powers. Wise and powerful men won the affection of the people and made sure that the realm was not seized by others. "Now what these sages devised is the so-called Way. Thus the Way in China, in the last analysis, has only two goals: to snatch away the domain from others, and to take care that the domain is not snatched away by others." [15] The Way was a man-made fiction: "Is the Way of the kings of antiquity anything more than the law of that age?. . . All it appears to be is a deception to win people over and control them. . . . It is an evil Chinese custom that men of latter times take the activity of the sages to be the model." [16] Motoori means to show that the Japanese have abandoned the true course in order to imitate false customs. In China, he noted, a commoner could become a king and a king a commoner, but in Japan a divinely appointed emperor had always been the "unshakable truth established since the beginning of heaven and earth." Owing to his descent, the Japanese emperor is beyond good and evil; he is not subject to a man-made moral role. Thus the Way, according to Motoori, can never serve as a fixed ideal to regulate the reign of the emperor. Rather the reverse: the rule of the divinely appointed emperor whose succession has been unbroken for ten thousand generations, the "administration of the country in fairness and justice," constitutes the only standard of political procedure. This was the great lesson of Japan's antiquity, recorded in the national chronicles, but almost forgotten. Echoing Ogyū Sorai's conviction that men are the makers of political systems, Motoori believed that the Japanese emperor since antiquity was both earlier and higher than any Way, and thus responsible for both its contents and its management. The Way and direct imperial rule were one and the same thing.

In Japanese Neo-Confucianism, reverence for the emperor was

---

[15] Koten Nihon bungaku zenshū, *Motoori Norinagashū* (Tokyo, 1960), p. 249.

[16] *Ibid.*, pp. 249–250.

expressed only in a literal esteem for "the kingly way," *ōdō;* the emperor's management of the Way was maintained only as theory. The real task of administering the realm, serving the Way, was in the hands of "moral managers" (*yūtokusha*). But in Motoori and his nativist followers there is a genuine esteem for the person of the emperor in the unbroken line of succession. In Motoori's writings the emperor is transformed from the Neo-Confucian idea of a heavenly *principle* to a *principal* of politics. The emperor's divinity, so essential to Motoori, is the guarantee of his eternity; thus the problem of authority is resolved for all time to come.

This development of nativism under Motoori's direction was assisted by contemporary socioeconomic dislocations. Motoori was acutely aware of his non-samurai background, and showed great sensitivity to the corrosive effects of official morality on social life. We know that his audience, recruited from the merchant and peasant classes, was more numerous than that of his predecessors; this fact by itself suggests the political character of his teaching. Motoori lived during the period when Tanuma Okitsugu was shogunal counselor, a period noted for its corruption and rising social failure. Peasant rebellions, Motoori noted, had become a regular feature of contemporary life. Famine among the peasantry prompted Motoori to remark that the peasantry resembled the sesame seed: both could be squeezed dry and yet yield something more on further squeezing. Everywhere, he wrote, there was progressive disorder and official mismanagement. Motoori did not see in these problems an opportunity for a new political arrangement; rather he sought order within the political endowment, the *bakuhan* order. He advocated a political restoration of direct imperial authority because it promised the popular acquiescence which the Tokugawa regime had failed to win. To restore, for Motoori, meant to conserve; but what he intended as a pattern for the flagging Tokugawa order became the pattern for a completely different political order.

This shift from an emperor who *has* absolute authority to one who *is* absolute authority had several important implications.

Direct rule by a divinely appointed emperor removed the Confucian possibility that the ruled might participate in political life. The incidence of peasant disorder raised for Motoori the threat of mass participation in politics; his imperial theory was an effort to prevent it. The role of the masses in society was to be the ruled. "Whatever constitutes the Way is to be conducted by those who are at the top. All things are bestowed on the lower orders by those who are above them; and people who are below are not the ones who must conduct and decide upon government." [17] Motoori's restorationist government, unlike the *bakufu,* was envisaged as effective without reliance on military force or coercion; for *kokugakusha* believed that the emperor, in his capacity as historical representative of the gods, could induce the ruled, for better or worse, to follow *voluntarily* the ordinances of the rulers. Motoori hoped to transform the country into the emperor's realm and to identify the political process with the person of the emperor. Submission to the emperor was religious recognition of the majesty of the national gods.

The nativist concern to locate the true interior psychological life of the Japanese possessed political consequences. Motoori's studies of the Japanese poetic tradition yielded a number of aesthetic notions. Such sentiments as *mono no aware* (a sense of sadness for things because they will pass) and *magokoro* were employed by Motoori to insure greater submissiveness among the ruled. He saw these notions, which informed the great poetic collections like the *Manyōshū* and the *Kokinshū,* as revealing among the ancient Japanese a depth of feeling not distorted by artificial norms. Motoori argued that this sensibility, if liberated from Confucian requirements, would dispose the ruled to submit voluntarily to the authority of the emperor and the national gods. The feelings of the people toward the emperor as suggested by the poems of the *Manyō* should be reinstated in contemporary life. Freed, people would be able to enter into the feelings of the

[17] *Ibid.,* "Uiyamabumi," pp. 9, 15.

emperor. This affection would prevent the people from wishing to participate in the affairs of the emperor—the political realm. They would bask in the light of his brilliant majesty (for he was the son of the sun), and know the distance between the one who was absolute authority and themselves who were merely subjects. (The implications of this idea were fully worked out in the Meiji Imperial Rescript on Education, which established a national morality founded on this notion of distance and submission.)

Although nativists saw the emperor as the bearer of absolute authority, inasmuch as he made norms, they never thought of him as an autonomous maker of rules. Motoori and his successors were more interested in preserving the political equilibrium of the shogunal order than in providing some alternative. Nativism, in its last *bakumatsu* phase, attempted to promote greater submissiveness among the ruled and especially the non-samurai sectors of society. It hoped to confirm the policies of the regime executed in the name of the "emperor's will." Hence Motoori's regular assertion that "all things come from the upper orders," and his admonitions to the ruled to accept everything as if it were a blessing. When he advised people to observe "the rules of the current authorities" and "follow the customs of the times," he meant that Tokugawa leadership, in the name of the emperor, was meeting daily demands with suitable norms. He also believed he was locating the true meaning of "the Way of the gods" (*shintō*). Neo-Confucianism, based on the possibility of a stable and perfect order, lacked techniques for adapting to contemporary change; but in nativism, contemporary facts could be used to serve the purposes of the leadership through the formation of new norms.

Nativism tried to secure an ironclad guarantee against mass social disorder by voluntary nonparticipation of the ruled; it also sought to give the ruling class a broader range of political action. The Neo-Confucian management of the Way through the exercise of moral principles (*ri*) was replaced by an emperor with human dimensions who based norms on actual reality. This shift liberated political leaders from the lifeless world of ethical abstraction into the more flexible world of fact and concrete values; and it destroyed the Neo-Confucian criterion of "praise and blame," because policies now, rather than reflecting timeless principles, had to be based upon an assessment of contemporary conditions and needs. Motoori and his late Tokugawa followers— Hirata Atsutane, Satō Nobuhirō, Suzuki Shigetane, Ōkuni Takamasa—opened the way for a rigorous political realism founded on an investigation of contemporary society.

Motoori Norinaga was not, as we saw, delivering an invitation to rebellion. He believed he was confirming contemporary Tokugawa rule in its legitimacy by linking it to the imperial favor. For the time being, it had been commissioned to express the imperial will; but his belief in changing realities argued strongly for study of contemporary social reality as a condition of successful rule. And he offered an unconditional legitimation for any political rule, whatever it was, in the imperial will: the emperor made any political regime into an imperial administration. This emperorism, which would be later adapted by the restorationists of the 1860s, sought to recognize political reality as it actually was, not as the fulfillment of some abstract universal principle. Politics, for Motoori, was not based on timeless moral imperatives carried out by passive ethical managers; it was relativistic, changeable, and comprehensible. As long as any system worked, it should be considered efficacious and worthy of continuance. If it failed, nothing could ward off its eventual destruction. The emperor always remained, to make the succeeding regime in turn into his imperial administration. Nativists like Motoori rarely considered the further problem how the imperial administration should be constituted, but they did open possibilities which were explored by late Tokugawa ideologues such as Sakuma Shōzan, Yoshida Shōin, Maki Izumi, and Ōkubo Toshimichi. For the *kokugakusha* it was enough to confirm the existing leadership in its imperial favor. But the suggestion that the choice of leadership depended on "the natural course of events" and political circumstances held out clear hope of legitimacy to any who might contemplate substantial changes in the imperial administration.

These political possibilities of restoration and emperorship lay behind the late Tokugawa discourse over domestic problems, and behind the foreign crisis which culminated in the opening of the country (*kaikoku*) in 1854 and the signing of "unequal" commercial treaties in 1857–1858. By that time, the domestic failure which Motoori Norinaga had perceived in the latter years of the eighteenth century had deepened: progressive economic deterioration among the samurai and peasantry, indebtedness, poverty, the continuing affluence of the merchant and artisan classes, endemic rural outbursts, and ineffective sumptuary reforms. In addition to this specter of internal decay, Japanese society in the early nineteenth century was exposed, by the growing frequency of foreign ships off its coast and by news of foreign adventures in India and China, to the threat of invasion and colonization. Something in the fixed Neo-Confucian landscape was changing. Yet not until the actual opening of the country were men willing to abandon old concepts and believe what they were seeing. This occluded vision was characteristic of several Oriental societies forcibly obliged to respond to a new situation; but the Japanese response was the most rapid and decisive. The Meiji Restoration was brought off in a little more than a decade's time after the first confrontation with a Western nation.

Until Commodore Matthew Perry rammed open the doors of Tokugawa seclusion, most Japanese writers believed that the problem facing their society was essentially domestic, and that it in no way called into question the premises on which that society was founded. Even Motoori and the nativists endeavored to ensure order and stability; and while they may have chipped away at the pattern, they always intended to reaffirm society as it existed in their time. Morality (they felt) was not undergoing judgment, but only the practitioners of morality—men who had willfully abandoned the moral principles which could maintain society in perfect imitation of cosmic stability. This conviction prevented most writers from perceiving the new reality announced by domestic deterioration and external peril. Late Tokugawa ideologues sought only to renew the received political order within received ethical standards. Until 1854 this meant concentration of activity on the domestic problem to the practical exclusion of the external problem. Behind this decision, as we saw, lay the old Chinese formula "internal disaster always leads to external catastrophe." Internal disaster in turn was seen as being produced by moral laxity among the leadership. A society weakened internally would, as Chinese dynastic historians consistently claimed, invite an invasion of barbarians from without.

This problem during the *bakumatsu* generation was first taken on by the writers of the later Mito school: Fujita Yūkoku (d. 1829), his son Tōko (d. 1853), and Aizawa Seishisai (d. 1863). Their solution was presented as definitive, to the generation which reached maturity before the coming of Perry. While the Mito statement in its syncretism shared the new vision offered by nativism, this fact was obscured by its celebration of the Neo-Confucian moral principles underlying the Tokugawa *bakuhan* system. Mito writers were mainly concerned with domestic economic failure, especially at the domainal level. They met this problem with a massive restatement of the assumptions governing life during the Tokugawa period—a choice which inevitably led them to consider the moral requirement of political society. In isolating the moral ligaments which held together social order as they understood it, like good Neo-Confucianists they argued that political authority lay with the emperor, who in turn delegated administrative responsibilities to the shogun. The shoguns, they had learned, were not playing the role entrusted to them: maintaining tranquillity and prosperity. Instead, the shogunate had been pursuing policies which prevented the domainal lords from doing their job. Shogunal autocracy (the Mito writers felt) had been accomplished at great expense to the realm (*tenka*), for it had weakened the domains financially and militarily; it was not only a rejection of the status order, but also a violation of imperial trust. The malaise had been caused by moral indifference; its resolution would be a moral rectification of "designations and duties" (*meibun*) and a restoration (*chūkō*) of the prosperity of the imperial realm—that is, the Tokugawa order. A solution of this internal moral problem, which was defined by the misleading slogan "revere the emperor" (*sonnō*), would allow the country—the domains, really—to turn to the secondary problem of a foreign threat; and this could be solved by a policy called "repel the barbarian" (*jōi*).

There were several reasons for the authority of the Mito statement. Most writers came first to know the crisis through the solution offered by Mito writers. The analysis was backed up by a prestigious domain, long known for its tradition of learning and its place in the Tokugawa arrangement of power. In the 1840s the Mito daimyo Tokugawa Nariaki gave forceful endorsement to the solution. Hence the Mito combination of Neo-Confucianism and nativism imposed itself on the generation of writers and activists growing up in the years before *kaikoku*—who then were left without recourse. Maki Izumi, one of the leading makers of events during the explosive years between 1861 and 1864 (the *Bunkyū* era), was, by his own admission, powerfully affected by the Mito learning at a formative time in his development. His friend Kimura Saburō, who shared his excitement on first discovering the Mito school, wrote of him: "Maki was the man most responsible for taking the initiative for bringing the Mito learning into Kurume *han*."[18] In a diary (*Tempō kanshin nikki*) which Maki kept of a trip he made in 1844, he tells of his brief stay in Mito. By a thorough reading of Aizawa's *Shinron* (*New Proposals*) Maki had become well versed in the main outlines of Mito thought even before his trip. Thus his journey to Mito was a pilgrimage in which he met Aizawa and discussed educational problems. Aizawa insisted that schools must serve as "places which inculcate the principle of loyalty," no doubt recalling the earlier establishment of the Mito domainal school, the Kōdōkan.

[18] Quoted in Matsumoto, "Sonnō jōi undō . . . ," p. 124.

Maki agreed that it was essential to carry this idea out because, he added cryptically, "the times, like friendship itself, cannot endure deep impressions." [19]

Yokoi Shōnan knew and approved of the Mito message early. Yokoi's commitment to it was cemented by a lasting friendship with Fujita Tōko. Yokoi, while studying in Edo during the 1840s, like many of his generation fell under the sway of Tōko's person and rhetoric. To the young men sent by their domains for study in Edo's fencing schools and academies, Tōko appeared an archetypal *shishi* (patriot), since he was both a respected man of letters and an outstanding swordsman. Through Tōko, Yokoi met Tokugawa Nariaki and was offered a teaching position in Mito; he turned it down in order to work out the ideas of Tōko and Aizawa in a practical program of reform in Kumanoto.

Another contemporary activist, Sakuma Shōzan, struck up a friendship with Fujita Tōko and wrote lengthy memorials in the 1840s in the Mito style, studded with passages in the idiom of the *Shinron*. The classical case of a late Tokugawa ideologue who acknowledged his debt to Mito was Yoshida Shōin. During the trip to northeastern Japan (Tōhoku) in 1851, Yoshida, like Maki before him, spent a few days in Mito. There he met Aizawa and Toyoda Hikojirō (Tenkō), spoke with them at some length, and faithfully recorded the highlights of his stay. Toyoda astonished Yoshida by "his extensive learning and exciting discussions," while his conversations with Aizawa moved him to write how deeply he was impressed by the whole experience. "The ways of Mito are a kind of hospitality that touch men of other areas. . . . It [Mito] is a place where one does not conceal but rather gives expression to his thoughts. If someone could have heard the discussion in our meetings, he most certainly would have grasped brush and recorded the way to achieve a strong country and to transmit [those ideas] throughout the country." [20]

[19] Arima Hideo, ed., *Maki Izumi no kami ibun* (Tokyo, 1913), pp. 332–333.

[20] Yamaguchi ken kyōikukai, *Yoshida Shōin zenshū*, 12 vols., 2d ed. (Tokyo, 1938–1940), X, 217.

Upon his return to Hagi, Yoshida Shōin was given ample opportunity to reflect upon what he had learned in Mito by being put under house arrest for insubordination. He summarized his newly found belief when he wrote: "If one is born in the Imperial Land but does not know it, how can he stand erect in the world?" [21] Immediately he plunged into a feverish study of the classical national histories (*Rikkokushi*). In 1852 his enthusiasm for Mito reached heights of uncritical admiration; he tells us that he devoured in one month's time both the *Nihonshoki* (*Chronicles of Japan*) and the *Zoku Nihonshoki* (*Chronicles of Japan Continued*), whose grand total amounted to seventy volumes!

Ōhashi Totsuan, the restorationist of the shogunal capital Edo, tried to give the Mito statement a new lease on life after the opening of the country and the signing of the commercial treaties. He also inspired Mito retainers to take direct action against *bakufu* officials who had undermined the proposals of Tokugawa Nariaki. Ōhashi's restorationism, like his ethics, was little more than an attenuation of Aizawa's central ideas. Finally we should mention Hirano Kuniomi of Chikuzen *han*. Hirano apparently read the *Shinron* in 1858 and was so stirred, he reports, that he abstained from smoking in order to train troops more earnestly. The biographies of late Tokugawa ideologues and activists are filled with such examples of devotion to the Mito achievement; whatever the motive, there can be no doubt that Mito learning reached most quarters of the Japanese intellectual world and strongly influenced the formative period of men who came to maturity at the time of *kaikoku*. Even for those, like Kusaka Genzui and Takasugi Shinsaku, who came of age during the 1850s, the Mito persuasiveness continued to excite and to inspire, to move and to direct. Through personal contact or through reading, samurai intellectuals from the 1840s on showed great dependence on the Mito rhetoric. Few books like the *Shinron,* which gathered the Mito argument up into a classic statement of purpose, have reached an entire generation as their audience, much less provided it with articles of belief. The Mito learning

[21] *Ibid.,* X, 331.

was much more than a starting point in the intellectual adventure of the late Tokugawa period. In its coherence and its synthesis of the past, Mito established a tradition of discourse within which contemporaries (and later writers) would have to work out their solutions. The generation which built a new intellectual synthesis into the Restoration took its selection of elements from Japanese tradition out of the Mito learning.

While the opening of the country in 1854 proved that the foreign crisis was both related to domestic decay and more critical, writers were slow in casting off the spell of the Mito solution. Some items were never rejected; for one, the Mito rhetoric. Mito writers, especially Aizawa Seishisai, used the language of nativism (*kokugakuron*) and mytho-history to dramatize their arguments and to provide bland Confucian moral principles with sacral authority. Moreover this language, stressing the "divine country" (*shinkoku*), the "prosperity of the imperial realm," and similar concepts, was especially suitable to the notion of a new political space, the country as a whole (*tenka*), imposed by Perry's intrusion. While Mito writers had no intention of abandoning the domain for the realm, they inadvertently provided the language for the transfer. Political experience was automatically expanded beyond what Mito writers had open to them at an earlier time, and writers, feeling obliged to account for this change, were forced to come to terms with a new arena of choice. In face of the threat raised by *kaikoku,* the world of the solitary *han* had little meaning to most writers and activists since, as Sakuma Shōzan observed even before the coming of Perry, the threat involved all of Japan.

Over and above the language of myth, Mito writers delivered to discourse the notion of *restoration.* They themselves were calling for a restoration of the traditional domestic order, the *bakuhan* system, to prop up the domain; but their call awoke later writers to other possibilities. Their summons for restoration of the *bakuhan* order was transformed into an active political movement, inspired by nativist political theology, which demanded the restoration of direct imperial rule.

The potentiality of such ideas as emperorism and restoration could not be explored fully until the external catastrophe, in the shape of *kaikoku,* came to dominate the counsels of state. Once Japan was opened to foreign contact, the center of interest shifted from the domain to the country as a whole; and within this expanded political space the notion of an all-powerful emperor and its nativist associations acquired new importance. The problem of *kaikoku* could not be treated by traditional assumptions. Not even the Mito writers had perceived that external threat might eclipse domestic deterioration in the scale of importance. Perry posed a threat of unknown dimensions to the country as a whole. Realizing this, the shogunal counselor Abe Masahirō was obliged to break precedent by petitioning the emperor and consulting several lords. In soliciting opinions from the emperor, who had remained outside politics for well over two hundred years, and from the lords, who in large part had been denied positions of political responsibility, Abe was acknowledging that the foreign crisis affected not just the Tokugawa house but the entire country. The decision about opening the country to foreigners was too great for the shogunal bureaucracy to handle; it was a national affair. While Abe acted merely out of fear and indecision, he recognized something unique about Perry's demands. Japan had been closed to foreign relations for over two hundred years, and Abe did not want the responsibility of breaking a historical precedent of such long standing. He was also fearful of making a mistake, since he knew from recent events in China that there was no second chance. In appealing to both emperor and lords for support, Abe broke with the tradition of decision making and created a new precedent. Nothing in the Tokugawa political arsenal seemed useful in dealing with Perry's challenge. If Abe had followed received practice, he would have driven Perry's ships off. But he knew that if he did this, he ran the risk of recriminations, invasion, and possible colonization. The echoes of British activity in India and especially in China were very audible in Tokugawa Japan. When news of British victories in China (1842–1843) reached Edo it was much amplified; but Japanese officials believed the reports. So Abe tried to make a decision acceptable to the major elements in Japanese society. His action became the object of discourse, dialogue, and debate.

Abe's appeal to the emperor spawned a political movement calling for the restoration of direct imperial authority. His break with tradition established historical change as a new means of validating actions. After 1854, men believed that only the emperor could represent the unified realm and support decisions that governed its fate. Hence the idea of the emperor as *principle,* upheld most recently by the Mito ideologues, was replaced by that of the emperor as *principal.* Abe's attempt to win support from the lords by inviting their counsel actually continued a practice he had begun before the opening of the country. He thereby opened the way for another kind of political solution: "consultation of public opinion" (*kōgi yoron*), broadening the base of political participation. In the end the Meiji Restoration of 1868 represented a confluence of these two political currents: an absolute emperor, presiding over a deliberative assembly composed of representatives of the domains. The removal of the shogunate was essential to the new political arrangement—although this fact was not perceived until 1866 or 1867.

This search for understanding, which is detailed in following chapters, is recorded in contemporary discussions. The failure of the Mito writers (chapter 2) was one of perception; they proved incapable of seeing the changes taking place in the landscape. Perry's appearance sealed their fate. In the wake of this retreat writers were left to their own devices and sought to adapt an inherited rhetoric to current changes. Even in the late 1840s Sakuma Shōzan (chapter 3) was alerting his contemporaries to the problems they might face if seclusion was abruptly ended. A decade before Perry, Sakuma warned his countrymen about the need for military defense and for a unified political effort that would overcome the weakness of domainal sectionalism. This rudimentary state could be achieved, he thought, if the *bakufu* and domains would jointly serve in an administrative capacity for the emperor, whose personal authority alone could hold the various

parts together. His proposal for a revised political arrangement
grew in part out of his advice to abandon "old standards" and
"the ancestral law." His search for a new political community,
embracing the essential features of the *bakuhan* system yet overcoming its sectional limitations, led him to appeal to an authority
higher than "the dignity of the Tokugawa house" or indeed than
"the august Imperial Court"—namely, to the "welfare of the people," which, he believed, was symbolized in the longevity of the
imperial line. Welfare, in his time, required defense, and defense
involved the entire realm. What Sakuma was writing about in
the late 1850s and early 1860s was a concept closely resembling
our notion of a national community, which he hoped would
provide Japan entry into the international comity of nations.

A new political space required a new kind of leadership. The
sages were good men, but their examples were inaccessible to the
present. Rather, Sakuma believed that the times demanded a new
political role. Filling this role was another problem; and in the
end Sakuma, not alone among his contemporaries, was inspired
by his own example. His leader was to be a hero passionately devoted to the political stream but distinct from it, one endowed
with knowledge and a capacity to act under changing conditions.
This role Sakuma assigned to the emperor, who was to preside
over the expanded realm. While accepting the nativist concept of
kingship and the need for divinity as an essential element of authority, Sakuma envisaged an emperor released from the shadowy world which Japanese sovereigns had inhabited from time
immemorial. But here his dependence on nativist theories ended.
Instead of calling for the restoration of an emperor based on an
ancient example, Sakuma modeled his imperial hero on contemporary examples. Since he felt that the new political realm in
Japan would be served best by a leader appropriate to the times,
he drew from recent history the happy examples of Peter the
Great and Napoleon who, finding themselves in comparable situations, went on to make history.

Sakuma's contemporary and student Yoshida Shōin (chapter
4) contributed certain elements to the discussion; but he made

his mark in the field of action, since he sought simply to drama-tize what he was thinking. Yoshida accepted the notion of an expanded realm and the need for a leadership suitable to it. He differed from Sakuma in his call for a movement of "unattached patriots" (*sōmō no shishi*) who would leave their domains in or-der to carry out a restoration of the emperor. It was Yoshida who saw most clearly the usefulness of an imperial restoration to deal with shogunal treason and ineptness in foreign affairs; and while he spared no invective for his enemies, until his last year of life he did not propose dismantling the *bakuhan* system. The reasons for his final defection are clear. After the *bakufu* ignored the em-peror's decree to expel the barbarians and signed commercial treaties with the United States and Great Britain in 1857–1858, Yoshida turned to organizing a "national" group of patriots will-ing to work for restoration before the country was lost to foreign-ers. He believed that neither the *bakufu* nor the lords were capa-ble of dealing with the foreign threat and asked, in a letter to a friend, "If that is the case, where will the restoration of Japan's prosperity come from?" [22]

Yoshida Shōin's goals were unclear. Even when he spoke of a restoration of the emperor, he was more concerned with an ac-tion that would seize power from the *bakufu* and avert foreign conquest and colonization of Japan. Yoshida devoted much of his energy to determining whether men were worthy of joining him in such an undertaking. In calling for a rising of unattached pa-triots like himself, Yoshida demanded fidelity of motive and complete self-sacrifice in execution. This he called loyalty to the emperor—a willingness to act out of selfless devotion, at any risk, to rescue the imperial court from defilement. Yoshida hoped that his own example would constitute a new kind of political loyalty transcending established arrangements between shogun and dai-myo, lord and retainer. In his obsessive search for fidelity and sin-cerity he found a shortcut which set up a direct line of loyalty be-tween emperor and subject. In contrast with earlier accounts of Yoshida, our evidence shows that toward his last days he re-

[22] *Ibid.*, V, 315.

moved all the ambiguity about the hierarchy of loyalty over which his youthful writings agonized. Yoshida was executed before he could translate his yearnings for loyal and righteous action into a political movement, but others followed after him to fill in the details of his vision.

Yoshida's call for an uprising of unattached patriots triggered the restorationist movement of the early 1860s. From 1861 through the summer of 1864 there exploded a rash of plots, assassinations of shogunal and foreign leaders, and larger plans for an imperial campaign against the *bakufu*. These events were centered on the imperial capital of Kyoto, which had become the rallying ground for loyalists bent on serving the expanded realm and its titular head, the emperor, rather than the domain and its lord. The man who provided ideological direction and political coordination in this moment was the Shinto priest Maki Izumi (chapter 5), who had just been released in 1862 after serving ten years in prison for seditious activity. Maki was then responsible for a number of abortive coups designed to bring about a restoration of the emperor and direct imperial rule. His rewards were failure and death; yet his premature restorationism showed, in its very failure, how restoration might work if certain elements in society were mobilized—patriotic samurai, peasants, sympathetic lords.

Maki Izumi was the kind of leader Yoshida Shōin would have approved of. Although they never met each other, many of Maki's followers were originally students at Yoshida's academy in Hagi. And Maki combined the various strands of nativist thought, especially its concept of restoring a Japanese-style emperor, with the work of men like Sakuma and Yoshida, who had dramatized the idea of an expended realm, a new political community. Maki also sought, in his writings before the 1860s, to equip the emperor with human dimensions, since he was to be actively engaged in the political process. Nothing would give greater reality to the idea of a restoration, he believed, than an actual campaign led by a living emperor. Epiphany was important if men were to be inspired for self-sacrificing actions. The emperor had to be taken out of the shadows so that he might be seen. While his divinity (which had to be preserved) had militated against this change in the past, Maki believed in the possibility of a "manifest deity" taking on the new political reality and inspiring men everywhere to follow. If a political movement was to be created, it was necessary to have an emperor who was both distant (by virtue of his divinity) and accessible (by virtue of his Japanese rather than foreign style). The earlier Mito concept of an emperor who merely authenticated the hierarchical order of society was not enough to generate a political movement. And Kusaka Genzui, an associate of Maki's and student of Yoshida's, went further to demand the complete dissolution of "the several domains aligned to the *bakufu* which prevented the association of red-hearted patriots and the emperor." What Maki hinted at, Kusaka made explicit: a Neo-Confucian utopia in which there was only emperor and loyal retainers.

Events were to show that Maki and his fellow conspirators did not understand the times as well as Sakuma Shōzan, Yokoi Shōnan, or Yoshida's student Takasugi Shinsaku. Hence Maki's plunge into restorationism when it had no chance of succeeding; he had no systematic plan. He failed miserably in the crucial item of finding military and financial support. Maki believed that the call for an imperial campaign would rouse men spontaneously from all parts of Japan to join it. In summoning "red-hearted" patriots to leave their domains and participate in a vaguely conceived imperial restoration, Maki and his collaborators also turned their backs on the one source of potential support for such an undertaking: the domain. This is not to suggest that Maki was oblivious to the importance of domainal support, or to the growing strength of the autonomous domain. But early disappointments in trying to recruit Satsuma and its lord in a restorationist undertaking made him skeptical later of securing domainal support. His disappointments also, apparently, persuaded him that he could carry off a restoration without domainal backing. Yet Maki's failure still led to a newly political emperor leading an anti-Tokugawa movement; restorers had to avoid Maki's mistakes. They would have to recognize the tenacity of established institutions such as the domain and the *bakufu;* they would have to admit (at least privately) the folly of a policy of expulsion; and they would have to face up to contemporary experience and to experiment without trying to satisfy the passion for heroism. Maki and his followers, in the end, succumbed to the temptation of going down in a blaze of glory. In the absence of a program they had no choice but to look good as rebels without a cause.

After 1864 the activists, recognizing that Maki's restorationism was only a rehearsal, turned to finding the financial and military support he had failed to secure. While ideologues such as Yoshida, Sakuma, and Maki did not find a political solution to Japan's ills in the 1850s and 1860s, they posed a crucial problem which demanded a response: How could the emperor be related to the growing autonomy of the domains? Or, equivalently, how could the traditionally autonomous power of the domain be absorbed into a new concept of political space? Ironically, the domain had emerged as a strong element in Japanese politics after two hundred years of dependence just at the moment when a new concept of political space was demanding the dissolution of sectional loyalties before the foreign threat. Hence the theory of emperorism (*sonnō*) after 1863 made the *bakuhan* system into a datum of political organization and called for revisions to allow its continued existence under the new dispensation. If the ideologues failed to deal with a new concept of the emperor, a new political space and the persistence of domainal autonomy, it was because they believed the foreign crisis required immediate attention. Paradoxically their efforts generate a more nearly adequate theory of sectionalism. Yet the final settlement of the Meiji Restoration was the work of others. What was done by men such as Yokoi Shōnan (chapter 6), Takasugi Shinsaku, Kido Kōin, and Ōkubo Toshimichi (chapter 7) was to develop a new political vision, which envisaged the overthrow of the *bakufu* and a revised political order based on the most powerful elements in Japanese society. Unlike their predecessors, they were willing to drop the moorings of Neo-Confucian morality, and to act upon an understanding of contemporary reality without relying on precedent. When they called for a new government staffed by "able and talented men," they meant that the measure of able administrators was their "practicality" (*jitsugaku*).

While restorationists had earlier gathered around the unifying symbol of the emperor to destroy domainal sectionalism, they ultimately had to admit that the most powerful force in society was the traditional authority of the *han*. After the failure of the restorationist coups there was a retracing of steps. Men like Takasugi, Yokoi, and Ōkubo were willing to promote a renewed sectionalism as an alternative to the "breach of conduct represented by the expulsionist policy." By this charge they meant that expulsionism, an integral part of the earlier restorationism, led to the dangers of Maki's attempted coups and to increased foreign naval attacks against Satsuma and Chōshū. In exchange for expulsionism, ideologues in some larger domains began supporting the policy of strengthening the realm. Sectionalism became the basis of the Restoration of 1868, because it balanced the demands of a unitary structure (the emperor) with tenacious domainal interests. Its theory, first hinted at by Yokoi Shōnan but developed by Takasugi and Ōkubo, argued that nothing was more real than the domain in a new political environment. Thus the strength of the realm depended on the collective strength of the domains, especially the large ones (*kakkyōron*). Expulsionists had tried to suppress the sectionalism of *bakufu* and *han* for a higher principle of authority (emperorism) without caculating the tenacity of domainal interests. Their successors, Yokoi, Ōkubo, and Takasugi, viewing internal and external realms as separate, worked to satisfy the requirements of each. Earlier theorists like Sakuma and restorationists like Yoshida and Maki were concerned with the external problem; hence their proposals for domestic reorganization (i.e., restoration) had little substance. Their primary emphasis on expulsion blurred the distinction between the internal and external realms. Sectionalists believed that the foreign problem could be met by domainal military preparedness through Western military technology and organization, while the internal situation required a strengthening of local authority so that the domain could play a more effective role in the formation of national policy. This new recognition is the source of Yokoi's crude theory of economic development, outlined in the *Kokuze sanron* (*Three Proposals for Domainal Policy*), in which he advised the *han* to "enrich itself and strengthen its military" (*fukoku kyōhei*). It also gives the probable meaning of Takasugi's concept of a "greater sectionalism" (*dai kakkyō*), now reformulated to serve the demands of political order; and Ōkubo's concern for "public discussions within the realm," and his plea for broader representation of other elements in society (lords and upper-ranking samurai) in the counsels of power. Finally, here is the culmination of a political consciousness that began in the eighteenth century—in which men abandoned moralism in order to construct a political society based on contemporary needs—and the beginning of a vision that was to inform the organization of Japanese society in modern times.

II *Mito and the*
Establishment of a Tradition
of Discourse

The concern of the writers who made up the later Mito school was the crisis of the domains of the realm: Were the political values consecrated by the Tokugawa shogunate being observed? Less urgent, but more basic, was the question how, if at all, these values could be regarded as permanently valid. The Mito writers argued that what they saw as a misguided response to domestic difficulties in their domains and to foreign probes proved that their society had departed far from true principles of conduct and of political procedure. The conclusion that the values set up by the first Tokugawa were being neglected by the shogunate itself led them neither to repudiate those values nor to criticize the institutions embodying them. The crisis led Mito writers rather to ask why ethical principles, which had promised an eternity to society, were not being observed, and to propose a reordering of traditional values which might arrest a failure of nerve by restating in ideal terms the organizational requirements of the *bakuhan* system. Ironically their awareness of crisis included a critical failure to locate the true crisis.

Whatever writers such as Fujita Yūkoku or Aizawa Seishisai

said about economics in their domain or the intermittent Russian
threats in the north, they saw the real crisis as a "weakening of
the spirit," the progressive relaxation of traditional ethical restraints. The urgent problem of financial failure in the domains
reflected an underlying moral decay. Similarly, the threat of foreign invasion only emphasized how helpless men were without
the security of moral purpose. The barbarian from without could
enter only if civilized men within abandoned eternal principles
of proper conduct. Thus the achievement of the Mito school lay
in locating the source of trouble in the deterioration of public discipline and in the effort to strengthen the realm by restating the
traditional assumptions of Tokugawa society.

The writings of Fujita Yūkoku, his son Fujita Tōko, and his
most outstanding pupil, Aizawa Seishisai, form the most complete statement of traditional values in Tokugawa Japan. Out of
the assumptions behind their concept of order, they consciously
selected from several historical traditions the one most suitable to
present problems. Fujita Yūkoku, with the aid of classical direc-
tives, defined the problems and produced a rhetoric which helped
his successors understand and evaluate. Aizawa, probably the
greatest of Mito writers and certainly the most cherished among
Japanese, organized Yūkoku's fears, perceptions, and proposals
into a classic reaffirmation of purpose. Finally Tōko, in response
to the actual needs of reform in the 1830s and 1840s, transformed
this theoretical program into a practical public discipline—and at
the same time weakened the statement of his predecessors.

Any restatement of tradition reveals problems that require attention, and results in reinterpretation by adding elements alien
to what is supposedly being conserved, even though they spring
from that awareness of present problems which prompted the
restatement in the first place. Japanese tradition was altered
when Mito writers became conscious of their traditionalism. Contemporary events had called into question not the validity of the
Neo-Confucian moral pattern, but only the adequacy of its realization. Under the impact of *naiyū,* the threat of "domestic calamity," Mito writers sought simply how best to renew the *bakuhan*

order. Renewal could involve creative transformation, but only within the limits of received moral standards. Mito writers believed they knew these moral standards; but in reformulating them, they were consciously choosing one tradition while eliminating others from possibility. They were not fully aware that their confident restatement admitted the existence of new facts demanding decisions, and perhaps a vague dissatisfaction with the task of defending an indefensible tradition. Their restatement forced them unconsciously to go beyond the limits of Neo-Confucian orthodoxy to make it work under new conditions—for example, by their willingness to incorporate native mytho-history into it.

Still, the past which Mito writers remembered or selected served as the avenue along which later thinkers would gain access to the Japanese tradition. For the generation of political writers after the attempted Tempō reform of shogunate and domains in the 1830s, tradition meant precisely the Mito synthesis. Only through the ideas promoted in the name of "tradition" by the Mito rhetoric did that *bakumatsu* generation have available a clear statement of the values underlying Tokugawa society. In their effort to recapture an assumed unitary Japanese tradition, the Mito writers wove together a syncretistic tapestry in which Neo-Confucianism was freely combined with nativism, *kogaku* (the "study of ancient texts"), historicism, and other elements. The synthesis was persuasive—coherent, systematic, authoritative, and comprehensive; it also met a deep need.

The Mito writers responded to a specific crisis in the *bakuhan* order: the social and political failure of the managerial class. They tried to arrest decay by elevating a status system into an absolute ethic: the "Way of loyalty and filial piety" (*chūkō no michi*). The Mito statement crystallized the hopes and fears of the obsolescent samurai class, recommending its "restoration" to its true position in society. But it could only concretize tradition at the expense of contemporary historical reality, when it offered consolation to a beleaguered and failing managerial elite. In the *bakumatsu* generation the Mito statement won the fullest sympathy from the samurai, because it sought to give their class (and by extension the system which defined its status) a new lease on life. The Mito illusion that a perfect society existed would be sustained so long as events appeared to conform to classical prescriptions about order and disorder; that is, so long as men could believe that their behavior was responsible for the quality of life.

A crisis which involved increasing peasant rebellions, the socioeconomic failure of the samurai class, and the shattering of the dream of eternal seclusion, was met forcefully by Mito writers in their reaffirmation of the Confucian *taigi meibun*: the "Great Principle of designations and duties." The proclamation of an ethic which supported the managerial claims of the samurai was intended both to remedy an ailing part of society and to arrest the crisis by repudiating the present which had generated it. In place of the rejected present, Mito writers celebrated a nonexistent past; in place of a society conditioned by history, they imagined a universal civilization realizable in all times and places. The informing principle of this civilization, according to Fujita Tōko, was "the Five Relations and the five elements." These relationships authenticated the division of all things; when a person knew his place in the social order, he showed that he knew the meaning of "discrimination" and was fulfilling the requirements of *taigi meibun*.[1] The Five Relations validated a status system, yet within it some relations were more important than others. Tōko argued that "loyalty and filial piety are the basis of name and doctrine," since the relations between parent and child, lord and retainer are prior to the others. This emphasis served the samurai claim to leadership well, since the class had employed the ethic of *chūkō* (loyalty and filiality) to maintain its internal solidarity and its distance from the rest of humanity. What began as a class ethic of "discrimination" was elevated by early Tokugawa writers and by the Mito school to a theory of leadership.

The most important element here (Mito writers explained)

---

[1] *Fujita Tōko-shū*, "Kōdōkanki jutsugi," in *Mitogaku taikei*, ed. Takasu Yoshijirō, 8 vols. (Tokyo, 1943), I, 68–69. This work will be cited hereafter as *Mgt*.

was the necessity to maintain "reverence for the emperor" (*sonnōron*). The imperial office gave ethical validation to a particular political system; the system prosecuted politics in the name of the emperor. Reverence for the emperor was necessary in any political theory, including the Mito one, and was in no way intended as an alternative to the *bakuhan* system. In order to restrain anti-*bakufu* sentiments among the lower samurai and indebted lords —precisely in order to preserve the *bakufu* system—Mito writers insisted on the theoretical position of the emperor as the highest authority in society. Obedience to the domainal lord displayed loyalty to the shogun, which in turn meant allegiance to the emperor. Thus respect for the emperor was the guarantee of all social order. Mito writers explicitly formulated the requirements for conserving the division of society. If "discrimination" was to be accomplished, "men must 'exhaust' loyalty and filial piety" in their daily behavior. Any effort to express loyalty directly to *bakufu* or emperor was a rejection of social discrimination and a breach of etiquette. Those who "exceed discrimination," Fujita Tōko argued, are committing "the crime of usurpation and rebellion."[2]

Closely linked in the Mito scheme to the Confucian notion of "designations and duties" was the theory of *jōi,* "repelling the barbarian." Just as society must conserve the moral principle of discrimination as the pledge of civilized life, so it must keep the barbarian outside the gate. Most countries, Aizawa Seishisai wrote in the *Tekii hen,* experience periodic "changes in name and withdrawal of mandates" (i.e., political revolutions); it was a special sign of civilization in Japan that the same imperial house had remained in power since the beginning of the state. Only Japan, of all the countries in the world, had known the security of an unbroken imperial succession and so had escaped the disorder of periodic rebellions for power and "name." This unparalleled example of legitimacy must be defended internally by observing the "way of loyalty and filial piety," and defended also from external encroachments. "To protect [the realm] from the

[2] *Ibid.*

four seas by relying on the imperial sovereign is the Great Way
of heaven and man." [3]

In their effort to authenticate the status ethic of loyalty and
filial piety (*chūkō no michi*), Mito writers added to the traditional
functions of learning and made its central object the dissemina-
tion of a "public ethic" (*shūshin*). If contemporary crisis had
forced the military estate to assert a dominant role, the other
classes also must play their parts voluntarily. Such acquiescence
was guaranteed if a public discipline, the "way of loyalty and
filial piety," was the purpose of education. When Fujita Tōko
wrote that "learning is really nothing other than its own encouragement," he was celebrating the traditional Confucian role of
education; [4] he was also doing something more. In the 1830s he
helped establish in Mito *han* a domainal school called the Kōdōkan, whose practice (widely imitated in the 1840s) enforced a
public moral discipline as a means of combating the crisis in culture; its purpose was to reinstate the status ethic as the focus of education.

Traditionally, a public discipline such as *chūkō no michi* had
not been the object of the learning enterprise. Confucianism assumed that individuals were already endowed with a sense of discrimination, and that its soundness was beyond criticism. Without status, civilization was impossible; recognition of social rank
and distance separated the world of civilized behavior from barbarism and the kingdom of animals and birds. Mito writers took
up the notion of status to overcome moral failure and promoted
the idea that education must be practical (*jikkō*) and therefore
provide instruction in a concrete moral discipline. But emphasis
on moral instruction as the purpose of learning did away with
the sense of a genuine intellectual pursuit found in original Confucianism. In fact Mito writers ignored the central advice of the
Great Learning (*Ta hsüeh*): In order to confirm the correctness
of universal principles, men are obliged to "investigate things"
(*kakubutsu*) and to "penetrate principle" (*kyūri*). If this injunc-

[3] Aizawa Seishisai, "Shinron," in *Mgt.*, II, 5.
[4] Fujita Tōko, "Kōdōkanki jutsugi," pp. 97–98.

tion failed to prompt Neo-Confucianists to study nature, it certainly urged them to study the world of human affairs in all its manifestations.

Kakubutsu kyūri meant, for Neo-Confucianists, an intellectual pursuit of external reality, particularly human affairs. They believed that a proper examination of several things would reveal that the external world is informed by the same principle as the individual, while the penetration of the original principle in the heart is applicable to all other things. Only through studying the actions and words of sages and moral men, as shown in the classics and history, can contemporary man learn about behavior informed by principle. Hence Neo-Confucianists rejected experimental knowledge and the authority of immediate experience from the world of external reality as worthy objects of learning and education.[5] Although Neo-Confucianists showed a disposition to protoempiricism, it was limited to the categorization of human phenomena. And although Confucianism was rationalistic, its rationalism was hemmed in by its emphasis on morality. Yet despite the limitations of a moralistic rationalism, Confucians still placed great reliance on the intellectual capacity of individuals to "reach what the sages have learned." And while Mito writers interpreted this narrowly as an invitation to follow up the promise of a status system, earlier Confucians viewed it as authorization for many kinds of intellectual inquiry.

Mito writers reorganized Confucianism, disregarded *kakubutsu kyūri,* and went directly to *shūshin,* moral teaching. The Mito concept of learning discouraged the acquisition of knowledge or any other intellectual activity unrelated to moral instruction. Failing to get in touch with an empirical reality that might be important to the carrying out of received principles, Mito writers rejected both metaphysics, especially the Confucian involvement in life and destiny, and any systematic study of economics, especially capital and profit. For example, Fujita Yūkoku's *Kannō wakumon* (*Questions and Answers on the Encouragement of Agriculture*) discussed domainal economics from this

[5] Maruyama Masao, *Nihon seiji shisōshi kenkyū* (Tokyo, 1954), p. 27.

antiempirical position; and Aizawa wrote off economics completely because it was an activity "that has nothing to do with loyalty or filial piety." [6] The emphasis of Mito writers on moral instruction was designed to have predictable political consequences—namely, a submissive population. Thus Aizawa wrote in the *Shinron* (*New Proposals*) that "there is nothing other than the Way which teaches the people of the sages to discipline the self and govern the realm." [7]

Mito ideologues rested an efficient polity on the availability of virtuous men (*yūtoku*), which for them meant the samurai class. Fujita Tōko acknowledged that the martial values which had once differentiated the samurai from the rest of society had been transmuted into virtues of civilian officials who were warriors only in name. Yet by arguing that the end of politics was to establish a public discipline stressing status, Mito writers sought to reduce politics to individual ethics. In a mood of reaction they sought to undo what time and Ogyū Sorai had accomplished: a separation of ethics and politics. In their conviction that individuals inherently knew how to behave in the public realm, Mito writers denied the sovereignty of politics and invoked the unpolitical *chih-kuo p'ing t'ien-hsia*, the ethical realm and benevolent polity of Neo-Confucian theorists; they promoted an internalized ethic—the Way of loyalty and filial piety—in place of an objective evaluation of the changes and political institutions of their society.

People can be ruled, Aizawa announced, only by *chūkō no michi*. Behind this dictum was a very low view of human nature. Mito writers were confident that the rule of *chūkō no michi* would serve as a guarantee of civilized life because most people were, in Aizawa's language, ignorant fools (*shungu*). Behind their optimism about achieving a benevolent realm was the conviction that the masses were naturally ignorant by virtue of their incapacity to be virtuous. And this was the criterion which decided who ruled and who was ruled. When they called the masses "ignorant," they meant "mean" as the word was used by Brit-

[6] Aizawa, "Shinron," p. 13.
[7] *Ibid.*

ish authors in the eighteenth century. The masses were mean because they were forever prevented from acquiring virtue and, as all Mito writers agreed, were capable only of being led. If left to their own devices they pursued profit and luxury; because they were fearful of spirits and ghosts, they would be gradually led to embrace Christianity, "a cruelly unjust and shallow doctrine." [8]

Behind this sentiment there is more than a little fear of mass disorder; contempt for the peasantry barely concealed a fundamental uncertainty of the ruling classes in the 1830s and 1840s. That peasant uprisings had become a familiar part of the landscape was a constant warning that the system was not working. The ruling classes saw the revolts as a symptom of moral failure and hence undertook the extensive reform activity of the Tempō years. By the mid-1840s, as a result of obvious widespread failure, the leadership concluded that reform was no longer a guarantee of order or a solution to the increase in peasant revolts. In the late Tokugawa period, only Mito writers reminded the leadership of its obligation to love and revere the people. And this love and respect, translated into concrete measures, would allay the fears of the samurai class, who saw worse things to come, by arresting disorder in the countryside.[9] Even though Aizawa believed that order could be established because the masses were ignorant, he also knew that "loving the people" required hard commitments from the leadership.[10] He could agree with Tokugawa Nariaki who, upon his succession as domain lord in Mito, stressed that it was a primary concern of the leadership to love the people. "Virtue is the root, commodities [food, clothing, tools] the branch," he remarked; a virtuous leadership could in no way "prevent themselves from bestowing blessings on the people." [11]

When Mito writers complained that even a "good government" based on "rewards and punishments" was feared by the

---

[8] Aizawa, "Shinron," pp. 78ff.

[9] Shibahara Takuji, *Meiji Ishin no kenryoku kiban* (Tokyo, 1965), pp. 125–131.

[10] Aizawa, "Shinron," p. 78.

[11] *Mito han shiryō, bekki*, I (Tokyo, 1935), 312–314.

people, they were registering a respectable Confucian distrust of
political institutions. The government was best that governed
least; for Neo-Confucianism this meant "loving the people." The
"good teachings" of etiquette and civilization were the guarantee
of permanent order. Mito writers simply equated the status ethic
with "loving the people" and argued that if the leadership
"bestowed the proper blessings on the people" by feeding and edu-
cating them, the realm would administer itself. Behind this political moralism was the conviction that "good government," however efficient, would "frighten the people" and deter them from
chūkō no michi, while "good doctrine" would "win the heart of
the people" and "preserve the realm for eternity." But contemporary events already confirmed that if "good doctrine" was abandoned, the people would "avoid political laws as one avoids an
enemy; their yearning for instruction will be like the yearning of
a child for an affectionate mother." [12] At bottom the Mito writers had a profound fear of the masses and the disorder they could
unleash. Order was "love" and love meant social acquiescence.
This was the premise on which Mito writers based their rather
hopeful view of achieving social happiness—but a premise which
promised order only if the people were brought under moral suasion.

Contemporary events showed that the worst fears were being
realized; treachery was everywhere, Fujita Tōko reported, and
the link between the masses and the managerial class appeared to
be weakening. When people are not under moral control, he said,
they are like a "product which first putrefies and then gives way
to worms and maggots. First the Way is abandoned, then later
people enter into heresy. People who are heretical are similar to
people who are ill. Men who govern the sick well will first promote their health; men who expel heresy well will first cultivate
the Great Way." [13] Nariaki, less concerned with philosophical
expression, simply stated that if the peasantry "bears a grudge or
resents the upper orders, it will not stand in awe of them." In

[12] Aizawa, "Shinron," pp. 155, 163ff.
[13] Fujita Tōko, pp. 79, 87.

these statements is all the panic which the leadership in *baku-matsu* Japan felt as it observed the signs of social failure. Here too is the meaning of the Mito statement as presented to a beleaguered managerial class which discovered that contempt for the peasants was not adequate to revive the flagging *bakuhan* order. To their generation the Mito writers offered both a renewal of the social order by reaffirming the imperative of status, and a concrete method of social reform; they tried to rejoin the outer and inner realms, inner goodness to correct behavior, which had become separated. Once they had finished with their task, it was as if nothing had changed. But events were to show that everything had changed. Still, for a moment they convinced their contemporaries that the landscape was not changing and that around them on land and sea they saw only the ghosts which accompany moral failure, but which can always be exorcised.

Mito *han* had a unique position in the Tokugawa order; since along with Kii and Owari it was one of three collateral branches (*gosanke*) of the Tokugawa house, it possessed unusual opportunities to help national policy. Mito was far from enjoying unlimited access to the counsels of power, but since it might always produce the next shogun, it commanded substantial respect in Edo. Moreover, since the seventeenth century it had been blessed by a succession of able and vigorous lords (daimyo), in spite of the inevitable incompetents such as Narinori, under whom Fujita Yūkoku served and wrote. In addition, Mito had earned, long before the crisis of the early nineteenth century, a widespread respect for its intellectual achievements. Thus even apart from its enormous prestige as a *gosanke,* it is not surprising that the intellectual activity attending the late Tokugawa quest originated in Mito.

Ever since the seventeenth century Mito had sponsored a monumental *History of Japan* (*Dai Nihonshi*), whose original compilation was the work of the "early" or "former" Mito school.[14]

[14] Takasu Yoshijirō, *Mito gakuha no sonnō oyobi keiron* (Tokyo, 1940), pp. 24–312. Also Herschel Webb, *The Japanese Imperial Institution in the Tokugawa Period* (New York, 1968), pp. 175–192.

This massive work shared with other domainal "histories" of the seventeenth century the purpose of showing the triumph of morality and political legitimacy, by means of classical Chinese canons of historiography. It is more interesting than most of the others, but it is no more reliable. Initiated by the second lord of the domain, Tokugawa Mitsukuni, it was to include the history of Japan down to the end of the Southern Court. Its organization on the principle of dynastic succession was the key through which its patron and compilers hoped it would vindicate legitimacy. This nonhistorical purpose made the *Dai Nihonshi* a sustained exercise in political theology. And while its editors worried over objectivity, principles of selection, and so forth, their work was vastly different from that of Arai Hakuseki, who was also writing history in the eighteenth century, but who was much more interested in actual facts. The Mito history stressed status and loyalty; while it was later appealed to by imperial loyalists in their struggle with the *bakufu,* there is nothing seditious about the work. The poet Rai Sanyō, in his widely read *Nihon gaishi,* popularized its ideas of loyalty and status and pressed them into the service of the imperial court. It was an ongoing project which recruited the brightest young men in the domain as part of their education. Under later lords it lost its original Confucian character and acquired the rhetoric of native mytho-history. By the late eighteenth century it had become a repository of native and Chinese sentiments on political order and kingship, which would find new expression in the crisis tracts of Fujita Yūkoku, Aizawa Seishisai, and Fujita Tōko.

THE PROBLEM OF WITHIN AND WITHOUT: FUJITA YŪKOKU

The intellectual pilgrimage of the later Mito school was begun by Fujita Yūkoku, who interpreted the signs of failure as the separation of inner morality from outer reverence. Aizawa Seishisai, Yūkoku's most distinguished student, in his autobiographical book *Kyūmon ihan,* wrote of his teacher in his characteristic way: "The master's thought is based on the principles of *sonnō* (reverence for the emperor) and *jōi* (expulsion of the barbarian) as they are found in the Spring and Autumn Analects. He has also been prudent in the theory of duties and designations (*mei-bun*), clarifying thoroughly the division between Chinese and barbarian, inner and outer." [15] Aizawa located the governing motif of Yūkoku's thought: unification through discrimination. For Yūkoku, *sonnō* meant a reaffirmation of the principles underlying the domestic moral order, the *bakuhan* system; while *jōi* dealt with the other side of the coin, the outer realm of the barbarian. This differentiation merely enlarged the more basic duality distinguishing the morally superior man: "inner cultivation, outer tranquillity." It was the framework within which Yūkoku both viewed the world around him and proposed to reshape it.

Fujita Yūkoku never saw contemporary problems—peasant uprisings, domainal indebtedness, the appearance of Russian adventurers in northern waters, the slow erosion of class lines—as contradictions of the received endowment. By his belief that nature was a reality-principle underlying the organization of society, he saw only the dissolution of status and the rejection of moral "discrimination" (*chūkō no michi*). "Designations and duties," he concluded, were being thrown to the wind; individuals were showing daily that they no longer felt obliged to fulfill the duties of their status, "to abide in reverence." Since the Tokugawa order gave human expression to an ethic based on the paradigm of natural organization, Yūkoku warned that society would dissolve because of "internal troubles" (*naiyū*) and "external catastrophes" (*gaikan*). Just as the individual's interior morality was prior to his outer reverence, so a correct domestic order was the surest safeguard against external threat. For classical Chinese political theory had taught Yūkoku that, while the end of a dynasty was always accomplished by the peril of the barbarian at the gates, the reason for this lay in a prior moral failure within the society. What Yūkoku saw in peasant uprisings and the appearance of foreign ships was not challenges unrelated to his concept of order,

[15] Quoted in Tamagawa Haruzō, *Sonnō ron* (Tokyo, 1943), p. 6.

but only symptoms that the ligaments of society were loosening. None of these events could be considered a cause of decline by itself, but only a warning of moral paralysis.

Fujita Yūkoku was born in 1774 and died in 1829. His father, who did not hold samurai status, managed a business which "manufactured a product of the times" in Mito. Yūkoku's biographer, like all good panegyrists, locates his genius as early as possible in childhood, and even says further that his father, because of his great ability, was not suited to the life of a merchant.[16] Nobody of Yūkoku's caliber, that is, could possibly have descended from modest origins; even though his father remained outside of the major class, he obviously behaved with the nobility of a samurai. It was the father's hope that his son would in some way serve the domain; hence, we are told, Yūkoku was encouraged very early in life to take up learning as the surest road to the *han*. Typically, Yūkoku responded to encouragement; untypically, he was tardy in development, showing at first a strong liking for play. But even in play he demonstrated precocity. At the age of ten, after repeated pleas from his mother, Yūkoku began to change his ways—after all, he was getting older—and plunged into a new life of scholarship. Since he already possessed "unusual ability," he progressed rapidly in his studies, writing respectable poems when he was eleven and composing essays a few

[16] It is exceedingly difficult to write biographies of Japanese personalities since we have few if any psychological cues to go on. This is especially true of historical personalities. Contemporary reports and personal letters are often cast in a moral framework, and the figure emerges as a one-dimensional man. This is, of course, the stuff of *denki,* but *denki,* however disguised, do not add up to biography. What I have done in this study is simply to include a few salient facts about a man's life and then proceed to an analysis of his writings. The best we can do under the circumstances is to write a meta-biography in which the personality is revealed in his official writings. Until we are supplied with a genuine theory of personality —and I suspect this is a task for which Japanese themselves are better suited than foreigners—we have little choice. For a fuller discussion of this problem, see my review essay of Masakazu Iwata's *Okubo Toshimichi* in the *Harvard Journal of Asiatic Studies* (1965–1966), Vol. 26.

years later that easily could have been taken for the work of a mature mind. One of his major moral tracts, the *Seimeiron* (*Essay on the Rectification of Names*), was written when he was only eighteen years old.

When he turned thirteen, his father enrolled him as a pupil of Tachibana Suiken, a teacher in Mito famed for his political approach to education. A few years later Yūkoku, on Tachibana's recommendation, joined the prestigious Shōkōkan, the historiographical bureau in which the *Dai Nihonshi* was being compiled. In 1789 he accompanied Tachibana to Edo and was given the opportunity of study and contact with the leading scholars of the day. There he met one of his childhood heroes, the vociferous loyalist Takayama Hikokurō. Actually Yūkoku had earlier written a poem in honor of Takayama's monomaniacal concern for imperial respect. Takayama represents one of those cultural landmarks peculiar to Japan, the humorless hero-loyalist promoting a private cause. But his endless outpourings on the state of coastal defenses in the north rang with authority. Yūkoku spoke with Takayama again in 1791 when the hero had just returned from an inspection tour of defenses; on this occasion he learned something about the foreign threat, and also was first introduced to a rhetoric critical of the *bakufu*. Takayama, as all Japanese children used to know, and as anybody who takes the time to read inscriptions on Japanese monuments can learn, went down in a blaze of glory. After a round of travel, during which he paid his respects at a number of imperial sites, he went to Kyūshū, always a safe place for hotheads, and committed suicide in the house of a retainer of Kurume *han,* bowing in the direction of the imperial palace.

Fujita Yūkoku's trip to the capital was a failure. Shortly after his arrival he decided to return to Mito and put his learning to use where it would do the most good. From this point on, his intellectual energies, inspired by the example of Takayama and of Gamō Kunpei (another contemporary single-minded loyalist) were enlisted into the service of Mito *han* and its moral and economic problems. Yūkoku learned through association with na-

tionally oriented ideologues such as Gamō that these problems
were local manifestations of a more general malaise: the financial
insolvency of the domains under the Tokugawa arrangement of
power. Neither Yūkoku nor his fanatical friends had any pre-
monition of a new kind of political space, the expanded and unified realm: they were not protonationalists. He believed that the
problems would be solved not by changing things but by getting
back to the way things had been and should be. This meant a
tightening of the ethicopolitical order, not its abandonment. At
seventeen, just before he wrote the *Seimeiron,* Yūkoku reflected
that the "moral order of Japan is not something that changes."
Despite the mere "political changes since the Kamakura *bakufu*,"
Yūkoku wrote, "and the removal of political power from the
hands of the emperor, nobody has committed an offense against
the respect of the emperor. The imperial line since Amaterasu
Ōmikami is unbroken and has not been stirred. Even during the
Tokugawa period the shoguns have led the several lords to honor
the emperor. Those literary scholars who today call the shogun a
king (*Ō*) forget the respect the shogun has for the emperor, and
it ought to be said that [such writers] have thrown into disorder
the teaching of the sages who stress morality and order." [17] Yet
in restating a basic order, Yūkoku laid down the foundations for
much of the innovative political discourse that was to follow.

Like most Confucianists, Fujita Yūkoku believed in the possibility of achieving a benevolent government (*jinsei*)—that is, a
state based on morality in which politics was subsumed under
general ethical behavior. The concept of *jinsei* had served since
the time of Mencius as one of the most enduring and dynamic
elements in Confucian political rhetoric. It had been modified
from time to time, but the indispensable requirements for realization of an ethical realm remained: a concern for contemporary
affairs, and the encouragement of "practical learning"
(*jitsugaku*).[18] Practical learning prepared men in responsible

[17] Fujita Yūkoku, "Seimeiron," in *Mgt.,* III, 380ff.
[18] See my article on *jitsugaku* in B. Silberman and H. D. Harootunian,
Modern Japanese Leadership (Tucson, 1966), pp. 83–119. "Hōji," in *Mgt.,*
III, 169.

political positions to formulate proper policies. Political practice in turn was an inexhaustible source of knowledge, consisting of precedents upon which future administrations might draw. Mencius had believed that it was the object of a benevolent polity to tranquilize the people and bestow happiness, and Yūkoku was quick to reaffirm his faith in this ideal. "People are considered to be the base of the realm," he wrote in a Mencian mood in one of his letters, "and if they constitute a firm base, then the realm also will be firm. Virtue is considered essential for good government and is exercised in promoting the people's welfare. In the course of promoting the people's welfare, a government must assist the weak and restrain the strong, foster the old and love the young, prohibit laziness and idleness, and establish a legal system that dispenses sure rewards and just penalties."[19] Despite the lofty moral tone of his requirements for a true *jinsei,* they were not intended to go any further than Mito domain. And this limited notion of political space is presupposed by all of his writings. Yūkoku was simply reaffirming the existing political structure; he saw no farther because he was partly unable, partly unwilling to do so.

In the *Anmin ron (Essay on the Tranquilization of the People)* Fujita Yūkoku uses Confucius' dictum that nothing exists outside of benevolence to show that benevolent rule must ensure peace and order, for "when the people are hungry they must be fed, and when they are cold they must be clothed."[20] Time and time again Yūkoku employs this classical vision of a polity whose sole aim is to bestow love and promote human happiness, in order to support his concrete prescriptions for problems of the domain. Aizawa does the same in even more lofty language; and while none of these writers envisages a new national realm, they supply the language for those who later do think in terms of a new kind of political space.

Chinese thought and practice had long presumed that an elite of classically trained managers would perform the routine of government. They were teachers whose moral superiority entitled

[19] "Hōji," pp. 179–180.
[20] Fujita Yūkoku, "Anmin ron," Mgt., III, 379.

them to govern, and the enterprise of government thereby became an exercise in moral instruction. Membership in the elite
was open to all who could prove the "talent and ability" (*jinzai*)
which consisted in understanding the true principles of nature.
Confucius' frustrated ambition to hold office turned him against
recruiting on the basis of hereditary descent, but in actual
Chinese practice admission into the mandarinate was regulated as
much by heredity as by a show of merit. Tokugawa Japan, while
subscribing formally to the fiction of political recruitment based
on the universal criterion of merit, staffed its bureaucracy with hereditary retainers, much more than did China. Yūkoku, the son
of a merchant, knew this, and was no doubt embarrassed by the
conflict between allocation on the basis of genuine talent and ascription by birth. The problem was intensified for him by his belief in the possibility of an ethical realm. He believed in the necessity of a qualified and appointed moral leadership; yet the
peculiar transmutation of the samurai from military class into a
civilian bureaucratic elite obliged him to make fundamental adjustments to bridge ideal and reality.

Fujita Yūkoku agreed with Ogyū Sorai, whose writings he
knew well, that political rule, while no doubt ordained by
Heaven, was in the end the work of men rather than of some indeterminate force such as *tendō,* the heavenly Way.[21] Following
Ogyū, he was aware that official Neo-Confucianism did not adequately account for change. He knew that eighteenth-century
thought had tried to make up for this deficiency. By the time he
began to write, the notion of change, its meaning and function,
had become current philosophical coin. Certainly, Ogyū's political relativism had not replaced a normative view of society. But
the emphasis on a first-class leadership in the shaping of affairs
was clearly at odds with the established view that man was no
more than the executor of an indeterminate command in political society.[22] For Ogyū, government, which he identified with

---

[21] See Maruyama, *Nihon seiji* . . . (n. 5 above), on Ogyū Sorai, pp.
71–241.
[22] *Ibid.*

the Way, was the work of men. Fujita Yūkoku agreed with this formula when he wrote:

Heaven does not of itself order the several peoples. If there are no leaders, there will surely be disorder. The several lords (*kun*) and their retainers are the persons obliged to govern the people. The emperor (*tenshi*) serves to unify the administrators and the people. In this task the emperor and the lords, unable to perform the duties of government alone, are assisted by the courtiers and the mass of samurai. Through understanding all things they will be able to formulate policies to rule all the people.[23]

As a theoretician Fujita Yūkoku acknowledged the role of the emperor, but only as an authenticating principle; the special role of the administrative manager is what he intended to illuminate and redeem. The exercise of principles springing from benevolence was not only a moral imperative but a necessary condition for survival. "If the people below are injured, a territory will never become a realm." [24] Elsewhere he argued bitterly how "haughtiness" in the rulers invariably produced severe weaknesses in the polity and the ultimate abandonment of all political wisdom.[25] Fearful of chaos, Yūkoku saw in continued leadership of the samurai class the best hope for order and civilization in Japan; but he also warned rulers, "even sagacious lords," to observe at all times the principles operating in the relationship between parent and child. "If we preserve the principle that people are as infants, it is possible to achieve a government that they will endure." [26] Strong words from one who sought to salvage the arrangement of power by preserving the samurai as a managerial class. And the goals of "loving the people" and "bestowing blessings" reached well beyond the boundaries of Mito, even though Yūkoku never said so. In taking the parent–child rela-

[23] "Anmin ron," p. 376.
[24] "Seimeiron," p. 380.
[25] *Ibid.*, p. 381.
[26] *Ibid.*, p. 382.

tionship as a guide to political rule, he felt that any political unit, whatever its size, was little more than an extended family.[27]

In 1789, upon the invitation of the shogunal counselor Matsudaira Sadanobu, Fujita Yūkoku wrote a politicoethical tract to restate the moral character and duties of rulers. Matsudaira had learned of Yūkoku's philosophical precocity and reported his admiration back to Mito; Yūkoku's teacher Tachibana thereupon requested the eighteen-year-old moralist to submit a short essay to the counselor. The result was the tract *Seimeiron* (*Essay on the Rectification of Names*), which revealed early his lasting belief in the inviolability of a hierarchic sociopolitical order. Its purpose was to state the conditions of a "correct society" and to show how Japan might avoid disaster. Social order was identical with civilization, and no alternative was conceivable to Yūkoku. But social order meant hierarchy and "discrimination" as revealed at work in the organization of nature, differentiating all phenomena. The political struggles of other peoples are an instructive map of hell where the weak are always devoured by the strong. But a society steeped in morality is pledged to order, good government, and human happiness. The basis of political order and its continuation, as Confucius said, is to "clarify the Way"; and this, Yūkoku added, means "rectifying the boundaries" of political order. And the only lasting guarantee of "rectification" is the principle that discriminates between parent and child, between lord and retainer. This principle is as natural to human society as the relationship between human being and beast, civilized and barbarian, inner and outer. A realm erected on such a foundation is one that will "remain unchanged and unmoved" for an eternity.

It is pointless to question Fujita Yūkoku's motives. He lived in a hierarchically organized society and enjoyed the dubious prestige of being a member of the managerial class. All his interests were on the line. Yet it would be a mistake to write off his praise of "discrimination" as a cynical power play to keep his class and himself on top. Yūkoku was, among other things, a committed

[27] "Anmin ron," p. 377.

moralist, an intellectual who believed (I think sincerely) in a specific paradigm for social organization and found it unimaginable that any alternative could promise civilization. Like many Tokugawa ideologues, he rationalized the existing structure with the loftiest pieties. The trouble was, his praise revealed a suspicion that the system was not functioning as it should. Why else would he have written? "In any country (*tenka kokka*)," he announced, "it is always a question how to define and straighten the relationship between lord and vassal, and the divisions separating the upper and lower classes." [28] "Discrimination" was normative, its soundness never became problematic for Yūkoku. What did pose a problem was the fact that these distinctions were no longer being observed. Eighteenth-century political history brought about at least one thing: the dissolution of the dreamworld inhabited by Confucian moralists. Now, while his notion of discrimination owed much to Confucianism, Yūkoku, as was the practice of his times, also invoked the authority of native mytho-history. Japan had an emperor who embodied on the one hand Confucian virtue and on the other the divinity of the sungoddess and of his historical ancestors. His presence made "discrimination" a sacerdotal principle, as well as an ethical one, since the divisions of the social hierarchy began with him. That is, society was ranked in such a way as to show a certain divine descent and the execution of the emperor's will. The realm was both moral and divine; the emperor both represented the highest embodiment of virtue and acted as a link between the national gods and the people. His presence as a "manifest god" not only made society possible but authenticated (as no other device could have done) the hierarchic nature of social organization.

This belief in a divinely appointed emperor gave Fujita Yūkoku grounds for asserting that Japan was superior to all other nations. He used the rhetoric of mytho-history to validate the moral principles of that social organization which he was trying to rectify. A divinely ordained land, established by the sun god-

---

[28] "Seimeiron," p. 382.

dess and directed by an unbroken succession of emperors, was the guarantee of order and the pledge of "discrimination." In syncretistic manner, Yūkoku identified Japan's divine origins with its possession of a universal ethic. Owing to the divine nature of society, respect for the emperor would never change; and by a process of descent from above, each social estate commands respect from the one immediately below it, as representing the emperor's will by its very place in the hierarchy. "Today," Yūkoku wrote in the *Seimeiron,* "if the *bakufu* respects and reveres the imperial court, then the several lords will revere the *bakufu.*" [29]

All other things might change—the shape of political organization and the managerial leadership itself—but respect for the emperor would remain the unshaken principle; and respect was revealed by observing the "discrimination" between high and low. In a certain sense Fukita Yūkoku, like Shinto ideologues, wished to recognize civilization as existing only in Japan. Although he was not explicitly racist, he certainly made racism a possibility for later thinkers. It appeared that one must be Japanese in order to be civilized, since Japan was the land of the gods. The token of this uniqueness was the unbroken continuity of the imperial line. A revealing passage in his *Kengenron (Essay on Reforming the Calendar)* which compares the Japanese and Chinese practices of imperial succession could have been borrowed from Motoori's *Naobi no mitama.* Beginning with the aim of understanding the character of the regnal periods during the time of Han Wu-ti, Yūkoku went on to explore the whole nature of imperial succession in China.[30] While the practice of regnal periods began with the former Han dynasty, he observed, the profusion of reigns representing several families struggling with each other reveals the purely human character of Chinese kingship.[31] Japan, in contrast, was known to have "established the reign of the august Imperial court in the Taika period; and from Shōtoku

[29] *Ibid.*

[30] *Ibid.,* pp. 372, 374.

[31] *Ibid.,* p. 374.

Taishi down to the present it has remained the same for over a thousand years." [32]

"Rectification of names" for Fujita Yūkoku meant that although he accepted without reservation the existence of a status order, its continuance required it to be restated. Disorder occurred when either party to the status arrangement failed to observe the principles of discrimination. "In the country," Yūkoku wrote, "there are lords and retainers, and there are the upper and lower orders. If the designations of lords and retainers are not corrected, the division between upper and lower orders will weaken. The division between the aristocratic and nonaristocratic classes will blur, and the distinctions between the upper and lower orders of society will vanish. The strong will despise the weak, and the masses will be thrown into confusion and disorder." [33] For Yūkoku, the realization of order hinged on setting straight the various "designations and duties" (*meibun*), that is, the classes which constituted Tokugawa society. The observance of *meibun* was sanctioned both by ethical imperative and by divine appointment. The divinely ordained hierarchy of these classes "passed from generation to the next down to the present undisturbed in its solemnity"; Japan's superiority in the world was marked out by the fact that it alone had preserved the lord-vassal relationship since its divine inception.

Fujita Yūkoku's vision of order demanded also acceptance of the Confucian notion attributed to the *Ch'un-ch'iu,* the *Spring and Autumn Annals* (but in fact worked out in the *Kung Yang* commentary), that in society there cannot be conflicting sources of authority; as "there are not two suns in heaven, so there are not two rulers on earth." [34] The emperor was the sole source of authority and there could not be a duplication of roles. If this, as some writers argue, was a gentle slap at the shogunate, it was

[32] "Seimeiron," pp. 382, 393. Motoori, by contrast, was inhibited by a lack of historical evidence and went back to Jimmu Tennō.

[33] *Ibid.,* p. 382.

[34] *Ibid.,* p. 383; also Tamagawa (n. 15 above), pp. 7–8.

also a reminder that society could function only if its several members, from the highest lord to the lowest peasant, played the roles to which they were assigned. Let us look in turn at the role assigned in his thought to emperor, shogun, lords, and peasants.

The emperor. Japanese history, Fujita Yūkoku argued, clearly revealed the unchanging position of the emperor. "Toyotomi Hideyoshi abandoned the reign titles of the Fujiwara regent; but that he did not choose to be called a king ($\bar{O}$) shows his observance of correct designations and duties."[35] More relevant to his times was the way that Tokugawa Ieyasu himself demonstrated respect for the imperial position, when he accepted the title which only the emperor could confer.[36] As Hideyoshi was reluctant to take on the title of "king" out of respect for the emperor, so Ieyasu was content to accept from the emperor the office of shogun. Moreover, Ieyasu, according to Yūkoku, showed in all his acts—the pacification of the realm, the establishment of institutions promising peace and order—how scrupulously he observed the status which the emperor conferred on him. So devoted was he to his task and position that he went about setting the rest of society straight on the basis of the relationship which as shogun he enjoyed with the emperor. It was in this manner that society was organized around the relationship between lord and vassal, and the division between high and low was "hardened for all times to come."[37] I suppose there is some irony in Yūkoku's idealized version of how Tokugawa Ieyasu went about his task; still, it was his purpose to show that a correctly functioning status order had been ordained by heaven through the agency of the imperial will and had been executed by the imperial messenger, the shogun. Tokugawa Ieyasu administered the emperor's will after he received his "title and rank." He was not the emperor's rival, nor an independent source of authority apart

[35] "Seimeiron," p. 386.
[36] *Ibid.* In ancient China, lords received, as a symbolic gesture, the calendar of events from the emperor and in return pledged their loyalty.
[37] *Ibid.*

from him. "Since the emperor is truly a descendant from heaven, the shogun should not be called a king. However, even though the shogun is not to be called a king, he must act in an imperial way if he is to govern." [38] The shogun acted in the political realm in lieu of the emperor; and while he was not an autonomous maker of rules, so Yūkoku claimed, his actions possessed imperial authority: "The men who govern this country act in place of the direct administration of the heavenly descendant. . . . Because the emperor has merely withdrawn from the personal administration of his realm, these men have for some time directed the course of government. Owing to the length of time [since the emperor ruled directly] it is difficult to change customs today." [39] History taught what early Tokugawa theory confirmed: the emperor served as the source of authority—as the center of gravity, so to speak,—for political society, but no more.

While Fujita Yūkoku repeated common currency, he also hinted at a new notion which nativist writers were already promoting. The idea that the emperor served only as a *principle* of authority was consistent with the belief that the "realm was public and not the private possession of one man." But an emperor who was a *principal* in his own right and a personality—as the nativists and certainly Yūkoku also saw him—implied the opposite conviction: that the realm belonged to one man, the emperor.[40] Although the shogun administered the realm, Yūkoku wrote, it still belonged to the emperor. This idea, in spite of its possibilities for subversion, was never so exploited by Mito ideologues, who only emphasized how the emperor served to authorize Tokugawa political organization. Perhaps the notion of the country as the emperor's private realm was meaningful only after its opening (*kaikoku*) shattered the myth of a "public realm." In any case it was Yoshida Shōin who set up the idea of a private imperial realm as the sole object of devotion and action. After 1854, as

[38] *Ibid.*, p. 388.
[39] *Ibid.*, p. 387.
[40] Ono Hisato, *Meiji ishin zengo ni okeru seiji shisō no tenkai* (Tokyo, 1944), pp. 169–170.

we shall see, he spoke increasingly of "imperial retainers" serving
the private realm of the emperor.

The shogun. In order to avoid confusion over leadership, and
to remind society that "the emperor has not taken charge of
countrywide affairs but only received the attendance of the several lords," Fujita Yūkoku tried to clarify the meaning of status
in unmistakable language. It was his purpose to show how the
shogun's service to the throne revealed a sense of "propriety."
"Propriety is the same as duty," he stated; and even though the
emperor did not participate directly in the exercise of political
authority, he was still the highest authority in the land. Shogunal
power was limited by the nature of the position itself; ruling in
place of the emperor, the shogun serves only as a regent
(*sessei*).[41] Yūkoku's insistence on affixing the proper title to each
office, as in the case of emperor and shogun, was intended to
point up the limitations of the *bakufu*. He hoped to show that
the shogun was merely the most powerful among the lords in administering the emperor's realm. Other lords had duties corresponding to their "name," which they must be allowed to execute
without interference. Yūkoku was more interested in rescuing
the domain (and by extension its lord) than any other institution
of Japanese society. Much of his moralizing is merely a preface to
taking on the problem of "duties and designations" relating to
the lord and his true relationship to the *bakufu*. And he concluded both that the shogun functioned only as a lord among
lords—as was already implied in his redefinition of the relationship between shogun and emperor—and that the shogunate, in
bolstering its own authority, had undermined the power of the
several daimyo.[42]

The lords. If the shogun was simply a lord among lords, as Fujita Yūkoku believed, what then of the lords themselves? In his
circular rhetoric he tried to resolve uncertainty about the lord's
expected role: "When the *bakufu* respects the position of the emperor, then the several lords will respect the *bakufu;* if the

[41] "Seimeron," p. 388.
[42] *Ibid.*

several lords respect the *bakufu,* then they are revering the court." [43] Clearly he was expecting the lords not only to recognize the emperor as the sole source of authority, but also to acknowledge the distance existing between themselves as retainers and the shogun as lord of all lords. Yūkoku reveals here his opinion that the *bakufu,* owing to its peculiar relationship with the daimyo, had assumed some of the functions of the emperor; and while accepting this in the spirit of tolerance, he also urged the *bakufu* to maintain strict observance of status in all the tiers of Tokugawa society. History never confirmed that the Tokugawa arrangement was anything more than it appeared in his day, yet Yūkoku argued as if historical propriety were being violated. In his criticism Yūkoku elevated the daimyo to an importance not suggested by history or tradition; but he was sure that only this new role could arrest decay and preserve the social order.

The shogun's office was regent to the emperor; the duty of the daimyos was to govern their domains, which collectively made up the realm. But this division of duties was not being observed. The shogun, playing a broader role than his "name" called for, pursued a policy which prevented the several lords from exercising correctly the duties of their office. Fujita Yūkoku knew how the *bakufu,* since its inception, had tried to enhance its own power and eliminate potential alternatives to its rule; but he chose to explain its current advocacy of these measures as a sign of mere incompetence. By the late eighteenth century this policy had produced an evident decline of the daimyo; and while this centralizing tendency was no departure from practice, Yūkoku chose to interpret it as confusion of roles. The lords were not being allowed to perform the duties required by their office; but since these were essential to the "realm of his Majesty," it followed that the *bakufu* was responsible for introducing a disruptive element into the polity.[44]

Fujita Yūkoku claimed that the *bakufu* willfully followed a

[43] Ono, *op. cit.*
[44] *Ibid.*

policy of self-interest in which "the base is strengthened while the ends are weakened." [45] When he argued that upper social levels should show compassion toward the lower, he was writing not only about relations between ruling class and peasants, but also about relations within the ruling class. On every level of society there were divisions between high and low; hence there must be standard rules governing their conduct. "To complete the Great Way of heaven and earth," he explained, "lords must be compassionate to the people (*ōdōron*) and the people must respect the lords (*sonnō*)." [46] Within the range of possibilities suggested by these two concepts, Yūkoku meant that the "imperial Way" of compassion (*ōdō*) was fully consistent with the accepted Tokugawa theory of sovereignty, while "respect" (*sonnō*) enjoined the rule to submit to the ordinances of the emperor's realm. If internal disaster was to be avoided, the *bakufu* must show "compassion" to the several lords, just as the lords must be moved by benevolence toward the people they administered. Only after *ōdō* was shown could *sonnō* be expected; if both could be realized, "duties and designations" (*meibun*) would be fulfilled. "How can we strengthen the rectification of duties and designations? How is the country of the *bakufu* to be governed today? . . . At the top we live under the heavenly descendant and at the bottom we are tended by the several lords." [47]

The peasants. Precisely how the "bottom" should be tended by the lords occupied Fujita Yūkoku's attention after he wrote the *Seimeiron.* In his belief that learning had to serve a practical purpose, Yūkoku tried to apply his concept of order to the operation of Mito *han*.[48] "It is a treasure of government," he states in one of his letters, "to know how to bestow blessings upon the people. How is contemporary man to achieve this?" Not by teaching people about the Way, he answered, nor by "accustoming [good people] to luxury and laziness," but by encouraging them to carry

---

[45] See Sakata Yoshio, *Meiji ishinshi* (Tokyo, 1960), p. 35.
[46] *Ibid.*
[47] "Seimeiron," p. 388.
[48] "Hōji," in *Mgt.,* III, 199. "The aim of learning is efficiency."

out productive enterprises. The lord in turn should perform meritorious works everywhere; first, then, he must insure an adequate food supply and a strong military organization able to preserve order. But in actual fact "people everywhere have become accustomed only to inadequate merit [in the rulers] and benefit." He despaired of continuing the Tokugawa peace. "The administration of Mito *han* today is based on the division between rich and poor, separate [standards of] virtue and separate behavior. All this has to be changed. If there were a great crisis, how could we adequately accept responsibility in the several sectors of society?" [49] How indeed? Interests were too disparate and discipline too lax to permit a common effort. Moral malaise showed itself in economic failure that was impoverishing both samurai and peasant. Yūkoku demanded a "correction of finances" throughout Mito. But he knew that the real solution depended solely, in the end, on efficient leadership; the "selection of men of ability" who knew how to exercise virtue and to achieve the great end of all governments, "a rich realm and a strong army" (*fukoku kyōhei*).[50]

Fujita Yūkoku believed that while reform should be initiated by the *bakufu*, it must be executed by the domain. He knew that the problems of Mito were in some respects unique, but that no domain could escape certain problems. However, the *bakufu* had failed to seize the initiative; and so the mandate of reform passed into the hands of the domainal lord. In investing the domainal lord with the responsibility for reform, Yūkoku was elevating the domain to an unprecedented level. He had written earlier that the domain's weakness was due to shogunal policies; reform would both rescue the domain from destruction and also give it a chance to play the role it was supposed to. Yūkoku's rhetoric bears down on one conclusion: the responsibility of the daimyo, despite the practice of the recent past, to act out his "historical" role. But we know, as Yūkoku knew, that the "historical" role he was assign-

[49] *Ibid.*, p. 178.
[50] See *Mgt.*, III, "Kannō wakumon," 86, 93; "Hōji," p. 170.

ing to the lord was a fiction and an invention of his own. If (as
several interpreters suggest) Yūkoku was attacking the shogun-
first policy of the Tokugawa *bakufu,* he was also proposing an
alternative autocracy by making the domain and its lord central
in the arrangement of power. History had shown that reform, to
be effective, must be promoted by the *bakufu.* Yet the *bakufu* during his own day had consistently failed to initiate reform. Under
the shogun Ienari (1793–1838), shogunal administration was
nominally controlled by the counselor Mizuno Dewa no kami.
Ienari's own life was wrapped in luxury, and Mizuno was unable
or unwilling to inaugurate countrywide reforms. Knowing this,
Yūkoku suggested to his own lord, Narinori, that, as head of one
of the *gosanke,* he should take the lead and establish a precedent
by transforming his domain himself. Previously Yūkoku had reminded Narinori of his illustrious predecessor Osamasa who (in
1786) had helped the shogunal counselor Matsudaira Sadanobu rid
the *bakufu* of Tanuma Okitsugu. After the removal of Tanuma,
Osamasa had worked closely with Matsudaira to bring about the
reforms of the *bakuhan* system during the Kansei era. In admonishing Narinori "to follow the footsteps of Lord Osamasa who
aided in the deposition of Tanuma," Yūkoku hoped that if
Narinori failed to persuade the shogunate to begin reform, then
he might do it himself. Yūkoku, although jarred by Narinori's
ineptness, continued to believe that reform in one *han* would lead
to a countrywide movement.[51] In the special case of Mito, Yūkoku
called on the examples of the first two domainal lords and recommended both emulation of their achievements and return to
their principles; in fact, such a "return" was no return at all, but
rather a formula for rearranging the power relationships in the
bakuhan system.

    Faced with the decline of the Tokugawa economy, the Mito
statement proposed to tighten the existing "feudal management." [52] But the program also had to produce a concrete theory
of political and economic reform and of "civil administration"
(*minseiron*) if it was to express the concepts of "good govern-

[51] "Kannō wakumon," p. 85.
[52] Shibahara, *Meiji Ishin* . . . (n. 9 above), p. 128.

ment" and "loving the people." This program was designed not to prevent peasant uprisings from without, but rather to promote "correct instruction" in order "to gain the heart and mind of the people." This theory was developed by Fujita Yūkoku in his most mature work, the *Kannō wakumon,* and was later carried out by Tokugawa Nariaki as an active program of reform for Mito. It also came to serve as a guideline for an entire generation of reformers throughout the country during the Tempō years.

Fujita Yūkoku argued that it was a fundamental responsibility of the domain lord to uproot twin diseases, "fondness for money" and usury.[53] He traced the origins of the contemporary malaise back to the late seventeenth century:

> In the beginning of the feudal order (*hōken*) there was an abundance of skills in our domain; and we did not suffer, as we do today, from an insufficiency of national production. During the time of Tokugawa Mitsukuni, the administration of government was conducted with frugality and economies; but owing to the preparation of *han* military affairs, there had to be a small but ordinary increase in expenditures. [To meet this increase] Mitsukuni not only taxed fields and paddies, but also took steps to cut costs by eliminating superfluous offices. Despite these efforts, despite even the availability of new land from reclamation, Mitsukuni was not able entirely to overcome the inadequacy of production.[54]

Mitsukuni's successors, Yūkoku noted, were even less successful, since they had to extort gifts and loans from wealthy merchants and peasants. Yūkoku did recognize that the malaise was not simply moral; not all of Mito's troubles could be attributed to human weaknesses. Between 1729 and 1749, he recorded, the population in the domain increased steadily, and even if new habits of consumption had not been popularized, in daily life the gross domainal product would not have been nearly enough to feed new mouths.[55] Moreover, he observed that the problem of population increase was complicated by widespread "abuses" which

[53] *Mgt.,* III, 181, 194.
[54] "Kannō wakumon," p. 161.
[55] *Ibid.,* p. 4.

local authorities out of indifference had allowed to develop. He was aware that normal expenditures had risen, but he failed to see the economics of a society in which new forces were demanding attention. Yūkoku, like other defenders of a natural economy, had no way of understanding the growth of a commercial sector. Whatever he cited as a symptom of economic decline was usually a promising development toward commercial economy. Economic failure—which he saw in the "love of money" and increase in loans—had resulted in five abuses: luxury, disunity, forced labor, oppressive local standards, and "annoying disturbances" (peasant revolts).[56] Fujita's belief in a natural economic order ruled out solutions to these grievances as costing a political price too high to pay.

The abuse of luxury. The abuses which, for Fujita Yūkoku, constituted *naiyū* explained why consumption exceeded production. "Luxury," he wrote, "begins with wealthy peasants who boast of splendid homes, clothing, and elegant goods . . . and this change in style is eventually imitated by poorer peasants." [57] The habit of luxury is furthered by artisans who produce "useless goods" which originally were valued only by merchants but "today have become [items] of daily usage." His remedy for these excesses in consumption was to invoke traditional frugality and strict economies.

The abuse of disunity (*kanpei*). By this he meant the growing disparity between rich and poor.[58] Disparity of wealth could be easily removed if land surveys were conducted on the Chinese system of wells and fields. Such surveys would show which landholders were holding large tracts and not paying sufficient taxes, and would discourage further alienation of property. He was less concerned with the plight of the peasantry than with the somnolence of the samurai class. To resolve samurai poverty he recommended that the class, on a fifteenth-century example, be "re-

[56] *Ibid.*, p. 23. The first book of the "Kannō wakumon" expresses the five abuses; the second book is where Fujita offers his prescriptions.

[57] *Ibid.*, p. 24.

[58] *Ibid.*, p. 39.

turned to the land" (*dōchaku*). This merger of samurai and agrarian interests, a scheme used later by the Meiji government to break up the class as a coherent social unit, was justified by a notion of historical change. "Knowing how there have been changes in human conditions and circumstances from past to present," he argued, "we must today have methods that correspond to the times." [59] Yet even though an understanding of the times was to help formulate policy, policy would also have to follow classical precedents—the timeless principles of "heaven and earth." Yūkoku saw no need to resolve the inconsistency between his contemporary relativism and his inherited moral norms. Later writers, facing even more severe crises, would find in the conflict between ideals and reality the means of a genuine historical consciousness.

The abuse of forced labor. The classics had taught Fujita Yūkoku that "while exactions of physical labor had existed since antiquity, they were always trifling"; thus in times of peace the peasant should not be required to work more than three days per year to fulfill his public obligations.[60] Moderation was advised in the *Analects,* but, Yūkoku complained, times had changed and people in his day were being forced to perform labor for inordinate stretches of time. Puzzled because "ancient practices employed men only where they were needed," he confessed, with unconscious irony, that he failed to understand why peasants in his day had to be used at all for public service. If public projects demanded a large labor force, the people should not be recruited away from their own fields for more than a few days. And again Yūkoku's relativism comes out: because the times have changed it is essential "to change laws so that they are united to principle," [61] where "principle" means "loving the people" and "winning their mind and heart."

The abuse of local standards meant the way the rice yield was allotted: four portions to the lord, six to the peasant. Yūkoku

[59] *Ibid.,* p. 59.
[60] *Ibid.*
[61] *Ibid.,* p. 69.

called for stricter observance of the traditional system of appor-
tionment and its uniform application throughout the domain.

The abuse of "annoying disturbances": the growing frequency
of peasant revolts. Fujita Yūkoku may not have understood what
pressures moved the peasantry to strike out against authority, but
he was not far wrong in laying the responsibility on the managerial class. Since Yūkoku considered the masses ignorant and also
believed the leadership should love them, he argued that if the
managerial class wished to preserve control of society and rescue
civilization (he identified its control with civilization) it must
give concrete expression to its responsibilities. "Annoying disturbances" was an abuse caused not solely by the peasants (even
though Yūkoku believed they were aspiring for a style of life beyond their reach), but also by a leadership which did not fulfill
minimum requirements of benevolent government. Instead, managers relied excessively on laws and ordinances (*hōrei*)—always a
sign of moral failure in Confucian social theory. "Ordinances are
like utensils, particular tools with which to govern the people.[62]
But "no matter how many good ordinances there are available,
if there are not virtuous men to employ them, it is as with an
unskilled worker who has good tools but no craftsmanship." [63]
Only when laws reflect the reality of human conditions can the
lord and his retainers rely on precedents. The past showed that
men made laws in response to the conditions of their times; and
while Yūkoku urged the leadership to "select from old practices
those which are still good and usable," he insisted that a moral
leadership would always try to ascertain the requirements of its
own society.[64]

Fujita Yūkoku called for a program to "enrich the country"
(*fukoku*) and "increase domainal wealth" (*kokuri*), with strict
adherence to a "traditional mode of agricultural production" (*nō-
honshugi*). Thus he advised his lord to conduct his administra-

[62] *Ibid.*, p. 73.
[63] *Ibid.*, p. 74.
[64] *Ibid.*, p. 85.

tion within a fixed yearly domainal income collected from peasants, to end "loose standards," and to regularize samurai and peasant life. If a domain could measure accurately "what comes in and what goes out," "rectify economic boundaries," and exercise frugality in all economic behavior, he was confident that it could return to a purely natural agrarian economic order. All peasants and samurai living in the castle town must be returned to their original homes. "Peasants must be discouraged from intermarrying with merchants . . . and they must be registered separately. They must also be prohibited from dealing in the affairs of merchants. . . . Merchants should be limited in the amount of land they possess . . . and placed in a position beneath the most humble peasant. . . . Among the products merchants seek to sell, only those which aid humanity should be permitted. Those of inferior use, such as gems, jewelry, and pleasurable products, and those which are unsuitable to people's daily use should be prohibited." [65] In one sweep Fujita Yūkoku rejected not only the present but also the changes which had happened in the *bakuhan* system since its inception two centuries earlier. This denial of the present and call for restoration of an earlier and simpler life, transformed later by Aizawa and Fujita Tōko into a theory of political action, was the most attractive feature of the Mito statement to a managerial class fearful of losing power to a mass uprising. To eliminate "abuses" Fujita Yūkoku was calling for the abandonment of contemporary life; for they were part of the texture of life in the late eighteenth century. Virtually ignoring significant growth in commerce and technology, Yūkoku called for the reinstatement of a natural economy where change and increase of wealth had no place. His plan was simply to return to agriculture as the base of society, and to make it more attractive and beneficial. It is true that his purpose of restoring an anterior ideal presupposed agreement between manager and managed that it would lead to happiness. But Yūkoku was no illusionist. Men could believe that in rejecting the present it was possible to deny the results of unnatural development. But a

[65] *Ibid.*, pp. 85ff; Sakata (n. 45 above), p. 31.

major crisis stemming from the problems of the present revealed
that agreement was not accessible to them, and the past was not
redeemable. Fortunately for Yūkoku, he never lived to see the rebellion of Ōshio Heihachirō in Osaka or the coming of Matthew
Perry.

If the threat of *naiyū* could be dealt with through a rectification of "economic boundaries," then moral discipline would help
Japanese society meet the lesser challenge of *gaikan*. Domestic
renovation through strengthening of what was "inner" and thus
civilized, in a united effort to restore public discipline and "enrich the country," was both essential in itself and prior to the
tightening of military defense. He considered a strong army
(*kyōhei*) the solution to the problem of what was "outer" and
noncivilized. "Men who hope to strengthen the army in the manner of antiquity must first enrich the country. But men of today
have not yet sought to enrich one domain." [66] While his order of
priority, dictated by classical practice, blurred his perceptions, he
was not unaware that Western ships were appearing in Japanese
waters with increasing frequency. Thus the problem of *naiyū*, although it had to be dealt with first, concerned only the decline of
the domain, while the specter of *gaikan* imperiled the Tokugawa
arrangement of political society and by extension civilization itself.

Fujita Yūkoku berated complacency in a protracted peace as
expressed in the indifferent adage "When there is order, rebellion
is not to be feared." He wrote anxiously: "The military estate has
erected a regime that down to the present has lasted two
hundred years. . . . People have become old and died without
ever experiencing military reform. . . . The whole country has
rapidly become dead drunk and forgotten the crisis of war. In
the extreme north there are barbarians prying at Japan (*shinshu*)
because they have plans aiming at the south." [67] Worse still was
the low level of military discipline within the samurai class.

[66] "Hōji," pp. 178, 194.
[67] Quoted in Inobe Shigeo, "Mitogakuha no jōiron," *Shirin* (Tokyo,
1921), Vol. 5, no. 2, p. 22. Also "Hōji," in *Mgt.,* III, 176.

Long used to peace, and now plunged into economic desperation, the samurai had lost the qualities which once distinguished them from the rest of humanity. To survive a foreign crisis, he argued, the country would first have to reform the *bakufu;* this could be done if the lords seized the initiative. Yūkoku wrote to Narinori:

If we are not able to relieve the errors of the past by petitioning the *bakufu,* how will we be able to encourage the main actors in the domains? The teaching of war in times of peace is disliked because it raises troubles when there is no cause. But capable lords will not forget dangers, and will maintain the ordinances by keeping domestic administration in line. In order to warn us of the northern barbarian [Russia] the *bakufu* has recently issued decrees to those lords closest to the sea, admonishing them to prepare for emergencies. We should not lose this splendid opportunity to strengthen the military. Your Excellency, should we not pay attention to this? [68]

Yet after all this, it should be said that Fujita Yūkoku did not take the threat of "external catastrophe" as seriously as his words imply; rather, he used it to provide additional support for internal reform.

The foreigner was upon Japan. To secure success in domestic affairs, Fujita Yūkoku made the urgent military problem a condition of internal reform. He probably saw a strong military establishment more as protection against inner sedition than as bulwark against the outer barbarian. It was in this context anyway that he worked out the idea of *jōi,* "expelling the barbarian," which Aizawa later made more concrete. Writing to his son Tōko, then about nineteen years old, Yūkoku explained what *jōi* meant: "In antiquity the Hōjō family took hold of the government, negotiated with the Mongol emissaries who threatened invasion, and cut off their heads. The Mongols could have attacked when we were unprepared, but generals throughout the country requisitioned all materials for military use. In this way the country was put into military preparedness to meet the Mongol invasion." [69] The Hōjō had not forgotten the ever-present possi-

[68] "Hōji," p. 197.
[69] "Hōji," p. 196. Inobe, *op. cit.,* p. 3.

bility of war, and their example should remind the *bakufu* of its
duty. Yūkoku advised the *bakufu* immediately to take into counsel the opinions of the several lords—another illustration of his
desire to redefine the role of the lord. To establish the right kind
of civil administration and meet "the trend of the times," he
called for a leadership of talented men equipped not with "empty
theories," but rather with a "practical knowledge of contemporary affairs" (*jitsugaku, jikkyō*); for a tightening of the public
spirit; for "the opening of discussions among the leaders of the
country" (*chōkugen no michi o hiraki*); and for an understanding of the conditions existing in the upper and lower classes.[70] It
is almost as if Yūkoku used the myth of a foreign crisis to
achieve the reforms he saw as necessary: to elevate the domain,
and to reduce the shogunate. If the problem of the inner could be
resolved (and Yūkoku offered an answer), then the problem of
the outer would take care of itself.

Fujita Yūkoku's program of "benevolence" had an inner con-
tradiction. In one direction it was expressed in return of samurai
to the land (*dōchaku*), increased military preparedness, and so
forth, as means to arrest the growing frequency of peasant uprisings. In another direction it meant reorganization of politics: the
transfer of power back to the domains, so that through the "rectification of economic boundaries" they might prevent mass insur-
gency of the "ignorant people." This double-edged policy earned
for Yūkoku and later Mito reformers the criticism that their vision suffered from irreconcilable contradictions. Actually it is the
whole point of their effort. The moral pieties which they felt
obliged to defend left them no choice but to deny the present and
to reject the datum of immediate experience as counterfeit and
unnatural. On one hand they desired to preserve the power of
the managerial class by identifying it with civilization; on the
other they despised and feared the masses. It is then hardly surprising that Yūkoku would resort to both intimidation and bribery. What is important about Yūkoku's thinking is less its "contradictions," instructive as they are, than its order of priorities.

[70] "Hōji," p. 199.

Both his selection of problems and his modes of solution produced an abbreviation of reality; he also established important precedents for further discourse on problems of authority, order, and the survival of the *bakuhan* system.

THE MYTH OF THE PAST AND THE HISTORICAL CONSCIOUSNESS OF THE PRESENT: AIZAWA SEISHISAI

Fujita Yūkoku located the crisis in the *bakuhan* order; Aizawa Seishisai magnified his insight into an epic statement of purpose. Yūkoku by his formulas of the "imperial Way" (*ōdōron*) and "designations and duties" (*meibun-ron*) had reaffirmed the principles of loyalty and respect underlying the Tokugawa arrangement of power. He could only do this by rejecting the present in favor of a remote past closer to the paradigms of order. His insistence upon the "rectification of names" presupposes that duty is a fixed principle unrelated to the practice of contemporary politics. History proved that name and reality could be separated; men had ruled in the past without the authorization of status. Yūkoku was very clear about this when describing the rise of the Hōjō family. Although he confessed his approval of their performance during the Mongol crisis, he condemned them in the end as mere usurpers "without name"; they had exceeded the limits of the duty of their rank in political society. In this way Yūkoku explained the "political ups and downs" of history, without relying on theories such as the "transfer of the mandate" which Confucianists employed to justify a new political authority after the fact. Despite his espousal of the "imperial way," Yūkoku also believed in the sanctity of the Japanese imperial house as shown by its unbroken line of succession. But *ōdō* could never be squared with belief in the emperor's divine descent; for it required even his acquiescence in a transcendental Way, while the theory about his descent placed him beyond all political rules, making him in part transcendent. Moreover, *ōdō* put in the middle of history a criterion of ethical behavior, while the idea of a divinely appointed emperor removed him from the judgment of history. Fujita Yūkoku never really acknowledged this dilemma, but later writers, notably Rai Sanyō and Aizawa Seishisai, consciously directed their attention to it.

Furthermore, Fujita Yūkoku by his idea that the formation and execution of policy obeyed the changes of the times and contemporary requirements, delivered to writers such as Aizawa a powerful technique with which to assign meaning to the present. By suggesting that different times required new adjustments if the leadership was to accomplish a "benevolent administration," Yūkoku equipped Neo-Confucianism with a concept of change. He was arguing that history is not changeless, and was inviting other writers to make qualitative distinctions between past and present, to ask how the present came to be what it is. Yūkoku was also suggesting that something more than moral example was required to meet new needs—namely, an elaborate political apparatus, long rejected by orthodox Neo-Confucianists. This new conception of history implied that political leaders should be judged not by vague ethical imperatives, but by the criterion of success in formulating policies suitable to changing conditions.[71] In this view, politics was no longer dependent on the ethical behavior of the sage whose superior virtue has entitled him to rule. It was no longer reducible to ethics, since ethical behavior, especially the exercise of *meibun,* had little to do with the success of political experiments. While it would be ideal to have a leadership that was both politically astute and ethically upright, history had shown that morality did not guarantee astuteness.

Fujita Yūkoku also argued that, whatever the nature of political administrations, absolute authority rested with the divinely appointed emperor. Administrators would succeed or fail, depending on their skills as politicians. The imperial house would remain intact, providing moral legitimation to political regimes. In Yūkoku's thinking, an emperor who already *has* absolute authority is the same as one who *is* absolute authority. Neo-Confu-

[71] Bitō Masahide, "Nihon ni okeru rekishi ishiki no hatten," in *Nihon ni okeru rekishi shisō no tenkai* ed. Nihon Shisōshi Kenkyūkai (Sendai, 1961), p. 56.

cianists had simply identified the emperor with the moral Way and explained his divinity as just an expression of his virtue. Yūkoku reasoned, on the contrary, that his divinity was prior to his morality and the two were not always the same thing. In theory an emperor might be immoral, but since he was beyond good and evil he could not be judged or deposed by history. The emperor's divinity alone made the political process possible. Still, he was not bound by temporal political conduct. This was the responsibility of men who rule and administer in his name. If they failed, as they often did, it was not out of any defect in virtue or in the emperor, but out of their inability to satisfy contemporary political necessities. The emperor got off scot-free, since he only authorized politics and made it possible, but he was not responsible for its mismanagement. Fujita Yūkoku, following nativists such as Motoori Norinaga, presumed that political leadership should always make contemporary needs a datum in the formulation of policy. Success or failure depended upon the extent to which the leadership could "penetrate" social reality.

Of course, a political regime seeking to usurp the "name" of the emperor would be acting unvirtuously, but Japanese history offered few such examples. For this reason, Yūkoku claimed, Tokugawa Ieyasu refused to arrogate to himself the title of king, even though he was obliged to subject himself to the "kingly way." Success was possible only to men who recognized that the present is not the past; even Yūkoku called for a rejection of the present *only after he recognized* that his present was different from an ideal past. All that was required of political leadership, with respect to the emperor, was acknowledgment of his absolute authority and observance of the decorum proper to the relationship of lord and vassal. This argument, hinted at by Yūkoku, was brought to a high level of sophistication by his student Aizawa. Behind Aizawa's majestic restatement of tradition was the conviction that morality—namely, assigning "the right name" to each function—had become obliterated by time. The present had the unique task of rejoining ethical skills and policies to the exigencies of the times. Aizawa's was the last creative effort to rejoin history to ethics, but in his recognition that his present was different from the past, he was delivering to discourse a new concept of present-mindedness. Instead of giving to the future a convincing argument for the reunification of politics and ethics, morality and history, as he hoped, his idea of a unique present dramatized the impossibility of such an achievement. While he believed that the present was uniquely appointed to put society back on the correct course, others would argue that its uniqueness demanded unprecedented measures and policies. Even Aizawa's celebrated attempt to restore to his present the meaning of a remote mythic past confirmed this line.

Aizawa Seishisai, a Mito retainer and Fujita Yūkoku's outstanding pupil, spent his long life observing the currents of change which his teacher only dimly perceived. His life spanned such formative events as the first Russian and British probes in Japanese waters, the Tempō reforms, the crisis of *kaikoku,* and the demise of Mito *han* in countrywide affairs. Yet his writings, more voluminous than those of most *bakumatsu* writers, reached their greatest fullness and popularity early, in the 1820s and 1830s. He said what he had to say from the time when the crew of a British whaler was detained in Mito, down through the Tempō reforms; when Perry's squadron forced open the door of seclusion, most of the Mito rhetoric, as expressed in Aizawa's writings was outmoded. Aizawa, reputed the foremost spokesman of "expulsionism" (*jōiron*), probably acknowledged how far his thinking had been discredited by the opening of the country, when in 1862 he wrote an essay justifying *kaikoku* as a means of preserving independence.[72] Entitled *Contemporary Policy (Jimusaku)*, the work failed to conceal Aizawa's instinctive suspicion of foreigners, even though it approved *kaikoku* as a temporary defensive expedient. But it did little to alter the fixed image of the Mito position as formulated by Yūkoku, Tōko, and Aizawa himself. The eminence of the school had faded through failure to accommodate itself to a national crisis. Also the domain of Mito,

[72] Nishimura Fuminori, *Aizawa Hakumin* (Tokyo, 1938), pp. 356–362, and Arakawa Kusuo, *Ishin zenya* (Tokyo, 1965), pp. 102ff.

owing to the death of its vigorous leader Nariaki and a protracted internal struggle, was removed from center stage of national affairs. Aizawa's effort to keep up with the times was too
little and too late, for his new line had been anticipated by former followers of the Mito school: Sakuma Shōzan, Yoshida
Shōin, Yokoi Shōnan, and others.[73] Events had overtaken Aizawa and relegated his vision to the status of a historical curios-
ity.

Aizawa was early enrolled as a pupil of Fujita Yūkoku, and in
his autobiographical *Kyūmon ihan* tells us something about the
education he received:

First the teacher [*Yūkoku*] lectured on the *Classic of Filial Piety*
(*Hsiao ching*), and followed this up with the Four Books and the
Five Classics. Often when we were reading exercises, he would dwell
on points that were difficult and clarify them for us. . . . Following
this, we were made to read the *Shih chi, Tso Chuan, Kuo yü, Han shu*
and so forth. Because he was able to manage a high degree of excitement in his lectures we would never lose interest [in the text]. Sometimes we would pass through poems and try to penetrate their sentiment; at other times we would discuss the merits, in antiquity and in
the present, of the rites of etiquette and music, political teachings and
punishment, the status obligations of lord and vassal, father and son,
the changing conditions in the countries of the world, and the discrimination between Chinese and barbarian, within and without.[74]

To his pupils, Fujita Yūkoku stressed the principle of loyalty in
all human relationships, a particular consequence from the notion of discrimination. Aizawa, seizing this lead, refashioned the
idea of *shinkoku,* the "divine realm," as the source of all truth
and value. As J. R. Levenson said of Chinese Confucianism in the
nineteenth century, he transmuted what had been "a consideration of space" into a "consideration of time." That is, taking a no-

[73] Nishimura here tries to make a case for Aizawa's defense of *kaikoku.*
He adds that it was different than that promoted by Yokoi and Sakuma
because it was still based on a firm belief in cultural discrimination (*jōi*).
Aizawa, pp. 356–362.

[74] *Ibid.*

tion like *shinkoku,* which originally possessed only spatial significance, he turned it into an idea no longer bound by time or
place, valid for all ages and all times.

Aizawa's education was continued by association with the Mito
historiographical bureau (the Shōkōkan) and by a brief period
of study in Edo. After his return to Mito in 1820, he opened up
his own lecture hall (*juku*) and began to teach. At the same time
he became involved in domainal administration and, necessarily,
in political factions; he held responsible positions in the Shōkōkan
and district magistracies in and around Mito. In 1829, together
with Fujita Tōko and about forty other retainers, Aizawa became hotly involved in a dispute over succession, since the *han*
lord Narinori had recently died. Narinori had left no male heir,
and one group of domainal administrators favored a son of the
shogun, while the "Reform Wing" in which Aizawa was a leading figure supported Narinori's brother, Nariaki. Fujita Yūkoku,
before his death in 1826, had also come down on the side of Nariaki, arguing that adoption ran counter to traditional practice of
the Mito house. Through the efforts of Aizawa and Fujita Tōko,
the Reform Wing made its case known to the *bakufu* and won
the appointment of Nariaki.

Aizawa served as an adviser of Nariaki during the crucial years
when the new daimyo was trying to carry out a broad reform
(Tempō), and at the same time participating in decisions in the
counsels of state.[75] In 1841 Aizawa became general adviser and
lecturer in Nariaki's new school, the Kōdōkan, and was elevated
to the rank of *kōshogashira* with a stipend of 250 *koku*. In the
following years his fortunes fluctuated as Nariaki fell out of favor
with shogunal authorities. But despite these ups and downs, Aizawa's prominence as defender of traditional values continued
until his death in 1862. Through his most eloquent statement, the
New Proposals (*Shinron*), he became the teacher of a generation
of prerestoration activists, who reached beyond domestic politics
to the perilous future of Japanese civilization, even though Aizawa himself was never prepared to go beyond the world of the
domain.

[75] Aizawa, pp. 69–81.

In days when British ships kept appearing off the coasts of Japan, Aizawa wrote the first of a series of tracts which applied the canons of traditional learning to contemporary problems. This genre, inaugurated with the *An-i monshō* in 1824 and fixed with the *Shinron* in 1826, characterized his writing, including a dozen books, for the next twenty years, his most prolific period.[76] Aizawa, completing the *Shinron* when he was forty-four years old, had already distinguished himself as a teacher and philosophical expositor of the Chinese classics. The *Shinron* came out when the Tokugawa *bakufu*, in desperate need of a foreign policy, issued the ill-conceived *mu-i uchi harai rei*, "don't-think-twice expulsion edict," as a rejoinder to the mounting British probes. The edict was little more than a tired restatement of Tokugawa isolationism, which revealed the incapacity of the *bakufu* to see beyond the immediate implications of events. Therefore Aizawa, despite his initial approval of the edict, put together a statement to make up for the deficiencies in the "new" policy.

The *New Proposals* and later writings of this genre were efforts to explain Japanese civilization in the context of world movements and to justify an antiforeign policy as the only proper defense of *shinkoku*, the divine realm. In Aizawa's hands, culture in the name of *shinkoku*, which had earlier described historical experiences in a specific geographical environment, become a universal designation. For Aizawa, *shinkoku* with all its rich mythic associations was a more elaborate way of describing the *bakuhan* order. The difference between Aizawa and Fujita Yūkoku is one of language. Aizawa's decision to use the rhetoric of native mytho-history (as restyled in the early nineteenth century by men like Hirata Atsutane) made the *Shinron* a general statement moving beyond the *han* to civilization itself—before political events forced such a transfer, and despite Aizawa's purpose to exalt the ethical integrity of the domain.

Aizawa used the amuletic word *kokutai* ("national essence") for the power destined to protect Japan. The confrontation with the West, though slight in the 1820s, obliged him to summon up

[76] It should be noted that the *Shinron*, owing to its "incendiary" theme, was not published until much later.

the power and mystique of *kokutai* in order to decide why Japan, now transmuted into *shinkoku,* was superior to all other societies. On one hand, Aizawa affirmed Neo-Confucianism as a body of universal truths which had long shaped Japanese social behavior and political practice; on the other hand, he felt it meaningless to restore another people's history, which had given original expression to these truths, and like earlier writings invoked native experience. Then, by arguing that the beliefs produced by the Japanese experience were similar to those of China, Aizawa could have his cake and eat it: he could claim universality under the forms of a unique history. And because Japan alone was the repository of universal human values, developed first in China but subsequently abandoned, its defense was the defense of civilization. Against this argument the nativists, especially Hirata and his followers, could only affirm emotionally the uniqueness of Japan, but without the authoritative support of Confucian universalism. To summon the glories of *shinkoku* before it had been corrupted by Chinese culture was not enough to appeal to the most literate and sophisticated group in society, the samurai, for whom Confucianism remained the most advanced and perfect statement about human society. In his critique of Motoori Norinaga's *Naobi no mitama* Aizawa demonstrated how intellectually unsatisfactory the pure *kokugaku* ("nativist") statement seemed to those educated in a Confucian idiom who thought of themselves as the Japanese equivalent of the Chinese literati.[77] And while nativism, in its late Tokugawa form, offered a theory of vocation and called for the routinization of status, it did not, like Confucianism, provide a historical validation for the rise of the military estate and its assumption of managerial power.[78]

Aizawa, then, started as a good Confucianist, illuminating ethical precepts which would make good government possible. The

---

[77] Aizawa Seishisai (Yasushi), "Zoku Naobi no mitama," in *Mgt.,* II, 394–481. Also, Itō Tasaburō, "Edo jidai goki no rekishishisō," in *Nihon ni okeru rekishi shisō no tenkai,"* p. 243.

[78] Matsumoto Sannosuke, *Kokugaku seiji shisō no kenkyū* (Osaka, 1957), pp. 65–111.

function of government was to preserve an arrangement of power in which the "sovereign acts and thus rules for heaven" and exercises his political authority through "good teaching," not through rewards and punishments.[79] Order requires the "Way of the lord" (*kundō*), that is, imperial rule. "In times when there is no *kundō*, there can be no administration or political affairs. Nor is there anybody to manage skillfully the necessities of daily life for the people. There would be nobody to prevent thievery, the strong would defy the weak, and the masses would be reduced in numbers through bloodletting."[80] If lords fail to instruct the people in proper conduct, it will be impossible to distinguish between humanity and "the birds and beasts." Beneath all human organization lie the Five Relationships which the emperor, after receiving his mandate from the sun goddess, perfected by distinguishing between lord and retainer and designating filial loyalty as the key duty of all. "Those who govern the people," he wrote in this connection, "are the samurai (*shi*). The peasant, artisan, and merchant provide the lord and *shi* their daily necessities. . . . Those who work with physical strength nourish men and are governed; those who work with their mind are nourished and govern the people. . . . They [high and low] mutually assist each other and constitute the Four Estates."[81] The functions of the several estates might change, but the ethic of discrimination which supported the leadership in its claims was timeless, "without beginning or end."

Aizawa viewed the *bakuhan* order as a representation of this timeless pattern. He was therefore forced to ask how the position of the emperor fitted in with this universal scheme of things. So was Fujita Yūkoku; but his pupil Aizawa, under pressure of events, while retaining the old concept of emperorship, expanded the possibilities of the emperor's role. In evoking the elaborate claims of myth and its imperial associations, he had no intention other than rehearsing what most Tokugawa ideologues agreed

[79] Aizawa, "Tekii hen," in *Mgt.*, II, 350–351.
[80] *Ibid.*
[81] *Ibid.*, p. 357.

on as the role of the emperor. The emperor was a principle of political authority which provided ethical validation of the *baku-han* system. Aizawa did not mysteriously rediscover the emperor (as many writers have argued) at a crucial time in Japan's political history. He had always been there, because without him the system of things was not ethically possible. He was the keystone of the social edifice, even though it was not customary for him to exercise direct political rule. "Receiving nature, which is the creation of Heaven, the emperor broadens the work of nature. The *bakufu* assists the imperial court and manages the country (*tenka*). The several territorial lords all serve as the bulwark of the imperial court (*toku wa mina tenchō no hampei ni shite*), and enforce throughout their *han* the political ordinances of the *bakufu*. Their retainers and the people, by following the edicts of their respective lords, are therefore obeying the ordinances of the *bakufu*, and thus of the imperial court also. To depend upon the imperial court is the Way by which the heavenly ancestors are compensated." [82] Aizawa, despite the authority he lavishes on the emperor, believed that the "realm still belongs to the realm because it is a public realm." If he had entertained the nativist notion of emperorship, he would have held on the contrary that "the realm is the private possession of the emperor." He could endorse the notion of a public realm because he did not conceive of the emperor as a personality playing a vigorous political role; for Aizawa he remained what he had been, a lifeless principle authenticating a timeless order. For Aizawa, as for early Tokugawa ideologues, the emperor was still identified with the Way, whereas contemporary nativists made him prior to the Way or above it.

Even for Aizawa this meant that the emperor was without personality, a shadowy figure who contributed little to the making of history. What was important, for Aizawa and most Neo-Confucianists, was an emperor who could manage the Way—and who therefore was subject to it. If he failed to meet its requirements, he would contribute to political failure and chaos and lose

[82] *Ibid.*, pp. 358–359; "Shinron," pp. 181–182.

his position. But an emperor with the regulative task of validating the social order had an impossible moral role. His only guarantee of survival was nonactivity—ceremony and ritual. He could not be involved in *doing;* for his occupying a ceremonial role, his *being,* was all that mattered. For Aizawa the emperor was not a creator, in contrast to the views of the nativists; for "heaven created nature," and it was owing to this act that he existed, like other elements in the universal order of things, without beginning or end. Men would come and go, serving temporarily in the capacity of emperor, but the position was timeless, a reminder of the unchanging order of things. When historical change intruded, he could act to readjust things back to timeless regularity. Undoubtedly Aizawa, with his syncretistic position which included both nativist and Neo-Confucian elements, was unclear in his views of the ideal order. But he was not unclear about locating the emperor as the source of authority over against heaven, and as the validating principle of loyalty between lords and vassals.

For Aizawa, just as there were many levels of political authority, so loyalty existed on many levels. He had to admit that all loyalty was ultimately directed toward the emperor, even though he used this admission to strengthen the loyalty between ruler and ruled on all levels. He never anticipated any possible conflict in loyalty. When he argued that the *"bakufu* is obliged to suppress calamitous rebellions and is thus the pillar of the court," he added that the lords, by performing the duties of territorial administration, were serving the emperor and heaven. "The lords of the several domains have the status of heavenly officials," he declared, "and thus they form the bulwark of *shinshū.*" [83] Only after the emperor became more than the ethical validation of the system and acquired a new set of clothes—a personality and a historical role—would the problem of loyalty arise for men searching to justify what shogunal and domainal authorities would judge as disloyalty. In suggesting that the emperor "broaden the work of nature," Aizawa was simply taking a fix on his cosmic

[83] "Tekii hen," p. 349.

location.[84] "Heaven and earth," he wrote, "are the origins of man. Because he receives the body of his ancestors, he is born to embrace the spirit of heaven and earth. The imperial throne worships heaven and earth externally; men impart their sincerity to heaven and earth by submitting to their duties, and internally they worship their ancestors and endeavor as individuals to be sincere." [85] Aizawa's logic is inescapable. The emperor merely represents the great cosmic order, heaven and earth; outwardly men show their devotion to this order by performing their natural duties, while inwardly they express respect to their ancestors for the "blessing" of existence. Here Aizawa showed more than a casual dependence on the nativist notion that all duties are divine vocations.[86]

Aizawa believed that the teachings of living sages could be steeped in the utterances of gods and Heaven, and that the emperor illuminated such teachings. People entrusted "their sincerity to the imperial crown, who then transmits it to the gods." [87] But in assigning this function to the emperor, Aizawa makes him more than the validating agent of an ethical order. The emperor is not merely serving as an intermediary between earth and an indeterminate heaven, which in the Confucian scheme was little more than an immanental or consensual source of authority. Even though he seeks only virtue, he also is involved in power. By the emperor's direct link to the gods or the national ancestors, his authority is beyond good and evil and is liberated from the judgment of society. And the divinity of the imperial family was the guarantee of Japan's eternity. Aizawa knew that the principle of discrimination, as enforced by the presence of a divinely appointed emperor, had little to do with political history. The emperor acted in history but was not part of it. Neither China nor the West had known such an eternal principle; in all their history dynasties had changed through disorder. "The custom of

[84] *Ibid.,* pp. 349, 382.
[85] *Ibid.,* p. 382.
[86] See Matsumoto, *Kokugaku seiji shisō* . . . , p. 106; *Mgt.,* II, 357–359.
[87] "Tekii hen," p. 346.

Russia," Aizawa wrote, "is that during the upheavals within the country lords are murdered and rebels rise to take their place. . . . Among the ten thousand countries only Japan has had one imperial line, transmitted by the descendants of the sun goddess since the founding of the country." [88] Despite his simple intent to show how the emperor authenticates the system, *he* authenticated possibilities which later writers would explore in their effort to dismantle the system. Implicit in Aizawa's confused rhetoric was the idea of an emperor who was both virtue and power, who was being but was involved in doing, who adjusted but also acted.

Aizawa's anxiety over the present motivated a flight to the past. He wrote that the great fourteenth-century loyalist Kitabatake Chikafusa had complied his *Jinnō Shōtōkiji* to correct the confusion of rival claimants to the throne, and to remind his contemporaries of the divinity of the imperial line in contrast with the impermanence of political rule both in Japan and elsewhere. "Today these subjects [retainers] are the grandsons of those who originally received the benevolence of the heavenly grandson, and they are the ones who follow the political ordinances of the *bakufu* and the territorial lords. Even though there have been ten thousand changes during the last thousand generations that have passed, the great principle (*taigi*) of lord and retainer and the obligation of son to father have not changed from the beginnings of the country down to today." [89] History and ethics (it seemed) had parted ways, but real politics was possible only if they were rejoined. Yet Aizawa knew that there had been "political ups and downs," even though the continuity of the imperial line had been preserved. He also knew that political failure was not the same as moral failure, though political leaders might incur some terrible wrath if they usurped the emperor's "name." Rather, the success of a regime depended upon how well it understood the historical conditions of the times to formulate policy within the established limits of order.

[88] *Ibid.*, pp. 335–366.
[89] *Ibid.*, p. 382.

Much of Aizawa's writing, especially during the Tempō years, was called out by contemporary conditions. "There are two great problems today," he announced in the *Shinron*, "and they are changing conditions and abuses." [90] This was not a moral indictment of change. Change was the "natural course of heaven and earth," and through an understanding of history and of the present, shogunal leaders will formulate proper policies.[91] But first they must understand certain historical exemplars which earlier had given expression to the great moral principles of loyalty and filial piety. Aizawa's appeal to history combined the Neo-Confucian stress on the unity of history with a new view which distinguished the past from the present. While he argued for the inevitability of political change, he was not entirely at home in the new relativism—a present that might be different from other presents, process which intruded upon timeless patterns. To soften this sense of isolation he had recourse to historical norms of loyalty and filial piety. Aizawa could not yet (as later writers did) accept process and change in the present as a new source of authority. Rather he used Japan's antiquity to restore and expand the "emperor's work" (*tengyō*) in the present. Later writers would concentrate exclusively on the meaning of the present; but for Aizawa the precedent of the past, "even though it is remote from the present," would inform Japan how "to reform the spirit of the people and preserve the country. By relying on imperial power, which is the Great Way of heavenly beings, we should so conduct ourselves . . . as to return to that which is the warp and woof of the realm." [92]

In this pursuit of the past Aizawa settled on the task of examining the exclusive concept of *kokutai*, which becomes the central metaphor of his writing. Already in the preface to the *Shinron* he discloses to his generation the meaning of Japan's divine foundation in antiquity for all times to come: "Our land of the gods has emerged from the sun, from which it derives its natural

[90] "Shinron," p. 91.

[91] *Ibid.*, pp. 68–69; 146–147.

[92] *Ibid.*, p. 38.

vitality. The successors of the sun have occupied the throne from generation to generation, from the beginnings to the very end." [93] He finds additional proof of Japan's divinity in its geographical position, by obvious design, at the center of the world. This notion comes from the much earlier Chinese effort to map out the boundaries of civilization. The late Tokugawa period, continuing Yamaga Sokō's innovation of identifying Japan with the "central kingdom," held that only Japan qualified for the status of civilization, since it alone had preserved the ideals of antiquity. This feat, unparalleled (according to Aizawa) among the countries of the world, had made Japan the political center of the globe, whose influence, like the rays of the sun, reached out in all directions.

No less important for Aizawa was the eternity of imperial descent which had sustained the unity of Japanese civilization since time immemorial. It was no accident that the imperial line had survived so long in one family. From the inception of the ancient state, the Japanese people had been of one mind in their devotion to the emperor. "The people, respecting the heavenly descendants, know how to revere the sun goddess; and by so doing they unite their will to the heavenly deities (*tenjin*)." [94] The relation of lord and retainer, exemplified eternally in the relation of emperor and people, is the mark of civilization; Japan is its latest and only extant expression. Aizawa, despite his homage to the imperial genealogy, will not betray Confucian pieties and rhetoric. Thus he compares the relation of emperor and people to that of parent and child, shaped by prescribed duties but mediated by kindness (*on*). It is kindness that "permeates all things existing between heaven and earth," and serves as an unbreakable link between ruler and subject.[95] But despite these vestiges of Confucian social theory, Aizawa is more concerned to clarify the loyalty between ruler and ruled, and uses the family as an example of the

[93] *Ibid.,* p. 42; also "Gegaku jigen," in *Mgt.,* I, 199–202; "Tekii hen," p. 330.

[94] "Shinron," p. 13.

[95] *Ibid.,* pp. 5–6.

sentiment that must inform this relationship. Here is the stuff from which *kokutai* is made.

In making *kokutai* out to be the guarantee of Japan's uniqueness as a civilization and eternity as a state, Aizawa examined *shinkoku,* the paradigmatic age of gods and heroes, and found that Japan had drifted far from the true norms of human conduct, *taigi meibun.* This analysis, despite its ethical purpose, relies on the native mytho-history in ancient texts such as the *Nihon shoki,* from which he lifts verbatim long passages. The merger of Shinto mytho-history and Confucian morality becomes complete in this investigation of the ancient polity; for Aizawa the Tokugawa order becomes the political identity of *shinkoku.*

At the inception of the state, when the sun goddess established the foundations of political life, all was made to conform with heaven, for "the position of [Amaterasu Ōmikami] was a heavenly one, her virtue a heavenly virtue." Following the nativists (*kokugakusha*), notably Motoori Norinaga, Aizawa identifies the attributes of the sun goddess with the three items of the imperial regalia: "Her virtue is comparable to the jewel, her brightness to the mirror, and her stern authority to the sword." They were turned over to the great-grandson of the heavenly progenetrix, as was the administration of the country, and became the divine symbols of imperial office, handed down from generation to generation, furnishing the holder an emblem of divinity and a guarantee of eternity. "At the time the heavenly progenetrix handed down the divine utensils, she took the treasured mirror, consecrated it, and said: 'To look at this mirror is to look at me.' From this time, ten thousand generations have celebrated this as the divinity of the heavenly progenetrix. . . . Looking into this treasured mirror they saw her reflection, and when praying they saw their own bodies, bequeathed to them by Amaterasu. In this way they felt a mutual communion between the gods and men." [96] This myth shows the inviolable link between sovereign and subject, maintained by timeless obligations—reverence for

[96] *Ibid.,* pp. 6–7.

ancestors and filial devotion. Hence the moral character of *shin-koku:* "If kindness is prosperously achieved from within, and the great duty (*taigi*) made clear from without, loyalty and filial piety will be established as the Great Way of heaven and man." [97] Aizawa's analysis, like Fujita Yūkoku's, rests on the complementarity of opposites, within and without, whose proper balance was the pledge of a harmonious social order.

Loyalty and filial piety, moral counterparts of within and without, had a single source and unified man with heaven, since they were, from the beginning, bound up with the divine appointment of the imperial clan. Aizawa argued therefore that government could not be separated from religious exercises. Once more he turned to nativism; his equation of religion and polity demanded a priest-king, wholly at odds with the Confucian sovereign. Also, since no differentiation could be made between sacred and secular, the realm was divine and the private possession of the emperor. By his divine descent, the emperor was both political and religious leader. Since the emperor has taken over "the heavenly duties," he wrote, "*matsuri* ('religious ceremony') is government . . . and government is teaching; teaching and government are inseparable." [98] Here nativism is combined with the Confucian doctrine that good government instructs through persuasion rather than legislates through coercion. But, he observed, the imperial charisma was never directly exercised, since it was the duty of the several lords to administer the imperial realm. Aizawa, like Motoori, conceived of the emperor, not as an autonomous agent in political decisions, but as a symbol of absolute authority. History, he admitted, often showed how men reaffirmed their basic belief in imperial authority by administering in "the name of the emperor." Certainly, he continued, the Taika reform of the seventh century aimed at nothing less than a restoration of a country unified under the mantle of imperial authority. Under the guidance of Shōtoku Taishi, land was reorganized and redis-

[97] *Ibid.,* p. 7.
[98] *Ibid.,* pp. 12–13; "Tekii hen," p. 354.

tributed, personal property and slave-holding were abolished, and "all was returned to the emperor; all became imperial retainers." [99]

Ancient Japan witnessed also to a unity of state and military—for example, in making the sword one of the three items of the imperial regalia. This connection enabled Aizawa to criticize contemporary unpreparedness and defects in Tokugawa military organization. It is irrelevant that his ideal unity of government and army was not realized in any one historical period. He rejects the notion of a professional military class separated from the land; for in the emperor's realm, a private possession publicly administered, there are only "imperial retainers." He knew how a military élite had evolved in history, but believed it to be an unnecessary evil; the realm had available in times of need a loyal army of subjects, which when normalcy was restored would return to the land. The divine realm (*shinkoku*) had no need for a specialized military class, and raised a militia only in times of emergency.

Actually Aizawa's argument here was based not on social conditions in the pre-Taika period, but on the idea of conscription in the post-Taika reforms. "In antiquity weapons were stored in the shrines (*jinja*), and men, before going off to war, used to celebrate their duties to heaven. . . . The emperor received the edict from the gods and through this the will of the people was unified with heaven. Thus the people become soldiers performing heavenly duties." [100] Aizawa projected this ancient practice into the present to argue that only a united effort could meet threats from without. To this end he stressed unity between "heaven, earth, and man" in ancient Japan. Once man was separated from the soil, he could no longer fulfill his "heavenly duties." Just as taking up arms in response to the emperor's call was a sacred obligation, so tilling the "emperor's land" during peace was equivalent to "celebrating heaven." He described antiquity in this manner, not out of desire to understand past relationships, but to find

[99] "Shinron," p. 23.
[100] *Ibid.*, p. 39.

conditions of contemporary survival. Those who, as in the past, work the land in normal times will wish to defend it in time of war. By contrast, a professional military class such as the samurai (*shi*) removed from the land is useless in peace and less concerned to save the land in war. "It is for this reason," he concluded, "that the military must defend the land, for the land nourishes the military. The two cannot be separated; if they should be, the land will lie fallow and the army will be reduced to a weakened minority." [101]

Aizawa also believed that *shinkoku* had economic prosperity. He rejected both a professional military class removed from the land and the consolidation of land in the hands of merchants. Since the land was the "emperor's realm," it should not be subdivided into estates controlled by moneylenders or usurers.[102] Aizawa, like many of his contemporaries, viewed land as the only source of wealth and power. This view served the interests of the *bakuhan* order; it was also rooted in the cosmological assumption of classical Chinese naturalism that man and all other forms of life owed their existence to heaven. But later generations had reduced this generative principle to a passive force.[103] Reverence for heaven, by the sages in China and the emperor in Japan, meant the exercise of virtue in "expanding heaven's work" by leaders who would act in heaven's place, because they understand how to tranqualize humanity.[104] Aizawa wrote approvingly of the Taika reform because it sought to abolish private property and return the realm to the emperor; abolition of private property, despite political ups and downs, would mitigate poverty.[105] To measure precisely "what comes in and what goes out" was the true index of adequate agricultural production. A major abuse of contemporary economic life was the increase of "unproductive people": merchants, artisans who produced luxury items, and the

---

[101] *Ibid.,* p. 48.

[102] *Ibid.,* p. 22.

[103] "Gegaku jigen," I, pp. 238–239.

[104] *Ibid.,* p. 239; "Tekii hen," pp. 358–359.

[105] "Shinron," p. 58.

Buddhist clergy.[106] Contemporary agricultural production, especially in "grains and cereals," was insufficient to feed a growing population—not because it was growing, but because energy and money were being diverted into nonagricultural pursuits. He saw money as the symbol of contemporary economic problems, since in antiquity little money was in circulation and people were free from its debilitating effects. The production of gold and silver encouraged luxury and indebtedness. The country should check the use of money, refrain from importing food, and through the equalization of land and other practices of ancient Japan grow all the grains necessary for consumption. (Consumption itself would have to be reduced to minimal requirements.)

Aizawa's evocation of antiquity no doubt had a restorationist motive, common to Neo-Confucianism in both Japan and China. For Aizawa restoration meant *shinkoku,* in which a divinely appointed emperor is central. But Aizawa also knew that emperors usually reigned without ruling, and that real administrative power was held by imperial ministers. He also knew that different times demanded different policies, which meant approval of Motoori's "recurrent leadership." Aizawa's restorationism invited criticism of the Tokugawa regime by later writers on the grounds that contemporary needs were not being faced in the making of policy; it hints then at a vague dissatisfaction in his own thought. He was aware that restorationism, more than a reassertion of imperial authority, would require investigation of social reality.

But Aizawa's embrace of restoration (*fukko*) was, however, different from the religious revivalism of Hirata Atsutane.[107] The two writers differed in their attitudes toward history. Despite the nativist stratum of his thought, Aizawa's restorationism remained

---

[106] *Ibid.,* pp. 58–59.

[107] Itō, *op. cit.* (n. 77 above), pp. 238–242. Tahara Tsuguo has written a brilliant intellectual biography, *Hirata Atsutane* in Jinbutsu sosho, (Tokyo, 1963). For our purpose see pp. 287ff. See also Matsumoto Sannosuke, "Kokugaku no seiritsu," in Iwanami kōza *Nihon rekishi* (Tokyo, 1963), Kinsei 4, vol. 23.

true to Neo-Confucian political philosophy. Though he recorded change, he never accepted indefinite continuation of change; change must mean improvement, and as a Neo-Confucianist Aizawa was committed to the ideal of a stable society which has achieved perfection. More concretely: Aizawa, unlike Hirata and the *kokugakusha* of the late Tokugawa era, accepted the historical and ethical meaning of the samurai class. Therefore he could not deny the relevance of history down to the establishment of the Tokugawa system; it was a necessary prelude which explained the role of the military estate. On the other hand, Hirata and his supporters, seeking a literal revival of ancient Shinto, turned away entirely from the immediate past to a remote time where the military estate played no role. In embracing pre-Taika antiquity, Hirata abandoned all history after the establishment of the Nara state. This meant a wholesale denunciation of foreign philosophies—Confucianism and Buddhism—and also of the history for which they were responsible. He also had to deny any historical role of the *bushi* (samurai) in the making of the Japanese state, and came close to attacking the ethical basis of social discrimination.[108]

These differences help explain the appeal of Aizawa to late Tokugawa ideologues and the failure of Hirata's nativism. Both writers invoked antiquity in response to contemporary crisis. But in rejecting the immediate past, Hirata failed to understand the

[108] Itō, p. 240. Also Itō Tasaburō, *Sōmō no kokugaku* (Tokyo, 1966). Itō argues in this book that because the Hirata persuasion in nativism rejected the "historical meaning of the middle ages," especially the period in which the samurai class was emerging to power, it found little support in the intellectual world of Edo and Kyoto. Rather it recruited its adherents from among priests of Shinto shrines, the spiritual center of village life. From the shrines Hiratagaku was transmitted to the post-town officials, *mura* chiefs, wealthy merchants and peasants, in short, to the leading groups in Japanese rural society. Enrollment, even at its peak, never exceeded 600 members, most of whom came from villages. To this subject Shimazaki Tōson has written an eloquent and epically long novel on the appeal of Hirata's nativism and revivalism among commoners and the utter disillusionment of one of its adherents after the restoration, called *Yoakemae.*

complexity of contemporary needs. And it was absurd, certainly
to Neo-Confucian rationalists, however tinged by nativism, to believe that a restoration of ancient Shinto could solve the crisis.
Hirata was using the concept of restoration, not as an analytic
tool, but as a serious solution for present problems—but in fact it
inhibited any understanding of them and compelled him to abandon the present entirely.

The novelist Shimazaki Tōson tells a poignant story in his
Yoakemae of how the pious Aoyama Hanzō believed that the Restoration of 1867 would bring a return to older religious and political values, as the school of Hirata had promised. This illustrates
precisely how Hirata and his school envisaged restoration. No
Confucianist could ever suffer such a delusion. Aizawa nowhere
in his writing suggests that a literal restoration of a specific past
is possible. For, while he accepted the principle of restoration
(*chūkō*), he never denied the past, remote and immediate, from
which the present evolved. Concern with contemporary conditions induced him to search in Japanese history for standards of
conduct and judgment, which he found in *shinkoku*. As a Confucian he might disapprove certain phases of the past but he
could never deny their reality, for the continuity of human experience recorded in history was the pledge of the ethical way and
of its universality. The section of the *Shinron* dealing with *jisei*
("circumstance of times") illustrates Aizawa's concern with the
question how the past came to evolve into the specific present.
Jisei provided Aizawa with a vague but genuine concept of historical causation; it allowed him to explain present actions, not
by the moral character of contemporary acts, but as in inheritance of the immediate past and the actions of one's predecessors.

Aizawa could not claim that history always showed how the
virtuous would succeed and the wicked fail. When he wrote that
in the "changes in the movement of time, peace and rebellion are
normal conditions," he was saying that moral conduct is *not* the
axis around which history moves. His type of restorationism required him to confront present problems before he rejected them,
and not to flee straightway to some distant time before the spirit

was corrupted by history. Hirata's romantic alienation nowhere appears in Aizawa's restorationism. Aizawa, although a romantic of a different sort, was forced to accept social responsibility. For history revealed not only mythical paradigms but also the necessity that leaders understand their times well enough to formulate appropriate policies—which had nothing to do with morality.

History was the crucible in which the "status order" (*mibun chitsujo*) had been forged. To abandon it, as Hirata and his followers proposed, would have meant for Aizawa denial of that order, the only ethical principle by which social life was possible. History also showed how the rise of the military estate preserved the principle of order. Aizawa in his judgment of history did not restrict himself to Confucian "praise and blame," but used this standard only when convenient, and a more objective one at other times. The quality of leadership should be judged not only by its commitment to the moral principles of discrimination, but also by its ability to base policies on an investigation of social reality. Regimes collapse, he argued, because political leaders fail to understand the demands of the times. Here Aizawa agreed with the nativist idea of political accommodation, whereby Motoori's "recurrent leadership" admitted into their policy-making the datum of experience. Despite the rise and fall of political regimes, the emperor remains; and praise and blame could not be leveled against the leaders without also touching him. By a more realistic criterion Aizawa could assess the "recurrent leadership" of any period without involving the emperor.

A knowledge of history could assist leaders in making reality, rather than theoretical ideals, the operative norm—not because history showed a dialectic between virtue and vice, but because it recorded political deeds, how men faced contemporaneity. History revealed which policies were successful, which rulers were wise, how changes were brought about in accordance with the conditions of the times.[109] "Persons who govern the country well," Aizawa wrote, "must first observe the great conditions before them," and he explained elsewhere that this was so that they

[109] "Shinron," pp. 21–27ff.

might "know how to expand sufficiently nature's work."[110] History taught Aizawa the distinction between ordinary and extraordinary times and the need for policies suitable to each. Yet, although he supports a realistic relativism at the expense of abstract principles, he was not jettisoning them, but rather trying to find a place for them in a broader approach to history. Often Aizawa, after recommending a complete understanding of the times, refers to men who use "normal principles" to guide their policies—especially in his critique of Tokugawa society, whose problems led to traditional principles in the first place.

Tokugawa Ieyasu and his immediate successors, Aizawa believed, received their trust from the emperor in good faith, and by ordering the country, achieved a two-hundred-year peace. He saw this as a great accomplishment. But for this protracted peace Japan paid a high social and economic price. Order was established at the expense of principles, and now the signs of mismanagement and decline were everywhere:

In our times daily customs have tended to become excessively haughty. The several lords indulge in luxuries to the extent that in their hearts there is no other loyalty. Without men to oppose these practices, luxury continues to increase and the pain of greater poverty is inflicted. Moreover, the bitterness of the poor (*hainin*) is not without consequences; that they have not yet taken up arms is due to their fear of the samurai spirit and their own lack of leadership. . . . The oppressed (who rise up against authority) must be repelled throughout the country. While the signs of calamity have shown themselves, only gentle benevolence and makeshifts have prevented violent changes. It is for this reason that men must work hard, without changing the country.[111]

Aizawa knew that luxury and the "bitterness of the poor" were inherent in policies which produced peace, though a peace whose disadvantages were greater than its benefits. In its pursuit of peace the *bakufu* encouraged "luxury" and "laziness." Aizawa is

[110] *Ibid.*, p. 146.
[111] *Ibid.*, pp. 48–49; Matsumoto Sannosuke, "Sonjō undō ni okeru kindaiteki seiji ishiki no keisei," in *Meiji ishinshi no mondaiten,* ed. Sakata Yoshio (Tokyo, 1962), p. 129.

arguing that these abuses, even though not directly inspired by Tokugawa policy, served shogunal interests. This policy, according to Aizawa, was "to strengthen the base [shogun] and weaken the ends [domains]." [112] The *bakufu* had been fortifying its own control at the expense of the domains, which in theory constituted the managerial arm of the *bakuhan* sysem. Earlier writers like Ogyū Sorai and Kaibara Ekken used the metaphor of trunk and branch to convey the same concern for balance between the political body and its limbs; for them and for Aizawa alike the principle of balance was reciprocal recognition of status. The debilitating system of *sankin kōtai* ("alternate hostages"), the exclusion of outer lords (*tozama daimyō*) from government, and similar policies prevented full participation of the domains in the management of society. Harmony was merely a euphemism for autocracy. Moreover (Aizawa believed) shogunal indifference had encouraged a new style of luxury rooted in a non-Confucian urban culture, which attracted the daimyo and enriched the merchants, but weakened the financial structure of the *han* and of the country. Aizawa argued that when the Tokugawa proposed to eliminate opposition from the domains, they refused to see that this policy would endanger the country itself. The declining fortunes of the samurai and the growing distress of the peasantry were proof of how this policy was operating. Aizawa formulated it epigrammatically. "By weakening the country [locally], the country is weakened; to encourage foolish [local] leadership, leadership becomes foolish. If we are both weak and foolish how can we hope to move (*dōjō*)?" [113]

Behind these tautologies lay a deeper one, the regular assumption of Chinese political philosophy that the country was not the possession of any one person, but "belonged to the country." That is, while the country was the emperor's realm, it was administered in a "public fashion" by ministers to whom authority was delegated by the emperor. Aizawa invoked this formula to remind the shogun of his dependent position, at the risk of rais-

[112] "Shinron," pp. 51–52; Sakata, *Meiji ishinshi,* p. 34.
[113] "Shinron," p. 49.

ing the suspicion of disloyalty to the *bakufu*. One way of avert-
ing this suspicion, stated by Motoori and accepted by Aizawa,
was to view "the emperor's government" as a "public institution"
(*kōki*). This meant a policy in which the decisive elements of society, particularly the lords, played once more an active role in
the affairs of the realm (*tenka*). "Today," Aizawa wrote, "in
order to take advantage of the opportunity to repel the barbarian,
we must promote this strength [autonomy of the domainal lords]
throughout the various areas. It is our duty to promote it and use
it in our daily life. . . . To use strength . . . it must be transported into the country, so that the public institution of the
realm does not become the private possession [of one person.]" [114] Fujita Yūkoku had once expressed a similar sentiment; but for him a "public administration" of the "emperor's
realm" was a speculative possibility, which proved only his faith-
fulness to his Neo-Confucian education. In Aizawa's hands the
idea is articulated into an active principle; and combined with
criticism of shogunal policy, it came to occupy a central role in
the *bakumatsu* discourse on policy.[115]

Aizawa believed that "weakening the end to strengthen the
base" had paralyzed the organs of the *bakufu;* a dramatic illustration was inability to decide upon a "policy of war or peace."
He called for general "rectification" in society: full observance of
ōdō by the leadership in showing compassion to the people; full
observance of *meibun* by the people in displaying respect to the
lords. Aizawa's metaphor of "ends" and "base" covers not only
the relationship between the general social category of high and
low, but also the numerous fine gradations between *bakufu* and
lords.

What did Aizawa mean by a "policy of war and peace?" Be-

[114] *Ibid.*, p. 53.

[115] The idea of *kōgiron*, which served as one of the chief political metaphors in the new arrangement after 1868, meant modestly a broader base
of political participation in the administration of the "public" (emperor's)
realm. See for an analysis of this relationship, Haraguchi Kiyoshi, *Boshin
sensō* (Tokyo, 1962).

fore him stood the mounting foreign probes and the *bakufu*'s me-
chanical response in the expulsionist edicts (*uchi harei rei*). Domestic weakness, brought about deliberately by the shogunate to
strengthen itself, prevented the "realm from pursuing military
preparations." A decision on "war and peace," because it affects
the *bakuhan* order and requires participation of all its parts, involves cooperation between *bakufu* and domain. This is possible
only if the *bakufu* ceases to "weaken the end to strengthen the
base"—that is, abandons policies designed to keep the domains
impotent. Aizawa despairs in Book II of the *Shinron* that
"knowledgeable men are not able to plan, while men of valor can
do no more than show anger." [116] Invoking the politics of *ōdō*
and the morality of *meibun* once more, Aizawa advises that the
top (the shogun) must show compassion to the bottom (the
lords), while the bottom must respect the top. Yet the shogunate
which had upset the balance could also be the first to exemplify
for the ruled their duties to rulership. In alerting his generation
to the threat of invasion and in calling for a speedy decision on a
"policy of war or peace," Aizawa was attributing responsibility
for domestic decay to the shogun-first policy.[117]

Aizawa's novelty in the Mito school lies in the fact that, following a lead first hinted at by Fujita Yūkoku in the *Seimeiron,*
he combined the requirements of *meibun* with those of *ōdō* to assess the present and to attack shogunal policies. Earlier Mito writers merely stressed the obligation of the people to respect the
lords, which is what they meant by "revering the emperor" (*sonnōron*). Thus in the later Mito school Yūkoku called for the *bakufu* to revere the imperial court, and for the lords to respect the
bakufu. But Aizawa, seeking to resolve the domestic crisis, joined
this notion to the idea of the "imperial way" (*ōdō*), where the
lord (shogun) shows compassion to the people (now identified
as domainal lords), to demonstrate that shogunal policies were
not satisfying established ethical standards. The shogun had, after
all, received a commission from the emperor to administer and

[116] "Shinron," pp. 99ff.
[117] Sakata, *Meiji ishinshi,* p. 35.

"tranquilize the realm"—that is, to preserve the life of the people, and to defend the realm (*kokka*) from invasion. To carry out this responsibility the shogun was required to revere the emperor, as had all his predecessors. The foreign threat reminded society that the shogun was not fulfilling his obligations. Thus Aizawa, seeking simply to reform an existing system, elevated the status of the emperor by locating the source of the shogun's authority. Aizawa hinted at a new concept of power—an emperor who in transcending political responsibility was the highest authority in the land. But this was the emperor of the nativist vision.

This criticism of the *bakufu* lies behind Aizawa's theory of "expelling the barbarian" (*jōi*). When Tokugawa Nariaki and his adviser Fujita Tōko combined *jōi* with "reverence" (*sonnō*), expulsion became a powerful theory of political reform calling for basic revisions in shogunal policy. Yet Aizawa, by his prior concern for the domestic crisis, in which the managerial class and the domainal system seemed imperiled, failed to take the foreign probes as a serious threat. "These conditions [the appearance of foreigners in Japanese waters] have not yet come to enclose us," he wrote, knowing, as a good moralist, that resolution of *naiyū* was always prior to resolution of *gaikan*.[118] In the end he advised a policy of war on the grounds that preparation for war was the best defense of peace. "Offense and preparation are one and the same thing." [119] But this policy demanded participation of all the domains and again put the *bakufu* on notice about the domestic crisis. "Today," Aizawa wrote, "the policy of *jōi* has been transmitted throughout the land. The question of war and peace has been resolved, and the realm knows which way it must go." All that remained was to work out a policy of defense, whose central task was to restore the balance between ends and base, *bakufu* and daimyo. Just as the decision on "war and peace" required broad deliberation within the *bakuhan* order, so preparation involved participation of the domains. Aizawa rested the success of the policy on "first setting into order the various areas

118 "Shinron," pp. 150–151.
119 *Ibid.*, p. 100.

within the realm, and managing the four directions; the emperor, through an understanding of conditions, will tranquilize those who are closest and then turn next to those who are distant. This will result in the work of a restoration (*chūkō*)." [120]

In short, Aizawa's concerns were domestic; he used the opportunity of a foreign crisis to reassert the autonomy of the domains. "Internally," he wrote, "we have to practice military defense"; but defense was the lever by which he hoped to rescue the system.[121] This attempt to "overcome the present" required changes in four fundamental areas.

First and foremost he urged a change in the "pursuit of internal administration." This included "a reassertion of the martial spirit" among the samurai of the domains; prohibition of luxury among the people; "tranquilizing the people" (which meant that the leadership should fulfill its responsibilities toward them, while the people lived a simple agrarian life); and recruiting men of talent and ability for administration.[122] Aizawa noted that domainal integrity was being destroyed by failure of martial spirit, but could be restored if the criterion of merit was reintroduced in filling positions and granting rewards. Luxury was an old problem, and Aizawa's prescriptions for it were inspired by Fujita Yūkoku. And his endorsement of more rational recruitment for officialdom in the decades to follow set off an avalanche of criticism.

Aizawa's second proposal involved "preparing military ordinances," a specific plan to strengthen the domain. Here he called for the "selection of courageous soldiers," an "increase in a mass popular army," and "a purification of discipline."

He advocated the "enrichment of the domain" (*fukoku*). Like Yūkoku, he argued that military defense must be combined with a hardheaded economic policy stressing austerity, and a careful calculation of "what goes out and what comes in."

The most important domainal reform was to limit the eco-

[120] *Ibid.*, p. 147.
[121] *Ibid.*, p. 155.
[122] *Ibid.*, pp. 101–130.

nomic activity of merchants and artisans, since it promised "not to injure finances nor harm the people." Aizawa was sure that economic failure in the domain arose from the excesses of merchants and a lavish style of living which all were beginning to emulate. "If poverty is to be exchanged for wealth," he argued, this style must be eliminated, agriculture must be encouraged, and all (including the samurai) must be returned to the land. In his sensitivity to *jisei* ("understanding the tendency of the times") he recounted the achievement of Peter the Great and recommended the adoption of Western military technology in Japan. He was careful to dissociate this program from foreign trade, which might in fact have rescued the domestic economy, but which, he warned gravely, "corresponds to useless items of luxury" and drained the country of silver and copper.

Aizawa's proposals presupposed that men of responsibility must have the "great conditions of the world . . . in the palm of their hands" before making policy.[123] This conviction, as we shall see, rationalized the speedy adoption of Western technology, and later of Western political and social ideas. Together with the idea of "practicality" (*jitsugaku*), *jisei* was a powerful impulse for change. "Viewing the great conditions today," Aizawa concluded confidently, "we should make Japan a castle, the Pacific Ocean a moat"; and if the realm was unified or "completed," a proper defense against the barbarian would take care of itself.

Despite his bellicose xenophobia and expulsionism, Aizawa's proposals for defense were not original. In intent they resembled the *bakufu*'s policy of *uchi harai rei;* in content they repeated almost word for word Fujita Yūkoku's earlier statement on wealth and power, *fukoku kyōhei.* The important thing in his theory of *jōi* and military defense was relating them to what he saw as the principal purpose of his day: reordering the *bakuhan* system and overcoming the threat of domestic chaos. *Gaikan* was merely the occasion to carry out domestic reforms. A return to moral stabil-

---

[123] *Ibid.,* p. 137.

ity promised the leadership security against popular disorder. Although Aizawa supplied the rhetoric for criticism of shogunal policies, its promise was not realized until the Tempō reforms begun by Tokugawa Nariaki under the guidance of Fujita Tōko. For Aizawa even the shogun-first policy as a cause of malaise was secondary to moral failure. "Since the signs of calamity have shown themselves," he wrote darkly, only "benevolence" could prevent violent changes.[124]

To invoke the principles of Neo-Confucian morality in such a time was hardly enough, since the ethic of status was meaningful only to the samurai, and not to the masses who were threatening to snap the bonds of civilized life. Popular education translated Confucian precepts into understandable maxims for mass consumption—which were easily abandoned in time of economic distress. Pure morality, as European history reveals, fails to sustain expected behavior where religion succeeds. To secure submission from the ruled to social order and to realize permanently the promise of civilized life, Aizawa summoned the sacral language of myth. Yet precisely the ethical principles which he hoped to promote through the myth lost their authenticity in the process. In making mytho-history a condition for accepting a status morality, Aizawa undermined status morality both as an outer guide for behavior and as an inner imperative disposing men, like homing pigeons, to righteous and loyal action. In recompense, externally his stress on sacral duty provided behavior a new point of reference; internally, he felt that the nature of man, if it was good, would automatically be identified with the mind and heart of the emperor.

The Confucian principles that the rulers should "love the people," "bestow benevolence and compassion," and "provide proper doctrine" were linked by Aizawa to the continuity of the imperial line and its divine purpose. This new connection called forth sacral-religious associations which a rational morality could never provide. "The heavenly ancestors introduced the way of the gods (*shintō*)," he says in the *Shinron*, "and they have established doc-

[124] See n. 111.

trine; by clarifying loyalty and filial piety they began human history." These duties had been transmitted to the emperor by the gods from their home in Takamagahara, which serves as the "great foundation of the Japanese state." Since that time the position of the emperor, a direct appointment of the gods, had remained unchanged. The emperor joined these ordinances, "the great morality of heaven and earth," as they were handed by the heavenly ancestors, to his "own body." Just as the emperor looks up to the virtue of the heavenly descendants, Aizawa continued, so the people, receiving into their bodies the heart (*kokoro*) of their ancestors, have respected and served the emperor for an eternity. When the emperor has received the will of the heavenly ancestors in his body, and the people have received the will of their ancestors in their bodies, then there can be no change in history. All these ideas are expressed in the "way of filial piety." The emperor, in worshipping his ancestor the sun goddess, has realized the principle of filial piety himself and revealed its obligations to the people.[125]

"If the whole country reveres the heavenly duties [filial piety and loyalty]," Aizawa promised, "then all will know how to respect the emperor."[126] And respect for gods and emperor, since they are united in past and present, produces respect for the realm also.[127] By converting ethical duties into the currency of religious submission, Aizawa saw a way of securing mass consent to the ordinances of the ruler. "The chief deities instructed their descendants to remind the people of this respect, and those who administered the realm learned how to make their minds one with the will of the emperor, in order to follow the emperor's expectations." In Chou China, Aizawa recounted, kings established shrines at which the people could worship the gods of the earth. Similarly the spirit of ancient Japan (Yamato) was preserved, and therefore Japanese down to the present worship these gods. Likewise, because since antiquity "the land relied on the people,"

[125] Arakawa, *op. cit.* (n. 72 above), pp. 109–113; "Shinron," *Kokutai* 1.
[126] "Shinron," p. 126.
[127] *Ibid.,* pp. 156–157.

it was the practice of the people "to respect the gods of the land by way of the emperor." [128] As a contemporary expression of gratitude, Aizawa advised the establishment of national shrines (*kunisha*) where people could offer respect to gods and land through reverence to the emperor. The shrines would link sacred to secular, past to present, and would "preserve the unity of the divine ancestors and their descendants." Obedience to the emperor would express respect to the deities of the realm—and to the realm itself. The "public spirit" invoked by Aizawa is the people's reverence for the emperor and for his administration. "People in antiquity," he lamented, "knew how to revere the emperor, but this knowledge has been all but forgotten in the present." If civilization in Japan was to survive, the present had an opportunity that came once in a thousand years "to inform the people of this principle and purify the public spirit." When this enterprise has been accomplished, "we will unite past to present" and emperor to people.[129]

Just as government and religious ritual are indistinguishable, so instruction in "public spirit" through "clarification of the national essence (*kokutai*)" will bridge the gap between past and present. Past and present are not different if it is recognized that Japanese history has continued without rupture or revolution in the ruling dynasty. In the face of crisis, Aizawa offered restoration in men's minds and hearts of the timeless principles on which the state had been founded, through religion and ritual. People everywhere would know that order and civilization depended on their moral support, and that moral support depended on their knowing the Five Relationships, since "there is nothing greater to enshrine." [130] Moral knowledge as sacral duty will dispose them "to respect the imperial court; and to respect the imperial court is to respect the heavenly deities themselves." "[By sacred duty] the administration of the *bakufu* and the several lords

---

[128] *Ibid.,* pp. 128ff.

[129] *Ibid.,* p. 169.

[130] "Tekii hen," p. 353. "The heavenly grandson erected a doctrine of filial loyalty." Also, "Shinron," p. 170.

are unified." Disloyalty to the domain is registered on a cosmic scale as disrespect to the gods. Neither Motoori Norinaga nor Hirata Atsutane could have expressed the claims of religious devotion better. The difference was that those nativists rejected the claims of an ethic in favor of a psychology, where the pure heart (*magokoro*) of the people will automatically reach out to the emperor.

What better guarantee for order was available to Aizawa than turning ethical responsibilities into religious duties? He saw the failure of Hirata's efforts to revive "pure Shinto" among the non-samurai masses, and the false hopes which his concept of restoration raised. With the command to "purify public spirit" and "clarify *kokutai*," when "past and present are once united," Japanese society must undertake the "great task revealed in the present." "If we accept this task, we will go on to erect the Great Warp. We must reform the evil practices of the barbarian; and although it is said that the great task of building a state is difficult, when we establish the Great Warp today we will make the inhabitants of the four seas as one family, and the ten thousand generations of the past as one day. . . . *Shinshū* will rank at the head of a great continent because it possesses the imperial spirit, the true spirit." [131] If *kokutai* can serve once more as a united basis of action, if history through mythic exemplars can be put back on track, Japan will be prepared to meet contemporary events. In this way Aizawa rejected his present; it was this rhetoric which kindled confidence in a beleaguered managerial class trying to sustain its position in the face of an imminent volcanic eruption. Reassertion of *kokutai* alone could reconsecrate Japan's historical destiny in the present, since it was the only ordering principle powerful enough to unite the country. It was *kokutai* that distinguished the Japanese from all other people and gave their historical experience its integrity. When unity was restored, Aizawa was confident that the leadership could exact the fullest from the people; for "just as the feelers of a mantis will be insufficient in the face of a chariot, so foreign soldiers will be no

[131] "Shinron," p. 166.

match for the masses. A unified realm is supreme, while a disuni-
fied country will most certainly be inferior." And when the
threat of "domestic disorder" is overcome, the possibility of an
"external catastrophe" disappears.

LEARNING FOR LEADERSHIP: FUJITA TŌKO
AND THE EDUCATION OF SHINKOKU

According to Aizawa, *kokutai* would realize a national personality; but it must first be transformed into a practical public discipline. Aizawa also believed in religious observances where the
masses revered the divine virtue and the imperial blessing. He
sought to routinize his understanding of Shinto as an integral
part of national life. To this end he wrote in Japanese a book
which popularized the main arguments of the *Shinron* and
might, he hoped, be understood by a larger part of the population. This book, *Soen wagen,* was written in 1834, at just about
the time of the Tempō reforms in Mito; it explained in clear language the requirements of Shinto and the principles of worship
and religious ritual. But the *Shinron,* like most of Aizawa's writings, was a statement of protest, gathering up the main currents
of the Tokugawa period and providing a rhetoric and body of
cultural slogans for later writers to borrow from. And despite his
own effort to popularize his message, Aizawa found no lasting
way to work his ideas into a public educational discipline, although certainly he believed in the necessity of a proper education.

And even though Aizawa later participated actively in the
Mito reforms, his principal role was as a consoling theorist. In
the 1830s, mass peasant rebellions, long a part of the Tokugawa
landscape, were Aizawa's fears. The number of what Eric Hobs-
bawm calls "pre-political" movements like these portended worse
things to come. Even though their motivation was not political,
their result (as Aizawa and Fujita Tōko observed) certainly was.
Fujita Yūkoku had hung the success of his social proposals on
the hope of able leadership, which only began to be realized by

the Tempō reforms. Ōshio Heihachirō's call to arms in Osaka in
1837—the single most important rebellion of the late Tokugawa
period—showed the need for an able leadership armed with the
moral purpose of *kokutai,* which was possible only from the proper education.

Under the leadership of Tokugawa Nariaki (a model leader
himself) Mito began to work out a new kind of education for
able leadership. The impetus came from Nariaki himself, recently victorious, as we have seen, in a struggle for succession,
who was trying after 1830 to put Mito back into order. His effort
is called the Tempō reform in Mito *han,* and his procedure was
followed throughout the country by other domains. On the eve
of the reforms, Nariaki was complaining that contemporary leadership was shamefully inefficient, and while he had Mito in
mind, his charge had wider significance. "Officials," Nariaki
wrote, "have made insincerity their chief concern. Although we
must seek out diligence, in truth there are few men of diligence
today occupying official positions." [132] Nariaki was unspecific,
but apparently, like most *bakumatsu* writers to follow, he was directing his protest against the shogunal bureaucracy. Since most
domainal administrations were staffed by lower-ranking retainers,
many as a result of actual talent or skill, it seems unreasonable
for Nariaki, who was putting his own house in order, to criticize
so strongly the state of local leadership.

On one hand, Nariaki had a genuine devotion to certain humane Neo-Confucian pieties. On the other hand, he was a leader
brought up for his task who, with his class, stood to lose everything if the burden on a heavily loaded peasantry was not light-
ened. Almost immediately after he took office he expressed both
sides of his character: "Since the people are the base of the
realm (*kuni*), even though we have done nothing outside of no-
ticing this, we have succeeded to the inherited realm and serve it.
And this means to make loving the poeple a principal concern.
As for loving the people, though it can be done by several methods, the principal concern is to end the administration of severity

[132] Tokugawa Nariaki (Mito Rekko), "Kokushi," in *Mgt.,* V, 175–176.

(*oren*). Severe rule since the Genroku and Hoei eras [literally, "since the time of the official Matsunami Kanjuro"] has led increasingly to impoverishment among the people. In this connection, if severe rule is removed, then it is known how the people should be raised up." [133] Nariaki never tired, in his pronouncements, of saying that "the lords are the parents of the people," "virtue is the base, finance the ends," "handicap at the top is profit below." He was committed to reviving the status ethic and the morality of leadership. He therefore endorsed for the retainers of the domain a "moral learning" (*dōtoku*), and for the peasants an education which might once more identify their role in society. And while his first business in order of time was to reconstruct *han* finances, education stood as high in order of importance.[134]

Nariaki's financial reforms in the domain, as one facet of his overall plan for reform, show his restorationist vision in the effort to regain a pure agrarianism. But in his concern for designations and duties, he knew that economic reform must be accompanied by moral and practical learning to instruct leaders and people in their responsibilities. Nariaki's interest crystallized at about the time that news of British victories in China during the Opium War was beginning to leak into Japan. With the assistance of Fujita Tōko, son of Yūkoku, he sought a solution to the failure of nerve in officialdom, which he analyzed as a failure in training, in a new kind of *han* school. Nariaki had long felt the need for better education than existed in Mito to serve both his retainers and the populace. He had previously set up lecture halls in the domain, and asked the wealthy to provide funds and books.[135]

In 1841 after these experiments, he set up his domainal school, the Kōdōkan. Apparently Nariaki had thought of it in the mid-1830s, but had not been able to establish it then because of the

133 *Mito han shiryō* (n. 11 above), pp. 312–314.
134 Shibahara (n. 9 above), pp. 133–164; also Sakata, *Meiji ishinshi* (n. 111 above), pp. 38–44.
135 Takasu, *Mito gakuha* . . . (n. 14 above), pp. 96ff.

122

priority of financial reform, and also because of opposition by domainal elders (*rōshin*), who rejected his proposal on the grounds
that "education follows wealth." The school was organized to
teach a practical discipline, to renew the military spirit for contemporary needs, and in general to promote the classical Japanese
ideals as restated by Aizawa. The Kōdōkan was intended to serve
as a national model to dissolve particularism and restore agreed
universal standards in training potential leaders. Fujita Tōko was
appointed a school magistrate; and some years later, after consultation with Nariaki and Aizawa, he produced a general statement of aims, the *Kōdōkanki,* in which Aizawa's contribution is
perhaps dominant.

Learning for leadership was possible only if leadership had a
theory of social action and a political purpose to serve. To this
end Fujita Tōko crystallized the cultural statement of Aizawa
into the formula *sonnō jōi:* "expulsion of the barbarian through
reverence for the emperor." Both concepts had been formulated
separately by Fujita Yūkoku in his theory of inner and outer
"discrimination." Aizawa had elevated *jōi* to a cultural necessity.
Even before them *sonnō* had been something of a subversive idea
in the hands of the courtiers such as Yamagata Daini and Takenouchi Shikibu during the mid-eighteenth century.[136] Tōko (and
Nariaki behind him) combined them to deal with specific social
and political problems. Once combined, they became intimately
associated with the specific crisis, not as a hollow litany celebrating status order, but as a plan to arrest decay and promise reform. Nariaki and Tōko wanted to prevent a coalition of two
potentially destructive forces: a tendency, dramatized by the increase in peasant outbursts, to discredit the managerial competence of the leadership; and an imperial restorationism, prompted
by Ōshio's rebellion in Osaka, taken up as a theory of political reform by déclassé samurai. The Kōdōkan was designed to pro-

[136] See Tōyama Shigeki for a brilliant cameo-like sketch of this early
inarticulate expression of *sonnō* in the eighteenth century. *Meiji ishin*
(Tokyo, 1954), pp. 66–68. A longer and drier account is found in *Ishinshi,*
ed. Ishin shiryō hensankai henshū, 8 vols. (Tokyo, 1942), I, 190–224.

vide correctives to these dangers. The important thing in Tōko's reformulation of the Mito rhetoric is his incorporation of an item of contemporary experience—the concrete signs of decline during the Tempō period—into an effective theory of political action. Aizawa had no theory of action, only a theory of culture— namely, the principle which distinguished Japan from the barbarism of the West. In response to the crisis of the managerial class, Tōko made Aizawa's culturalism into a theory of political action which might allow the managerial class to overcome the crisis of the day. But ironically, this theory of action, which he called *sonnō-jōi-ron* ("respect for the emperor and expulsion of the barbarian"), unleashed in the early 1860s the very forces of change which it sought to stem.

The *Kōdōkanki* became the quintessential expression of Mito thinking because of its political purpose. Fujita Tōko in his commentary on this document (the *Kōdōkanki gijutsu*) sets up as tradition a morality practiced only in Japan because of its divine founding. Here he summarizes the *Kōdōkanki* in neat slogans: "the unification of Shinto and Confucianism," "the inseparability of loyalty and filial piety," *sonnō jōi*, "the union of military arts and civilian skills" (*bu-bun*), and "the indivisibility of learning and practice." It was the special duty of the samurai class to conserve this unique inheritance.[137] Preservation of this tradition was the promise of *sonnō jōi*, which was no more effective, however, than the leadership behind it. The *Kōdōkanki* tersely states that "Ieyasu eliminated rebellions and turned toward the rectification [of names]; he revered the emperor, expelled the barbarian, and established the basis of peace by permitting both military arts and civilian skills."[138] Tōko's elaboration calls for a new leadership committed to these goals and insists that the union of military (*bu*) and civilian (*bun*) is central to their education: "In this gloriously Divine Land, with the succession of the Heavenly Sun, we have for generations and generations revered the sacred regalia, and they have reigned over all things.

[137] "Kōdōkanki jutsugi," in *Mgt.*, I, 50–51, 54.
[138] Nakamura Kōya, *Fujita Tōko* (Tokyo, 1942), p. 176.

The discrimination between high and low, inner and outer is as unchanging as heaven and earth. In that case *sonnō jōi* is, in reality, the highest duty (*taigi*) of loyalists (*shishi*), who 'exhaust' the loyalty of benevolent men in repaying the realm." [139] Here is one of the earliest expressions of the kind of leadership which captured the imagination of activists in the late Tokugawa period, especially at the time of Perry. There was no better example of a *shishi,* a man of high purpose, in the *bakumatsu* than Tōko himself, who became, for the younger generation trained in the lecture halls and fencing academies of Edo, the example of a new leadership. Tōko, known principally for his writings and his poetry, was also an extremely proficient swordsman. His training was the basis of his educational theory: samurai must be as proficient with brush as with sword. This unification of military (*bu*) and civilian (*bun*) was, of course, a Tokugawa innovation; civilian skills among the samurai had become an accommodation to peace.[140] Yet the threads of romance, though frayed, were retained, and the samurai was obliged to keep up his military skills. While *bakumatsu* writers consciously revived the example of the samurai of the civil-war period (*sengoku bushi*) in the new situation, the late Tokugawa samurai with his civilian skills and administrative responsibilities had little in common with his illiterate sixteenth-century ancestor. And while Tōko insisted on both skills for the leadership, fearful that military training was lagging, his principal concern was still to establish an able officialdom for shogunate and domain.

While Fujita Tōko was wrestling with the *Kōdōkanki,* an advance reader of the manuscript, Satō Issai, urged him not to neglect military training for civilian arts. Satō wrote:

I'm sorry to say, but I must find fault with your general outline. . . . The sages possessed both heart and mind. This is true even of T'ang Confucianists as far as the evidence shows. They never divided scholarly studies from the kingly way. Today the military style is not correct. The conduct or preparation of useful political duties is

[139] "Kōdōkanki jutsugi," p. 50.
[140] *Ibid.*

trifling. This training must blossom out so as to unify military arts and civilian skills. If a civilian administration is the only way, the warrior who does not possess letters is not a true warrior, while the scholar who has not prepared in military affairs is not a true scholar.

In response to this admonition, Tōko and Nariaki devoted much of the curriculum of the Kōdōkan to the traditional military arts, but they were more interested in training "diligent" and efficient administrators. For the malaise in both domain and *bakufu* had been brought about by official incompetence. According to Tōko, the purpose of the school was to train talented samurai, however low their class rank, in diligence.[141] The school's statement of principles, the *Kōdōkan gakusoku,* written in Nariaki's name but in all probability drafted by Tōko, endorsed a benevolent government administered by "superior men" (*kunshi*) and enjoined all domains to encourage "talent and ability" as criteria for recruitment.[142]

Since the unification of military arts and civilian skills was the condition for a new leadership, then practicality (*jitsugaku,* "the inseparability of learning and practice") must be the style of education. Fujita Tōko's plan for a learning eventuating in practice was more than a classical cliché, since it guided curriculum and was a primary requirement in the training of all officials. "Officials," he wrote in his commentary, "must never abandon practical studies." A major abuse of the times, he complained, had been to "abolish practical studies" and pursue "useless" literary learning which failed to inform men of affairs about "changes in conditions" and needed policies. This idea is constantly echoed in the late Tokugawa discourse on men and politics. It explains why Tōko and others found it easy to accept technology as a serious object of education; despite Tōko's special attachment to traditional Japanese military skills, he was early on record, like Nariaki, as supporting the adoption of Western military technology.

In order to realize "diligence" in public affairs, training of

[141] *Ibid.,* pp. 84ff, 94–95, 97–98; also in "Hitachiobi," in *Mgt.,* I, 304–305.
[142] *Mgt.,* V, 183ff.

officials also had to emphasize "sincerity" (*shisei*), single-minded commitment to the responsibilities of political office. Fujita Tōko conceived of loyalty as an expression of responsibility to one's office. The official who brought efficiency and diligence to daily tasks, he wrote in one of his letters, was being sincere; yet "sincerity" earlier had been identified with blind loyalty and devotion. Most domainal education during the Tokugawa period turned out obedient and loyal retainers whose only qualifications for office were conformity and abject devotion. Within the traditional framework of social class, Tōko redefined the role of the *shi* as carrying civilian duties in fact prior to military prowess. "If they [*shi*] possess only prudent behavior," he warned, "but shirk their duties by failing to serve diligently, they must be compelled to seek out the way of sincerity."[143] "Prudent behavior," the outward display of virtue and blind obedience, was not enough in official duties. Elsewhere in the *Hitachiobi* Tōko condemns contemporary officials who have acquired the finely honed gestures of "virtuous conduct" but can barely read and write.

As a contemporary witness of Ōshio's uprising in Osaka, Fujita Tōko relates in his diary how the whole affair was proof of a corrosive political mismanagement poisoning the land. Its surprising (though temporary) success worried him, since the political incompetence which provoked rebellion and the military unpreparedness which permitted it some success existed throughout the country. He blamed the malaise in political leadership on the system of hereditary ascription, and claimed that loyalty and ability were entirely different things. "Even though the personal conduct of an official is jaundiced," he asked, "is it not more jaundiced to forget the duties of civilian office and to possess only prudent behavior?"[144] Tōko was not willing, of course, to repudiate loyalty or overlook "little honesty and crooked prudence" in the exercise of official duties. But it was not enough for samurai-administrators to approach their duties with only an understanding of the values regulating social relationships.[145] To avoid this

[143] "Hitachiobi," p. 304.
[144] *Ibid.*, p. 305.
[145] *Ibid.*, pp. 324–325.

kind of leadership he prescribed an ideal, brilliantly exemplified by Nariaki himself, where the performance of administrative duties was informed by "intent, certainty, devotion, and selflessness" —values which once characterized a military class in war, but which were now pressed into the service of a civilian administration.

The practice of the times, Fujita Tōko noted in a long letter to Aoyama Enu, who served as a dean (*sōsai*) of the Kōdōkan, was to "abandon practical studies"; yet if practical studies are promoted, "you will also increase the number of righteous men and decrease the volume of lesser men" and drive off the contemporary craze for empty learning.[146] Empty learning, typically represented by "useless literary studies" or Zen Buddhism, was for Tōko and many of his contemporaries that which failed to promise material success.[147] That is, learning should at all times serve the political enterprise, no matter what its content might thereby include. Personal cultivation was worthless in daily problems, as the Ōshio rebellion so clearly disclosed, because it reflected selfishness antithetical to a benevolent polity. It is not surprising to find Tōko urging the study and adoption of Western military techniques which promised to defend the realm from without and within. Even though he and his colleagues failed to realize the full potential of Western technology, they still opened the way for later men, even die-hard reactionaires, to incorporate it into the framework of *jitsugaku*.

The upshot of Fujita Tōko's work was not to destroy the classical definition of learning and leadership, but to reaffirm the true meaning of *jinzai*, "talented men." If such men had occupied positions of administrative responsibility, he never tired of repeating, Japan would have been spared the rebellion of Ōshio Heihachirō.[148] Tōko insisted that the values of intent, certainty, devotion, and selflessness were the prerogative not of birth but of men who by natural intelligence and ability stood apart from the rest of humanity. Through the criterion of merit as objectively

[146] *Mgt.,* I, 438, 440.
[147] "Kōdōkanki jutsugi," pp. 98–99.
[148] *Mgt.,* I, 234–241.

measured among samurai alone (no question as yet of putting lower classes into office!), he sought to circumvent the practice by which "men without ability, . . . because they are born into certain families, are permitted to manage political affairs." [149] Here is the meaning of Tōko's educational theory; the redemption of *shinkoku* was possible only if it was entrusted to a new kind of leadership, the *shishi,* who brought to their task ability, purpose, and proper training.

[149] "Hitachiobi," pp. 352–354.

III *The Action of Culture:*
Sakuma Shōzan

The logic of classical thought forced Mito writers to the conclusion that external problems were possible only because the domestic machinery was ceasing to function and the defensive barriers were thereby weakened enough to invite the intrusion of a barbarian power. Chinese history disclosed (they believed) an eloquent reminder of the unyielding nature of this nemesis. In the world of the 1830s and 1840s there was ample evidence for them to organize reality in terms of the formula *naiyū gaikan;* for domestic disorder called into question not the paradigm of nature or reality, but merely the application of moral behavior which nature required if reality was to be achieved. Although their statement offered consolation to a weary and beleaguered managerial class, their commitment to arresting *naiyū* blinded them to the foreign threat and to real social and economic domestic changes. They dutifully proposed to tighten coastal defenses and steel the populace in discipline, but they could not acknowledge substantial change or adjust to its demands.

The Mito view of society hung on the assumption of perfectibility; knowing the principles of a perfect moral order, Mito writers knew how to construct a perfect social order. This complacency accounts for their failure to view the foreign problem seriously as one bringing in new concepts of social and political order. In their view, isolation had served Japan because society, as it approached perfection, had no need of contact with lesser peoples and lesser social systems. If there was a sign of uneasiness throughout the country—and many believed their days as managers were numbered—it was a sign not that their concept of society was wrong but that men in positions of responsibility had grown indifferent to perfection. On their own premises, they had forgotten that a society informed by *meibun,* while indeed the only possible civilized one, also required the utmost effort if it was to be sustained. Hence Aizawa's constant insistence that unity was the goal of social perfection, and that social perfection required all groups to fulfill their obligations. The past (Mito writers were confident) had taught them how men had forged civilization out of chaos. Therefore, they called first for unity of purpose in acknowledging the inviolability of *taigi meibun,* and then for socioeconomic measures which might restore a prior life. No analysis of the profound economic problems agitating Tokugawa Japan was required, since nobody saw the need to question the moral principle underlying a "natural" economic order. The truth of this principle motivated their optimistic vision of society, and to the end Mito writers, despite their lavish syncretism, remained true to the Neo-Confucian conception of social reality.

Because of the boundaries of discourse which they had established, Mito writers were hopelessly committed to the idea of "discrimination" as the only possible basis of civilized life. An act of faith enabled them to celebrate a tranquil political order without ever confronting the prospect of change, and hence to dwell interminably on personal conduct. Yet this preoccupation yielded no new theory of personality. Rather, they reaffirmed the notion of a public personality, whose inner self corresponds to his outer behavior, and whose meaning was revealed in the exercise of duties corresponding to status. For this image of personality nothing was more important than the ethical nurturing of the

whole person, since it promised an inactivity and reverent quietism toward the social order, while the guidelines of behavior
were marked out by accumulated precedent relating to the whole
range of publicly accepted situations. In their reaffirmation of the
public personality, Mito writers strove to put humanity into harmony with nature and to restore the undifferentiated simplicity
of the natural order. Investigation of social reality would show
how to stay on an even course, and how change always represented a departure from the "natural" norms informing civilized
life.

Yet this investigation of reality, if carried out by other men,
might reveal a greater variety to "practical studies" than merely
economics; perhaps then it was time for Japan to go further and
examine the speculative possibilities of Neo-Confucianism itself.

Once *gaikan* was forcibly recognized as a new principle of reality, especially after the opening of the country, the Mito statement, whatever it merits, could no longer serve the needs of the
Japanese. By their commitment to an ideal social order reflecting
natural principles of organization, the Mito writers found it difficult to account seriously for *gaikan*. In their scale of values the
problem of an "external catastrophe" was merely a further symptom of the decaying domestic order. Yet when the specter of *gaikan* intruded upon the Japanese scene, and events brutally confirmed this warning in the opening of the country (*kaikoku*),
writers were obliged to move *naiyū* down the scale. And then the
way was open to question the ideal of social order itself. No
longer could men like the Mito ideologues believe their society to
be a representation of social perfection; no longer could they take
refuge in the belief that the real problem was only laxity in application of principles to conduct; no longer could reality be
identified with the Neo-Confucian natural order.

After Perry's intrusion, Japanese society found itself compelled
to accept change and its unknown consequences. This accommodation, painful and shocking, required a confrontation with a
new principle of reality. Writers began to abandon the claim of
social norms which had informed their perception for a direct en-

counter with the reality of new social claims. Thus writers from
Sakuma Shōzan through Yokoi Shōnan declared their willingness
to abandon "empty theories" and "useless learning" for concepts
of analysis rooted in the "investigation of contemporary conditions." They could then analyze either the validity of the Neo-
Confucian speculative relationship between abstraction and the
reality of contemporary society, or the question whether change
represented an inevitable decline of civilized life. In either case
this shift in concern—acknowledging change and serving it
through some investigation of social reality—liberated political
leaders from abstraction into the more flexible world of fact and
value. This return to reality destroyed the Neo-Confucian criterion of "praise and blame," because policies could be based no
longer on timeless principles, but rather on an assessment of contemporary conditions and needs.

This new frame of mind, as we saw, was inherent in the Mito
statement, even though it was never so expressed. And ironically
it was seized upon by men nurtured through Mito rhetoric with
an unyielding concept of social ideality, who sought to save that
concept from the destruction threatened by its failure to accept
new events and knowledge. If they preserved some core of the
Mito statement, they nonetheless contributed to its shrinkage.
The price for survival was diminution, and Mito was reduced to
an intellectual anachronism by the 1850s, a reminder to men everywhere of the impermanence of all systems of social order. Defender to the last of order and tradition—or of what it imagined
these to be—by 1856 the Mito school had seen its achievement become its epitaph.

Confrontation, even though oblique, with a new reality-principle required a psychology or theory of personality which, as we
saw earlier, Confucianism failed to provide. The disparity between ideal conduct and new needs destroyed the Confucian
model of public personality. Liberated from history—in this
case a moral past—the late Tokugawa personality was increasingly less obliged to submerge private impulse in order to realize
unchanging social expectations. The opening of the country led

activists successively to question the concept of social order which they had inherited from Mito; to attack the normative bases of behavior and leadership; and finally to hint at a conflict between private choice based on a perception of reality, and the public expectation which fixed how reality should be perceived. But in the absence of a concept of the ego they were left few choices in dealing with the challenges of the day. In Sakuma Shōzan's celebration of a "historical emperor" and eulogies of Peter the Great, in Yoshida Shōin's unattached heroes (*sōmō no eiyū*), in Yokoi Shōnan's new managers (*yūtokusha*, Confucian reformers resembling George Washington more than any Chinese culture-hero), the sociohistoric reality of the *bakumatsu* generation inspired writers to find a theory of personality that might serve the requirements of political leadership. The late Tokugawa period disclosed the range of personality and behavior possible to a society liberated from history and in process of accommodating itself to a new principle of social reality. Once the contemporary situation was accepted as a datum in perception—a recognition that Mito writers tried in vain to avoid—personality and leadership became indissolubly linked.

But in spite of all this, the example of Mito did not fail to reach men. If there is heroic pathos in grandiose systems which fail, here was one testifying to the richness of the Japanese intellectual imagination; and its failure was not an indictment either of the impulse to its construction or of the imagination which decided for a generation what constituted history and tradition. As men witnessed the rapid failure of the Mito statement, they were still unwilling to bury it. Nor were they willing to use *gaikan* as the occasion for a total abandonment of the Mito effort with an indifferent shrug. They had been nurtured on the Mito rhetoric and had accepted the Mito resolution of contemporary crisis; even though it no longer delivered the promise of consolation, they still had to go on with the job of living. And this meant, especially for a generation of writers and activists raised in the 1840s, replacing the parts of an intellectual edifice with new and more durable ones. As they worked from inside a failed system, they had to make the conditions of failure a datum in constructing new modes of intellectual defense. To have been schooled in the Mito rhetoric was an emblem of intellectual seriousness and respectability; and to ignore this inheritance—the only link of most intellectuals with the past—was to ignore Japan itself. Their various efforts must be considered a repayment of debt or a sustained attempt to make Mito work under new conditions. The centripetality which Mito represented earlier, where men gathered around central pieties, gave way to centrifugality, and agreement on all points was no longer possible. Men then seized upon those vestiges of a broken center which they believed to be of lasting value. In their hands tradition became several things, and none again could ever be so confident that he had the right answer. But a tradition of vestiges indicates the failure of coherence: the center did not hold. By the 1840s younger men were turning to other ideas and new forms of knowledge.

There was little agreement among ideologues why Mito failed. Precisely because so many factors contributed to undermining this achievement, men differed widely in the choice of new organizing principles. The diminution of the magnetic appeal of Mito was due to several causes of different sorts: dissolution of Neo-Confucian norms governing inquiry by interest in Western medical and military technology; the uniform failure of the Tempō reforms to establish new moral precedents; the exaggerated reports during the first Anglo-Chinese war that the ignominious fate of India was in store for Ch'ing China; the opening of the country (*kaikoku*) and the signing of commercial treaties, which after 1858 made Japanese ports available to Western nations. Like enormous hammer blows, each event struck hard at the complacent Mito achievement and dislodged a decisive element of its structure. The rapidity of these hammer blows prevented the planned retreat that was possible for nineteenth-century Chinese thought; and all that remained by the 1860s was a memory of the optimism which only a decade earlier had swept the country and comforted an entire managerial class. As discrete factors chipped away an element here and there, different writers stressed the aspects of the Mito achievement which appeared essential to laying the basis of a new unity. The threads that Mito thinkers had woven into a whole cloth could no longer cohere. And Aizawa's late but feeble attempt to come to terms with *kaikoku* merely confirmed this fact.

Most writers in the 1850s and 1860s tried, under new conditions and with new knowledge, to use Mito as a nucleus for a reconstituted intellectual order. But there was nothing like agreement in the details of reconstruction among writers from (for example) Sakuma Shōzan down to Takasugi Shinsaku or Ōkubo Toshimichi. In response to changing conditions, writers and activists reached beyond the narrow limits of Mito ideologues and explored a whole new range of ideas and programs which ultimately included the overthrow of the *bakufu*. From the modest beginnings of romantic restorationism and fanatical antibarbarism, they went on to formulate a new political consciousness and ideology on a trial-and-error basis within the context of late Tokugawa political history. The new ideological constructions represented a change from an inflexible position to political realism. While some sympathized with a theory of "reverence" (*sonnō-ron*) based on the normative ethic of designations and duties (*meibun*), others clung to expulsionism as the basis of a unified Japanese society, and still others opted for a Confucian emperor-ism (*ōdō*) and the cultivation of a "public realm" to resolve immediate political problems. Agreement on specific plans was rare, even while the uncertainty of the future linked all writers and activists in a common effort. But the common effort ultimately produced an operational plan which called for the destruction of the *bakufu* and the building of a powerful and wealthy state through modern skills and knowledge. And this was a long way from Mito.

The celebration of modern skills and new knowledge was possible because writers, despite their incapacity to agree elsewhere, shared a disposition toward practicality (*jitsugaku*) and an identification of rational techniques as the way to solve Japan's problems. However disparate, the several efforts showed the shape of a common struggle for liberation from established thinking and for acquisition of a new concept of social reality formed by the investigation of contemporary conditions. In the task of salvaging the usable elements of the Mito statement, practicality and the impulse to investigate were better equipment than Chinese intellectuals had at their disposal in a similar situation. In this quest to emancipate thought from moral abstraction and to establish a more flexible foundation for action, no man in the late Tokugawa period was better prepared than Sakuma Shōzan.

THE FOREIGN THREAT AND THE PROBLEM OF DEFENSE

Sakuma was one of the earliest of *bakamatsu* ideologues to take on the new reality; suitably, the encounter was inaugurated by a man more committed to the pursuit of knowledge than to action. He was, as Maruyama Masao put it, "a type who is the complete intellectually rational thinker." [1] In his time Sakuma's breadth of knowledge was unparalleled. And his commitment, as a concerned intellectual, to share his learning rather than make a mystery of it shows how far he believed in the necessary relationship of knowledge and investigation to action. The emergency of *gaikan* and the peril of colonization could be resolved only if men investigated new knowledge and techniques. Sakuma showed that if Japan's new mood was to be something more than an anxious emotional nationalism, it would have to be informed by a "rationality" and an empirical consciousness leading to an investigation of the wider world. His greatest contribution to the late Tokugawa discourse was, I think, his insistence on abandoning inherited moral standards—conceptual equipment which acted as a prism to filter knowledge through—in favor of the authority of immediate experience which yielded a direct confrontation with the conditions of the world. The stimulus for this awakening was the news of the British victories in the first Opium War, which reached Japan about 1841, and which in the following years was to reorient Sakuma's career and thought.

[1] Maruyama Masao, "Bakumatsu ni okeru kenza no henkaku," *Tembō* (May, 1964), 77:19.

In his time Sakuma Shōzan (1811–1864), a retainer of the Ma-
tsuhiro *han* in present-day Nagano, was the hope (his contemporaries attested) of a generation of young samurai intellectuals left
defenseless after the dissolution of the Mito statement. His range
of associations was truly prodigious and included most of the outstanding ideologues of the time, while his own students constitute an even more impressive testimony to his intellectual mag-
netism. Apart from Yoshida Shōin, who died years before the
Restoration, Sakuma's list of pupils includes late Tokugawa personalities such as Katsu Kaishū, Kobayashi Torazaburō, Hashimoto Sanai, and Sakamoto Ryōma; and early Meiji writers and
thinkers such as Kato Hirōyuki, Tsuda Mamichi, and Nishimura
Shigeki.[2] Even though he was by the age of thirty-four (in 1845)
an accomplished scholar of Neo-Confucianism who had made his
mark on the world, Sakuma, after learning about China, turned
to the study of Western military technology. This did not constitute a fundamental break with his prior commitment to Neo-
Confucianism, but was rather, I think, an effort to explore possibilities inherent in this intellectual tradition. Sakuma reached
back into the Neo-Confucian tradition and found sanctions for
learning and knowledge which had long been smothered in Japan—most recently by Mito writers in their treatment of the purpose of learning. His was the last creative attempt in Tokugawa
thought to accommodate Neo-Confucianism to technology.

Within the revitalized Neo-Confucianism which he hoped for,
Sakuma sought to define the cultural basis for action—that is, a
culture through which the Japanese could confront the challenge
of the day and preserve their political independence. In the
action of a reconstituted culture Sakuma hoped to conserve essential elements of the received endowment in a creatively transformed way, as a condition for taking on new knowledge without fear of total erosion. Since he saw that time was growing
short and Mito was failing on all fronts, Sakuma treated the
problem facing Japan in the 1840s in terms of the totality of culture. Culture, he believed, would yield adequate standards of ac-

[2] Minamoto Ryōen, *"Meiji Ishin to jitsugaku,"* in *Meiji ishinshi no mondaiten,* ed. Sakata Yoshio (Tokyo, 1962), p. 60.

tion and guidelines for behavior, but only if it was in tune with contemporary reality. Sakuma was confident that full investigation, both of contemporary conditions and of his own philosophic endowment, would offer sanctions for new behavior and new knowledge. Yet time still allowed Sakuma to think in terms of the totality of an ethicopolitical culture that would permit the Japanese to view the mystery of Western technology as naturally consistent with established moral precepts. Within the orbit of a culture where ethical limits were always agreed, Sakuma argued that technological knowledge could find a natural place. Unlike Chang Chih-t'ung, whose solution is often compared with his, he did not succumb to either desperation or cultural conceit, and refused to regard the acquisition of moral knowledge as prior to technology.

The acceptance of technology under the protective sanction of Neo-Confucianism was a genuine effort to vindicate the universality of Neo-Confucianism by showing its capacity for change to meet the requirements of new knowledge. Because Sakuma was able to overcome cultural complacency and conceit, he went beyond his Chinese contemporaries and saw that Western learning was useful not only in military defense but also in the political order. Once he began to apply the idea of *kakubutsu kyūri* ("investigation of things through penetration [or exhaustion] of principle") it was natural that he would try its possibilities in the realm of politics and policy. With Sakuma's disposition to practicality, *kakubtsu kyūri* was a technique that allowed a direct experience of information wherever necessity dictated. In this formula Sakuma delivered to political discourse a powerful relativism, implicit in the Mito statement, but submerged under the weight of traditional norms and morally oriented learning. Here Sakuma, whose response always reflects a felt dissatisfaction with the Mito school, went beyond his original intent and helped further disrupt the Mito achievement, whose faults he was no doubt trying to redeem. After Sakuma, the response of activists, however hysterical, would always be tempered by a concern for appropriate knowledge. To know was a prior condition to acting correctly.

Sakuma Shōzan's early years were spent in studying the classics under a domainal elder, Kanebara Tōzan; in studying traditional Japanese mathematics under a retainer, Machida Harazaemon; and, of course, in the practice of traditional military arts.[3] His biographers are quick to record his precocious ability to learn rapidly and well in the inevitable incident where the hero in infancy clearly showed a sign of his later intellectual greatness. Sakuma's later eminence as a scholar was foretold when at three years, so the story goes, he wrote Chinese characters by himself without being taught by anyone.[4] Such accounts tell us more about the biographer than his subject. As far as it can be determined, Sakuma's real intellectual career began in 1834, when at the age of twenty-three he was sent to Edo for advanced study under the direction of the Hayashi school, the shogunal college or academy. Always the emblem of promise and ability, the study tour in Edo brought him into contact with Satō Issai, who was then at the school and who was one of the few original thinkers of the time. The story of his encounter with Satō is a familiar one, but worth recounting since it reveals something about Sakuma's intellectual commitments.

Despite his public approval of Neo-Confucianism, Satō apparently harbored a strong sympathy for Wang Yang-ming's "intuitionism" (*ōyōmei shingaku*). This meant for Sakuma that Satō was favoring the authority of speculation over against moral precedent in guiding behavior; interiority was prior to exteriority, public behavior followed private impulse. This kind of intuitionism discredited the more orthodox emphasis upon a natural order and the need for constant investigation of social reality to determine the proper mode of conduct. It held that men always know how to act correctly, without recourse to investigation, and that learning can only confirm this self-knowledge. In a reminiscence of 1860 Sakuma disclosed his earlier attitude toward Satō's intuitionism, and his own retention of orthodoxy: "Issai favored

[3] Biographical information on Sakuma is taken from Ōhira Kimata, *Sakuma Shōzan* (Tokyo, 1963), pp. 31ff., and Miyamoto Yū, *Sakuma Shōzan* (Tokyo, 1936), p. 53ff.

[4] Ōhira, p. 26.

the school of Wang Yang-ming and did not care for Chu Hsi's
conception of the principles of nature. . . . I follow mainly the
precepts which correspond to the Ch'eng-Chu [system] by which
one investigates the principles (*ri*) of nature and all other
things." [5] Elsewhere Sakuma gently but self-righteously condemns Satō for dwelling only on poetry and prose to the exclusion of the philosophical classics because he felt no need for
moral knowledge.[6] Wang Yang-ming had suggested at one point
that a study of the classics was not really essential to proper conduct; and Satō Issai, while he made no real effort to discredit the
classical texts in the eyes of his talented students, offered more en-
thusiastically his own insights on conduct and his thoughts on literature and poetry. What could be more galling than a celebration of "empty learning" to a young samurai disposed to practicality, hard work, and self-righteous seriousness?

A number of writers, searching for influences, see in Sakuma
Shōzan (as also in Yoshida Shōin) an enormous intellectual debt
to intuitionism, and argue that both failed to conceal their indebtedness. The burden of proof lies not with Sakuma whose pattern of renunciation was consistent, but with those who assert
that the activism found in him and in the restorationists was possible only by intuitionism. Even if this were so, it still remains to
be demonstrated that Sakuma's attitude toward action, which
throughout his writings is constantly justified by Neo-Confucianism, resulted from intuitionism. And this theory hardly explains
why he expended so much time and energy in securing new
knowledge. Indeed, it would be difficult to say what kind of action was conceived by Wang Yang-ming, and how it was distinguished from Sung Neo-Confucianism. Meditation rather than
action, self-cultivation rather than "outer tranquilizing," are the
associations of intuitionism.

The episode is further illuminating because it occurred just

---

[5] Shinano kyōikukai, eds, *Shōzan zenshū,* 2 vols. (Nagano, 1922), I,
608–609, "Dai Issai iboku." Hereafter this source will be cited as *Sz.* See
also Miyamoto, pp. 53–58.

[6] Miyamoto, p. 6.

prior to Ōshio's rebellion in Osaka (1837), which Sakuma, like Fujita Tōko, condemned without equivocation. Ōshio was said to be sympathetic with intuitionism; and his rebellion, an attack on the established authorities, was alleged to be a natural outcome of this commitment to an unorthodox theory of action.[7] Sakuma urged that this abuse or intellectual excess should be dreaded, and "since intuitionism (*ōyōmeigaku*) has spread throughout the realm (*kokka*) we ought to reject it with all our might."[8] But the rebellion was instructive. Sakuma (like Fujita Tōko, whose writings he was then reading) believed that the uprising, having exposed why intellectual training should be corrected, argued for the reassertion of Neo-Confucianism. Satō Issai was well intentioned but his intuitionism blurred distinctions; it was too permissive. Just as "from the standpoint of a fencing pole (*shinai*) there is no discrimination between lord and vassal [so] from the standpoint of reason (*dōri*) there is no discrimination between teacher and student. When theories are different, even though one might be the teacher, he will not be able to gain obedience."[9] Here Sakuma reveals the intellectual affiliation which he was to sustain throughout his writings. Yet this affiliation was not merely the lip-service to daily ethics common among Neo-Confucianists of the time.

In a preface to a new edition of the writings of the Sung philosopher, Shao K'ang-chieh, completed on his second tour of study in Edo in the autumn of 1831, Sakuma shows that his involvement in Neo-Confucianism was more than an affected gesture:

The essence of learning is in *kakubutsu kyūri*. . . . Men of today only talk about things (*butsu*) and principles, but do not investigate human ethics and daily necessities. When does one investigate the principle (*ri*) from daily necessities and human conduct? Hitherto we have been in the dark about things and principle. But, "things are the boats and vehicles of the body, and men who do not study these things and

[7] *Ibid.*, pp. 54–55.
[8] Quoted in Ōhira, p. 47.
[9] *Ibid.*

their principles ride on rudderless ships, stand on hubless carts.". . . We can say that it is our desire to investigate things and penetrate principle, and this certainly is how we can enter and apply the thought of master Shao.[10]

Shao Tzu was a contemporary of Cheng Tzu, who lived before Chu Hsi, and he contributed a formidable element to the making of the so-called Sung school. His special interest was an application of principles found in the classic of augury, the *I Ching,* which guided him in his pursuit of the principles and laws informing the universe and "the ten thousand things." [11] In conscious emulation of Shao, Sakuma began his early studies with the *I Ching.* Sakuma's special reliance on Shao K'ang-chieh is explained by a particular turn of Shao's thought: the doctrine that if men failed to know the principle behind things (a knowledge possible only through investigation), then they were doomed never to know correct moral conduct. The kinds of *ri* Sakuma proposed to investigate were principles operative in the natural world whose manifestations were found in society. With Sakuma as with his Sung master, the concept of "investigation" involved an exploration, not into the natural world, but into social reality, since it was there men learned what necessities had to be met. Such an inquiry was essential both for correct individual conduct, as we shall see, and also for proper political policies. The "investigation of things" promised an escape from abstraction and norms by establishing the precedent of a powerful relativism; it was the technique by which Sakuma and others to follow would separate history from moralism.

During Sakuma's second trip to Edo in 1839 he began to study the relation between technology and Neo-Confucianism and to apply it to the resolution of domestic disorder. Even before then he had been forcibly obliged to reevaluate the purpose of his scholarship and the relevance of learning to the realities of *naiyū.* The countrywide famines of 1836, followed by Ōshio's rebellion

[10] *Sz.,* I, 379–380, "Shao K'ang-chieh bunshū yo."

[11] Fung Yu-lan, *History of Chinese Philosophy,* trans. Derk Bodde, 2 vols. (Princeton, 1953), II, 550ff.; *Sz.,* I, 380–381; Miyamoto, p. 58.

in the following year, had prompted him to put his learning to the service of the domain and its economic problems. This first exhibition of a practical learning prepared Sakuma for his later response to news of Britain's victories in China. To deal with local manifestations of what clearly was a national problem, Sakuma drafted a proposal, the *Gakusei Ikenshō* (*Opinions on the Educational System*), which, following the Mito precedent, located the source of the trouble in moral paralysis.[12] An echo of Mito writers is heard in his proposal that learning must always serve practical ends. The same dependence on Mito inhibited him from seeing at this time the real source of problems. The answer to domainal ills, he felt, lay in propping up moral education; and his recommendations show how far he was committed to conserving the Mito view of social order. "In tranquilizing the realm (*kokka*), it is essential to correct customs and to nourish talent and skill by making them fundamental concerns. When there is a shortage of talent, duties cannot be accomplished, even though there is an abundance of offices. In correcting customs and nourishing skills, it is necessary to stress the educational system where the arts of the Way are clarified."[13] This moral training for social leadership, well articulated by Sakuma's friend Fujita Tōko, involved an austere practicality and a fusion of military and civilian skills. Once this disposition toward practicality had displaced Confucian metaphysics and had taken on the technique of *kaku-butsu kyūri,* Sakuma was prepared to consider the possibilities of Western military technology.

Sakuma Shōzan did not take up the study of Western weaponry after a thorough metaphysical appraisal, as many of his contemporaries did. Sakuma's second trip to Edo coincided with the Morrison incident; with the ensuing punishment of pioneer enthusiasts for Western learning, Watanabe Kazan and Takano Chōhei; with news of the first Anglo-Chinese wars; and with the presentation in 1840 of Takashima Shūhan's timely memorial

---

[12] See, for example, Numata Jirō, *Yōgaku denrai rekishi* (Tokyo, 1960). Miyamoto, p. 60.

[13] *Sz.,* I, 67-78.

calling for the study of cannon casting. While residing in Edo, Sakuma also witnessed the first of Mizuno Tadakuni's shogunal reforms, which included the appointment of Sakuma's lord Sanada Yukitsura to the Office of Naval Defense. Sanada in turn immediately selected Sakuma as his adviser. This appointment, and the command to study military arts, led Sakuma to enroll in the school of Egawa Tarōzaemon. This sequence of events suggests that Sakuma did not enter on the study of Western technology (as it was available in Edo in the early 1840s) through Neo-Confucianism; rather he found himself involved in coastal defense and cannon casting out of his lord's initiative—and also perhaps out of a growing awareness that the nature of problems was changing. The practicality inherent in his intellectual endowment is shown in the reform policy he formulated during the period of training under Egawa. And these new duties prompted Sakuma to think about the relation between the claims of the new knowledge and of Neo-Confucianism.

When Sakuma turned to finding a place for the new learning within the received intellectual tradition, he raised questions that have continued to exercise thoughtful Japanese down to modern times. In the early 1840s he did not think of anything so elaborate as the notion of two distinct cultures informed by two different principles (*ri*). No more does his later slogan *Tōyō dōtoku, seiyō gei*. ("Oriental ethics as base, Western technique as means") assume a radical cultural difference on the grounds that the *ri* of Japan was different from that of the West. This conclusion has been drawn from the Chinese experience where, as in the thought of Chang Chih-t'ung, two distinct cultures—China and the West—respectively illustrated *t'i* (substance) and *yung* (function). Sakuma could escape this dualism because he thought of Japan as an independent entity, no more tied to the Orient than to the West. From the standpoint of the Japanese (he wrote in a Chinese poem in 1844), both Westerners and Chinese are foreign; how then could Chinese learning be called "within" or "ours" and judged good, while Western learning was "other" and bad? Since Sakuma was prepared to spare Japan from the responsibility of being "Oriental," he urged return to a cultural independence which would permit free inquiry into "the conditions of the world." To release inquiry into the world from the rigid categories imposed by Chinese learning, it was essential for the Japanese to draw out their own individuality from the Orient. Such a liberation involved repudiation of the earlier Mito insistence on "inner" and "outer"; and it promised Sakuma a new scientific knowledge and an independent Japanese political community following the course of thought whichever way it was moving.[14]

Sakuma saw better and earlier than most of his countrymen the importance of the foreign threat. Before the coming of Perry and the opening of the country, much of his activity and thinking was poured into meeting the challenge. At the same time he learned a respect for the adversary that changed his whole attitude to culture. Thus in 1850 he wrote a petition for more translations of Western (i.e. Dutch) technical books. He calls not for trade but for useful information. The intellectual equipment for a proper coastal defense was available but had been neglected. The promise of *kyūri* had been smothered by excessive concern with textual studies, and its true meaning, "the investigation of all things," had been dissipated. Since the time of the Duke of Chou and Confucius, Chinese and Japanese had been robbed of the fruits of investigation, and thus of the means to strengthen national power.[15] Elsewhere he argued that it was essential to survival to know the enemy, and that such knowledge was blocked by cultural conceit and complacency. The overwhelming fact of his times, he noted, was the presence of a foreigner who, even though he failed "like birds and beasts" to discriminate between high and low, constituted a threat which could not be ignored. "The urgency for preparing to meet a foreign invasion (*gaikō*) does not begin just by knowing them [the foreigners]. The method by which you know them lies not just in exhausting their skills, but in combining their learning with ours."[16] This is in dramatic contrast to the view of Fujita Tōko, who had

[14] See Maruyama (n. 1 above), pp. 22–23.

[15] *Sz.*, I, 124.

[16] *Sz.*, I, 128.

charged that even though the "barbarian has acquired some knowledge, his doctrines follow the Way of birds and beasts. They must not be used in the imperial land. Our land is the only country near to China; but if we imitate their customs, then we would pass into their Way." [17] Sakuma hoped to establish a view that would broaden the base of Japan in the present and ensure the "long independence of the realm in the world." [18]

After the opening of the country Sakuma remained convinced that the meaning of Neo-Confucianism had been obscured by time and by the "customs of the realm." It had become customary to deny the dynamism of Neo-Confucianism; hence scholars, faced by new knowledge which they did not understand, differentiated cultures and assigned priority to what had been achieved in the Orient. Surely (he wrote in one of his last petitions) it was the basic intention of Chu Hsi from the beginning "to cross over to the five continents in our times in order to investigate their skills and things." [19] Earlier in 1849, on the occasion of trying to publish a Dutch dictionary, he saw the development of the "five continents as continuous from the beginning down to today." He urged studying the "military skills of the several nations" and the ways they had realized prosperity and strengthened national power. While this had been the practice in China down to Confucius and the Duke of Chou, the precedent had been lost, and Sakuma asked why.[20] He never answers the question, but notes that China, the land of sages and the home of Chu Hsi, had paid a high price for its indifference in its recent war with the English.

He continued that Western science and technology should not be thought incompatible with the teachings of the Ch'eng-Chu school. Rather "the meaning of Chu Hsi is to penetrate the *ri* in conformity with the realm so as to increase knowledge. When

[17] Fujita Tōko, "Hitachi obi," in *Mgt.,* I (see chap. 2, n. 1).
[18] *Sz.,* I, 128.
[19] Inoue Tadashi, "Kyūri no hatten," *Rekishigaku kenkyū* (Tokyo, 1940), Vol. 10, No. 7, p. 33; also *Sz.,* II, 549–551, "Letter to Kawaji Toshiakira."
[20] *Sz.,* I, 123–130.

the meaning of the Ch'eng-Chu school corresponds to such things as the investigation of Western conditions, the explanations of those two teachers will correspond to the world. If we follow the meaning of Ch'eng-Chu, even Western skills will become part of learning and knowledge, and will not appear to be outside our framework." [21] Sakuma saw no conflict between his concept of an ethical civilization and the acceptance of Western knowledge, which he understood as a natural concomitant of Neo-Confucianism that would inflict no damage on its governing principles. If conflict were inevitable, he would have to postulate two distinct cultures each with its principle (*ri*), and make a differentiation between "ours" and "other." But in a letter to Kobayashi Torazaburō he states that "there are not two real principles of the universe that reside in different places. The learning skills developed in the West are conducive to the learning of the sages. . . . In the universe there are not two real principles. . . . All the sages of a hundred generations would not be able to move or change this fact." [22] The principles of ancient sages and Western empirical skills were one and the same thing. Neither was limited to a special country or culture; rather (as the sages of antiquity revealed) both were accessible to all peoples in all times. The problem, as he saw it, was not a conflict between the relative merits of Chinese and Western learning, but determining the true principles underlying each. If they were true principles they must be mutually compatible. Hence Sakuma could never have conceived of two different cultures informed by two different *ri*. Culture, the possession of true principles, was its own boundaries; its development was not restricted to those areas "closest to China."

Sakuma Shōzan's enthusiasm for science and the new learning was a response to his shaken confidence in Confucianism. In a

[21] Inoue, *op. cit.*, p. 33; *Sz.*, II, 549–551.

[22] Miyamoto (n. 3 above), pp. 63–64. For a different view see Albert Craig, "Science and Confucianism in Tokugawa Japan," in *Changing Japanese Attitudes Toward Modernization,* ed. Marius Jansen (Princeton, 1965), pp. 133–160.

letter to Katsu Kaishū he confessed the personal price he had paid for the decision to study technology, but he expressed no regrets. "When an eccentricity in the school of Chinese learning occurs and a person pursues Western studies prosperously, he receives the contempt of scholars of Chinese learning."[23] They close ranks, he continued, despising the eccentric in unison out of fear that he will establish new explanations. Sakuma complained that he had earned disapproval because he had departed from accepted practice, but he also said that those who condemn were small and mean. He knew the consequences of taking on a new learning. "Observing that the customs of other areas are different and not the same as our conventions, one can compare these to different varieties. When these [foreign] studies are conducted prosperously, the lovely customs of our country will gradually change because of this," but if there is distrust and doubt, then they will be impeded.[24] Independence in political culture made it as natural to entertain what was distant and different as what was close and familiar—without fear of corruption. Free of its affiliation with Oriental-inner culture, which is simply geographical, Japan (shinshū) is also free to determine the conditions of its own survival; nothing is foreign if it is useful in preserving the independence of the realm.

The immediate stimulus for technology was the need for defense measures; its adoption was rationalized by an appeal to practicality and to the requirements of the times. Sakuma was not much different from a number of contemporary thinkers who were calling for an abandonment of "past customs" and an evaluation of contemporary world conditions. This new historical consciousness in much of late Tokugawa thought was dramatized by the shogunal decision to break precedent and consult both the emperor and several *tozama* lords in order to achieve a broad-based decision on Perry's demands. Unlike late Ch'ing thought, which failed to see any real difference between past and present, Japanese writers saw in the coming of foreign ships a unique event which broke with the past and thereby inspired a

---

[23] *Sz.*, II, 631, "Letter to Katsu Kaishū"; p. 710, "Letter to Katsu."
[24] *Ibid.*, p. 710.

new understanding of history in which one age could differ from another. While Sakuma believed that it was necessary "to use the times" and "have a fondness for changing conditions," as he put it in a letter to one of his pupils, he was also fearful of change that might simply serve self-interest. Change, he urged, requires knowledge, but it also must reflect a basic intention to serve the realm. This, he believed, must be the motivation of "sympathetic samurai" (*yūshi no shi*) who formulate suitable plans for the realm. When they initiate necessary changes, they must "not change this purpose; they must pursue unusual success when confronting unusual times." [25]

This concern which Sakuma early felt was exacerbated by news of the first Anglo-Chinese war and by fears of disaster awaiting the Ch'ing state. He responded so forcefully to the news because of its likely results for the Japanese if they did not learn why the Chinese were failing. The war, he noted, spelled a special doom for the Ch'ing state—that is, for a crucial segment of civilization.[26] The impact of this war and the problems of defense it raised spurred him to write a petition in 1843 in which he set out an Eight Point Policy on Naval Defense. Beyond the technical challenge which the Chinese failed to take up, the poor performance of the Ch'ing state meant, he believed, a further withdrawal of civilization, leaving whatever was left to defend in Japan. The Chinese, he wrote on numerous occasions, had lost the real meaning of true principles and, in place of inquiry and investigation, had substituted conceit and complacency. The remains of the true principles were left in Japan, and it was essential for the Japanese to enhance this inheritance in order to protect it. Defense was necessary, he argued, not because "it related to the honor and disgrace of the Tokugawa family, " but rather because it was a measure in response to "the fate (*anki*) of the imperial house whose line of a hundred generations is without comparison in the world." [27]

In his memoirs, the *Seiken roku,* which he wrote in prison,

[25] Maruyama, "Bakumatsu ni okeru kenza no henkaku," p. 25.
[26] *Sz.,* I, 89–94.
[27] *Sz.,* I, 93–94.

Sakuma Shōzan records how he had tried to awake the country
to the necessities of defense, and how he had been punished for
his prescience. Describing his developing awareness, he notes his
reactions in reading Wei Yüan's *Hai-kuo t'u-chih,* and the sympathy he first felt on learning of the efforts of a kindred soul in
China. But the sympathy soon dissolves into criticism. Sakuma is
quick to point out that while Wei showed some sensitivity to the
problem of defense, his approach revealed how little he understood the problems of China and the requirements of an adequate defense. He compares Wei's notions about defense and
gunnery with his own recent experience and concludes on the
disparaging note that his Chinese compatriot brought to his
awareness all the cultural conceit of his class and education.[28]
According to Sakuma, Wei had followed the ancient practice of
deploying a defensive navy to protect the coast from direct incur-
sions. Apparently this procedure had fallen into disuse, and certainly in the early nineteenth century it proved ineffective against
both pirates and opium smugglers. Sakuma believed that this
kind of defense was necessary, but only as one aspect of a larger
defense network. A navy, he argued, should be supported by a
tight organization of land-defense units. This presupposed considerable knowledge of Western military technology. He agreed
with Wei that it was important "to manage foreigners by knowing how they feel," but disagreed over the means to achieve this
policy.[29] Further, to know how foreigners feel and think, one
must not think of them, as Wei does, as "birds and beasts" or as
barbarians. The essence of his critique of Wei's policy, which
events in China were already confirming, is disclosed in the expression of a doubt: "In this book of Wei's is described an opinion similar to mine; that is, we should establish schools in our
country that will teach foreign languages and translate foreign
books in order to seize the thoughts of foreigners. This is fundamental to managing foreigners. . . . But I am not sure if they
[the Chinese] can master the necessary foreign languages." [30]

[28] *Sz.,* I, 13ff., "Seiken roku."
[29] *Ibid.*
[30] *Sz.,* I, 14.

Again Sakuma notes how interested Wei is in the problem of gunnery, but how little he knows about the technology behind it. Just as languages are the key to foreign technology, technology in turn will remain a mystery if the principles underlying it are not taken seriously. Wei's views, he writes, "are childish and unbelievable," and he has compounded a mistake into a legacy of error that will surely "lead those who follow him into wrong ways." [31]

This analysis of Wei Yüan, sketched earlier in Sakuma's memorial of 1843, points to an abiding conviction: culture can yield adequate action when a sincere investigation of reality is conducted, but it will not do so automatically. Culture presumes the acquisition of knowledge, since action and policy cannot be properly prosecuted unless informed by knowledge of contemporary conditions. "Culture" here is both more and less than it was conceived by Wei and the members of his class. Sakuma formulated it as a tool serving the interests of a political community, which decides what knowledge is useful and what is not. But (Sakuma is insistent) knowledge, learning, and investigation are essential to culture. As the demands of the political community change (he observed) so do the contours of culture.

The example of Wei elicited another response from Sakuma. Suitable measures and policy depend on the availability of talented men and their placement in positions of responsibility. Virtue, he believed, does not ensure knowledge, and knowledge is essential to policy and action. Men of "talent and ability" were for Sakuma those (like himself) committed to the acquisition of knowledge. Wei Yüan, he noted, always stood at arm's length from Western technology; he admired its power but never took it seriously enough to study it actively. Here was the reason why the Ch'ing state had failed in its struggle against the English. In his prison musings Sakuma constantly returned to the theme of "talent and ability," understood as passion for learning. This traditional notion was later expanded by Yoshida Shōin and Yokoi Shōnan, but Sakuma Shōzan first formulated it to deal with the contemporary crisis.

[31] *Ibid.*

Sakuma's criticism of contemporary leadership had a double edge: failure was both political and intellectual. Each failure arose from a weakness in character. "Officials in recent times," he complained, "are very careless, ill-mannered in speech and in conduct. They feel that it is important to behave this way so that others will follow them. What an absurd misunderstanding this is!" [32] Contempt, he continued, was a poor substitute for knowledge and real courage in dealing with the foreigner; and yet contemporary leadership in Japan as in China constantly relied on it. For Sakuma, virtue was measured only by conduct, and proper conduct was possible only if a man possessed ability and talent. "Ability" here meant capacity or will to investigate social reality; "talent" meant success in applying knowledge to the management of contemporary affairs. Sakuma's writings reveal, over and over again, how his own career was an effort to realize this moral superiority.[33] Talent and ability were natural heaven sent gifts which had to be utilized, as with Sakuma himself, by men so endowed, even at the risk of punishment and imprisonment. His commitment to talent and ability provided him a basis on which to act, even though it would surely invite official disapproval. Ability was its own justification, and its exercise would serve the best interests of the Tokugawa house, of the realm of culture, and of the new political scene.[34] In contrast to this criterion of acceptable action—prior possession of knowledge—Yoshida Shōin, as I will show later, equated talent and ability rather with the impulse to act loyally. Loyalty is virtually invisible in Sakuma's thought, and while he no doubt viewed it as crucial to behavior, he did not see it as a real problem. This difference, which I will return to later, arises from the ways Sakuma Shōzan and Yoshida Shōin saw the major problem of the day.

Sakuma's condemnation of intellectual leadership was even stronger. "What are the scholars of today doing?" he asked. "Do

[32] *Sz.,* I, 18.
[33] See the opening passages of *Sz.,* I, 13ff., "Seiken roku"; also "Memorial to Hitotsubashi" (1864), *Sz.,* I, 302ff.
[34] *Sz.,* I, 223, "Petition of 1862 to the *bakufu*."

they know the righteousness admired at the time our country was established, and under the government of Yao and Shun during the Three Dynasties in China? Do they, on learning of rites and music, punishment and rewards, go on to apply such things in the real world? Do they exhaustively study geography; the conditions of land and sea routes; the ways of preparing for an enemy's attack; the methods of constructing forts and barriers; the ways of relieving the people; mathematics, physics, and geometry? They might, but I have not yet heard about it. And so I say, what are the scholars of today doing?"[35] The shortcomings of officials could always be explained away; but the resistance of scholars, men of recognized ability, to new knowledge was injurious to the realm, since official policy was usually formed upon their advice. Even a real understanding of the classics and of ancient precedent was beyond their reach, because they had failed to distinguish between useful and useless. Learning, Sakuma argued, was no longer linked to daily affairs as it had been in antiquity; no value was to be found in reading books, studying hard, or discussing theory for the sake of theory. Little would be lost if the empty learning of contemporary scholars did not exist. "Learning that is truly significant," Sakuma announced, "is like a hemp gown in summer and a fur coat in winter. Everybody would be inconvenienced in his daily life if he did not have one or the other at the appropriate time."[36]

He is showing the importance of a practical learning (*jitsu-gaku*) that would ascertain and serve daily needs, and change as they changed. This indictment of contemporary learning was dramatized by calling attention to the unpreparedness of Chinese scholars for the consequences of the first Anglo-Chinese war. In a confessional letter written to one of his closest confidants, the poet-loyalist Yanagawa Seigan, Sakuma disclosed in detail the kind of practicality required of contemporary scholars:

If there is one thing I dare worry about, it is that nowadays the knowledge of Chinese and Japanese learning only is not enough to cover ev-

[35] *Sz.*, I, 11–12, "Seiken roku."
[36] *Sz.*, I, 12.

erything, and that we should be versed in current events found throughout the world. If we look at such circumstances today through the exercise of investigation, we will learn that Columbus discovered a new continent, Newton the Law of Gravity, and Copernicus the heliocentric theory. . . . There is no other way for our country to retain power . . . than to become versed in these arts and try to invent similar things like the Europeans.[37]

Ultimately he would conclude, in contrast to all other thinkers of the time in both Japan and China, that mathematics was the basis for all learning and investigation, and that mastery of Western learning involved, not superficial techniques, but rather the "penetration" of the principles underlying inventions and discoveries. Sakuma understood early and consistently how a mastery of scientific principles preceded the development of technology. He called for "basic studies" which would first yield an understanding of the general problem before any attempt at application. This constituted no surrender to Western learning, but only a refinement of his own sense of practicality and view of culture.

In all this, Sakuma Shōzan had shifted the grounds of argument as it had been earlier established by the Mito ideologues. But the nature of events had also changed. Sakuma's petition of 1843 to Sanada acknowledged the priority of the foreign problem. This recognition impressed upon him the necessity of a new kind of preparation; and his consistent attempt to combine the Neo-Confucian investigative technique (*kakubutsu kyūri*) with Western experimentalism, and to demonstrate the universality of the *ri* (principles) found in Oriental morality and Western science, was directed to requirements of this new "problem consciousness." In Sakuma's mind *gaikan,* the threat of an external catastrophe, acquired a new ethical importance, and replaced *naiyū,* the preoccupation with putting the natural order into proper adjustment. Mito writers had seen the problem in neither social, political, nor technological terms, but rather as a corruption of the moral order. If correct adjustments to the Neo-Confucian paradigm of nature were made, then social (and indeed all

[37] *Sz.,* II, 845, "Letter to Yanagawa Seigan."

other) problems *would be solved along the way*. This solution
was rejected by Sakuma. Moving *naiyū* down the scale of significance, he saw the problem from a different perspective. If the
threat was an external enemy with a superior technology, then
the problem was technological, not moral, and required a technological solution. This explains why so much of his writing,
public and private, is given over to problems of defense and an
understanding of naval technology, and why he said so little
about "adjusting" the natural order or "rectifying" the moral
boundaries of political society; these were not problems any
longer. Sakuma likewise sought to demonstrate the universality
of knowledge informed by *ri* in order to render it an accessible
and respected object of attention for Japanese. But in saying that
technology provided its own solution and that all other problems
would take care of themselves along the way, he was neither
adopting the view of Chang Chih-t'ung that a culture with
moral knowledge was superior to one which was merely scientific, nor suggesting that technology would defend Japanese cultural values.

Almost all of Sakuma's writings after 1843 reveal his commitment to serving "the welfare of the realm" through his own efforts and knowledge. How did his investigation offer to serve the
"welfare of the people?" In his memorial *Kannō ko ni agarite
tenka tokon no yōmu o chinzu* containing the famous Eight
Point Policy on Naval Defense, Sakuma revealed anxiety about
consequences from the threatening probes of Western ships if
coastal defenses were not tightened. The petition was a slow start
at interest in the West, since a strong expulsionist sentiment is
embedded in it. His policy for naval defense is little more than a
dressed-up version of Aizawa's earlier proposals. And this same
expulsionism, while it underwent a transformation after the
opening of the country, still played a decisive role in his thinking. He transmuted it into a concept of an independent and unified political culture. Sakuma was also able to jettison cultural institutions which were found, on later inspection, to be without
any value to the new independence. The need he felt to do away

with institutions which only presented obstacles to change was
inspired by his observation of events in China. A few months before his naval petition, he wrote about the war between England
and China and its possible meaning for Japan, in a letter to Katō
Nagatani (October 1843):

Have you heard recently by hearsay about the war between England
and China? Even though it is a rumor, it is one which we cannot take
lightly. According to what I've heard, the situation is that the Europeans [British] have polluted (*seiai*) the district of Li-yüeh, which had
existed since the T'ang dynasty. It is very grievous. And on this occasion there have been a great number of changes in the Ch'ing state.
Our country is only a short distance by sea [from China], and no country in the East will be able to remain out of the reach of the yearly attacks of British ships. Although this information is not based on an official report, there is actual proof of it.[38]

Sakuma took the bold step, even on his then meager information,
of calling for a general alert and the speedy establishment of
a defense network: "We must be prepared to meet the barbarian." [39]

Preparation required a multistage policy; the Eight Point proposal was an early and partial answer. In it he outlined the steps
necessary if the specter of *gaikan* was to be exorcised. While the
statement owes much to Mito formulations of defense and expulsion, it reveals a considerable shift in the ground of argumenta-
tion. It reflects also his lifelong conviction that a proper merger
of inner and outer, of the private and public realms, required
their redefinition: namely, as "Oriental ethics, Western technology." This merger is not to be understood in terms of an attenuated contrast between substance (*t'i*) and function (*yung*). Political culture, identified by Sakuma as the "welfare of the people," or more exactly as the space in which that responsibility is
prosecuted, demanded accommodation to changes; and technological borrowing realized through a policy of naval defense,

[38] *Sz.*, I, 109–110.
[39] *Ibid.*

since it would be informed by *ri,* offered the best solution. His
policy required a personal involvement in learning technology
through gunnery school, difficult language study, and experiments in the new sciences.

Sakuma's naval policy made many proposals: the establishment
of forts equipped with large cannons in strategic areas on the
coast; halting the export of copper in order to use the metal in
the casting of cannons; construction of large ships, in the Western
style, for the transport of rice and other commodities; establishment of a Bureau of Naval Supervision to manage commerce
with foreign countries; construction of Western-style warships
and the teaching of naval strategy; the establishment of a countryside school system to teach "ignorant men and women" loyalty and filial piety; clarification of rewards and punishments;
the achievement of a benevolent but firm government to
strengthen and unite the popular will (*minshin*); and the creation of a system to recruit men of talent and ability for positions
of political responsibility.[40] Sakuma's major concerns are listed
first and involve hard practical matters; his concern for morality
appears secondary. He summarized his own priorities thus:
"Within the Eight Points we have two obligations: emulating
Western manufacturing methods in the production of a variety
of firearms, and learning about naval science and the equipping
of ships." [41]

To realize these priorities Sakuma put first the effort to understand the foreigners and their feelings—the familiar Chinese device of managing the barbarian with barbarian techniques. Sakuma's residual expulsionism down to the early 1850s allowed him
to view the acquisition of technology—barbarian technique—as a
mere gesture. But unlike Wei Yüan, Sakuma was subtly transformed by the very technology with which he sought to "expel
the barbarian," since he had taken the extra step of trying to understand the feelings of the foreigners. In pursuit of this more
difficult knowledge, Sakuma's expulsionist mentality underwent

[40] *Sz.,* I, 62.
[41] *Sz.,* I, 62–63.

a profound change which set the pattern for the future. It was no longer possible to keep the barbarian at arm's length, or to bisect the world between culture and barbarism. The key to this transformation was his involvement in the technological enterprise. On the one hand he plunged into a study of Dutch—an impossible task in the absence of linguistic aids. Since it was essential to know the barbarians, "nothing is more important than to be proficient at their languages." [42] Unfortunately Sakuma and a whole generation of samurai expended great energy in learning the wrong language. Sakuma's ill-fated effort to win official approval for the publication of a Dutch dictionary is well known. Yet this failure (he wrote in the early 1860s) only illustrated the government's refusal to accept responsibility; without language study, the secrets of naval defense would remain forever beyond Japan's grasp. So would political independence, he hinted.

Closely linked to his interest in foreign languages was the study of naval technology and tactics, during which he discovered that this body of knowledge rested on principles which could not be taken lightly. "Mathematics," he wrote, "is the basis of all learning. In the Western world, after this science was discovered, military tactics advanced greatly." [43] Here Sakuma invoked the authority of Sun Tzu, the legendary philosopher of war in ancient China, who in his *Art of War* wrote about "estimation, determination of quantity, calculation," and recommended "advancing from basic studies to higher learning." [44] Sakuma identified "basic studies" with mathematics, and "higher learning" with technology. Not even the Chinese had paid much attention to Sun Tzu's admonition, he went on. Military studies had, as a result, failed to develop. Their stagnation illustrated another principle, that learning was a cumulative effort which could not be realized "in a morning or in an evening." [45]

[42] *Sz.*, I, 225, "Jigi wo tsūran shitaru bakufu e jōshōko."

[43] *Sz.*, I, 10, "Seiken roku."

[44] *Ibid.*

[45] *Sz.*, I, 305, "Hitotsubashikō ni agaru kokka no jiran wo chinzu." See also Maruyama, *loc. cit.* (n. 1 above), p. 26.

During the two decades between the first Anglo-Chinese war and Sakuma's death in 1864, he saw the terrible unfolding of *gaikan*. A strong defensive network would prevent the barbarian from holding Japan in contempt and ensure her survival. In existing installations he saw only weakness and incompetence: "The existing coastal defenses all lack method; the pieces of artillery that have been set up in array are improperly cast. . . . The situation being such, even though we wish to avoid incurring the scorn of the barbarians, how can we do so?" [46] His early answer is an unrestrained commitment to naval defense and tactics, which became the occasion for a wider commitment. Despite his unquestioning faith in the ethical civilization shaped by Confucianism, he refused to let it interfere with technology and defense.

Sakuma never doubted the superior value of the inherited ethical culture, and his intellectual work testifies that he felt a need to defend that culture. We can assume from the general tone of his earlier writings that he would see technology as adapted to the interests of culture; in his scale of priorities, technology was clearly subordinate. After the opening of the country he began to introduce qualifications into this position. During these years he began to think of the realm less in ethical terms and more as a unit of political space, and by 1860 the process was complete. Political culture had replaced ethical culture as the scene of human action. This does not mean that he had abandoned his earlier commitment to a specific morality; it means that he had moved this morality down on his scale of priorities. Morality had a genuine position within the new idea of political space which he developed; but if it interfered with larger considerations such as the independence of the realm, it would have to be abandoned for a more functional standard. Sakuma was not blind to the weakness of ethical culture. The true tradition of culture, as he conceived it, enjoined men to entertain the possibility of change when their investigation of social reality required it. But after the country was forcibly opened, he quickly saw that no domestic moral re-

[46] *Sz.*, I, 8–9, "Seiken roku."

vival could defend the country from cannon and warships. Sakuma pared down culture to political dimensions because his
investigation of reality made it a prerequisite for retaining independence. A unified political community was essential to a unified defense; and technological change required central political
coordination. Even when Sakuma was most committed to Neo-
Confucianism, in the early 1840s, he argued that passive observance of ethical principles could not be considered adequate protection against a threat from outside.

He criticized the contemporaries who held that loyalty alone
was sufficient to defense. "In the *Chou shū*," he charged, "It is
said that if both sides, friend and foe, have the same power, then
the possibility of victory will be decided by loyalty." But Sakuma
knew that loyalty and morality were not enough in his times,
since Japan was not equal to its potential rivals. What was most
irksome was how little contemporary officials had learned from
recent events in China. "I have learned," he continued, "that
many domains today [1859] insist upon loyalty above all other
methods in defending the realm." [47] He rejected both the excessive Chinese reliance on traditional ethical superiority and the
dependence upon military bravado in the Japanese military tradition. Both were useless. Nothing could take the place of understanding and preparation. What was needed was a plan based on
a careful assessment of the situation and its possibilities. He complained about scholars who lectured on military affairs to little
avail, since their teaching corresponded to things of little use.
Sakuma was not openly disparaging the usefulness of Neo-Confucian ethics; he was distinguishing realms or modes of experience
and action. And while he was disposed to dissolve human nature
—mind, speech, conduct—into the morality of a status order, this
did not inhibit him from taking science and technology seriously.[48]
Yet he never considered his commitment to new knowledge
revolutionary.

[47] *Sz.*, I, 311.

[48] See Matsumoto Sannosuke, "Sonjō undō . . . ," in Sakata (n. 2
above), p. 142.

TOWARD A NEW POLITICAL SPACE

We have seen how Sakuma appealed to the "welfare of the people" as authorization for new policies and modes of action, how he severed Japan from the Orient, and how he began to think of culture more in political than in ethical terms. He rejected the Neo-Confucian denial of a political order, but also envisaged broader political space than the Mito ideologues. Aizawa and Fujita Tōko had called for a restoration of the *bakuhan* order, in which the domain, unfettered by the shogun, would function as a real center of authority. As they conceived it, the reconstituted *bakuhan* system was a concrete manifestation of the moral order, not political but ethical. Even though the Mito statement came down hard on the Tokugawa, its purpose was not to undermine the institutional arrangement but to strengthen it. The object of their criticism was the moral failure of personal leadership and what they saw as a politicization of the moral order. Sakuma no doubt agreed with this analysis down to the time of his involvement in shogunal politics and the news of the first Anglo-Chinese war. But his experience in defense and military technology, and the fact of *kaikoku,* altered his angle of vision into accepting the possibility of even greater politicization. Whatever his personal opinion on the opening of the country, he was realistic enough to accept it as given in his investigation of contemporary reality. In the process of alerting society and government to the necessity of naval defense and military technology, Sakuma had to change his view of what he wanted to protect. Culture was meaningful only if it served a larger political purpose; and political purpose was possible (Sakuma argued in the mid-1850s) only when it was associated with a specific concept of space—the expanded realm (*tenka*).

The revisions in Sakuma's own attitudes in response to the Anglo-Chinese war were not a complete break with the Neo-Confucian conception of an ethicopolitical order, or with the classics in which the political enterprise was always judged by the criterion of proper moral conduct. But new interests and necessities produced significant alterations in a mind long trained by an orthodoxy which simply denied all alternatives. Practicality and a quickened sense of contemporary requirements—the welfare of the people—liberated him from dependence on coded responses and moral abstractions to the real world of fact and value. "The teachings of Confucianists," he wrote in a letter to a friend, "relate only to loyalty and obligations (*giri*). They have been received from the sages of antiquity, Yao and Shun. Nevertheless, they do not distinguish between calamities in human nature and in moral sense." [49] This is an early announcement of Sakuma's disposition to separate morality from politics and history. On the one hand, it led to one meaning of his favorite formula—"Oriental ethics for the base, Western technology for the use." On the other, it produced a division between an inner and an outer realm; ethics ruled in the former, but the latter, the world of politics and history, could be served only after an investigation of contemporary social reality disclosed what needed to be done. Morality was the pledge that such an investigation would be carried out by men of superior talent and ability. [50]

For Sakuma, then, the natural moral order of personal behavior was governed by changeless principles, while the outer realm, political action and history, obeyed laws of change ascertained by constant investigation. As the times and needs changed, so would policies and roles. [51] The meaning of history, he explained in his petition to the *bakufu* on current developments, was no longer to be found in ethical exemplars; the judgment passed by history could no longer be made on the criterion of the ethically good ruler. Men could still be praised or blamed on the criterion of personal moral behavior; but this rarely had anything to do with their performance as political leaders, or with their success in the political enterprise. Rather, Sakuma argued, success or failure constituted the only criterion of political behavior; and success

[49] Quoted in *ibid.*
[50] *Sz.*, I, 240–243.
[51] *Sz.*, I, 223–253.

depended on "a daily observation of the conditions of the times." [52]

Sakuma's interest in the new knowledge was a prelude to his politicization of Neo-Confucianism, since it led him to question morality as an instrument of policy. His new vision of politics and history is already visible in his petition of 1843 to the domainal lord Sanada Yukitsura, the object of which was "to explain the important duties of the country and to raise them to the level of public concern." [53] While this petition anticipates a British attempt to open up Japan and suggests how it might be averted, its principal purpose is to show the ineffectiveness of "strict adherence to the ancestral law (*sakoku*)." A decade before the coming of the Perry squadron, Sakuma was already warning Japanese of the real threat posed by *gaikan*. In the 1840s Sakuma was still alone in this conviction, and his warnings, while supported, as we saw, by real evidence, had to compete with the Mito assessment of the problem and its presuppositions. So vivid was his apprehension of the threat that he was able to say that nothing in Japan's past, not even "the ancestral laws" and the "customs of the times," could cope with it. He saw in the 1840s what others would only conclude after 1854 that the foreign menace was an unprecedented event for which Japan's historical experience was insufficient preparation.[54] Hence he lashed out against "the thick curtain of tradition" and demanded the abandonment of laws and procedures which had served the Japanese so long. This separation of *gaikan* and *naiyū* presupposed a separation of political history from moral conduct and allowed him to see that the uniqueness of the foreign problem required a unique solution. But this forced a decision to break with a conventional historical awareness in which men imitate moral history, for a consciousness of history in which history follows the actions of men. He also found, along the way, a new source of accountability: change.

[52] *Sz.*, I, 231, 240, 309.
[53] *Sz.*, I, 99.
[54] *Sz.*, I, 93.

What faced Japan was an emergency. "However important these rules [of the past] have been until the present," Sakuma reasoned, "we have to replace them, because of the hardships they have brought, for the sake of the welfare of the realm." Rules which were current in earlier generations are superseded by "new facts which crystallize into principles of later generations." [55] It is natural "to reform the august laws which have been erected for the realm," since "it is a moral principle of Japan and China to follow ordinary laws and procedures in ordinary times, while in times of emergency employing emergency measures (*sei*)." [56] Sakuma argued that although recognition of this principle of change had always been possible, it had been neglected in the deliberations of leaders. The classics, especially the *Chung Yung* (*Doctrine of the Mean*), had long authorized this procedure, but society "failed to discern the drift of the times (*jisei*) and seize the opportune moment (*jigi*)." If men were to change this generation, in accordance with the precedent of change set by former generations, they must not be limited to rules handed down from a distant past. Rather they should "not adhere to the old system but follow the times and obey change." [57] This, he held, was the reverent procedure of sincerity (*makato*), the principle which corresponds to the "Way of the Chung Yung."

This concept of change, which provided the political leadership with a sanction for new policies, allowed Sakuma such flexibility as Neo-Confucianism never could allow, and served as the organizing principle in his political thought. In one of his last petitions, written in 1864 and submitted to Hitotsubashi Keiki, he returned to this theme and called on the authority of the classics. But whereas his earlier notion of historical change was used to justify a policy of naval defense, in this later proposal it becomes a fundamental principle of sound leadership.[58] For a leader to

[55] *Sz.*, I, 98.

[56] *Sz.*, I, 98–99; also relevant is Sakuma's earlier petition, "Shokuhō gunhō shokushō seiton ikenshō, especially pp. 80–81.

[57] *Sz.*, I, 98–99.

[58] *Sz.*, I, 303–304.

know the requirements of change meant the difference between order and disorder. Here Sakuma relies on a metaphor found in his favorite text, the *I Ching*. He was very early affected by the naturalism of the *I Ching*, especially as it was accessible to him in the writings of Shao K'ang-chieh. "If we grasp the currents and developments of the present," Sakuma wrote, "we will be able to foretell disorder." There is a play on words here which is intended to evoke associations from the *I Ching*. To express "disorder" he used Japanese *ko*, which refers to a passage in the *Book of Changes* that describes the process of decay. The corresponding Chinese character *ku*, he explains, is a bowl containing worms, which mean defeat and destruction. "If one uses vessels and bowls for a long time, they will give rise to worms; if the body indulged in too much banqueting, it will become ill; if a realm is idle or inactive it will produce abuses. All of this must be decay (*ko*)." Decay for Sakuma meant too long reliance on habit or rigid adherence to tradition. But he knew that decay was not the product of an unyielding fate, nor so complete that it could not be remedied.[59] He recognized that political decay was the work of indifference and weakness, and also that rigorous action, in particular a liberation from the old habits of history, could remove its causes. Each age, he exhorted Keiki, must by investigation and the penetration of social reality ascertain its own needs, for only this will permit rulers to escape the threat of *ko*, the decaying vessel.

Disturbance and decay provide the opportunity for creative political response. "If," Sakuma went on to argue, "there exists the fact of disturbance and decay (*koran*), it is a principle that order must be restored." One follows the other naturally, since "from antiquity it has been a natural principle for political tranquillity to follow prevalent disorder, and for disorder to follow the creation of tranquillity."[60] Here is the meaning of the *Book of Changes*, which advises: "If one investigates (*kiwamera*), one will achieve change; when one changes, he will pass over to pros-

[59] See the *I Ching*, tr. Richard Wilhelm, 2 vols. (New York, 1950), I, 79–82.

[60] *Sz.*, I, 304.

perity." The cryptic language of the *I Ching* can only serve his purpose if he can show its applicability to contemporary conditions. In the definition of decay (*ko*) it is said that people "have to start well" and that "it prospers a man to cross the great water." For Sakuma, to "start well" means that the right time must be selected and the appropriate methods devised; proper deliberation constitutes a good beginning. Sakuma recalls that in the definition of *ku* an interval of three days before and after the beginning is advised to avoid the dangers of haste. A man prospers if he "crosses the great waters"; this means commitment to action, to movement, to a realization of what is needed. It also means "overcoming profound difficulties and rescuing society from the age of degeneration. . . . If one observes profound difficulties and is overcome by fear, he will not advance; if one stops short in idleness and inaction, he will end in decay and disorder." [61] There is no way to begin except to confront the problem. This confrontation must from the outset be informed by a desire to correct the relations between lord and vassal, high and low. It will also yield the Way to order and disorder which, in turn, will require "pushing and penetrating the front and rear of things in order to relieve old abuses."

Sakuma's language of decay and predictable disorder suggests that he was measuring what he observed by private standards of political excellence. He knew that Japan was on the brink of decay and disorder, and also how this fate could be avoided. Whereas the Mito statement celebrated classical antiquity, an anterior Arcadia, Sakuma had a view of history which did not rely on precedent. To be sure, Sakuma was too much enmeshed in "contemporary conciliation," too much committed to the politicizing of contemporary reality, to explore any possible future polity. He did indeed reformulate the famous Confucian statement in this form: "When I reached twenty I realized I had a part to play in the affairs of my domain; at thirty I realized I had a part to play in the life of the entire realm; at forty I realized I had

[61] *Ibid.*

a part to play in the life of the entire world." Still his political concerns were rooted in the problems of Japanese polity as it was forced to confront an outside challenge. But although there is little utopianism in his thought, he prepared the ground for a new view of historical change, realized in part by Yokoi Shōnan, that would make utopian expectations possible.

Sakuma's advice to abandon the "old standards" and "ancestral law," so intimately linked to the Tokugawa concept of authority, suggests that he was trying to work out a new political community that would include the essential elements of the *bakuhan* structure yet eliminate its sectional limitations. The expanded realm, as we saw, was his answer. Culture had to be served by an expanded political structure, a new polity, that would in time become indistinguishable from culture. To this end Sakuma appealed not to an abstract moral culture, nor to any contemporary political authority, but rather to an authority higher than moral culture, higher than "the dignity of the Tokugawa house," and higher than "the great plan of the Imperial Court" itself—namely, to what he called "the welfare of the realm." He claimed that the struggle facing Japan could be entered upon only by a unified country. "However important standards and laws have been in the past, they must be changed today"—not just for the Tokugawa family, but "for the welfare of the imperial line whose hundred generations of unbroken succession are without comparison in the countries of the world." [62]

The expanded political space of the realm in its widest sense (*tenka*) is defined by Sakuma at first in reference to a unified military defense. Japan could not be defended sectionally. In a characteristic tautology he urged that "the defense of the realm is in defending the realm, not in protecting the Tokugawa family." [63] A comprehensive defense plan could be produced neither by Tokugawa autocracy, which was based on a weak domainal structure, nor by a powerful sectionalism, which could exist only at the expense of the Tokugawa house, but only by a

[62] *Sz.*, I, 93-94.
[63] *Sz.*, I, 1165, "Meyasusho."

proper balance of the two. At the same time, such a comprehensive defense policy required a permanent centralized political structure. These needs aroused Japanese activists and writers to a new political consciousness, from which there was no return, that the realm was something more than the Tokugawa house and the several *han*. After all, Sakuma reasoned, the problem of a foreign invasion threatened all Japanese and thus required a collective response, which was possible only if the appropriate machinery was available. "An invasion would be completely different from the conflict taking place within the realm among the several domains. It would affect not only the Tokagawa house but also the nobility which have existed for over one hundred generations. As it is an urgent and important problem for the entire realm, all people should be concerned and serve the realm." [64] (Sakuma confessed modestly that he was merely offering his assistance to the government, but despaired, like the loyalist Umeda Unpin, at the thought of how few men knew what was going on.) Elsewhere he argued specifically that the realm, to be a realm, had to include full participation of all the lords. This meant relaxing control over them so that they could play a more meaningful role in military defense. "When one turns anxiously to the threat of foreign invasion," he stated, "it is a special urgency today to strengthen and enrich (*kyōsei*) national power." [65] But to achieve this goal a total effort was necessary, "an exhaustion of the power of the realm."

If the threat of invasion should pull together a unified political structure and break down the sectionalism of the *bakuhan* system, the purpose to be served was civilization itself—a civilization that had more to do, however, with the historical identity of the Japanese people than with the preservation of a universal ethic. Earlier Sakuma, still under Mito influence, located Japan's uniqueness in the possession of morality. And this uniqueness was reason enough for expulsion and defense. His early criticisms

[64] *Sz.*, I, 93–94; also p. 125, "Haruma o hangyō nite kaihan-sen koto o chinzu."

[65] *Sz.*, I, 110.

of Westerners as "barbarians" who "pursue only profit" and "fail
to discriminate" were indignant pieties handed down from Mito
writers, joined to an equally pious celebration of Japan as the repository of all cultural values—since China, as events showed,
had lost its birthright. Japan's divine origins and unbroken imperial line were the emblem of moral superiority and the pledge of
its eternity. There was nothing new about this view, but it exercised a profound influence on the younger Sakuma and on many
of his contemporaries. After 1854, this philosophical expulsionism
was to find new expression in the eloquent statements of Ōhashi
Totsuan and Maki Izumi. Yet writers until this time did not see
any real difference between the Tokugawa system and *shinshū*.

Sakuma saw the difference and when he elevated *shinshū* to
the status of a unified political realm, by necessity he contrasted
it with the Tokugawa polity. The contrast revealed a new alternative. The Tokugawa house had lasted only "ten generations"
while "the imperial line has succeeded for one hundred generations." The Tokugawa regime, like its predecessors, was part of a
continuing political manifestation of the great moral principles
bound up with the existence of the imperial line. The idea of the
realm (*tenka*), which is made concrete in the concept of the divine land (*shinshū*), "fulfills in this way over and over again the
promise of heaven." [66] Despite the intellectual distance he traveled, in which a moral realm was politicized into a nascent national community, Sakuma never entirely abandoned this religioracial conceit as an identifying emblem of Japan's independence and uniqueness.

Even after he had accepted the use of barbarian techniques to
deal with the barbarian, Sakuma still spoke of the necessity of
"manipulating the wild beast." [67] In the *Seiken roku* he announced that, despite Japan's technological handicaps, the special
qualities of *shinshū* would see the country through the crisis. "I
have not yet seen, since antiquity, inadequate strength to preserve

[66] See Matsumoto, "Sōnjō undō ni okeru kindaiteki seiji ishiki no keisei,"
in Sakata (n. 2 above), p. 144.

[67] *Sz.*, II, 561, "Letter to Kitayama Yasuyo."

the country. Will not the emperor esteem this power?"[68] However, Sakuma did not retain full confidence in the power of religioracial uniqueness to protect Japan, and in the end he employed it only to distinguish the Japanese from other peoples. It became the equipment of a national style, but it was not styled to protect the nation. When events shook his confidence, the first casualty was the notion of a morally superior realm. This change was anticipated by his contrast between the imperial line and the Tokugawa house; it was full-blown by the late 1850s, when *kaikoku* was an accepted fact and it had become clear that Japan must do much more in the way of taking the West seriously. Therefore Sakuma abandoned seclusion, as we noted earlier, and liberated Japan from reliance on an expulsionist policy. He wrote Yanagawa Seigan of the necessity to treat the Western nations as carriers of a respectable tradition, and confessed his anxiety over policies steeped in contempt and disrespect which could only lead to disaster. He marvels at the scientific acumen of the West, and how its inventions had contributed to its "power and dignity."[69] Here Sakuma is beginning to refer to Westerners no longer as "barbarians" but as "foreigners"—a distinction which he elevated in 1862 to the level of public advice.

Residual beliefs and attitudes still plagued Japanese statesmen, both in their reluctance to take the learning and power of Western nations seriously, and in their direct dealings with consular representatives. This, Sakuma observed, was best illustrated by the way diplomats addressed Westerners or referred to them in official correspondence. Particularly irksome was the continued usage of the term "barbarian" (*i, iteki*), for it revealed a contempt for international protocol, as well as the ineptness of Tokugawa leadership.[70] "Now that we have frequent contact with foreign countries, I wish that official correspondence would be drafted with more special care . . . for the appellations used are not at all suitable for those countries." Not only were they

[68] *Sz.*, I, 9–10, "Seiken roku."
[69] *Sz.*, II, 827–833, "Letter to Yanagawa Seigan."
[70] *Sz.*, I, 244.

wrong, but they inhibited Japan's efforts in "spreading its own dignity abroad," and they might lead to international complications. Sakuma knew that the usage was inspired by Chinese practice and was intended to dramatize the difference between those who possessed morality and those who did not—that is, between civilization and barbarism. But the Chinese were mistaken, and the Japanese, in following them, were even more so. This mistake was enormous because the Japanese described as barbarian "countries which possess better arts, learning, legal systems, and culture." [71] Rather, he suggests, it would be more polite, and more consonant with the fact of the Five Continents, to refer to them as *gaiban,* a term which implies that these countries are foreign and different but not inferior. But this was to acknowledge a community of nations that were different from each other but equal.

If the foreigner was no longer a barbarian, and possessed a culture in no way inferior, what would become of Japan's claim to moral superiority? Once seclusion was dissolved, the realm joined a concert of national powers. The failure of isolation ended expulsionism and with it the moral distinction between inner civilization and outer barbarism. Sakuma wrote in one of his last petitions (December 1862) that *jōi* was unreal and impossible. Membership in the international community was the condition of survival, and this meant abandoning Oriental reality for a Western reality; that is, pursuing true principles wherever they might be. To Yanagawa he wrote: "The foreigner (*gaiban*) today has come out ahead of the Chinese in learning and skills. He has clarified and explained things which the classics have not yet illuminated." [72] Yet even after *kaikoku* and the commercial treaties, little attention had been paid "to such things as naval defense and the protection of the imperial palace." [73] The way to achieve a realistic policy was to know the true principles of real-

[71] *Sz.,* I, 244–245.
[72] *Sz.,* II, 487, "Letter to Yanagawa Seigan." Also, cf. Maruyama, "Bakumatsu ni okeru . . ." (n. 1 above), pp. 30–32.
[73] *Sz.,* II, 279.

ity; and this would require men "to change conditions which date back to Ieyasu's period," abandon the policy of seclusion, establish intercourse with foreign countries, obtain the advantages of foreign technology, and pursue national defense through the new political structure of *kōbugattai,* "the unification of the court and the shogunate." These proposals had to be accomplished, for "where heavenly destiny (*ten-un*) has decreed, the imperial land (*tenkoku*) can in this way alone obey what has been willed." [74] Sakuma never explained what this "heavenly destiny" is, except to suggest that it will be manifest when true principles are sought out and observed.

The "divine land," [75] however unique, had acquired the dimensions of a national community (*tenka kokka*) competing with others "throughout the Five Continents." The realm was no longer defined in terms of the Neo-Confucian polarity between inner and outer, and it was no longer associated with Oriental culture or reality; it was merely that which is "ours" (*ware*) united to a new Western reality. Japan conformed to the true principles which had been satisfied by the "several countries of the Five Continents," and which had earlier been formulated by Sung thinkers such as Chu Hsi when he advised men (in his exegesis of the *Great Learning*) "to investigate all things on earth if understanding is to be achieved." Sakuma explained that the characters *oyobu tenka* (Chinese *chi t'ien-hsia*) "do not express the China of Southern Sung in which Chu Hsi lived, but rather expresses the world at large which he designated as the object of study." [76] When Sakuma recommended following the learning of the West and international protocol, he was referring to another realm—a world civilization made up of the participation of several countries, where membership required observance of true principles. "When strength [between countries] is similar, then virtue must be measured; when virtue is comparable, then princi-

[74] *Sz.,* II, 280. The Meiji historian Yamaji Aizan argued that this document is the most important of Sakuma's corpus of writings.

[75] See Sakuma's Chinese poem titled *Ou fu* in *Sz.,* I, 571–575.

[76] *Sz.,* II, 241.

ple is measured. . . . This is the correct procedure, the real principle, the public principle of civilization." [77] Sakuma was calling for a comity of nations, where each country would retain a uniqueness that would not disturb harmonious relations; where all would remain independent but united in observance of "universal principles of humanity and justice"; where each would have its own voice contributing to a single chorus. Here is the meaning of Sakuma's declaration that at the age of forty he realized he had a part to play in the entire world. The "divine land" would become Japan, and Japan would earn a place among the nations of the Five Continents through the exercise of the "correct principles of civilization."

Abandonment of ethical history and liberation from external norms allowed Sakuma to view political society from a different perspective. Like many others, in resolving contemporary domestic problems Sakuma supported the moderate *kōbugattai* position, the "unification of court and *bakufu*," as the more rational political formula. The nation could be defended only by pooling the strength of the imperial court and the shogunate. [78] This arrangement would minimize the possibility of abrupt changes and political dislocation. To this end Sakuma called for a "general consultation among the domainal leaders" (*kochō kōkan no shidō*) on national affairs and a general strengthening of the domain. [79] He was proposing what Mito ideologues had already seen as essential if the *bakuhan* system was to prevail. He saw success only if shogunal autocracy was diminished and the domain proportionately strengthened to meet its new military obligations. The speedy enactment of *kōbugattai* required reconstituting the *bakuhan* system. Such a program, hastily conceived and ultimately unworkable, seemed to be preparation enough for the more important problems of international affairs and a defense network. But Sakuma recoiled sharply when he discovered

[77] *Sz.*, II, 280.
[78] See Kaneko Takanosuke, *Sakuma Shōzan no hito to shisō* (Tokyo, 1943), pp. 164–178; *Sz.*, I, 281.
[79] *Sz.*, I, 302.

that others were using *kōbugattai* as a front for large-scale political reforms.[80] Nothing, he believed, would more damage national defense than a civil war between partisans of throne and *bakufu*. This fear explains why Sakuma ultimately consented to play the role of mediator in implementing the formula and assigned an exaggerated value to his part.[81]

Sakuma's scientism was no help in resolving the political crisis. If the "national essence" (*kokutai*) and Japan's unique "political order" (*seiji*) were useless in dealing with the foreigner, as he explained to Katsu Kaishū, there was still good reason to preserve the basic elements of its political heritage.[82] Reform promised disorder and should be avoided. His relativistic view of history hinted at a drastic political change but never authorized one—least of all one inspired by Western example. Anything that might inhibit a defense network was suspect, and though he anticipated the demolition of the status order, he tried though *kōbugattai* to give it a new lease on life. His attitude toward domestic reform reflects less a residual Neo-Confucianism than a desire to put first things first. Despite his initial approval of the reforms of the early 1860s, Sakuma was quick to plead for moderation. What irked him most in the plan was the proposed reform of the "alternate hostage" (*sankin kōtai*) system hailed by Sakuma's talented contemporary Yokoi Shōnan, who of course had a hand in it. Sakuma, sounding like the Confucianists he had criticized in his younger years, claimed that reduction in the retinues accompanying the domainal lord to Edo would not result in drastic economies. "Though lords will not hereafter be accompanied by as many retainers as in the past, it does not mean they will save expenses. People in high ranks are accustomed to having retainers serve them . . . and if it were not for the help of such retainers they would not be able to take care of themselves." [83] It would be more in keeping with precedent and traditional respect to maintain retainers and to make more use of their time.

[80] See *Sz.*, I, 230.
[81] To his mistress, see *Sz.*, II, 1322–1326.
[82] *Sz.*, II, 223–252, 1141–1142, "Letters to Katsu Kaishū."
[83] *Sz.*, I, 236.

Sakuma feared that reductions in the *sankin kōtai* system would weaken the status structure. The halfway measure of eliminating retainers would create new social problems and undermine the position of the lord, which Sakuma hoped to strengthen in the new political situation after 1854. Political systems, he pointed out, differ from one country to another on the basis of indigenous experiences. It was no solution to replace a shaky system with a totally different one which had grown out of an alien experience. This view was fully consistent with Sakuma's belief that nations, despite their participation in an international community, must retain their historical individuality. A domestic problem could only be resolved by materials at hand. Hence the *sankin kōtai* system should be retained in a more rational form. "Those involved in politics," he advised, "are the lords, and they should have sufficient retainers at their disposal." Time actually spent at Edo should be used for study, and "the retainers should be compensated with an adequate salary for their service; this is a natural prerogative of the lord." The proposal to reduce retinues shows (he admits) sincere intent among policy makers, but "it is too extreme and will surely bring evils in the future." History showed the results of excess: "When Han Kaotzu conquered the Chin he tried to change manners and morals and simply everything. As a result most of his retainers forgot about politeness, drank too much wine, desired public recognition, and finally turned against each other. As in the case of Kao-tzu, I'm afraid a complete change might introduce new evils to us today." [84] While it is necessary to base political deliberations on knowledge of contemporary circumstances everywhere, "it is natural that lords and noblemen have their own escorts. We have very good reasons for rank and status in our country, and we should always keep them in mind in our deliberations." [85]

This vindication of the status system reads like a page out of the *Shinron*—or out of Sakuma's own biography. But his rejection of the reforms of 1862 did not mean rejecting the possibility

[84] *Sz.*, I, 237.
[85] *Sz.*, I, 238.

of change, for his image of political society was new.[86] By his repudiation of the ancestral law in the interest of country, Sakuma was dropping a view in which humanity is formed by obeying fixed norms of social behavior, in favor of a view in which humanity is formed by adaptation to a constantly changing reality. Instead of holding man up to conformity with a fixed concept of reality, he argued that man was free to make and change norms, since reality was no longer fixed.

Sakuma's criticism of the reforms proposed by the *bakufu* reveals a coherent political method. Since change was inevitable, men could accept it if it showed a concern for the "people's welfare" and "the destiny of the whole of *shinshū.*" "Today," he wrote to Katō Nagatani, "we must exhaust our powers for the realm (*tenka*) and try to fulfill a great aim." He urged his countrymen to overcome the great grief confronting *shinshū.* Self-knowledge and skill were not enough. "We must carry on our shoulders the affection and love of country." He counseled moderation and calm: "It is good to be cheerful, and it is not good to be angry and excited." There was need for distance and deliberation if the great purpose of the polity was to be served. Investigation showed, he was confident, that the "great aim" required military defense, which was possible if supported by a united political effort. Hence, on one hand he advocated *kōbugattai;* on the other, he attacked the shogunal reforms of 1862 as weakening the power of the domains precisely when military defense called for a strong domainal system. We saw how the earlier Mito ideologues supported local autonomy in the face of traditional shogunal despotism out of moral and economic reasons. Sakuma, unconcerned with ethics, saw a strengthened *han* as a vital link in a comprehensive defense policy.

This political realism rested on Sakuma's rejection of abstraction in favor of fact and value. It was folly, he wrote, to believe that passion and self-righteousness alone "will whip the great ships of the West." Failure to ascertain contemporary conditions resulted from failure to release knowledge from abstract moral

[86] Cf. Matsumoto (n. 66 above), p. 144.

principles. In his petition on the "great aims" he clarified the proper course Japan had to follow: "The Chung Yung says: 'Confucius succeeded to the aims of men and transmitted the deeds of good men.' By not discriminating among the events of today we will not be able to pass into good and prosperous times. Discrimination is not to be found in an adherence to the old system. If we obey the drift of the times, and follow changes . . . we will be following the Chung Yung as well as the Confucian Way of sincerity." [87]

It was Sakuma's achievement to combine the spiritual obligation of serving the country's welfare with insights derived from attention to changing conditions. This implies a view, strongly reminiscent of Ogyū Sorai, that laws and customs are utensils of a political realm; when no longer useful they should be discarded. Politics is conceived of no longer as a static operation, barely visible in the splendor of morally perfect leaders, but rather as a dynamic process where new "laws" are constantly replacing older laws.

By the same token Sakuma abandons an objective human nature, its needs fixed for all times, in favor of a subjective human nature in constant flux. The welfare of the realm and this subjective humanity were vitually the same thing, even though they might appear as disparate goals in the polities of leaders. On the one hand, the leadership was guided by the high principle of the "welfare of the country" (*tenka no anki*); on the other hand, they must carry out the subjective activity of making judgments about the reality which stimulates change. But these responsibilities cannot be at odds; pursuit of the "welfare of the realm" must alert the leadership to the subtle changes in contemporary conditions. Here Sakuma says something important about leadership: devotion to the political process had to be mediated by skillful observation and by a capacity to remain distant from men and events. He was calling for leaders both in and out of the political stream, since it was their principal obligation to change laws in order to make new ones. Only a proper leadership could cope

[87] *Sz.*, I, 99.

with contemporary requirements; and here, Sakuma argued over and over again, the Tokugawa officialdom had been woefully inept. Shogunal leadership, however able personally, had been fated to serve a most narrow circle of interests; hence the incompetence and stupidity of the *bakufu* administration.

A new political space and a dynamic political process required a new kind of leader. Sakuma, like many of his contemporaries, had himself in mind as a start. His own person, he tells us, possessed all the qualities of a good leader. But Sakuma distinguished grades of leadership. While he always considered himself a man who could perform effectively in a position of great responsibility—say as a high-ranking bureaucrat—he also envisaged a leader of leaders who would guide, initiate, and inspire. The sages—Yao, Shun, Wu, T'ang—had beeen leaders of this order; their example was good but inaccessible, and might lead to slavish emulation. Hence Sakuma recommends "overcoming the example of the sages of antiquity" in order to "follow humanity." [88] He had in mind a hero endowed with both knowledge and the will to act.[89] This role he assigned to the emperor, who was just emerging, after the opening of the country, as an important principal in Japanese politics. Sakuma's imperial standards are astonishingly similar to the nativist ones popularized by writers such as Ōkuni Takamasa, Suzuki Shigetane, and Maki Izumi. Since the emperor in his divinity was by definition both in and out of the political stream, Sakuma had available and ready-made a leader who could reject history in order to make history. The nativists had been concerned only with preserving the equilibrium of the shogunal order, confirming current leadership and their policies in the name of the emperor. In his support of the *kōbugattai* formula Sakuma saw a means to put the existing arrangement of power under the authority of an all-powerful emperor. To this end he called for a more even distribution of power between *bakufu* and *han*. He assigned direct leadership of this reconstituted arrangement of power to the emperor, who had al-

[88] *Sz.*, I, 280.
[89] Matsumoto, p. 147.

ways been a *principle* of authority, and who now became a *principal* of authority as well. Sakuma's leader, the emperor, was not the shadowy figure of Japanese history and of handbooks on political theory; rather he was a pulsating personality, human in his concerns, vigorous in his capacity to act.

Not only did Sakuma advise abandonment of classical models, Chinese and Japanese; he also specified the kind of leader most suitable to Japan at this time. He wrote of heroes who were also emperors—a new phenomenon in Japanese political thought. He had available to him several modern figures, from among whom he settled on Peter the Great and secondarily on Napoleon. Despite scattered vague allusions to "restoration" (*chūkō*), Sakuma was not a restorationist in any proper sense; [90] his "revival" of the principle of direct imperial authority was not a condition for restoring the prosperity of a prior age, either literally or metaphorically. His celebration of heroes such as Peter and Napoleon shows both antipathy for classical Chinese and Japanese models and rejection of the typical restorationist romanticism.

Sakuma's view of Peter the Great and Napoleon as makers of history was shared by many of his contemporaries and was also exported to China later in the service of the "Hundred Days Reform" by intellectuals like K'ang Yu-wei and Huang Tsun-hsien. However, by that time the Chinese reformers had available the more immediate model of the emperor Meiji.[91] "What country, what age," Sakuma asked in a poem of 1859, "has not longed for a hero like Lord Napoleon?"[92] Napoleon knew how to deal with changing conditions and extended the dignity of France throughout Europe; all who confronted his banners "swayed like grass before the wind." His importance, Sakuma noted, was found in decisive acts which "in a short time smashed contemporary

[90] *Sz.*, I, 196.
[91] See Richard Howard, "Japan's Role in the Reform Program of K'ang Yu-wei," in Jung-Pang Lo, *K'ang Yu-wei, A Biography and Symposium* (Tucson, 1967), pp. 280–312.
[92] *Sz.*, I, 904; II, 111, 175, "Letters to Yamadera Gendafu."

abuses . . . and responded to the people's needs." His achievements inspire because they teach people not to pursue little
things, not to be content (like the Japanese) with "childish enter-
tainments." His countrymen should "know the mind of a hero"
such as Napoleon in order to "construct a Great Plan." Nothing
in Japan's history offers a comparison to his achievements. Even
though his "triumph was short-lived" and he knew defeat in
Russia, his vision commands respect. Such a man (as Sakuma
had written earlier in a letter to Akamatsu Mizutani) would
know how to relieve Japan of current difficulties; but he must
come from the lower orders of society, since experience will have
familiarized him with the depths of social and economic problems. "He will devise a comparable plan, enlist cooperation, drive
out wickedness; and in the end he will wrap up the world and
return it to the imperial court, which shall be revered by the
world for a long time." [93]

Sakuma's celebration of Peter the Great is just as enthusiastic
and more explicit. Starting from a confused Voltairean image of
Peter as an enlightened despot who illuminated with rationality
the dark corners of medieval Russia, Sakuma held that Peter
obeyed the necessities of the times because he made it his business
to know them. It was not irrelevant that Peter "pushed back the
eastern borders three thousand miles, learned Dutch science and
taught it to his people." [94] In contrast to the Russians, Sakuma
complained, the Japanese were sitting idly and ruminating on
past glories irrelevant to contemporary problems. Victimized by
narcissistic concentration on their own history, the Japanese had
failed to produce heroes since Tokugawa Ieyasu. His argument
is, once more, startlingly similar to Ogyū Sorai's theory of leadership. Russia offered a perfect parallel to Japan: Peter had first
unified the realm, in policy and in his person; had encouraged
the adoption of Western technology and the construction of a
maritime fleet; had elevated Russia to an honorable place among

[93] *Sz.,* I, 905; Miyamoto (n. 3 above), pp. 263–265.
[94] "A Song of History: Peter the Great," trans. Burton Watson, in *Anthology of Japanese Literature,* ed. D. Keene (New York, 1955), p. 439.

the "nations of the Five Continents." His efforts strengthened
Russia and prevented colonization, "being swallowed up." "Before Peter," Sakuma continued, "Russia was an impoverished and
benighted country within Europe," but since his reign "it has not
been inferior to any other country." [95] It was Sakuma's anxious
hope (he confessed to Yanagawa Seigan) that, once the inherited
system was revised, the government would select only the most
able men for positions of responsibility and, like Peter, first send
them abroad to learn something of the world and acquire new
knowledge. He also hoped that in time the Japanese would invite foreign technicians to their country and treat them with respect and courtesy, so that they might help renovate Japan in
that defense and technology which alone would raise it to eminence among the nations of the Five Continents.[96]

Sakuma was one of the early casualties of the drive for Restoration. He was assassinated for his part in mediating between court
and *bakufu* in 1864. Even during this enterprise his moderate
message was no longer heard, and younger samurai activists were
marching to a different drummer. To the last, as Tokutomi Sōho
has said, he was committed to things, rather than to men and
their behavior. He saw technology as a means of completing "a
circular pattern" (he wrote in the *Seiken roku*), "so that half of
the earth should not be missing"; this was the answer to Japan's
problems, and a good reason for him to offer his life. He knew
the risk he was taking, but he knew he had made the decision
long ago. He was pompously self-righteous in his convictions; his
letters show the monotony of one who knows he is right. Because
of his consuming interest in knowledge of things, and because of
his claimed (and actual) proficiency in this pursuit, Sakuma's
personality rarely emerges from behind the screen of a single-
minded purposiveness directed toward a "Great Plan." Compared
with his younger contemporaries like Yoshida Shōin, or with
older but more colorful associates such as Umeda Unpin and
Yanagawa Seigan, Sakuma is a shadowy academic figure who re-

[95] *Sz.*, I, 109.
[96] *Sz.*, II, 830–831, "Letter to Yanagawa Seigan."

veals very little about himself. But if Sakuma was a bore, he was
a courageous one.

Just as he begins to emerge differently when he writes to Ochō,
so in his letters to his mistress we are given all too infrequent dis-
closures of his personality. His writing changes from pompous
and stuffy Chinese or epistolary *sōrōbun* to a softer, more personalized Japanese syntax in the *kana* syllabary. For a moment we
see Sakuma as an extraordinarily sensitive man, not always as sure
as he seemed in public, not always as righteous as his contemporaries were persuaded to believe. In one of his last letters to his
mistress, written on the eve of his assassination with a prescience
that danger awaits him, Sakuma provides a last glimpse of the
character he industriously concealed. He describes his fears, his
doubts, his anxieties; but he also furnishes his life with an epitaph more suitable than anything his contemporaries or we today
could compose:

You are correct in your surmise that I am worried. Yet other people
are not really concerned about the things I worry about. . . . I have
heard that I will be attacked [lit., cut down] in my house, and whenever I go out I am confronted by opposition in several directions, but
I've thought little about it. During this time, when I am out, I have
been using a Western-style saddle on my horse. . . . Even though
there are foolish men who have criticized me for this, it is because they
are not open (*hirakanu*) to good things, and it is for this reason that I
use the saddle. Even though there have been many who have opposed
me and who have tried to change my views, especially military ones, I
have defended them single-mindedly for nearly thirty years. This has
not begun today. Since it has been my hope to plan for the future of
Japan, I do not intend to change this possibility. For thirty also I have
taken pain in this enterprise, and for nine years I have received censure. I will not exchange them now. During this time I have also felt
deeply about the Emperor and the shogun. . . . I am convinced the
fall of the country will accompany my death. I am not afraid of the
criticisms of people; my mind is always at peace.[97]

Yet Sakuma's intellectual achievement was impressive. Despite
private admissions of self-doubt, more than any of his contempo-

[97] *Sz.*, II, 1322–1323.

raries he was able to convert an inert intellectual endowment into a dynamic theory of action. His early interest in science and military technology, combined with his conception of a new political space devoted to defense, obliged him to review the inherited notion of an ethical polity (*jinsei*). His vision of a comity of powerful, equal nations, which made force a precondition of peace, obliged him to reconsider Japan's policy of seclusion. Sakuma transformed a moribund ethical culture into active political culture. In the course of dismantling the Mito notion of expulsion, he completed his view of power by enlisting the aid of a new science and technology which repudiated the naturalistic assumptions behind the concept of society he inherited.

This transformation of virtue into power brought possibilities for action in later years which Sakuma never anticipated. He conceived of the shift to power as a tactic to aid adoption of Western technology to defend the independence of the expanded realm (*tenka*); but he never envisaged broad political change. But the replacement of the Neo-Confucian static ethic of *meibun* by power as represented by technology, justified by practicality, liberated men who followed him, like Yoshida Shōin, to explore political possibilities hitherto inaccessible. Sakuma's politicization of Neo-Confucian morality into power permitted men to act without worrying about relating their conduct to their position on a fixed vertical scale of relationships.

Sakuma's own concern was to work the new knowledge into a society which had organized reality on the principle of nature (*shizen no dōri*). His sometime student in gunnery, Yoshida Shōin, went on to experiment with the almost unlimited range of power now available.[98] Yoshida thereby moved beyond the boundaries of that culture which Sakuma had sought to preserve, and created a whole new culture of action. But already with Sakuma the shift from virtue to power meant an interest in material things; and this in itself was a long ways from the unchanging Mito "morality of daily affairs" (*jinri nichiyō*).

[98] See Uete Michiari, "Meiji Keimō shisō no keisei, seiyōkan no tenkai tono kanran ni oite," in *Shisō* (Feb., 1967), p. 842.

IV *The Culture of Action: Yoshida Shōin*

Once, when he was in jail, Yoshida Shōin (1830–1859) had a dream.[1] He saw the image of a samurai whose courage would be tested twenty-one times. On closer inspection it first appeared as the Japanese sign for twenty-one, and then took on the shape of his own name: it was none other than himself. "My name is Tora, and *tora* means 'tiger,' and the virtue of the tiger is courage."[2] Yoshida returned to this theme in April 1857 in his piece *To Be Born Seven Times (Shichisei-setsu).*[3] This essay had been inspired by the exploits of Kusunoki Masashige, a familiar example of loyalty to the emperor.[4] Kusunoki was reported to

[1] Yamaguchi ken kyōikukai, *Yoshida Shōin zenshū,* 12 vols., 2d ed. (Tokyo, 1938–1940), I, 388–389. Hereafter cited as *YSz.*

[2] *YSz.,* I, 389.

[3] I'm assuming that it was later, since the earlier report of the dream is undated. The later reference is titled "A continuation of the 21 times courageous samurai." In *YSz.* IV, 129-130.

[4] Kusunoki Masashige was a minister to the emperor Go Daigo in the fourteenth-century struggle between competing courts, north and south, and, rather than submit either to "bribery" or to threat, he remained loyal to the end, fighting for the cause of the southern court and taking his own

have said to his brother Masasue before the battle of Minatogawa, "If you have to die, what will you do?" His brother re-
plied, "I wish to be reborn as many as seven times, and each time
I will try to destroy the enemies of the royal family [lit.,
traitors]." Kusunoki was pleased and responded, "Your words
show that you understand my heart very well." After this they
both killed themselves.[5] It is important that the dream which
tells us something about Yoshida's obsessions was connected with
Kusunoki.[6] The extraordinary courage expressed by the figure 21
could be realized only by samurai who, like Kusunoki and himself, were willing to die seven times in defense of principle and
of imperial loyalty.

Although the dream reveals anxiety about the way Yoshida
Shōin conceived of his role, he was not indulging in Buddhist
imagery. He knew Kusunoki meant only a metaphorical rebirth:
his example would live and inspire men to unimaginable heroism. "There have been a great number of men who followed
Kusunoki . . . and this will continue forever. I have passed Minatogawa three times on my way eastward, and each time I vis-
ited their graves I could not help but weep."[7] Yoshida's older
contemporary Maki Izumi had worked out an elaborate worship
of Kusunoki's example which drove him to extremes of devotion
—and also to action. The example of the brothers confirmed
Yoshida's devotion to the interest of the public and of the emperor. Although separated by time, his mind was one with Kusunoki's; because they shared principle (*ri*), they shared a common
purpose. "I am sure," he wrote, "that others will later remember
and follow me, for it is my intention to be reborn seven times in
order to show my gratitude to my country."[8] Probably the last

---

life when all hope of success had vanished. The subject of the untarnished
loyalism of Kusunoki and his brother was confiscated by writers, and
they were elevated into semitragic and epic characters. In a sense this is
what kept their example alive for generations of Japanese to follow.

[5] *YSz.,* IV, 128.

[6] For Yoshida's numerology see *YSz.,* IV, 128–129, 130.

[7] *YSz.,* IV, 128–129.

[8] *YSz.,* IV, 129.

piece he wrote, considered by his apologists as the culmination of the hero's work, the *Ryūkonroku,* ends with a poem. The last stanza reads: "Though I may be reborn seven times/How will I ever forget to drive off the barbarian?" Solemnly he signed it, "The patriot who has the courage of twenty-one (*Niji ikkai moshi*)." [9]

This recurrent dream, with its numerology, is fundamental for Yoshida. Since he uses his thought as an example of the action he chose, we cannot, as we could in the case of Sakuma, classify his efforts in tidy categories. His life can only be understood as what the French critic Roland Barthes calls "an organized network of obsessions." [10] Of all late Tokugawa personalities, Yoshida is best suited for psychological analysis, both by virtue of his volatile and flamboyant character, and by the confessional nature of his writing. He offers us, as few among his contemporaries do, highly personal testimony to his fears, anxieties, fantasies, and doubts. We shall study how his perceptions of reality began to change, how they helped form his obsesssions, and how these in turn motivated his political and literary efforts. Yoshida was a contemporary of Sakuma Shōzan, Maki Izumi, Yokoi Shōnan; but neither his choices nor theirs can be explained by "objective social reality," although each witnessed the same events in the 1850s. Beyond the historical situations on which Collingwood insists, the reality of a man's times is seen through the lens of his personal perceptions, and its index of refraction accounts ultimately for his response.

Not even Aizawa remained indifferent to *kaikoku;* Sakuma changed his mind early about Japan's problems. But Yoshida differed from his contemporaries in the way that his changing perceptions affected the role he assigned himself. He was acutely aware of a failure of support from the "sense of identity" in social groups. Erikson has written that where technological developments encroach on a large scale upon deeply rooted or strongly emerging identities (e.g., agrarian, feudal, patrician), youth feels

[9] *YSz.,* VII, 330.

[10] Roland Barthes, *Michelet, par lui-même* (Paris, 1954), p. 6.

endangered, both individually and collectively; it becomes ready to support doctrines which offer total immersion in a synthetic identity (e.g., nationalism, racism, class consciousness) and to condemn without discrimination stereotyped enemies of the new identity.[11] The young Yoshida belonged to such a generation, conscious of an identity vacuum, estranged and alienated. Such periods are brought on more generally by historical dislocations where inherited concepts of space, time, or culture are expanded and changed; where new knowledge and intellectual alternatives arouse fears and uncertainties; where, as Erikson has written of Luther, inner anxieties are aggravated by the decay of institutions which have served as the historical anchor of an elite's identity.[12] Yoshida, more than most, sharply felt after 1854 such a historical dislocation.

"The great affliction of the country," he wrote in 1859, in *Words of a Madman* (*Kyōfu no gen*), "is not knowing the reason why it is being afflicted. . . . If the reasons for this affliction were known, would not some plan be devised to divert it?"[13] Just as his perception of reality quickened after 1854, his estimate of his own role in the new situation became exaggerated. Before his death he was convinced that he alone could save Japan from destruction, by a curious psychological link (which I will discuss later) between his youthful yearnings and the fate of Japan. Convinced of the rightness in his cause, Yoshida was willing to risk estrangement from his friends, and in the end his life, to dramatize his sincerity, his fidelity, and the veracity of his vision. The salvation of Japan provided him with "a will and a fatality" (as Malraux said of Marxism in *Man's Fate*). Once he was committed to an early spectacular death, his writings became studded with disclaimers of selfishness, extravagant declarations of devotion at a time when nobody else professed devotion, and fervent prayers that a few would remember him and follow in his footsteps.

[11] Erik Erikson, *Insight and Responsibility* (New York, 1964), p. 93.
[12] *Ibid.*, p. 204.
[13] *YSz.*, V, 94.

Yoshida Shōin, like Sakuma Shōzan, took the problem of *gai-kan* seriously. No longer was it possible for serious men, as it had been earlier for Mito ideologues, to identify reality with the natural order and argue for moral rectification. Yoshida's break with the Mito school came about the time Perry appeared in 1853–1854. Apart from his domainal training in the military curriculum, his education was limited to the artificial synthesis of Neo-Confucian and nativist sentiments with which Mito rhetoric celebrated the status order. We have seen what Mito writers did not: that their language implied a shift in the concept of political space from the domain to an expanded realm called *shinkoku*. For them *shinkoku*, the sacred realm, was merely another way of referring to the conglomeration of semiautonomous political units in the *bakuhan* order. If it was divine, so much the better. When Sakuma or Yoshida registered disenchantment with the Mito solution around 1854, they uprooted the rhetoric from its unnatural context and put such terms as *kokutai* and *shinkoku* into the service of their own situation.

Despite their seeming reliance on the Mito statement, writers everywhere in Japan after 1854 clearly acknowledged a new reality brought in by *gaikan*, even though their language might evoke other associations. Yoshida, following Sakuma, was very willing to abandon "empty theories" for "the investigation of contemporary conditions." Yoshida had an antipathy for the established scholarship which he dubbed "the abuse of nonlearning and nonthinking." By "nonlearning" he meant skill in such things as poetic studies inapplicable to contemporary affairs; by "nonthinking" he meant empty theorizing, intellectual activity which dissolved when forced to account for real facts. Hence Yoshida discarded Mito learning for more realistic alternatives.[14] But his commitment to practicality was not an abandonment of tradition or received pieties; rather, as illustrated by its acceptance of Western gunnery, it sprang from a sharp, indeed exag-

[14] *YSz*, IX, 19–123. Yoshida's record of his "western trip (*saiyū nikki*)" is filled with examples of this "celebration" of practicality.

gerated, sense of loyalty, which obliged him constantly to reject whatever he considered useless to the realm.[15]

Maruyama Masao has argued that, while loyalty was formally expressed in the Tokugawa period through the impersonal social relationships of Confucian ethics, there existed another tradition which could justify personal behavior. Throughout the Tokugawa epoch "loyalty" ostensibly meant simply blind devotion; yet, according to Maruyama, beneath the surface there lay another tradition which obliged the loyal servant to be his own judge, discriminating between benevolent leadership and wickedness. History in this view provided higher principles which men might invoke to support an action resulting from personal judgment.[16] This tradition is supposed to have gone back to the *sengoku* period of the sixteenth century, before social relationships were impersonalized by Confucianism, when the relationship between lord and retainer was based on personal friendship and affection developed in war. Samurai then had accessible a wide range of options: they could leave the lord if they were dissatisfied, or join him in death on the battlefield (*junshi*).[17] Maruyama's classic example of how this recessive tradition was revived in the *bakumatsu* generation is Yoshida Shōin. "The consciousness of a foreign crisis that pressed upon Japan in the late Tokugawa period aroused a sense of responsibility and honor which until then had been latent within the feudal ethic. If on the one hand the kind of action generated by activist *rōnin* was an attempt to renew the wild character of the *sengoku* disturbances, on the other hand we can detect clearly the tradition of the *Hagakure* [a pure feudal loyalty] ethos in Shōin's paradoxical 'selfless loyalty' and subjectivistic autonomy." [18] Maruyama infers from

[15] See Kano Masanao, *Nihon kindai shisō seiritsu* (Tokyo, 1956), p. 23.

[16] Maruyama Masao, "Chūsei to hangyaku," in *Kindai Nihon shisōshi kōza,* 8 vols. (Tokyo, 1961), VI, 391.

[17] It is interesting to note that the Tokugawa early in the seventeenth century abolished the practice of *junshi*.

[18] Maruyama, *op. cit.*

Yoshida's behavior that, although he (like all samurai) had been trained in a Confucianism that had depersonalized the warrior ethic, the original ethic of friendship was never fully smothered by Confucianism or absorbed by the Tokugawa bureaucratic state. Vestiges remained beneath the surface of expected behavior, ready to be resuscitated as by Yoshida in times of historical dislocation when established modes of conduct no longer offered support.

In reply to Maruyama, we may ask why it took over three hundred years for the submerged tradition to be exploited. Samurai acting on their own during the Tokugawa period, as an expression of what Yamamoto Tsunemoto (1659–1719) imagined the *sengoku* warrior to be in his romantic evocation of samurai behavior, the *Hagakure,* were few and remote from the late Tokugawa years. Yoshida and his contemporaries acted in an unprecedented way to satisfy the frustrations of youth, to search for identity and to rededicate it to Japan. Yoshida clearly felt he was living in a unique present, which corresponded to his unique personal development. His consciousness of a new present was linked to his conception of the public interest. If he was relying on a prior fugitive tradition, it is doubtful that he would have selected one which had lain dormant for three hundred years. Traditions simply do not remain pure for that length of time. Rather, I suspect that Yoshida appealed to another fugitive tradition, one more readily available to him and his contemporaries since it had already started to be revived: namely, *nativism.* In an essay written in 1856 Yoshida fully approved Motoori Norinaga's doctrine that the realm is the private possession of the emperor, in language that appears borrowed from the *Naobi no mitama.* He also accepted Motoori's emphasis on purity of feeling and the obligation of all people to revere the emperor.[19] The unclouded feeling of a "pure heart" (*magokoro*) automatically allows people to reach out to the emperor.

The actions of Yoshida Shōin and of succeeding restorationists confirmed Motoori's analysis. If the imperial realm (which in an-

[19] *YSz.,* IV. 139–141.

other sense was public because everything belonged to the emperor) was not being served because investigation of reality was being slighted in favor of fixed bureaucratic procedures inadequate to the current of the times, then men were obliged to reinstate efficacious politics. Belief in an "imperial realm," as Yoshida called it, liberated political procedure from unconditional norms. Politics, in his mind, had to be accountable to the emperor; this required observation of contemporary historical reality. This political relativism (which Yoshida took as his definition of loyalty and sincerity) was surely more powerful than some recessive tradition waiting beneath the surface of accepted behavior. Yoshida's appropriation of the nativist tradition permitted him to explore private impulse under the rubric of "pure heart," and to seek out a new personality to fit the changes taking place. By shifting the object of loyalty to the emperor, Yoshida could insist on a direct personal expression of fidelity. And since it was the emperor's realm that was being served, there was no necessity to defend a fixed system of political arrangements—the *bakuhan* order—if new arrangements could promise greater political stability.

Yoshida also expanded his quest for personal identity into the search for an adequate theory of political leadership. Sakuma Shōzan had moved in this direction through his celebration of a historical emperor. Yoshida transferred the responsibility for decisive action to the *sōmō no shishi,* the unattached patriots serving the emperor. Yoshida rarely took on the problem of political institutions, which he saw as subordinate to the problem of leadership. Much of his thought and conduct were spent in providing his contemporaries with a living example of how personality and leadership might be realized through loyal action.

Yoshida's short career made action itself into an investigative technique.[20] There are few major turning points; but in this life

[20] Yoshida's "biography" is quite familiar by now, and available in a number of works. As I stated earlier, since it is not my intention to write biographies on men, with a mode of expression which is virtually impossible at this time, I am bypassing all pretense at doing so. And, as the

he packed several lifetimes. If he had not spent periods in prison and under house arrest, he would not have written as much as he did. In his well-spent confinement he reassessed his opinions; the torrent of his confessional letters, poems, short essays, petitions, shows that when he was prevented from acting, writing became a substitute.[21] Yoshida's career rested on a belief that action in all directions would solve the contemporary malaise and reveal a new concept of leadership. He only insisted that action, however violent, must flow from a prior inner commitment to principle and loyalty (*gi*).

Yoshida knew that leadership, especially at the shogunal level, was hopelessly ill-equipped to deal with an unprecedented situation. Action was the only hope. His self-image became exaggerated, and his behavior took on more elements of childish reckless-

---

reader can see, I have included only the barest "biographical" data, and I have entered these only when they appear necessary or related to specific turns of thought, perception, and behavior. Perhaps J. P. Sartre was right when he said that this, after all, is the only way to write biography and capture or rescue a life. The wholeness of a life pursued by biographers in astonishingly minute detail usually does the life a disservice since it is organized around significant events which the personality may have achieved later in his life but which he could not have known when he was younger. Japanese "biographers" always equip their subject with an example or incident of youthful genius and prescience as if to suggest that the character's later life was already foretold when he was a child. Sartre, in any case, has put it much better than I ever could in his "autobiographical" book, *The Words* (New York, 1964), translated by Bernard Frechtman. While the problem was put much earlier in his novel *Nausea* (1940) he has made the problem of historical biography an object of analysis in "Question de Méthode," the long preface to his even longer *Critique de La Raison Dialectique* (Paris, 1960), Vol. 1.

For further biographical data and information on Yoshida, see the following: Naramoto Tatsuya, *Yoshida Shōin* (Tokyo, 1961), rev. ed.; David Earl, *Emperor and Nation* (Seattle, 1964), pp. 109–160; and Heinrich Dumolin, "Yoshida Shōin," in *Monumenta Nipponica* (Tokyo, 1938), pp. 350–377.

[21] It could be argued that Yoshida's writings, however repetitive and tangential, express an autobiographical attempt at confession. Often they say more about himself, his doubts, fears, insecurities, etc., than they do about the subject he is trying to engage.

ness, yet this very eccentricity disclosed his perception of a new principle of reality. His personal solution was to create a *culture of action* in which men, unfettered by fixed ideological pieties that would allow the establishment to control them, might engage themselves in the problem of historical dislocation. This culture of action demanded heroes with the will to test new conditions by experimenting with political possibilities. Risk was irrelevant. The greater the peril, the stronger the mystique of action. The right kind of death, for Yoshida and Maki Izumi, was preferable to inaction, and a greater achievement than the realization of specific goals. Yoshida was not a reformer but a revolutionary and, I think, a nihilist, who saw in action and destruction an antidote to compromise and accommodation. He made his judgment to act after a private assessment of the best interest of the imperial realm. But toward the end of his life Yoshida valued the nature of the action and its success less than he did commitment, fidelity of purpose, the way an action was carried out, and its expression of sincerity (*shisei*).[22] Along with the rest of traditional behavior, he also discarded the traditional standards of "loyal conduct."

The moment of truth for Yoshida came in 1853–1854 with the arrival of Commodore Perry. While this event did not push him to the same extremes as the signing of commercial treaties by the *bakufu* in 1858, it altered his perception of reality, and all his later moves depended on this initial response. His early military training in Chōshū had given him an interest in military studies. With it he combined Mito sentiments—and antibarbarism—fashionable in the early 1850s. Predictably he saw Europe and the United States as hostile realms of cunning barbarians who knew neither principle nor bravery. Only the constant pursuit of profit (*ri*), he believed, drove the barbarian relentlessly into Eastern Asia; and although they had been successful in India and China, he was convinced that loyalty (*gi*) and courage would ultimately defeat profit.[23] (It should be noted, here, that when Yoshida referred to profit as *ri*, he was using a character different from the

[22] See the *Kaikoroku, Record of Recollections,* in YSz., X.
[23] YSz., II, 50–53 (January 1848).

one used to convey principle [*ri*]. He was using a character which often in Tokugawa moral writings, was juxtaposed to *gi* —loyalty, selflessness, public service—and carried the opposite meaning—selfishness, self-seeking and privately ambitious behavior.) But even in his youth Yoshida could not make an absolute differentiation between *gi* and *ri*; for he already appreciated Western gunnery. Despite his support for cultural discrimination (*jōi*), by 1849 he suggested that traditional military studies might profit by closer imitation of Western military technology. This was not, of course, an unusual position, and Yoshida justified imitation by practicality, since military studies revealed ways to win battles. "Men of wisdom surely always win." [24] This practicality could be approved, at least in theory, by existing ideas of loyalty. His journey to western Japan in 1850 (as recorded in his diary, *Saiyū nikki*) opened new vistas. He traveled throhout Kyūshū, visiting Kokura, Saga, Ōmura, Nagasaki, Hirado, Shimabara, Kumamoto, Kurume, and other places; everywhere he noted things seen and friends newly made. He wrote also that this trip convinced him about the essential soundness of Western military technology—which in fact was already serving the *bakuhan* system.[25] Yoshida's acceptance of new military possibilities still rested on an optimistic Neo-Confucian view of society.

But when on this trip he left his domain, Yoshida entered into friendly relations with several like-thinking men of other *han*. From these associations he later called for greater contact among retainers of different areas, and finally for an uprising (*kukki*) of patriots from all over Japan, men willing to shed domainal affiliations. Paradoxically, the more he moved toward the idea of "great loyalty" to the domainal lord, the more he came to believe in the possibility of an interdomainalism that would bring together the most able men in the realm. This dual allegiance hardened about the time of his eastern trip in 1851–1852. The stronger his sense of loyalty, the stronger his urge to leave the

[24] YSz, II, 48. In addition to this plaint, Yoshida also argued here that "victory represents the norm, while defeat means change."

[25] *Saiyū nikki* in YSz., X, 19–123.

domain. But Yoshida was working out a new concept of loyalty, and no doubt his effusive declaration of loyalty to the Chōshū daimyo was prompted by the fact that he took the second trip without official permission.

Yoshida made both of these trips before the coming of Perry. Nowhere in his accounts of them does there appear the obsessive emperorism of his last days. In a letter (August 1857) written to his priest friend Mokurin some time after the eastern trip he confessed how recently he had come by his imperial loyalism, even though the trip had taken him to Mito. "Even though there are men who revere the emperor today, the reliable ones have done so only for a short period of time. I have been trying for five years to find a way to express my reverence for the imperial court. But previously I had not known anything about the great principle of loyalty." [26] During his stay in Mito he talked with Toyoda Tenkō, a local intellectual, and in a burst of enthusiasm wrote: "If one is born in this land and does not know that it is the Imperial Land, how can he live as a true subject? To do so we must read first the thirty books of the *Nihongi* and then continue by reading the forty books of the *Zoku Nihongi*." This exuberance may have been simply a way to justify what domain authorities considered an illegal trip. While he seems to be talking about restoration of the emperor, he was still under the sway of Mito rhetoric, expressing an orthodox expulsionism.

Restorationism played little part in Yoshida's thinking, and even though he later called for a revival of ancient prosperity, his interests always lay in the present. Yoshida's flirtation with the Mito scheme obliged him to support a restoration of the true *bakuhan* system. He felt in fact so vast a distance between a classical past and a unique present that past solutions were of little value for present problems.[27] In a petition of 1848, Yoshida revealed a consciousness of time that became important in his later

[26] YSz., VIII, 518.
[27] Naramoto, *op. cit.*, pp. 83–84, hints at this interpretation and offers Yoshida's penchant to record happenings, "news" as an expression of a contemporaneously oriented journalistic mentality.

thought; he saw action as possible only after recognition of the distance between classical order and contemporary life. "Since there has been a long-standing peace," he wrote, "the gulf between high and low has gradually widened. I submit that we have to listen to, and be well versed in, the conditions of the lower orders. The first principle of prosperity is to manage the common evils of the past and present, and gradually to reform these abuses. Because of this long-standing peace we tend to give expression to our understanding of conditions with extreme rhetorical flourishes. In the present we are guided by old standards, and by neglecting real facts (*jiji*) we have lost the basic purpose of social life." [28] Later Yoshida recalled how in prison he had mastered the book on Mencius, only to conclude that it was "cut off from real facts," and how he retained "only that which is real or of practical use to mind and body." [29]

Yoshida conducted his eastern trip to investigate social and military conditions, knowing that he would be punished for it. "Practicality" obliged him to violate domainal procedure. His new higher loyalty, the consciousness of the present, always justified action. He equated loyalty with the search for real facts on which to base policy. Unlike Sakuma, who knew Western science better than Yoshida, and hence what kind of investigation was required, Yoshida's quest for "real conditions" was aimless and was replaced in time by action itself. In his last years, Yoshida made little attempt to define the ends of action or to tell his followers what had to be investigated.

On leaving Chōshū in 1851, he was put in a domainal prison and struck from the *han* register. "Since I did not receive permission to take leave from the domainal government, I will most surely be exiled. Yet if I had hesitated in this, the retainers of Chōshū would no doubt have been accused of being indecisive. This charge would have brought humiliation upon the domain. Although the punishment is administered by the *han*, it is limited to one person. When you compare this individual punish-

[28] *YSz.*, I, 241–242.
[29] *YSz*, IV, 84.

ment to the shame that would have been heaped upon the entire domain, what are the pros and cons?"[30] Yoshida suggests that, by assuming sole responsibility, he was shaking up the established structure of loyalty. His decision to leave the domain without official permission conformed to the requirements of loyalty, as informed by a sense of practicality. Years before his eastern trip Yoshida had asked, in an essay called "Answers to the Question of Loyalty" (1845), "What is the Way of loyalty?" He answers:

The Way of loyalty is not hearing or receiving orders; it is not running obediently; rather, it is found only in balance. What then is balance? It can be said, "doing practical things which result in achievement." But even if you accomplish a great achievement, if it is not done with practicality, loyalty will not be gained. Bravery without wisdom makes loyalty impossible; and when knowledge is absent, can the limits of loyalty be exhausted? If ignorant men exhaust themselves with practicality, they will surely achieve loyalty. But these results cannot be compared to those of knowledgeable men. If it is hoped to achieve a greater loyalty, men must study the Great Way.[31]

Here is an early example of the loyal conduct Yoshida was to pursue obsessively throughout the 1850s. The key to his later extreme declarations that he alone understood the true meaning of loyalty is his rejection of that blind obedience which was standard practice in his day, and his insistence that practicality and a sense of the present determined loyalty.

In 1845 Yoshida had learned from one of his military instructors, Yamada Matanosuke, about the conditions "that have made the barbarians prosperous and strong, and how they have corroded the Far East."[32] His early training in military studies gave him a speculative interest in coastal defense, reinforced by his surveys of 1848 and 1850. Just before Perry arrived he petitioned his

[30] YSz., X. *Tōhokuyū nikki,* pp. 187–328.

[31] *YSz.,* I, 122–123.

[32] Quoted in Matsumoto Sannosuke, "Sonnō jōi undō ni kindaiteki seiji ishiki no keisei," in *Meiji ishinshi no mondaiten,* ed. Sakata Yoshio (Tokyo, 1962), p. 149.

domainal lord to encourage greater training in Western military technology.[33] The new technology, he said, was much different from the small skills of the individual *bushi*.[34] Unlike his teacher Sakuma, Yoshida retained to the end his expulsionism, an outgrowth of a more basic differentiation between within and without, civilized and barbarian, which kept the problems of defense and colonization before him even when the foreign threat was not too great.[35] Perry's presence tested this speculative expulsionism and forced Yoshida to make a profound reassessment of reality and his role.

For Yoshida, Perry's mission discredited the established perception of reality and the pattern of nature on which it was based, and compelled him to entertain new possibilities. All the pieties he held up to that time, which had provided him personal and collective identity, were put to the test of relevance. His whole inherited world image was up for acceptance or rejection. Acceptance would have made him a reformer at most; his ultimate rejection transformed a contentious young man into a revolutionary. He recorded the event in the *Shōkyu kigen*. Japanese history showed numerous foreign threats, always the same and dealt with in a similar manner. But the appearance of the Perry squadron was different. "In reality," he wrote in his characteristic shrill hysteria, "the emergency before our eyes is the greatest illness of the last ten thousand generations."[36] He was also profoundly disappointed in the way the leadership responded to the demands of the intrusion, which revealed to him for the first time a fundamental weakness in Japanese society. The truculence of American demands threw the *bakufu* into panic and indecision. Thirty-seven officials, he observed, failed to break through encrusted political practice to see that the American presence was unprecedented and required new tactics. Failure of political ritual—a

[33] *YSz.*, I, 244. "Suiriki senyoku" is a youthful analysis of military tactics and defense.

[34] See Matsumoto, p. 150.

[35] *Ibid.*, p. 149.

[36] *YSz.*, I, 297.

change in reality itself—appeared in the *bakufu*'s total incapacity to deal decisively with the American proposals.[37] (Another contemporary, Yokoi Shōnan, immortalized the agony of the decision-making machinery in his *Kokuze sanron,* written a few years after the event.) Officials, Yoshida charged, hesitated and ultimately gave in to Perry's demands, hoping that deferment might persuade the Americans to sail away.[38] The whole affair was mishandled and merely invited the Americans to return a few years later and try to establish a consulate. Peace, Yoshida wrote somewhere, had too long turned men's minds from the possibility of war, which the situation demanded.

To meet the crisis of *kaikoku* (Yoshida tells us in the confessional *Yūshūroku*), "I expressed my opinions by writing several essays on ways in which Japan might avert international troubles." [39] He first put together proposals for defense. In this effort he was assisted by the classical idea (popularized by the *kokugakusha*) that the realm belonged to the country by virtue of belonging to the imperial court; it was not the private possession of the *bakufu*.[40] The sectionalism in the Tokugawa arrangement of power had lost sight of the "unshakable truth" that Japan was a unified realm. Despite the peculiar ambiguity of the *bakuhan* order, "all the land under the sun belongs to the emperor, and all the people in this broad imperial land must be his subjects." [41] Like Sakuma, he believed that the threat posed by the Americans affected not just the shogunate or the domains, but the whole country. The several lords, he announced, should not pay more attention to the safety of their own domains than to Edo. (Yoshida's follower Kusaka Genzui later repudiated both the daimyo and the domainal system.) Since emperor and realm were identical, *bakufu* and *han* must act in concert. "If any sector of Japan is eyed by foreigners, the *bakufu* and the lords together must

[37] *YSz.,* I, 333 (*Yūshūroku*).
[38] *YSz.,* I, 333ff.
[39] *YSz.,* I, 339, 340.
[40] *YSz.,* I, 298–299.
[41] *YSz.,* I, 298.

console the emperor by wiping out this stain on our country." [42]
Only the unification of the upper and lower orders would rescue
the country from the foreign invasion. In times of emergency the
domains and the *bakufu* must suppress sectional interests.

At this juncture Yoshida was content to remind the authorities
of their responsibilities; he was not yet mounting an assault on
the *bakuhan* system. In a letter to his monk friends Mokurin and
Gessho, he argued that it was inadvisable to sweep out the *bakufu* and usher in the emperor (*tenko*). A great enemy outside
called for cooperation among the lords, refining (*kiren*) the *bakufu,* and strengthening the country (*kyōkoku*).[43] A year later
(1855) he reaffirmed his faith in the *bakuhan* order in a letter to
his brother: "Loyalty to the *bakufu* and loyalty to the throne"
are the same thing, which had been Japan's great blessing for
over two hundred years.[44] (Yoshida changed his mind about this
blessing in a few years.)

Yoshida, then, conceived of an imperial unity larger than its
parts—parts which must still cooperate on important problems.
"In the past," he noted, "when the emperor was faced with a political question, he usually went to the shrine where his ancestors
were enshrined, gathered his retainers to discuss problems, and
listened to their opinions." [45] As time passed, the emperor was
removed from the counsels of power. But his dependence on the
advice of retainers had been tested only in times of peace, and "in
an urgent and dangerous time the country cannot be protected if
politics remains the way it has been." National crisis required a
national effort, which could be accomplished only under the leadership of the emperor. Yoshida, in urging the establishment of an
imperial focus of authority, suggested that even "outer lords"
might offer their opinions to the throne.[46] He stressed the invio-

[42] *YSz.,* I, 298–299.
[43] *YSz.,* V, 410–412 (1935 edition). See also Naramoto (n. 20 above),
p. 76.
[44] *YSz.,* VIII, 423 (Letter to Sugi Umetarō).
[45] *YSz.,* I, 299.
[46] *YSz.,* I, 300.

lable bonds between emperor and subject across all social division. In 1854 and 1855 Yoshida saw that *kaikoku* permitted the abandonment of established procedures. Cutting across familiar class lines, he implied that the fact that all people were subjects of the emperor was more important than their position in the status order. Peace had clouded the essential unity between emperor and people. "We have no reason to divide subjects into two categories [high and low] . . . court subjects and those outside the palace. Owing to the evil influence of peace, those subjects who are outside of the court have become estranged from the emperor." [47] Urgency required the end of differences based on distance, and discrimination must be made only in terms of ability—namely, "whether subjects are proficient in both military and literary skills." Yoshida, like many contemporaries, was invoking the classical requisite for leadership, talent and ability; but the context of crisis gave it a new lease on life. He overcame traditional restraints on recruitment by what had been at most a fugitive idea in Confucianism.

Years before the coming of Perry (1845), Yoshida saw the debilitating effects of a protracted peace and seclusion on Japan. "We are so relaxed," he wrote, "we are so addicted to luxury, that we are apt to waste money and forget about armament." This puritanical disapproval of luxury (which became more prominent in Yoshida as he got more involved in politics) was rooted in his concern for coastal defense and armament. It was senseless that men should die for the lords using old-fashioned equipment. "It is no exaggeration," he declared, "to say that weapons such as armor, swords, and so forth are useless." [48] Yoshida was concerned for a kind of victory with no historical precedent. Victory could be achieved only through a constant reassessment of military needs. Also policy had to precede a specific course of action; a "victory in government" was essential to "victory on the battlefield." [49] Thus in 1852, calling for the aboli-

[47] *YSz.*, I, 301.
[48] *YSz.*, I, 250.
[49] *YSz.*, 261.

tion of divisions between high and low, he urged the government to recruit only those who, regardless of status, showed proficiency in both civilian and military arts.[50]

LOYALTY AND ACTION

During the years 1853-1857 many of Yoshida's youthful ideas acquired new shape and direction through political action; and ideas and action grew so close as to be indistinguishable. Of all late Tokugawa ideologues, none was more concerned with problems of personality than Yoshida. Only he faced up to the knowledge that the hierarchic order had failed. The failure was most evident in the identity support it had promised to provide. Virtually alone in a new situation, he sought to deal with a new reality through encounter and action. While others around him looked to a superhero to arrest crisis, Yoshida pinned his hope on the "unattached patriots," *sōmō no shishi,* the model for whom was himself, a man unfettered by traditional behavior.

Yoshida's writings of 1853-1854 show the picture of a man scurrying around Uraga Bay to get a glimpse of the foreign ships, talking intently with anybody who would listen to him, and angrily tilting at imaginary officials who had failed to deal sternly with the Americans.[51] We can then imagine why he finally decided to take action by stowing away on one of the ships. He knew that this act, if discovered by the authorities, would bring longer imprisonment than that imposed by the domain authorities after his unauthorized eastern trip. He first tried to present his plan to a number of officials, but was not heard. Then he turned to Sakuma Shōzan for advice. Sakuma, Yoshida knew, had long favored serious study of "barbarian conditions" through firsthand observation. In this moment of indecision, Sakuma of-

[50] See *YSz.,* I, 263ff.

[51] *YSz.,* I, 339ff. The *Yūshūroku* is an eloquent journal, indeed a confessional account of the events during the years 1853 and 1854, and of Yoshida's perceptions and subsequent activity, written in jail. See also Naramoto (n. 20 above) for an analysis of this "world view" from prison.

fered a cryptic platitude which Yoshida interpreted in the light of what Sakuma had been promoting. There is something touchingly naïve about his encounter with Sakuma:

Whenever I faced an emergency I always turned to him [Sakuma] for advice. He always responded to me heartily. Cheering me up, he said: "It is never praiseworthy when one is without faults; rather we praise those who try to correct their faults. It is far more important for one to have corrected his faults, for nothing is greater than this. It can be considered a great compensation for one's faults if he makes an effort to perform some good or meritorious act for his country during a time of emergency, such as now when we face international troubles." [52]

Sakuma never explicitly urged Yoshida to board one of Perry's ships. But Yoshida knew from Sakuma that Japan would have to learn from the West if it was to survive. In his *Record of Recollections* (*Kaikoroku*) he remarked, in a way that Sakuma would have approved, that only by "crossing the seas to barbarian countries will we know their conditions." [53] Sakuma, I should add, never contemplated this possibility for himself. And in explaining his decision to work for the realm by stowing away on one of the ships, "to compensate for my deficiencies," Yoshida asked: "If we do not investigate the conditions of the barbarians, how can we ever drive them from our shores?" [54] This particular act, for which the *Yūshūroku* is an elaborate defense, brought "shame and dishonor" both to Yoshida and to many of his associates. But he calculated the risk of punishment and decided to push on. He was less bothered by imprisonment, the price for failure, than by the failure of the mission itself, because it was calculated to serve the "national interest." Unrepentant, Yoshida argued that his failure ultimately harmed the country; breaking the ancestral law enforcing seclusion was insignificant beside the potential national benefit.

[52] YSz., I, 340.

[53] *Kaikoroku* in YSz., X. YSz., III, 137. Through Sakuma Shōzan, Yoshida reports in the *Kōmō yowa*, he received encouragement when he decided to make the trip abroad.

[54] YSz., I, 343–345.

Yoshida conceived of his effort as pure and disinterested; he
was playing the sincere role required of a loyal retainer of the
"imperial land." Sincerity (*shisei*) had to flow from the individual; and though it might lead to disaster, it lighted the remaining years of his life. It also gave him (as we will see) a way to
judge the loyalty of others. In the new situation, action on the
basis of principled loyalty promised suitable solutions. In time
Yoshida moved away from this commitment to political action
toward the mystique of risk, action for the sake of action; its purpose was less to show his country the true path than to manifest
his personal integrity. His motivation was complex. At the beginning of his career Yoshida was expressing a class attitude
which distinguished samurai from other groups by their unique
responsibility to preserve "peace and order." In 1858, to explain
this theory in language accessible to his time, he codified the behavior expected of the samurai. Although he reminds the warrior
of his duty, there is much in his rules alien to his class colleagues.
The opening passages suggest that life is too short simply to
"follow the sayings of the sages"; men are obliged to say what
they feel and think.[55] For Yoshida, observance of the Five Relations is the key to samurai behavior, and of these the most important are loyalty and filial piety, in that order. "Born in the imperial land, we must know the reason why we are esteemed
throughout the world (*udai*). It is because the imperial court
has continued an unbroken succession for ten thousand years,
and the samurai inherit rank and stipends. The imperial lords
nourish the people and continue the work of the ancestors, and
the retainers and people show loyalty to their lords by continuing
the tasks of their fathers. Only in Japan is it true that lord and retainer are one, and that loyalty and filial piety are united."[56] Nothing is more important for the samurai than principle, the performance of loyalty. And loyalty is active; when it conforms to
courage, its true meaning will be revealed. Truthfulness, simplicity, and sincerity are the signs of character; effort, patience, and

[55] *YSz.,* IV, 19.
[56] *YSz.,* IV, 20.

quick decision are the power of duty.[57] As Fujita Tōko had noted earlier, peace had changed the samurai from warriors to salaried bureaucrats. And though Yoshida spoke of them as a bold band of committed and loyal men, in the end he wrote them off in his call for a general rising because they were no longer willing to sacrifice their meager stipends. Yoshida's idealization of samurai behavior owed less to any tradition than to his own imagination.

Between 1854 and 1857 he changed his view on expulsion. Originally he had accepted the Mito expulsionist policy and had learned from Sakuma the value of Western military technology in executing it. Even for Mito writers, *jōi* meant preparation and defense; Sakuma extended this notion by pleading for a national defense network along Western lines. And Yoshida for a while agreed.[58] But later he changed expulsionism as preparation and defense into attack and expansion,[59] and reformulated his theory of action accordingly. After 1854 he was convinced that the times were unique and that the crisis of *kaikoku* posed a direct challenge to the entire country. The same convictions in Sakuma only reinforced his belief in Western technology and mild political reform. With Yoshida they led to hysterical demands for attack, violent entreaties for a new kind of leadership, and a call for restoration of "imperial prosperity."

"We could discover," he wrote, "what emperors in the past have done . . . by studying the history of our country. But the circumstances today are completely different from those in antiquity." [60] At the time of failure of a "magic system"—that is, a whole system of belief by which a society rationalizes and regularizes behavior—there is a common tendency among intellectuals to over-authenticate the past. They use it increasingly to reassure the present that the beliefs which are called into question are still workable. Past relationships, held at arm's length, are in-

[57] *Ibid.*

[58] *YSz.*, I, 340; VIII, 215–216. Letter to his brother Sugi Umetarō in which he proclaims Sakuma the hero of the age.

[59] See Kano, *op. cit.* (n. 15 above), p. 31.

[60] *YSz.*, I, 353.

vested with an authority they never possessed. The *bakumatsu*
generation saw many attempts to find solutions in the past for
present problems; but in the end writers such as Yoshida saw the
past as remote and irrelevant. Japan had acquiesced to foreign demands for political relations and trade out of fear and weakness.
Indecision had harmed the country when officials failed to recognize the true nature of the foreign demands and threats. Yoshida
feared that when a country submitted to outside demands it
would lose its political independence. Perhaps it was too late, he
wrote elsewhere, but still a united effort ought to be made. True,
domainal lords attached great importance to their possessions;
but their domains were not all that was at stake. "In such a time,
are not people . . . obliged to make every effort to protect the
country? Why is there time to argue over this or that domain
when there is no time for cooperation?" [61]

Yoshida expanded his theory of defense to include the protection of key points. "Although, since Edo is the seat of the shogunate, we must pay special attention to its safety, we should also
defend other areas, since we must depend upon the various lords
of the realm who are ranked below the *bakufu*." Next it was necessary to prepare the defense of Kyoto; and "then we can follow
this up by setting up preparations for the several domains
throughout the realm. If we proceed in this manner, we will
achieve a *kokutai* which clarifies the imperial way, and we will
be able to restore the military power of the imperial court of
antiquity." [62] Yoshida's class consciousness "to assist in the peace
of the realm and tranquillity of the times" became a personal mission which few, toward the end of his life, were trusted to
share. [63] He was concerned with the preservation of domainal interests only because the obligations of the samurai (*shi*) were
rooted in the *han*. When crisis transcended the individual domain, as Yoshida believed, it was necessary to arouse all groups
and to dissolve all barriers. Hence increasingly he used "imperial

[61] *YSz.*, I, 299.
[62] *YSz.*, I, 325 (*Kyumusaku*).
[63] For duties of the *shi*, see *Bukyō zenshō koroku* in *YSz.*, IV.

land" as a new unit of political space greater than its parts. The symbol of this larger collectivity, the divinely appointed emperor, assumed for Yoshida new and concrete meaning. In both thought and conduct he cut through the chain of loyalties traditionally associated with the *shi* because he discovered, in his experiments with reality, that the duties of the samurai to the domain were simply not transferable to the imperial land. Despite his expectations that samurai would unite with other groups to "wipe out the stain of humiliation," he soon learned that local ties and sinecures blinded them to any transdomainal purpose. It was clear to him at the time of his eastern trip that domainal interests must at times be subordinated to larger tasks. Only after 1855 did Yoshida call for a new kind of activist who would, like himself, abandon the restrictions of domainal daily life to serve *shinshū* in its moment of crisis. I would also argue that Yoshida hoped to arm his new activist with a new kind of loyalty.

Yoshida's first impulse was, as we saw, expulsionist; foreigners threatened the sanctity of Japan. In July of 1854 he wrote: "American ships came to Yokohama . . . and demanded an answer which had been postponed for one year since their last visit to Japan. Unfortunately we had made no preparations whatsoever in the intervening period. Fearful of a fight, the *bakufu* welcomed them heartily and permitted them to do what they pleased; and even though they violated national law, nobody in the government dared to do anything about it." [64] A few years later Yoshida argued that, although it would have been foolish to follow a strict expulsionist policy and slay the American emissaries as Hōjō Tokimune had slain the Mongol representatives in the thirteenth century, it was necessary to size up the situation carefully and then take firm action.[65] It was evident to him that the American request was merely the first step in a plan to seize and colonize Japan; Americans were expansionists masking their true intentions. Yoshida took American exploits in Mexico to heart, despite the disclaimers of the consul general, Townsend

[64] *YSz.*, I, 335.

[65] *YSz.*, IX, 50–55; IX, 53–54 (Letter to Kusaka Genzui).

Harris, that they were not interested in territorial acquisition. He
wrote in 1858 that "the United States differs from other countries" in that "it is seeking to acquire a foothold in the Pacific."
Until recently, the United States had not been imperialist because
of insufficient strength.[66]

Fear of colonization and national extinction drove Yoshida to
unexpected acts and to revision of his notion of expulsionism.
The Americans could not be killed like the Mongols. He also rejected the defensive *jōi* policy promoted by Aizawa. While in
prison during the years 1854–1855 he read the Shinron and
wrote to his brother Sugi Umetarō how unsuitable this proposal
of the 1820s was for their time:

> Even though the works of Aizawa and Shionoya [67] are indeed very fa-
> mous, a policy of preparations calling for battleships and cannon is
> awkward today. Even if these men asked at this time for large ships,
> they would not know where to seek knowledge relating to methods of
> construction. In my viewing, Shionoya's petition is simply a policy
> which suggests buying ships from the Dutch. Buying . . . is not the
> same as constructing, which requires a profound understanding of for-
> eign conditions. The policy of purchasing today is . . . ludicrous, and
> those who have humiliated us with such empty theories are a
> disgrace.[68]

Yoshida feared Westerners but took them seriously. Although he
was writing of his present, he felt that the kind of expulsionism
promoted by Aizawa had probably been of little use even in the
1820s. These views were reinforced by the signing of the commercial treaties (1857–1858) and the opening of the ports. By

[66] *YSz.,* V, 228–279.

[67] Shionoya Tōin (1810–1867), an archetypal "conservative" sinologue
who served as an adviser to the shogunal counselor Mizuno Tadakuni during the Tempō reforms. Shionoya, who possessed some information on the
Opium War, wrote an essay, *Kakkaron* (1859), in which he revealed
both the cultural conceit of a believing expulsionist and the awesome sense
of helplessness before an unyielding nemesis. See, by all means, R. van
Gulik, "Kakkaron: A Japanese Echo of the Opium War," *Monumenta
Serica* (1939), IV, 478–545.

[68] *YSz.,* VIII, 354 (Letter to Sugi Umetarō).

1856 he wrote of expulsion as a lost opportunity. "In all countries," he wrote, "there is opportunity and there is duty. If conditions are not known, then opportunity is absent. By not knowing of changing duties there can never be talented [leadership]. Today we have lost the great opportunity of the country." [69] Yoshida at one time believed that the American presence should have received an immediate military response from the *bakufu*. But he never forgot that when the Americans had granted the time to make preparations that would have delivered Japan from the threat of colonization, the *bakufu* had done nothing and most lords had done nothing. To Kusaka a few years later he wrote in despair that only those who investigate contemporary conditions will know opportunity.[70]

Yoshida restrained his xenophobia and allowed Japan to enter into relations with the West. Originally in 1854–1855 he had disapproved of Japan's signing treaties with the United States, Great Britain, and Russia, because he saw no advantage in commercial arrangements. He was fully confident of the self-sufficiency of a "natural economy," as he wrote his brother in 1854, echoing the Mito view that trade "brings only useless items from foreign countries, while Japan will lose all of its useful products." But he concluded on later reflection that closer relations would provide some advantages. Although foreign trade was not important to national wealth, and the *bakufu* might lose something by signing treaties, military strength commanded barbarian respect and could be secured through cooperation with the West.[71] "Food and clothing produced in Chōshū are adequate to Chōshū; food and clothing produced in Japan are adequate to Japan."

In the end he came around to approving foreign contact in order to make sure that the "Americans and Russians do not lose trust in the Japanese." [72] The opportunities which contact presented were enormous. "The foreigners have approached us fre-

[69] *YSz.*, II, 269–270. See Matsumoto (n. 32 above), p. 153.

[70] *YSz.*, IX, 18–20 (Letter to Kusaka).

[71] *YSz.*, VIII, 340.

[72] In Matsumoto, p. 154.

quently and impolitely . . . while our country has crouched in
fear and followed their demands for trade and relations. . . .
Flatterers might find some justification for this, but I cannot permit such wicked and unreasonable opinions. A nation should
exist for itself and through the support of other countries. Only
in a country not coerced by the powers of a foreign state is
it possible to do what we desire." [73] Independence was the
requirement of the day and the guarantee of power. "When a
country is not prosperous it will surely decline. Now if we keep
our country powerful, we . . . must not only maintain what we
have but also extend [our territory] as much as possible." [74] The
emperor Jingu and Toyotomi Hideyoshi knew this secret well,
but their methods were of no value to the present. While carefully watching over what originally belonged to Japan, it would
be possible to occupy Hokkaidō and the Ryukyus "in an un-
guarded moment," then Korea, Manchuria, China, and even
India. "We should, so to speak, keep close watch on our country
and simultaneously spread our power to nearby countries." [75]
Only two alternatives were available: to colonize or be colonized.
Success in expansion would persuade foreigners to leave Japan
alone and would earn for the country a place of dignity among
the nations of the world. Here, Yoshida believed, was the great
opportunity missed by the *bakufu*. (This argument was used
later by liberals in the 1890s to justify the Sino-Japanese War. Tokutomi Sōho disclosed his own conversion (*tenkō*) in the revised
edition of his biography of Yoshida, where he used this argument in support of his own position.)

What Yoshida demanded of the *bakufu* was a domestic order
that could withstand foreign contact. This demand became more
urgent when the treaties were signed. In outrage he wrote:

Recently . . . our shame before the barbarian has unnecessarily sent individuals to their death. This in reality can be said to be the great op-

---

[73] *YSz.*, I, 353–354.
[74] *YSz.*, I, 350.
[75] *YSz.*, IV, 151–154.

portunity. Today we have signed treaties in fear. . . . What can we say about this? We have lost the great opportunity. What must be done is to harden the people's life and correct the public spirit. By reasserting life [in this way] we would not lament and mourn over death. Being loyal to those who are at the top, the people would hereafter never turn their back to death. Talking about ships and cannon is not performing this. We have turned our backs to these necessities . . . and we have lost by this policy.[76]

Preoccupation with naval defense and cannon reflected a panic and provided no guarantee of safety. But preparation for attack required more fundamental measures. "The people are inside, the barbarians are outside. It is disastrous to deal with the outside and leave the inside behind. It is better to govern the inside first and then to regulate the outside." [77] Too often, Yoshida remarked elsewhere, men have talked about the inadequacy of defense installations after events caused by the foreigner, but nobody has considered the necessities of a sound government (*minsei*). Moved by the recent defeat of the Ch'ing state, and by his belief in the formula *naiyū gaikan,* Yoshida argued that internal political reform was the essential condition of meeting the "outer barbarian." "We should combine sound government with naval defense." [78] The Ch'ing state had adopted a policy of strict expulsion; its failure revealed how little attention the government had paid to domestic disorder. Hence "the state had bogged down as a cart caught in a rut." [79]

To achieve sound government, Yoshida at first with Mito

[76] *YSz.,* II, 270.

[77] *YSz.,* IV, 37.

[78] In Matsumoto (n. 32 above), p. 155.

[79] Yoshida was obsessively preoccupied with events in China, and scattered throughout many of his letters and essays are observations on the failure of the Ch'ing state. Indeed, to this end he even wrote an essay on the rise and fall of the Ch'ing state. The central argument of the piece is centered on the failure of the Chinese leadership to resolve domestic problems, a failure to achieve a true *minsei,* which was not responsible for the foreign invasion but certainly made it easier for the barbarian to enter China. See *YSz.,* II, 219–259.

called on the classical relations (*meibun-ron*) between emperor
and shogun—for *shinshū* still meant the *bakuhan* order. After
1858 his increasing call for unity weakened any commitment to a
specific institutional arrangement; his effort to rescue the Tokugawa system dissolved into a repudiation of it. This conversion
sprang from his inability to relate inherited assumptions about social reality to perceptions of political change. The disparity between norm and reality forced Yoshida to employ a political
methodology rather than morality. Taking his lead from Sakuma, who increasingly favored power over virtue in the reorganization of society, Yoshida made Neo-Confucianism into a theory
of political action. In changing its orientation he sacrificed its
moral content. Later Yoshida's closest follower, Kusaka Genzui,
was to take this politicization of Neo-Confucianism even further.

This use of politics as a substitute for ethics was first made (as
we saw) by Ogyū Sorai in the eighteenth century. It freed political relationships from ethical restraints and made the judgment
of good and evil dependent upon the success of a political system.
Ogyū had believed that such a change was possible only when
leaders assessed the nature of reality and formulated policies con-
forming to what they believed contemporary necessity required;
his purpose was to preserve the Tokugawa order by providing a
flexible political structure which would meet changing social and
economic demands. Yoshida was prompted by the same motive,
but events pushed him beyond it to call for a different political
system.

Yoshida first showed this shift from virtue to power in his correspondence with Kusaka. In 1856 he chided Kusaka for being
too theoretical and inflexible in his assessment of contemporary
conditions. Responding to Kusaka's assertion that nature is always the same, Yoshida agreed, but qualified his agreement by
adding that virtue changes because "it is important for people to
measure virtue in terms of its actual utility." [80] He warned Kusaka that a view which saw nature and morality as unchanging
inhibited men from creative political action. Though paradoxically he continued to share the Neo-Confucian optimism that the

[80] *YSz.*, IV, 154.

organization of society will always reflect the organization of nature, he rejected the idea of a leadership so perfect in its ethical knowledge that it relegates political activity to a lower order of experience. Yoshida saw in the idea of moral perfection the danger of meditative inactivity; he feared that a morally perfect leader had no need to involve himself in the moral progress of the rest of humanity. Moral examples or instruction were not enough to meet the problems raised by social changes. Doing, for Yoshida, was far more important than being, action more necessary than meditation.

As action (that is, constant experimentation with social reality) became more important to Yoshida, he realized that ethical knowledge and a concern for pure feeling did not necessarily lead to meaningful political acts. He also recognized that the *bakuhan* order could not produce a flexible theory of political action. Political problems required political solutions, yet contemporary leaders had failed to see beyond morality. To Kusaka, Yoshida argued that the Neo-Confucianism guiding the leadership was shortsighted and led only to the meditative excesses of Zen masters. What could be more useless in these times? Moreover, feeling and intuition were useless impulses if they were not related to practical action. "Worrying is vanity," he wrote, and if it did not inspire the leadership to act creatively, "it is of no benefit to the realm." [81] When Kusaka confessed to Yoshida how distressed he felt, Yoshida responded self-righteously that he must break out of the lockstep of Neo-Confucian abstraction for the real world of practical action. "You have ignored my advice," Yoshida charged, "and you have still not liberated yourself from worthless paper arguments. . . . You have said much in eloquent language, but I dare say that you have no idea of reality whatsoever. Everything you have said is irrelevant to practical conduct [today]. . . . I am indeed sorry for you. Again I will try to persuade you . . . to get out of these paper arguments and turn your thinking to practical affairs." [82]

At this point in his thinking Yoshida drifted to what Matsu-

[81] *Ibid.*
[82] *Ibid.*

moto Sannosuke has called "political realism," a "gallop toward political practice with the aid of traditional rules of conduct characterizing the old retainer (*kashin*)."[83] Yoshida employed a trial-and-error method, and his recommendations up until 1857 still sought to rescue the traditional order. In the *Four Urgent Points* (1858) he outlined what would constitute a sound government in the new political environment. This theory had been articulated earlier in his large philosophical tract (also written while in prison), the *Kōmō yowa*.[84] This work related Mencius to contemporary conditions; while it represents a significant moment in his intellectual development, many of its pronouncements can be found scattered in essays and letters.

His prison miscellanies (*Noyama zōcho*) reveal a concern for a government which would serve the public interest. He asked, "How can we speak of a long-standing peace today when the barbarian poses a severe threat to the realm?" Men had failed to take into account "the experiences of antiquity."[85] Order is in accordance with the heavenly Way (*tendō*),[86] while disorder represents a departure from righteousness. History discloses how men in critical situations have seized the day to transform misfortune into fortune.[87] Yoshida warned that classical examples should not be taken literally because times are different, yet he did enjoin men to admire the spirit of innovation found in antiquity. The Korean invasion directed by the emperor Jingu, the examples of Hōjō Tokimune and Toyotomi Hideyoshi, clearly demonstrate how men in the past have responded to the oppor-

[83] Matsumoto, p. 154.

[84] David Earl, *op. cit.* (n. 20 above), has depended largely on the *Kōmō yowa* as a central source for explaining Yoshida's essentially intellectual position.

[85] *YSz.,* II, 264, 266.

[86] Maruyama has explained the concept of *tendō* in its late Tokugawa intellectual context in "Chūsei to hangyaku" (n. 16 above), pp. 268ff. See also, Ishida Ichirō, "Tokugawa hōken shakai to Shūshigakuha no shisō," *Tōhoku Daigaku bungakubu Kenkyū nenpo* (Sendai, n.d.), No. 13, p. 122ff.

[87] *YSz.,* V, 97 ("Kyōfu no gen").

tunities of crisis, clarifying the imperial way and expanding the national prestige.[88] The current opportunity required an effort "to discipline the life of the people, to rectify the public spirit, . . . and to exhaust the words and works of Mencius." For the "public spirit" (*minshin*) is the trunk of a tree, while acquired skills, technology, and weapons represent the branches. In a Mencian mood Yoshida advised strengthening the "public spirit" by increasing the wealth of the people, who would then have more reason "to love those who are above them and to die for the lord." He continued:

The essence of a public polity is the theory which governs the people. The essence of national politics exists in recruiting men of ability (*kensai*). Those who manage the government today have not exploited all the sources of talent in the country. What is required of able men in running the realm? If they practice principles leading to prosperity, if they demonstrate loyalty, if they stress rewards and enrich allowances, and if they employ the people of the realm in these efforts, then they will recognize military opportunities, then they will know what a sound government is.[89]

Yoshida argued that in his time the notion of a true *minsei* had disappeared. The feudal period (*hōken no sei*) had brought severe distress to the peasant. During the Three Dynasties in China (Hsia, Shang, Chou), he recalled, even though each peasant was taxed a portion of his land's yield, the load was light and government was administered benevolently. But in the Tokugawa period in Japan, the taxation was such a burden that it undermined the peasant's personal livelihood, threw him into indebtedness, and turned him against the regime. It was an axiom of wise rulers, he argued, citing classical examples, to take from the wealthy and to enrich the poor. Such a procedure, he believed, was a sure guarantee of uniting ruler and ruled and of avoiding rebellion and revolution. Because unity was Yoshida's main purpose, he tried to define the limits of a sound government, pleaded for the dissolving of social barriers in a time of cri-

[88] *YSz.*, II, 270; also *Yūshūroku, YSz.*, I, 355–365.
[89] *YSz.*, II, 276–277.

sis, and in the end called for complete sincerity (*shisei*) among all groups. At one point he argued that it was the duty of the shogun and his ministers to defend the realm from foreign encroachment. We saw that he discarded this argument and looked elsewhere for defenders because Chinese history taught him that once governments resort to mismanagement, there is no way of avoiding mass disorder and revolution. Because Japan belonged to the emperor, he urged all people, despite the mismanagement of the *bakufu,* to assume responsibility for defending the "land of the gods" from the barbarian.[90] Officials should watch daily, listen to grievances in rural areas, attend to the hamlets, and distribute relief where it was most required.[91] This incipient populism also marked the various restorationist movements of the early 1860s.

It was a basic premise of the *bakuhan* system that the ruled played no role. Tokugawa practice gave the samurai a monopoly of power, but disguised its military basis by attributing virtue to them. Neo-Confucianists rationalized this distance between government and governed by a universal ethic of social discrimination. Yet Yoshida was calling for massive cooperation as a condition of the defense of *shinkoku*. The differentiation of high and low was dissolved in a higher expression of "sincerity," which here meant willingness of all to die for the imperial land. This plea for participation of the ruled in politics was contrary to the *bakuhan* system and its Neo-Confucian pieties. Further, Yoshida was a short step away from substituting the imperial land for the *bakuhan* system, the emperor for the shogun, the imperial retainer for the domainal retainer.

Yoshida, until his very last days, sought desperately to work within the traditional political framework. His insistence on rescuing as much of the older system as he could is remarkable. The reason for this is not clear: perhaps it was a lingering class consciousness obliging him, as a samurai, to preserve order and tranquillity. Old ideas die hard. Yoshida still held in 1858 that do-

[90] *YSz.,* III, 378.
[91] *YSz.,* VI, 391ff.

mestic order was possible if designations and duties (*meibun*) were observed—but with qualifications. "Those who occupy high-ranking positions carry out political doctrines; those who are *shi* and clerks must refine their scholarly skills; and the peasant, artisan, and merchant must work diligently at their various occupations." Despite the resemblance of these words to the Mito statement, Yoshida added a new tone to it. The discrimination he was talking about sprang not from inviolable moral categories but from occupations. "We must always prevent the lower order from showing contempt for their superiors," and this was possible only if they were governed benevolently and shared in the responsibility of defense.[92] But also in several passages Yoshida laments the relaxation of status rules. Society must be immediately restored to order, beginning with the samurai who have slipped into a shameful state brought on by peace and tranquillity. The weakness of the samurai was found both in their indifference to military training (documented since the eighteenth century) and in their neglect of civilian skills (*bun*). His ideal was far from the unlettered warrior of the sixteenth-century *sengoku bushi* period. Yoshida, like Fujita Tōko, accepted the inseparability of military skills and civilian arts in the samurai. This was what distinguished them from the rest of humanity. Yet he was careful to specify what kind of learning he meant by civilian arts: practical knowledge that pertained to administrative tasks and taught people world conditions.[93] This practicality would instruct the upper orders in their functions and correct boundaries of conduct.

Yoshida found himself after 1857 in an insoluble dilemma. He tried to retrieve traditional principles which he believed were universal. Yet when he stripped them of their historical associations, which he felt had replaced the principles they were supposed to illuminate, they were no longer recognizable. Classical writings, he wrote, should be respected, not because of their actual historical content, but because of the spirit of enterprise

[92] YSz., III, 85, 133–134.
[93] YSz., IV, 178ff (*Shōka sonjukuki*).

they reveal. But this was to hold the past at arm's length.[94] Yoshida believed that such writings were classics because they illustrated how men in different circumstances revealed sincerity, loyalty, and practicality in their conduct. The specific content of their action was not applicable in other times. Only an investigation of contemporary needs could reveal to men how they must proceed. "The realm is not made by heaven and earth," he wrote to Kusaka in 1856, "it is made by men. Our approach to affairs must always be based on our assessment of what is needed."[95] Only the present can be known—and this only after an evaluation of "opportunities." The present is the only stage on which the individual can act. The success of an action is measured less by its results than by the sincerity motivating it. "We have to be of firm belief," he wrote in another letter, "and we have to be prepared even for giving ourselves to a just cause." Action is measured by the willingness of the actor to assume responsibility for personal decisions and by a disposition to practicality. Mencius, Yoshida said, warned against those who refuse to assume personal responsibility for things said; words have meaning only when men are willing to put them into action.[96]

Yoshida's examples of loyalty show that he was more concerned with proving his own sincerity than with achieving a specific result for a superior. Loyalty had to be stripped of all historical associations. It served only the present, and since the present kept changing, so did the actual requirements of loyalty. Hence it is not surprising that he declared late in his life that his loyalty was undifferentiated. In 1855 he argued to Mokurin, one of his trusted friends who was also a Buddhist priest, that loyalty to the *bakufu* and to the emperor were really not two different acts; loyal devotion to both represented the Great Obligation (*tai on*) of the last two hundred years.[97] A year later he rationalized his

[94] Matsumoto, p. 154. For an interesting contrast see J. R. Levenson on the late Ch'ing writer Liao P'ing in *Confucian China and Its Modern Fate*, 3 vols. (Berkeley and Los Angeles, 1965), III, 3–15.

[95] *YSz.*, IV, 142. See also Matsumoto, p. 155.

[96] *YSz.*, IV 154.

[97] *YSz.*, VIII, 423, 424.

argument and said that as a retainer of the Mori house, "working day and night in their service," he was also serving the emperor. True, the last six centuries had shown how the lords of Chōshū (and by extension many others) had flagged in their devotion to the emperor. Under present conditions, he wrote, it was his duty to point out how his lord might once more express loyalty to the emperor.[98]

Yoshida rationalized received notions of loyalty and pursued what he called a path of righteous conduct. In an uncertain environment he decided for himself what had to be done, because his sense of loyalty was directed more within than toward some specific object such as the emperor. His reorientation of loyalty led him to attack the *bakufu* as traitorous. But this grew not out of confusion over the object of loyalty, but from an understanding of conditions. If problems arise in the territory of the shogun, they must be handled by the shogun; if in the domain of the lord, by the lord.[99] The problems facing Japan in 1856–1857 were not restricted to the shogun or the lord—they involved all because they pertained to the imperial land. It was necessary then to treat these problems with means suitable to the whole realm. It was the emperor, not the shogun or the daimyo, who commanded loyalty, because the crisis imperiled all of Japan. "This affair arose from within the territory (*shinshū*) of the emperor." Only a loyalty flexibly serving contemporary needs and stripped of historical associations and specific objects would do for such times. Just as Yoshida could say that service to the Mori or to the shogun was service to the emperor, he could also say that service to the emperor was service to his lord and to the *bakufu*. This reverse formulation made Yoshida a revolutionary.

A GATHERING OF HEROES

Until the signing of the commercial treaties, Yoshida supported a moderate policy in which the decisive elements of political so-

[98] *YSz.*, VIII, 518ff (Letter to Mokurin, 1856); also III, 595.
[99] *YSz.*, IV, 142.

ciety (court and shogunate) shared power to present a much-needed united front (*kōbugattai*). Yoshida had misgivings about the capacity of the *bakufu* to act decisively since the events of 1854, yet he settled on a policy less extreme than expulsion and cultural xenophobia suggested. By uniting "the sound arguments of the imperial court and the correct business of the eastern castle [Edo]," he wrote in February 1858, "unnecessary traditions and obstacles will be removed under the pressure of the day to preserve the divine land." [100] He called for a restoration (*chūkō*) of the true principles (*seiron*) of emperorism and of the *bakufu,* and reminded the Japanese that it had been long-standing practice of the shogunate to protect the correct theory of imperial authority. But this moderation dissolved into petulant impatience and extremism when the *bakufu* ignored an imperial decree calling for an end to treaty negotiations and for the immediate expulsion of all foreigners. Yoshida's response to this shogunal failure sprang from outrage at the danger in such a repudiation for political order and national survival. His turn to extremism was prompted more by a quickened sense of emperorism than by expulsionism, which, as his subsequent course showed, served as the condition for his theory of emperorism. Troubled and angered, he threw himself into the stream of political extremism, in which up to this time he had only dabbled in hopes of dramatizing his loyalty and sincerity and the need for a creative program.

His impatience spilled over first into a vicious critique of shogunal conduct and polity, and then into a call for the destruction of the *bakufu*. In the *Jigi ryakuron* (July 1858) he proposed a five-point program to deal with the *bakufu's* recent act of disloyalty: (1) to clarify in detail the *bakufu's* disobedience of the imperial expulsionist decrees; (2) to discuss how to rebuke the *bakufu;* (3) to support the emperor's rejection of the "ugly barbarians"; (4) to explore how to tranquilize the emperor and secure his pleasure; (5) to gather knowledge in anticipation of similar occurrences, and to prepare the right kind of policy "to manage revenge." [101] The guilt of the *bakufu* was clear; the violation of

[100] *YSz.*, IX, 18.
[101] *YSz.*, V, 199–205.

virtue in ignoring an imperial decree was intolerable and could not escape punishment. This program, Yoshida believed, involved the proper combination of time (*toki*) and of principled loyalty (*gi*). Paraphrasing Confucius' commentary on the *I Ching,* Yoshida proclaimed that true greatness was shown when contemporary conditions were dealt with by loyal action.

Yoshida, in the remaining two years of his life, relentlessly dramatized with spectacular deeds the tenacity of his belief, in hope of raising up a movement of men who, like himself, would risk everything to serve the requirements of reality. The twenty-one-times-courageous samurai of earlier dreams was metamorphosed into the madman (*kyōfu*) and the divinely inspired fool (*gu*). His identification with a madness and folly which undercut established pieties is the measure of his sincerity and willingness to act on what he perceived.

Around 1858 Yoshida began to employ in his writings these twin metaphors of madness (*kyō*) and foolishness (*gu*). Precedent for this usage could be found as early as the Muromachi period (fourteenth and fifteenth centuries). The celebration of "madness" in Yoshida Kenkō's *Tsurezuregusa* (*Essays on Idleness,* written in the fourteenth century), or by the outrageous Zen monk Ikkyu, had affirmed a new concept of personality willing to break with precedent to do justice to a reality which few were able to perceive. Madness was understood as the gift of those who see reality more deeply and sharply, and who must therefore behave in ways which most will interpret as eccentric. In the last years of the Tokugawa shogunate, men of high purpose—*shishi*—found no other alternative than to represent themselves and their exploits as mad and foolish. A good example is Rai Mikisaburō, a son of the illustrious loyalist author Rai Sanyō, a confederate of Kyoto loyalists such as Umeda Unpin and Yanagawa Seigan, and a close friend of Yoshida's; he explained that commoners do not recognize opportunity and are destined to follow custom and precedent in blind obedience. The "madman" must break through the stagnation of established procedure to pursue his own vision of reality. Likewise Fujita Koshirō, son of the *shishi* Tōko whom we know, related that he was called "a

vulgar, mad (*kyō*) traitor." And Seki Tatsunosuke, a participant
in the Sakuradamon incident, was, as he himself put it, "entitled
to be called 'mad.'" It was not rare among loyalists in the 1850s
to employ *kyō* as one of the ideographs in their names: Yamagata Aritomo, an original member of Yoshida's school (Shōka
sonjuku), was known as Kyōkai ("concerned with madness");
Kido Kōin as Matsukiku Kyōfu; Shinagawa Yajirō as Shunkyō;
Takasugi Shinasaku as Toyo Ichikyōsei; Hirano Kuniomi as
"Chinzei [the old name for Kyūshū] no Kyōkaku [mad guest]";
and Yoshida himself often used the name of Chomon Kyōgatsu
("mad fellow").[102]

Yoshida's essays "Kyōfu no gen," "Zoku kyōfu no gen,"
"Guron," "Zokuguron," and others, composed in 1858, use the
new tactic, and disclose the anguished but deeper sense of reality,
the paralyzing anxiety and fear, which this perception unleashed.
Hysteria was the emblem of the new fear, but it was reinforced
by an inner confidence that what he saw was true and what he
advised was right. "Since men do not yet perceive (*shirazareba*)
the crisis confronting the country today," he wrote shrilly, "I
have truly made an explosion with my plans and have been
driven mad. Despite madness I must, however, speak out; and if
my ravings are not heard or heeded, I have no doubt that the
state will collapse. How will the plan be carried out and the crisis
averted? Who indeed will carry out such a plan?" The madman
of course. But on closer inspection he is, as Yoshida says, none
other than the twenty-one-times samurai of an earlier dream.[103]
Yoshida no doubt had himself in mind when he envisaged the
death of the madman who would be "heard by the sages"; and
his subsequent call for a rising of like-minded men implies that
he is the leader. The hero, mad and foolish, but wise in knowledge of a reality that few perceived, needed a following. To Irie
Sugizō, his most trusted and lasting follower, he wrote in March
1858, how apposite he found Li Cho-wu's famous phrase—"finding a hero among the masses is like snagging a fish in the well."

[102] Haga Noboru, *Bakumatsu shishi no seikatsu* (Tokyo, 1965), pp.
15–16.
[103] *YSz.*, V, 106.

And while he called for a rising of men to take hold of affairs, he was already thinking about the contours of a *culte du moi*.[104]

Beyond these traditional elements, madness had new psychological implications. Norman O. Brown in his recent book *Love's Body* has called attention to the schizophrenic who sees and lives a reality more real than that which is accepted on consensus. This too has been the claim of mystics, and certainly the history of Taoism and Buddhism in Eastern Asia offers numerous examples of the madman who in one sense is not mad at all. Whether the sources of Yoshida's "madness" are located in the Buddhist-Taoist tradition or somewhere else is irrelevant, since he emphasized how much he was out of time by labeling himself a madman, a fool.[105] But who was mad and who was sane? What was real in the 1850s and what was illusion? Madness allowed Yoshida to dramatize the threat to national survival and also provided him with a new sanction for what Bernard Silberman has called "non-traditional behavior."[106] In one of his poems, Yoshida says that the madman is free of history and personal ambition, and should be loved because "he knows what must be done, while the fool shuns advantage and disadvantage."[107] He also affirmed that the presence of the madman really meant "a concern for intelligence and virtue," but he despaired because intelligence had become the instrument of opportunism and virtue had been eclipsed by hypocrisy. Yoshida knew that many "talented samurai have become opportunists and many villagers are virtuous," and this truth represented a reversal of conventions. But he also confessed that when he "viewed current events with the eye of an insect" and found nothing being done, "I emit anger and become a madman."[108]

Yoshida as *madman* was a critic who stood outside of society.

[104] *YSz.*, IX, 286.

[105] See Kano (n. 15 above), pp. 46–47.

[106] See Bernard C. Silberman, *Ministers of Modernization* (Tucson, 1964,) for the working out of this concept of nontraditional behavior in the late Tokugawa setting.

[107] *YSz.*, VIII, 205.

[108] *YSz.*, VIII, 65.

As *fool,* he was completely engaged; every action of his was informed by sincerity, he was a man without a shred of self-interest. All in all he shows us a new kind of personality intent on alerting Japan to what was happening, a new kind of leadership coming to terms with the new reality. In his last year, when he broke with virtually all his disciples, only Irie Sugizō and his brother Nomura Wasaku clung to his ideal. This suggests that his concept of leadership either made impossible requirements or was impoverished. But the mad fool who "corrected loyalty and clarified the Way, who was unmoved by profit and merit" became the model of the "unattached patriot" in whom Yoshida invested the defense of *shinshū.*

As we saw, the occasions for Yoshida's madness were the *bakufu's* decision to sign the commercial treaties and its disregard of an imperial decree. Yoshida no doubt overreacted. He reasoned that the *bakufu,* in acquiescing to foreign demands, showed an embarrassing lack of leadership and planning, and in disobeying an imperial decree, expressed contempt and disloyalty. The *bakufu* had committed a crime of unprecedented magnitude: "It has abjured heaven and earth, angered all the deities . . . it has nourished the national crisis of today and bequeathed to future generations national shame. Opposition to a heavenly decree invites the barbarian externally; internally it menaces the several lords. When a man becomes rigid like porcelain, then only one domain is injured; but when the shogun fails to act, then the entire realm is imperiled. . . . If the decree is honored, the realm is following the Way. To destroy a traitor is an act of loyalty (*gi*)." [109] In apocalyptic tones Yoshida spoke out, hysterically and angrily, and his words were the words of a "madman" who sought against all odds to expose deception and alert society to a terrifying future. Officials had lost sight of what was taking place in the political landscape, "of real facts, and are left without the will (*kokoro*) to act." [110] The absence of a plan showed how far

[109] *YSz.,* VII 192–193.

[110] *YSz.,* I, 242; also see Kano Masanao, "Kindai shisō no hōga," *Iwanami kōza, Nihon rekishi,* (Kindai I), p. 305.

leadership had been paralyzed by reliance on a hereditary system of recruitment. Chaos, he wrote to one of his associates, was everywhere because of government officials (*daishin*) who preached endlessly about loyalty but "whose hearts are filled with hatred." [111] His own plan was pointless enough: an attempt to assassinate a shogunal emissary, intended to demonstrate in action the meaning of devotion. But his incapacity to formulate a coherent plan suggests that he was only concerned to carry out "purposeful action" in the hope that a new program might be revealed to him through it.

Yoshida was less vague on the kind of leadership he had in mind for Japan. The *Words of a Madman* and his last letters center on the need for leaders who are competent, loyal, and sincere. He was reviving views already stated by Fujita Tōko, but with a new twist. *Kaikoku* and more recent events had gone beyond the narrow world of the domain. Hence it was useless, Yoshida argued, to depend (like Tōko) upon a traditional mode of conduct. *Hōken* was being replaced by *shinshū,* a wider political space, and the change required new kinds of leadership and political action. Yoshida's constant complaint was the survival of hereditary leadership which had been removed for generations from changing realities. "Political power today," he wrote, "is controlled by upper-ranking samurai. It is a private preserve of a hereditary aristocracy, and it does not extend to lower-ranking retainers (*koshin*)." [112] Hereditary officials, he complained to Irie, had become numbed to reality and were wrapped in a life of "wearing silk brocades, eating precious foods [lit. pearls], hugging beautiful women, and fondling lovable children." [113] There was a great deal of hostility in Yoshida's sneering condemnation of those who wielded power and enjoyed its emoluments, but his life-style revealed that he himself was really not interested in frivolities and pleasures. In his *Essay on the Times* (*Jiseiron*), writ-

[111] Kōsaka Masaaki, *Japanese Thought in the Meiji Era,* trans. David Abosch (Tokyo, 1958), pp. 38–39.
[112] YSz., V, 102–103.
[113] YSz., IX, 286.

ten in September of 1858, he warned that *"Shinshū* will become a possession of the barbarians," despaired how few lords were available to protect Japan from invasion and colonization—the fate of India and China.[114] It was useless to depend upon leaders at either shogunal or domainal level for the defense of the country.

To meet the challenge of a unique historical crisis it was necessary "to seize the day, for such an opportunity will not come again in ten thousand generations."[115] It was a crisis, he observed, in which the principle of reality was undergoing a profound transformation, the political landscape was changing before his very eyes. He alone saw it. To be sure, Yoshida called endlessly for "the gathering of talented men," a system of merit, rewards and punishments for the conduct of official duties, and even the consultation of "public opinion." But many other concerned contemporaries were invoking these traditional palliatives. Yoshida went further to designate the kind of leadership required by the crisis. He quoted with approval the famous phrase of a not-so-famous Chinese statesman of the lesser Han Dynasty, Ssu Ma-hui, that "those who know the exigencies of the times will become heroes."[116] It is possible that he always hankered after becoming a hero; and while much of his writing proposes cooperation with key domainal and shogunal figures, it does not identify *them* as heroes. Paul Claudel somewhere remarked that youth is a time of heroic intensity; and Yoshida Shōin, who was a very young man, conveyed heroism in his notion of leadership. In *Words of a Madman* he exposed the essential incompetence of class privilege and power and advised recruitment by objective standards of talent and ability. He also called for incentives to the lower orders, and urged that if talent were rewarded, "one hundred abuses will be removed." This notion of an able and alert leadership, only a rehearsal of established opinion, was transmuted to serve as the basis of Yoshida's "heroic leadership," which was announced early in 1858. Until then he could believe

[114] *YSz.,* V, 250.
[115] *YSz.,* V, 251; IX, 363 (Letter to Takasugi Shinsaku, April, 1858).
[116] *YSz.,* V, 144.

with Sakuma that a tightening of leadership was all the times required; his appeal to *jinzai* and *jitsugaku* was reformist. His decision to abandon this position in 1858 rested on the conviction that the problem of *gaikan* had become even more complicated and more perilous, and the the *bakufu* was responsible through its repudiation of imperial edicts.

It is a paradox in Yoshida's thinking that, while he clamored, down to the end of his life, for talent and ability as the criteria of official recruitment, at the same time he called for a unique hero and a loyal band of followers. This dual program was accepted by his younger contemporaries, especially his students Kusaka, Yamagata, Maebara, Takasugi, and Kido—men who went on to change the course of political events. And it also served, I would argue, as a guiding principle for the Meiji Restoration of 1868, which was inadvertently set in motion by Yoshida's desire to supply Japan with competent administrators and yet simultaneously find a place for leaders like himself.

Yoshida's achievement was impressive. More than any of his contemporaries he single-handedly defined for the future its standards of leadership and action. He took up the earlier (and at times subversive) Confucian principle of "talent and ability" (*jinzai*) and transformed it into a concept that by expressing his own discontent appealed to members of his generation. After Yoshida, personality and leadership were indissolubly connected. He rejected what struck him as the fixed norms of official conduct required for the leader in favor of the authority of his own feelings. In organizing reality, he trusted his own perceptions more than the official view that reality followed nature. But his personal feeling was accessible to others because it sprang from the problems of his particular generation. A survey of the ages of those who, like himself, became politically active in the 1850s and 1860s will bear out this assertion. Yoshida was twenty-nine when he died, and at this time his followers were all younger than he: Maebara Issei was twenty-six, Irie twenty-three, Matsuura twenty-three, Katsura (Kido) twenty-five, Takasugi twenty-one, Kusaka twenty, Okabe twenty, Yamagata twenty, Inoue Bunta twenty-three, Nomura Wasaku eighteen, Shinagawa seventeen, and Itō nineteen. Beyond his immediate circle Sakamoto Ryōma was in his twenties when he became involved in national affairs and thirty-two when he was assassinated; Nakaoka Shinatarō died of wounds in 1867 when he was twenty-nine, Mutsu was twenty-four at the time of the Restoration, and Iwasaki was thirty-three years. The oldest among major participants were Ōkubo Toshi-michi who was thirty-eight, Saigō who was forty, and Iwakura who was forty-three. The Meiji Emperor himself ascended the throne at the age of fifteen.

Political action at the lower levels of society had fallen into the hands of younger men. Much of Yoshida's conduct and thinking were shared by his contemporaries and represent a compulsion to find a role for himself in a changing society. Seeing that estab-lished means of identity support were failing, he tried to fashion a new personality suitable to the emerging reality, and combined it with an older concept of leadership. In rejecting what we have seen as the received notion of a public personality he worked out a more comprehensive concept of leadership embracing, unlike Confucianism, a psychology. These innovations resulted from the crisis of identity which Yoshida experienced on the threshold of maturity, a crisis so severe that he never overcame it. Its require-ments maimed him for the few years that he was to live as an adult. We know this because he tells about it. Only a few writers in the Tokugawa period were as autobiographical as Yoshida: Motoori earlier, who suffered a comparable crisis in youth; Umeda Unpin; Sakamoto Ryōma; Maki Izumi, whose ten years' imprisonment forced him back on himself; and perhaps Yokoi Shōnan. The very existence of confessional data shows that per-sonality was being deeply affected by new events; by new tech-nological knowledge; and by the failure of established institu-tions, behavior, and modes of perception to provide support and security. Yoshida supplies the clearest evidence, since he took on the problem of leadership in order to save Japan from invasion and colonization. Yet his concern for the destiny of Japan was inextricably linked with his personal psychological problems.

Like all youth, Yoshida no doubt was seeking permanence in the midst of change; his perceptions of change as it accelerated explain why he panicked and sought extreme solutions. Even in a normal time he would, as Erik Erikson has said, have experimented with the most extreme possibilities offered by society for identification.[117] *Kaikoku* created a sense of historical dislocation and removed existing possibilities for identification. A rapidly changing reality quickened Yoshida's natural disposition to find a public role. But all traditional roles available to someone like him seemed irrelevant to his own needs and to the new needs of society. Erikson has also written that adolescence is a time when the individual either achieves or fails to achieve historical perspective, "a sense of the irreversibility of significant events and an often urgent need to understand fully and quickly what kind of happenings in reality and in thought determine others, and why."[118] Yet youth is limited in its choice: that tradition at hand which is the legacy of its own civilization poses the dilemma of confirming or denouncing existing roles. This narrowness of choice is counterbalanced by youth's power to sit in judgment on what history is offering it. At the point of intersection where the life-history of the young meets public history, the cultural endowment of their fathers, a critical decision is made: individuals either are or are not confirmed in their identity, societies in their style of life. Historical estrangement of a whole generation is always a possibility; especially when youth, as in the generation between *kaikoku* and the Restoration, fails to find an identity that fits its childhood expectations of peace, order, stability.

The coming of Perry and the signing of the commercial treaties discredited the established belief in a natural order and exposed the *bakufu* as an ineffective and irresponsible institution which could not deliver the tranquillity and order youth had been taught to expect. Moreover, this human failure coincided with

[117] Erik Erikson, "Youth: Fidelity and Diversity," in *The Challenge of Youth* (New York, 1962). See also Erikson's brilliant handling of a historical personality, *Young Man Luther* (New York, 1958).

[118] Erikson, "Youth," p. 14.

failures in nature (a cholera epidemic, earthquakes, drought), which surely were interpreted by contemporaries as signs of imminent destruction. The ineffectiveness was at first located in an incompetent officialdom, rather than in a defective institutional system—although the criticism was none the less revolutionary. *Bakumatsu* ideologues led by Yoshida Shōin did not immediately attack the existing arrangement of power and mode of recruitment in the domainal administrations, which were already open to younger men of lower samurai status who demonstrated "talent and ability." Their criticism was leveled at shogunal officials, whom they pictured as older men, or as men whose techniques—custom and precedent—were obsolete. Yoshida's cry for "talent and ability," his search for an able leadership, his obsession with heroism, all reveal his anxiety to find an identity consistent with his perceptions of social reality, to secure a public role, to enter history. But it was a new history that he was trying to enter. Natural immodesty obliged him to count himself among the talented and able. The youth and anxiety common to himself and his peers made his message understandable to them. Others reached similar conclusions. Some of his closest friends, such as Kido and Itō, realized the promise of his expectations in a truly revolutionary event, the Restoration.

Yoshida, as I have tried to show, had abandoned the bulk of what passes for history. He demonstrated in an early willingness not to confirm the roles which society was passing down to him. His confusion appears after 1854 in his inability to decide between reform and rebellion.[119] Precisely this inability became the source of his later charisma. After *kaikoku* and during the treaty negotiations, Yoshida saw the steady dissolution of a history which he had been taught since childhood to view as an inheritance. Dissolution of history meant dissolution of roles; and this is one reason why, in his last year, he turned to urge the dismantling of the shogunate. It was not, as I will show, the only reason. Circumstances called for extreme measures; and yet, extremist as he was, Yoshida was reluctant to scrap his inheritance com-

[119] *Ibid.*, p. 24.

pletely, and justified his actions by invoking traditional sanctions. This reassertion of a fugitive Confucianism, though not unique with him, reveals something about the nature of his confusion; it suggests that he was trying to resolve his crisis by impulsive attempts to end what Erikson has described as the moratorium with sudden choices. It is true that for Yoshida "talent," "ability," and "practicality" as techniques were historical possibilities in theory only. The central problem, as he saw it, was to affirm fidelity, *shisei:* sincerity of intent, commitment to a course of action which would lead to his death.

The search for fidelity, according to Erikson, is characteristic of youth in its general struggle for identification. Youth confirms the received roles when it can accept the essential fidelity of the inheritance handed down by an older generation. When it cannot, it searches frenetically elsewhere. Yoshida Shōin, when he invoked terms such as *shinsei, makoto no michi* ("the true path"), *shinjitsu* ("real truth"), was reacting to the infidelities of late Tokugawa society. The balance between fidelity and diversity, between agreed morality and experimentation, between durability and change had collapsed, so he judged; and in the swamp of moral hypocrisy, where "black-hearted officials" were concerned with frivolities rather than with "correction," all that was left was the achievement of "a superior fidelity in the fatal pretense" of being mad and foolish.[120] Yoshida's consistent clamor that he alone was being "sincere" has a striking resonance today in those who denounce their elders and what they have to offer as hypocritical and irrelevant. His last testament—the self-pitying *Ryūkonroku*—is a final expression of his unwavering sincerity: if heaven acknowledges his fidelity, then surely so would the *bakufu*.[121] During his last imprisonment, when he was about to be sent to Edo for a high-level interrogation, his thoughts are constantly on sincerity; and he describes himself to his contemporaries, immodestly, with a fitting quotation from Mencius, "Never has there been one of complete sincerity who did not

[120] *Ibid.,* p. 6.
[121] *YSz.,* IV, 503–504.

move others." Actually, this was the advice he offered his student peers of the Shōka sonjuku.

The notion of a higher fidelity was not new, but Yoshida's understanding of it was. Preoccupation with fidelity and sincerity (*makato-shisei*) had become an essential feature of Neo-Confucianism during the Tokugawa period. It was associated with criticism of excessive emphasis on *kei*—reverence, duty, and loyal service.[122] Official Neo-Confucianism, for official reasons, was centered on *kei:* it was concerned with values guaranteeing public performance of duties. The various efforts to accommodate Neo-Confucianism to changing sociopolitical realities by writers as diversely oriented as Nakae Tōju, Kumazawa Banzan, Yamaga Sokō, Itō Jinsai, and Kaibara Ekken shared the celebration of *makoto*. The exterior realm of duty and service was eclipsing the interior realm; the heart was becoming shackled; men were losing the sense of a vital center, inner freedom.[123] While early Tokugawa critics sought to make this sense of interiority serve the requirements of outer duty, later critics put external conduct at the service of the internal realm. For the later writers, *makoto* presupposed that the contours of external reality were uncertain, and it placed the responsibility for suitable behavior on an intuitive sense of what was relevant and appropriate. This shift explains the investigation of social conditions which many late Tokugawa ideologues clung to as an operational technique in the new landscape. The new formula made action possible; but it often required, as with Yoshida, abandoning received modes of conduct. For Fujita Tōko, fidelity (*shisei* or *makoto*) meant competence in official service; for Yoshida it meant experimentation in the possibilities of action and commitment. Specifically, Yoshida equated fidelity with action rooted in reality (*jitsu*), and reality could not be found in "empty theorizing." Rather, the pursuit of reality "followed the real facts of the day." Closely associated with this analysis of fidelity is the idea of "concentration." Ac-

[122] Sagara Tōru, *Nihonjin no dentōteki rinriken* (Tokyo, 1964), pp. 15ff.

[123] *Ibid.,* p. 16.

tion, Yoshida insisted, requires choice; once a decision is made, the actor must "concentrate on this one thing" he has selected. Yoshida was trying to provide ethical guidance in the new situation where received moral norms were disintegrating. Ethics here is seen as proper choice and action. For Yoshida, Maki Izumi, and notably Yokoi Shōnan, fidelity was truthfulness toward others. As Yoshida often said, it passed to the heart of other men and moved it. When he lamented that "he does not yet believe this to be so," he was saying that he was not permitted to fulfill certain possibilities which fidelity required of him.[124]

Yoshida's experimentation with fidelity hardened into a disciplined devotion. The strength of mature fidelity is gained, writes Erikson, "in the involvement of youth in such experiences as reveal the essence of the era they are to join . . . as beneficiaries of its tradition, as the practitioners and innovators of its technology, as renewers of its ethical strength, *as rebels bent on the destruction of the outlived.*"[125] Yoshida selected, for reasons already enumerated, the last-named course; when he first tested the range of inherited possibilities, he stayed within acceptable limits, but in the end he chose extremism and revolution. He spent his last two years translating his youthful psychological maladjustments into political rhetoric, first as a teacher, and then as a would-be leader of a band of heroes. Teaching, however revolutionary, could easily be justified under the rubric of tradition; in Neo-Confucianism there were only sage-teachers, not political leaders. But teaching could not satisfy the requirements of his newly acquired perceptions. Just as he was willing to discard outlived practices, so was he willing to exchange the role of teacher for that of the patriot-leader. Teaching was inadequate to express a fidelity that might move men. Since his vision required constant action and practice, he sought to reshape his students into a band of hard-core activists willing to share the mystique and risks of *shisei*. He felt also that teaching was too passive and too closely resembled the "empty theorizing" he condemned in oth-

[124] Sagara, p. 28.
[125] Erikson, "Youth," p. 23.

ers. Action and practice (*jikkō*) satisfied his inner need to "order
the world" and served the great task of character formation. His
personal anxieties were thereby made accessible to others for his
generation, and together they sought to find in sweeping political
change a solution of the psychological problems they had inherited from society. It was Yoshida who provided the adhesive.
"The essential thing was the appeal of abandon and of action, the
presence of a danger which alone permits the spirit to gather
itself." [126] Yoshida defined the métier of danger and action. He
needed a following to whom he could offer the insights derived
from his youthful psychological malaise, and also the example of
his simple and austere commitment. This following in turn authenticated the new yearnings and frustrations of his vision. Austerity and simplicity, always emblems of revolutionary commitment, were inextricably a part of his program for action. His
statue at Hagi, although idealized, captures his character: frailty,
austerity, overpowering zeal in his chosen cause. To show his
good faith, he forsook all pleasures. He found salvation through
sloughing off all that was not essential: smoking, drinking,
women (the only woman he apparently had any contact with
was his sister Chiyo, to whom he wrote frequently). He was prepared to offer himself as an example which would show, he
hoped, that the steps of deliverance were solitude, danger, and
death. But he needed a following—not just because the task was
too great for one man by himself, but also because a following
would confirm his vision. In the end, to escape the collapse of his
cause and his failure to find fidelity even among his peers, Yoshida's mind turned to death. For the action which equipped him
with his will also gave him a sense of fatality.

Yoshida Shōin's *culte du moi* was to be realized in the rising of
unaffiliated patriots (*sōmō no shishi*).[127] These Japanese min-

---

[126] R. M. Albérès, *L'Aventure intellectuelle du XX*ᵉ *siècle* (Paris, 1959),
p. 52.

[127] There have been several efforts to date to pinpoint the "rising of
unattached patriots." See Kano, *Nihon kindai shisō* . . . (n. 15 above),
p. 56ff; also Naramoto Tatsuya and Matsuura Rei, eds., *Senkakusha no shisō*
(Tokyo, 1966); pp. 19–20; 91–93. These writers agree that Yoshida's letter

utemen were to be recruited from those samurai who, like himself, had abandoned regional commitments and had begun to operate across domains. His early wanderings around the countryside and his efforts to strike up lasting relationships with likeminded *shi* from other *han* were the origin of the *sōmō no shishi*. His call for a rising was not a means to recruit "heroes" from all walks of life.[128] Yoshida's appeal did transcend social boundaries to reach those of roughly the same age as himself, because he was speaking a language they could understand. True, Takasugi Shinsaku's later conscript army (the Kiheitai) in Chōshū cut across class lines, and has been seen as an enlargement of Yoshida's earlier theory of a rising. But Yoshida was calling for a band of followers willing to leave the domain, while Takasugi's conscript army was formed to defend the domain. Also, the members of Yoshida's academy (the Shōka sonjuku) were mostly samurai—only a few like Irie and his brother Nomura were lower samurai, *ashigaru*—while the Kihetai recruited peasants.

Yoshida Shōin's fear of invasion, his revulsion at the incompetence and contempt of shogunal officials, and his sense that he and others like him were denied roles of responsibility, all together forced him to take matters into his own hands. When he was convinced that no inherited public role was worth playing, he turned to creating new roles and a new history in which he might find a place. It was at this juncture that he changed his orientation from reform to revolution. His call for a rising was effective because it appealed to both private and public ambitions; disloyal hereditary officials, who had to be replaced, were leading Japan to the doom of foreign invasion and cultural ex-

---

to Kitayama Yasuyo (Sakuma Shōzan's nephew) in April 1959 is the first explicit statement of the theory. Actually, evidence can be mustered in letters and essays written in 1858; and, of course, the ideal was with Yoshida long before.

[128] Many writers have argued that his call included not just samurai but also peasants and merchants. Nothing in any of his writings I have seen even remotely hints at this conclusion, even though later restorationists, Kusaka and Maki, called for recruits from the lower orders.

tinction. Yoshida expected the new patriots to follow him into paths of action which he, not they, selected. Extremism replaced gradualism; cooperation with officials was abandoned for direct action. The *bakufu* had already dismissed any hope of coopera- tion when it ignored the court's decree to "ward off the barbari- ans" and consented to commercial treaties designed to sap the strength of Japan.[129]

It is difficult to determine whether Yoshida's isolated remarks about the shogun's disloyalty add up to the proposal (*tōbaku*) to destroy the *bakufu*; he did work recklessly to limit the *bakufu's* arbitrary exercise of power. But he never wholly made up his mind to destroy the world—the *bakuhan* system—in which he hoped to find a place for his talents. "There is an opinion," he wrote on one occasion to Kusaka in July 1858, "that by erecting towering devotion to the emperor, loyalty to the *bakufu* will be lost." [130] Elsewhere he wrote, at about the same time, that "men who are party to Kii [Ii Naosuke's wing in the shogunal bureaucracy] are all evil, while those who are assisting Hitotsu- bashi are all loyal retainers." I suspect that Yoshida's new theory of leadership proceeded in stages. Once he had determined on ridding the *bakufu* of incompetents, it was an easy step to call for abolition of the institution itself. He saw leadership as part of political structure; after he had exposed the inefficiency of the leaders, he turned to an evaluation of shogunal structure. "The world of today is like a decaying old house (*rōya*). . . . I think that a great wind will arise and topple (*tempuku*) it over. If later we replace the decaying timber and abandon the broken raf- ters, and if we construct it anew by introducing new lumber here and there, it will be a most beautiful sight." [131]

Yoshida was not sure of the line between renovation and demo- lition, but he knew that renovation was like "waiting for the waters of the Yellow River to run clear." The government should have recruited outstanding men who, from the very beginning,

[129] *YSz.*, V, 199–205.
[130] *YSz.*, IX, 70–71.
[131] *YSz.*, VI, 122.

could have dealt with the barbarian rather than ignore him until it was too late. But it had failed to do so.[132] Since cooperation had been rejected by the *bakufu,* the opportunity "to build a new house" had fallen to men, like Yoshida, willing to consider extreme possibilities. Ability gained men admittance to positions of responsibility; but courage and action in the name of loyalty distinguished them from their fellow samurai. Something of Yoshida's great plan is seen in his dealings with the extremist Courtier Ōhara Shigenori; in his plot to seize Fushimi prison; and in his proposed ambush of the palanquin which carried the shogunal official Manabe Akikatsu to Kyoto. The last-named scheme was "an opportunity that was lost and which must be regretted." "Living in the divine land at this time, can we sit by and look on as spectators?" Yoshida asked, in defense of the expulsionism which had been rejected by the *bakufu.* "How can we plan for heroes? We have to watch for opportunities and then seize them." Thus he and Ōhara, in dealing with the *rōjū* Manabe, planned to seize Kyoto and defend it by calling the unaffiliated patriots to the city where they might "fight off the *shi* from all directions." Failure to carry out some such plan, Yoshida feared, would dash all hopes of *jōi* and "lose the great opportunity of restoring the prosperity of *shinshū.*" [133] And he continued: "If there is no rising of unaffiliated patriots, there will be no prosperity. How will these unaffiliates reinstate a sage emperor and wise lords? Men who follow my aims and are of my domain must follow this rising. Through the unauthorized power of the rising, small men will be excluded, evil men will be thrown out, and correct and able lords will be able to gain their places. This good news will be spread throughout the divine land and our hand will be rewarded." [134]

Yoshida's "Great Plan" was indistinguishable from his personal ambitions, as he admitted several times in his last letters. Only imprisonment prevented him from continuing to carry out what

[132] *YSz.,* VI, 128ff.
[133] *YSz.,* VI, 222–223 ("Yōkasaku chu-i," 1859).
[134] *YSz.,* VI, 224.

he believed (as he wrote to Takasugi) to be an "unyielding obligation." "I am not one to bide my time," he wrote on many occasions; he hoped the untarnished example of his own devotion would inspire others to join this "rising." Self-sacrificing to a fault, he constantly reminded his disciples (who looked upon themselves as peers free to make their own choice of action) of abstinence and denial.[135] Echoing a saying of Sakuma's, Yoshida advised that "injuring the national spirit is no small thing," and because "loyalty to the emperor is an unusual fact, I cannot employ conventional means to accomplish it." In that tense time, "if heaven has not abandoned *shinshū,* there will be a rising of heroes." [136] True loyalty and true fidelity are absent among those who hold office (*zaikan*) and those who are on stipends (*zairoku*). Loyal men must be recruited, he insisted, in an obvious reference to himself. "When one aims at performing true loyalty, he is exiled, and if he plans a rising of patriots, he cannot be moved." [137] The classic statement of this rising he expressed in a letter to Kitayama Yasuyo, a nephew of Sakuma's, in April 1859. "We have arrived at the juncture where we must grieve for the security of Japan. There are none in the *bakufu* who know what is happening; there are none in the country who are able to come up with a plan. From the year 1854 down to 1856 or 1857 there have not been any ships. Yet how will we be able to stem the rush if it should come from Washington or London? Since most officials of the *bakufu* are concerned more with luxury than service, there are only one or two men of remarkable character among them." Yoshida feared that incompetence and official indifference would open the way to foreign control. He warned:

Japan has been free for about three thousand years. How, one morning, will we be able to bear its control by other men? If we do not give rise to a Napoleon and announce our freedom (*furēhēdo*), it will be

[135] *YSz.,* IX, 275–276. In this letter to Irie Sugizō he boasts of his abstinence.

[136] *YSz.,* IX, 297, Letter to Odamura Inosuke, Kubo Kiyotarō, and Kusaka Genzui (March 29, 1859).

[137] *YSz.,* IX, 238 (Letter to Sase Hachijurō).

most difficult to cure the pain in our heart. . . . Even though I have tried with little influence to do my best, since last year there has been little or no profit from my efforts. They have only gotten me into jail. When a person speaks recklessly of these various matters, he is charged with a crime. Today, since most officials in the *bakufu* and the lords are drunkards, they do not even work for their stipends. Nothing outside of the emergent patriots can be depended upon.[138]

So insistent was he in his call for men who would abandon everything, he established requirements that most could not meet or understand. Himself sparse, ascetic, and disciplined, Yoshida expected of his followers the same self-sacrifice. On more than one occasion he reminded those around him how he had not eaten or taken saké for long stretches of time.[139] It was not a time to drink or to dissipate, for the body must be free to act.

Yoshida's demands were so harsh that he eventually broke with many of his friends and disciples. In the end he believed that he alone understood the real meaning of fidelity or "righteous action." His last letters reveal loneliness, the conviction that only he was a true loyalist, and an awareness of suffering for his truthfulness. In the face of adversity he had always pursued loyalty, while his friends performed flamboyant acts for self-gratification. He did not celebrate "righteous and loyal" action to show valor and courage, as he warned his most devoted follower, Irie Sugizō, in self-pity, but to reflect principle. This loyalty and principle imply personal responsibility. Purposeful action and personal responsibility marked a new kind of leadership, and also helped form personality.

Yoshida's search for fidelity in leadership and personality was not a program but an example of commitment. His description of leadership reflects his own behavior. His concept of leadership served to justify his own exploits, which were as adventurous and thoughtless as those of his enemies. But when he condemned others for recklessness, especially his former pupils Takasugi, Kusaka, and Katsura Shōgorō (Kido), they thought they were fol-

[138] *YSz.*, IX, 325–326.
[139] *YSz.*, IX, 275 (Letter to Irie, March 16, 1859); 263–264 (Letter to several friends); 252 (Letter to Irie, February 5, 1859).

lowing the path of "righteous behavior" and "justice" which he
had charted. Still he felt that all they showed in their exploits
was self-interest. When he urged them to act with determination
in a righteous cause, "to rise above the superficialities of traditional behavior," and refuse "to be satisfied with the petty or
commonplace," he was inviting them to perform independent
feats.[140] Yet Yoshida never spelled out clearly what he meant by
righteous action or fidelity.[141] He condemned the very behavior
he had inspired. His followers had available only his own commitment to action. Yoshida's real purpose, despite his advice that
the hero must not rely on others or expect anything from the
world, was to establish a personal cult; he hoped that his example, rather than encourage his student-peers to perform "meritorious acts," would inspire men to follow him into a course of his
own choosing. His censure of Kusaka, together with Kusaka's
confusion after Yoshida had been executed, makes it clear that
his followers failed to grasp his central message: the hero whom
he spoke of was none other than himself.[142] The conflict between principled loyalty (*gi*) and self-interest (*ri*) was far more
real than most Tokugawa ideologues saw. For, while Yoshida
could rationalize his own conduct, however reckless, as an expression of "principle," he could likewise condemn comparable actions of others as an expression of self-aggrandizement. Yet he
did hope that the future would fall into worthy hands; that his
death, which he so compulsively sought, might inspire "one or
two men of steadfast will to rise up and uphold principle and
loyalty." [143] If Japan had not vanished, there might still be time
for a massive "rectification." [144] Only in death would the meaning of principle in the hero's life be fully understood. Death represented for Yoshida a way of overcoming that personal failure
which he feared more than anything else. His last letters are
drenched in the necessity to control one's death, and the impor-

[140] *YSz.*, II, 26; also IX, 122, 192, 239.
[141] See *Kōmō yowa* in *YSz.*, III, 145, for Yoshida's notion of bravery.
[142] See Kano, "Kindai shisō no hōga" (n. 110 above), p. 313.
[143] *YSz.*, V, 234, 254
[144] *YSz.*, IX, 470.

tance of dying well. For Yoshida suicide was too easy and the expected returns too slight.

Neither the *bakufu* nor the lords, he complained in his last letter to Sakuma, could be counted on. "Where will the restoration of Japan's prosperity come from?" Everybody, including the foreigners, he wrote elsewhere, "knows more than the *bakufu*."[145] It could be argued that the aim of Yoshida's insistence on leadership and action was restoration. Expulsion (he believed by 1858) was the means to meet the contemporary crisis, which, if unchecked, would prevent a revival of prosperity. Yoshida's romantic restorationism, as far as I can determine, was synonymous with retrieving the "security and prosperity of the divine land." Earlier in the *Kōmō yowa* he had argued eloquently that the emperor had always received reverence, since it was a requirement of the office, but that his elevation "above the clouds," completed in the Tokugawa period, was in fact a sign of decline and contempt.[146] The intensity of his concentration on the emperor and his celebration of *kokutai* are well known, but they do not explain why he sought restoration or what it meant to him.

Apparently the refusal of the *bakufu* to accept the imperial decree prompted Yoshida to call on the emperor as a legitimizing principle. The refusal imperiled Japan's political security; restoration then meant simply the defense of the country. The structure of loyalty was not shaken. The *bakufu,* which had always simply represented a link in this vertical chain, was being removed because it was no longer functioning the way it should. Yoshida never intended a conflict in loyalties between lord, shogun, and emperor. He announced his unwavering loyalty to his domainal lord, Mori Yoshichika; and argued earlier (letter to Mokurin, August 1856) that this expression of loyalty was also loyalty to the emperor. This sentiment marks the later *Jiseiron;* and also the hysterically argued *Taigi o gi-su,* where he declares the shogun a national criminal who deserves punishment.[147] He proposed that Chōshū *han* should take the lead in expressing *taigi,*

[145] *YSz.,* IX, 321 (Letter to Nomura Wasaku, April 4, 1859).
[146] *YSz.,* III, 261.
[147] *YSz.,* V, 192–194.

arouse the realm in a torrent of indignation, and ultimately isolate the shogun. He would have approved of Yanagawa's declaration that the title of *Sei-i-tai Shogun* ("barbarian-conquering gen-
eralissimo") is meaningless, because the shogun had failed to
carry out his jurisdiction. The national gods were worried too,
for the realm stood on the brink of total collapse. "No plan has
succeeded in rectifying loyalty and principle or in clarifying the
Way. It is the teaching of the sages that to revere an imperial decree is the Way; destroying disloyalty is principle." The great
duty for his time, he urged, was illuminating virtue; and this
could be done only by rendering the imperial court secure. The
safety of the court ensured the continued independence of Japan.
Public wrath, inspired by Chōshū, would point to *taigi;* "the
American barbarians would shrivel and retreat," and the "rise
and prosperity (*kōryō*) of the imperial court awaits the flick of a
finger." [148]

By 1859 Yoshida was willing to jettison the *bakufu* completely.
This did not necessarily mean abandonment of the *bakuhan* system. He merely was recommending the removal of one element,
and looked to the domains, notably his own *han,* as the new pro-
tector of the imperial court. "We cannot forget either the virtue
of the court," he wrote in 1859, "or the obligation of the *han.*
The strength of the unaffiliated patriots will maintain the main
domain [Chōshū] close at hand, and in the long run it will assist
in the restoration of the imperial court." If the example of Chōshū, he continued, is followed by others, such a policy of restoration is possible.[149] But Yoshida failed to set clear priorities in the
face of the foreign threat. Did his call for restoration mean simply expulsion of the barbarian? Or did he have in mind, now
that the removal of the *bakufu* was a condition of Japan's independence, a more comprehensive reorganization? Yoshida raised
such questions but never offered answers. His suggestion that the
unaffiliated would work immediately to shore up the *han,* but in
the distant future would assist in the restoration of the court,
hints that he was even prepared to abandon the domain for a un-

[148] *YSz.,* V, 192–193; also 204.
[149] *YSz.,* IX, 326–327.

itary political structure. In face of the conflict between the demands of a unitary structure centered around the emperor, and the growing domainal interests, Yoshida proposed to suppress sectionalism in favor of the higher principle of central authority (*sonnōron*). But he did not realize the tenacity of domainal interests.

He felt the trauma of *kaikoku* and the threat of colonization so intensely that he never saw the distinction between internal and external requirements. His reliance on *jōi* prevented both him and Maki Izumi from ever realizing the existence of two separate demands. Nothing in Yoshida's writings reveals any concern to rebuild the *han* as an autonomous unit or to enlarge its economic and military facilities. He looked to Chōshū first because he believed he could find unaffiliated patriots there. But his plan for restoration suggests that these men would ultimately operate in a wider political space, the imperial realm. His adherence to Mori was instinctive and sentimental; and while he never wished to do his lord any disservice, time and time again he disclosed in his actions that he knew what was correct and loyal. His actions were always undertaken in full knowledge that they would be interpreted as an affront to the lord and to the domain. This indifference attests Yoshida's willingness to write off the *han* along with the *bakufu* from any renewed political structure. In April of 1859 he wrote in despair to Mori Yoshichika, who was then on his regular spring trip to Edo; failing to persuade his lord to stop off in Kyoto and urge the emperor to move against shogunal treason, he once more resorted to personal initiative because he knew best. His words sting with indignation: "We do not talk about the times, nor do we talk about conditions. When we come up against things that are possible, we are either put in jail or put up for decapitation. It is useless to try to talk to our lord about acting directly for emperorism and expulsionism. It is better to prepare and present (*sashiageru*) him with something like an incident relating to *sonjō*."[150] This bold statement is a genuine expression of how Yoshida reacted to established author-

---

[150] *YSz.*, IX, 351 (Letter to Irie Sugizō).

ity. He had earlier indicated to Sase Hachijurō that none among the domain's officeholders possessed "true virtue, true loyalty." His actions after the unauthorized eastern trip are never bound by domainal restraints. "If emperorism and expulsionism," he wrote in late spring of 1859 to Ōkabe Tomitarō, "does not change the world today, then nothing will." Yoshida may not have been too careful about the objects of his loyalty; but his willingness to act leaves no doubt that he was serving the larger cause of national independence. And his decision to act, even at personal peril, liberated the idea of loyalty from blind obedience on the one hand and abstraction on the other hand.

Experience moved Yoshida toward an increasingly realistic and rational position. His ultimate concern, as he reminded his associates, was not "a deceptive plan" (*kensa*) but sincerity and fidelity; it was not power (*chikara*) but loyalty and principle. Discrimination alone, which informed him of loyalty and the Way, served as the unique standard guiding action. He explained this a year before his death: "Today the fidelity and sincerity of the emperor rules over the realm. If the universe were covered with this great truth, then the men of the realm would act according to sincerity." [151] No other consideration than loyalty to the emperor ever entered his deliberations, he tells us; and his short life is too well documented for us to question this assertion. His responses had accelerated as his perceptions quickened. There was still barely enough time to act and to create new guidelines for actions; to change principles of conduct into conformity with a new reality which he alone saw; to rationalize the value system in such a manner that men could bypass the failing chain of command and appeal directly to the emperor. When he wrote Mokurin in 1856, he argued everything he was to argue in his last year: an unambiguous announcement of purpose, and a fitting, though premature, epitaph.

There are some who grieve and worry about the barbarian; there are some who, having become indignant about the barbarian, are anxious

[151] *YSz.*, IV, 100–102 (1935 Edition).

about the imperial court. . . . We know that the barbarian is a national disease and must be resented. Taking into account the broad reasons of the barbarian, we know that the state could collapse. We know that the profound grief of the imperial court is not a temporary thing. Whether this anxiety is basic or peripheral we have not yet been fully able to decide. . . . Grieving or feeling anxious about the imperial court occurs when one gets indignant about the barbarian. Confusing essentials with nonessentials, we will in truth fail to grieve for the imperial court.[152]

Indignation and anger over the barbarian was a natural unreflective response. But it was the end result of a more basic feeling: anxiety for the fate of the imperial court. And this anxiety represents a basic shift in the orientation of his own thinking, and in much of the dialogue that was to follow in the 1860s. Yoshida's new awareness of emperorism suggests that in his mind *kaikoku* could be accepted if only the imperial court was protected. The shogun, as military leader in charge of defense, had failed to exercise his charge. Failure dissolved into acquiescence with continuing foreign demands. Yoshida changed from a simple samurai, obliged to face the enemy for the welfare of the country, to what he called an "imperial retainer" taking up his post on the side of the emperor. He was thereby creating for himself and others the possibility of new roles. Destruction of the inherited political structure and its restraints on recruitment might create a new public role which would allow him to exercise his ability. In the end this quest for such a role led him beyond modest proposals for reform to revolutionary acts aimed at the destruction of established institutional life. Just as he refused to confirm the endowment which was supposed to confer identity on him, he also repudiated, in the name of a higher loyalty, the role of domainal retainer for the larger and newer possibilities offered by the changing political landscape.

[152] *YSz.*, IV, 189–190, "Mata yomu shichisoku" (1856).

V *Rehearsal*
for Restoration

Among his many anxieties, Yoshida Shōin feared most that his death might go unnoticed. Death, he urged his youthful followers, was the price men of action always paid if they were "to rise above the superficialities of traditional behavior" and refuse "to be satisfied with the petty and commonplace." While he hammered on the theme that the hero must act without fear of death (*kanshi*), Yoshida anxiously hoped that these words and the action which vindicated them would not die with him.[1] His vision of leadership was never fully worked out, and somehow the unaffiliated patriot was transformed into an "imperial retainer." He never comtemplated an end to crisis, when Japan would move to a new stage of development and require a new kind of leadership. He did speak of "times for change" and "the period for the complete alteration of the country," and he saw hope in violence and bloodshed. But he could not see beyond the task of preserving Japan from invasion and colonization, for which he wanted to die. He hoped that the future might fall into worthy hands,

[1] See Maruyama Masao, "Chūsei to hangyaku," in *Kindai Nihon shisōshi kōza*, 8 vols. (Tokyo, 1961), VI, 390ff.

and that his death might inspire "one or two men of steadfast will to rise up and uphold . . . principle and loyalty." [2]

In part Yoshida established the Shōka sonjuku to recruit a personal following. It was a small, tightly knit group of fellow retainers in their late teens and early twenties. Even before Yoshida's execution several had tried to carry out his teachings about principle and loyalty, and afterwards they tried to outdo the teacher. In particular, a handful of recruits from Chōshū attempted to make once again the kind of history he had taught. With the assassination of the shogunal counselor Ii Naosuke in 1860, there began a new kind of play, a veritable *chanbara* (Japanese horse opera), with the imperial capital of Kyoto as its stage. Principle spilled over into passion, which hatched terroristic plots. In this drama down to 1864 major roles were filled by graduates of Yoshida's academy. The common residence of these activists in Kyoto diminished domainal affiliation. They had all come there either to promote or to prevent new schemes, in flight from their domains, to talk, to drink, to intimidate children and small animals on the streets, and to die. The name of the play was *Restoration,* and the restorationists who played Kyoto in the 1860s were forced to rewrite and recast the script. But like all rehearsals, the Bunkyū years (1861–1864) made opening night in 1868 a success.

These events cannot be separated from the contemporary political prophecies and justifications of terror and violence.[3] The actions from the assassination of Ii Naosuke down to the defeat of the *sonjō* groups in 1864 are often of doubtful motivation. Those who lifted their swords against foreigners and shogunal officials

[2] YSz. (chap. 4, n. 1), V, pp. 254, 334.

[3] The best, which is the most complete, account of events relating to Kyoto in these years is in *Ishinshi,* ed. Ishin shiryō hensankai henshū, 6 vols. (Tokyo, 1942), III, 24–58, 75–94, 207–223, 242–253, 329ff, 621; briefer accounts are found in Tōyama Shigeki, *Meiji Ishin* (Tokyo, 1954), pp. 81–115; and Sakata Yoshio, *Meiji ishinshi* (Tokyo, 1960), pp. 126–165. In English the best survey of this period is W. G. Beasley, *Select Documents on Japanese Foreign Policy* (London, 1955), pp. 47–90, which is a remarkable summation of information culled from the *Ishinshi* version.

(or, lacking them, against townspeople), who hatched vague restorationist plots in the back rooms of elegant Kyoto restaurants,
were often also writers. They could not lay claim to the scholarship of Sakuma Shōzan, which took more time than they could
afford; to the imagination of Yoshida Shōin, whose vision many
followed; or to the originality of Yokoi Shōnan, who was under
house arrest during the years before the restoration. Yoshida
hoped that revolutionaries like Ōhashi Totsuan, Kusaka Genzui,
Arima Shinshichi, Hirano Kuniomi, the fellow conspirators of
Nakayama Tadamitsu, and the instigators of the Yamato Gojō
coup would leave their domains to concentrate their devotion on
expelling the barbarian and restoring the court to prosperity. The
maddest of them all was Maki Izumi, the possessed Shinto priest
(*shinkan*) of Kurume. From 1860 on, the streets of Kyoto, the
quarters around the shogunal palace in Edo, and the foreign
quarters of Yokohama were unsafe for moderates. Broadsides
were posted everywhere condemning one official as a traitor, announcing the forthcoming assassination of another, demanding
the expulsion of all foreigners from the "divine land." Kyoto was
the most active, especially after the removal of the Satsuma daimyo Shimazu Hisamitsu in the spring of 1863. Power to intimidate lay in the hands of an eccentric group of activists from Chōshū and western Kyūshū, protected both by Chōshū *han* and by a
faction of extremist courtiers.

These years saw a rise of the court's power in national politics,
and hence the enlargement of Chōshū's role. The extremism
committed in the name of the throne and silently sanctioned by
the Chōshū domainal administration marks a shift both in the the-
ater of political activity and in thought. The national power of
Mito *han* declined after 1860, owing to its retainers' complicity
in the assassination of Ii, the death of Nariaki, and a debilitating civil war; so did the Mito school of political thought. *Kaikoku* had destroyed its vision, and events after 1854 had discredited its moderate admonition to rectify social relationships. Mito
writers had sought to restore the *bakuhan* order and to clarify
the position of the shogun and the daimyo within it; nowhere do

they hint at dismantling it. This was first proposed by Yoshida and carried out by *shishi* who came to Kyoto in the early 1860s. Despite their program of *sonnō,* Mito writers meant nothing more revolutionary than to tighten the system—even though at the expense of the shogun. The concept of *sonnō,* as we saw, was changed by Sakuma, and even more by Yoshida, who in his last years wished to end sectionalism and destroy the *bakufu.* The Mito solution was irrelevant by 1860, and only Ōhashi Totsuan made a desperate attempt to renew it by politicizing its central ideas. The new understanding of *sonnō* corresponded to a radically new concept of the emperor, inspired in large part by nativists from Motoori through Suzuki Shigetane. Both Sakuma and Yoshida helped give the emperor human dimensions and a political role. Literary activists like Maki Izumi, trying to take contemporary political experience into account, gave even fuller expression to this new vision of an emperor who would lead a movement of patriots and rule the country. Through his devoted commitment to action in the 1860s, Maki tried to initiate political events that might lead to the elevation of this new-style emperor. Behind the respectable screen of "restoration" Maki's real purpose was to raise the emperor to direct political authority. This change was closely associated with Yoshida's general injunctions to act out of principle and loyalty. While Chōshū displaced Mito as the extreme element in national politics, while Kyoto displaced Edo as the setting for the new politics, the idea of *sonnō* underwent a corresponding change. The Mito view of reverence as an abstract principle of political authority did not inspire men to self-sacrifice. But an emperor who was also an active principal in politics could lead men to perform the maddest actions in the name of devotion. Men came to Kyoto to act and to die, not because of expulsionism but because of emperorism.[4]

Emperorism, as Yoshida had argued, attracted men who believed the *bakufu* was denying them roles of political responsibility, by the hope of more and different official posts. Hereditary allocation was indissolubly linked to shogunal foreign policy. This is

[4] Cf. Sakata, *Meiji Ishinshi,* p. 140, for another view.

the meaning of Yoshida's call for the destruction of the *bakufu* and his declaration that he was an "imperial retainer." Expulsionism was employed by "disaffiliated" activists to force the issue between court and *bakufu,* and to bring about sweeping reorganization. I have no doubt that ideologues such as Yoshida, Maki, Arima, and Kusaka were sincerely if neurotically antiforeign. But shogunal officials also embraced expulsionism, and they openly acknowledged their dislike of foreigners. To argue that activists embraced *sonnō* merely to underline their expulsionism is only possible under the hypothesis that such men as Yoshida and Maki were operating under Mito presuppositions; and I have argued that this was not the case.

The emperor of the Bunkyū era had already acted politically by issuing an imperial ordinance, or allowing it to be issued under his name. The activists saw him as no longer a prisoner of an abstract ethical system (*ōdōron*) but rather the maker of the Way, a personality who no longer needed the *bakufu* as his mouthpiece. When Maki Izumi called for an imperial army to march on the *bakufu,* he was summoning not a philosophic principle but a human emperor who would lead his forces directly into the campaign. Mito speculation saw the emperor only as an ethical anchor, never as a visible leader animating devotion among the new generation to destroy the *bakufu*. Men could never have found in Mito a theory leading to the destruction of the *bakufu* under imperial sanction.[5] The Mito retainers who assassinated the shogunal counselor Ii Naosuke at the Sakuradamon in 1860 were dramatizing how far the system celebrated by Fujita Tōko and Aizawa was out of line.[6] Nothing in their act suggested either the speedy removal of foreigners or the imminent dismemberment of the *bakufu*. Yet in the span of a few years this attitude changed. The change is already noticeable in Yoshida, who finally called for demolition of the *bakufu* as the surest way to deal with the foreigner; it was ambiguously stated

[5] See Sakata Ikuto, "Bakumatsu ni okeru kindaiteki tōitsu kokkaron seiritsu no zentei," *Nihonshi kenkyū* (July, 1966), Vol. 85, pp. 74–75.

[6] *Ishinshi,* II, 716–723.

in Ōhashi Totsuan's crude restorationism, and in the abortive plot to assassinate Andō Nobumasa in 1861 (when he saw first the necessity of removing the *bakufu*); and it reached a crescendo in Maki Izumi, who provided intellectual inspiration and political leadership to what came to be known as the *sonnō jōi* movement of the early 1860s. The major aim of this movement was restoration of direct imperial rule to combat shogunal incompetence and foreign encroachment.

Despite the announced expulsionism of the *sonnō jōi* activists (better referred to as restorationists), xenophobia defined only their mood, not their program; although it was sincerely felt by the *sonnō jōi* activists, it often misrepresented their efforts and concealed their projects. We may characterize the movement in six points.

Activists in the early 1860s employed the idea of expulsionism (*jōi*) to what they correctly perceived as a dangerous penetration of foreign capital now that several ports were open to trade. Thus the major essays of Kusaka Genzui (the *Kairan jōgi* and the *Kaiwan shirigoto*), written in the early 1860s and restorationist in mood, deal with the financial drain threatened by the commercial treaties. Kusaka and his associates saw, rightly I think, not only the inequality imposed by foreign nations in these treaties (especially, low tariffs on imports) but also the disastrous flight of specie from Japan threatened by such trade.

The moralistic slogans which *sonnō jōi* intellectuals confiscated from the Mito rhetoric gradually, during the early 1860s, acquired a warlike tone. As Yoshida had predicted a few years earlier, action suggested new political goals more relevant to problems of the day than moral pieties of another time.

Seizing new political possibilities made available by experiment took activists along a route which ended by denying the system itself. Despite Yoshida's final advice to destroy the *bakufu*, activists of the *sonnō jōi* persuasion arrived at this conclusion only after their involvement in political events in the early 1860s. The emperorism in their thinking prepared them to face ultimately the problem of "shogunal guilt." Respect for the emperor provided them, when the time came, with a broader arena of political action, the nation—since the emperor, unlike the Tokugawa, symbolized no special interest but rather all of Japan. Also in the early 1860s Yoshida's theory of "a rising of unaffiliated patriots" was realized. The various coups of the Bunkyū years testify how far this idea was put into practice. The *sonnō jōi* activists found in Yoshida's theory of an uprising and in his academy a theory of organization stressing horizontal, not vertical, relationships. The restorationist groups of the 1860s provided an organization where disaffiliated men might meet to pursue a common purpose, as equal comrades, freed of narrow domainal obligations and the restraints of status.

Thus the various restorationist groups drifted toward an uncompromising emperorism that rejected any such figure as the shogun and denied the basic principles of the *bakuhan* system. These restorationists in Kyoto aimed at seizing power, nominally for the emperor; to achieve this purpose they unleashed an impressive number of lightning-like coups or "incidents." The rebellion of Yamato Gojō (engineered by a disaffected group called the Tenchūgumi), the military rising of Ikuno, and the disturbance of the Tengu party suggest how far activists could put themselves outside the boundaries of established order. A cursory examination of the social organization of these groups strongly suggests that they recruited supporters from different regions of the country and status groupings (varying degrees of samurai, wealthy peasants, rural moneylenders, lower-ranking courtiers); and that they emphasized camaraderie, which had little in common with the rigid behavioral expectations of the vertical loyalty system in the domains.

The theorizing of the *sonnō jōi* activists deepened awareness of crisis and sensitized contemporaries to shogunal incompetence and its indifference to imperial opinion. Hence activists argued that when the imperial will was ignored, denied, or frustrated, there was cause enough to pass beyond the structure of authority (the

Tokugawa arrangement) and restore power where it belonged. This was certainly the case with the famous political change of August 1863, when an imperial campaign, composed of troops from Aizu and Satsuma, was called to oust the Chōshū loyalists from the streets of Kyoto. This symbolic possibility was later translated by restorationist activists into a major principle in the formation of an anti-Tokugawa army consisting of disaffiliates. Loyalists such as Hirano Kuniomi and Maki Izumi pinned their vague dreams of an imperial restoration (*fukko*) to the efficacy of the imperial will to raise a "righteous" and "loyal" army for a campaign against the *bakufu*.[7]

Those adherents of the *sonnō jōi* groups who survived the coups of the early 1860s were regrouped into a domainal movement calling for "destruction of the *bakufu*" (*tōbaku*). After extremists were driven from Kyoto in late summer of 1863, they sought to retrieve their lost opportunity. This effort was planned by Maki Izumi, but when the restorationist coup against shogunal officials in Kyoto came off prematurely, violence exploded after the Ikedaya incident of July 28, 1864. (Ikedaya was a shipping agency of the Satsuma *han*, where Maki and his followers fought with troops from Satsuma sent to dissuade them from acting.) A few weeks later Sakuma Shōzan, serving as a *kōbugattai* mediator in Kyoto, was unexpectedly assassinated. The clash which claimed the lives of Kusaka and Maki, the "Disturbance of the Forbidden Gate" (*kimon no hen*), took place later in the summer of 1864; loyalists, mostly from Chōshū, were routed at the Imperial Palace, dispersed, hunted, and killed. Out of the ashes of this defeat was formed an anti-Tokugawa movement deriving its strength from large domains, which, through a policy of *fukoku kyōhei*, prepared themselves for the life-and-death struggle with the *bakufu*. This theory was first set up by the Kumamoto retainer Yokoi Shōnan; it was executed by former loyalists like Takasugi Shinsaku and Ōkubo Toshimichi. I shall return to these men in chapter 7.

[7] See Tanaka Akira, "Bakumatsu no seiji josei," in Iwanami kōza, *Nihon Rekishi* (Kindai I), pp. 147–148.

The loyalist activists called for by Yoshida in his naïve theory of a rising (and who later congregated in Kyoto to make the city unsafe for man and beast) were probably inspired by the examples of Rai Mikisaburō, Umeda Unpin, and Yanagawa Seigan. Yoshida knew these men, especially Umeda; he was lumped together with them by the shogunal authorities during the purge of 1859 (*Ansei taigoku*). The loyalists Umeda and Yanagawa were members of a group called *oshitsu shōsei-ha* devoted to serving the court. They were finally stamped out by the purges of 1859; but they provided activists not only an example of an organization centered in Kyoto, but also an emperorism (*sonnōron*) stripped of Neo-Confucian moralism.[8] The *oshitsu shōsei-ha* combined two traditions: the loyalism of eighteenth-century courtiers such as Yamagata Daini and Takenouchi Shikibu, and the restorationism of the nativistic followers of Motoori Norinaga. As Yoshida was beginning to call for action against the *bakufu*, Umeda, acting as spokesman for the Kyoto loyalists, expressed his unhappiness at makeshift domainal organization and the inability of lords from large *han* to arrest the decline of the realm.[9] Before Yoshida, Kusaka, or Sakamoto Ryōma had expressed such doubts, Umeda publicly gave up on the lords. And like his younger colleagues, Umeda reposed confidence in people like himself. "How many men are there like me," he asked solemnly, "who have moved the country in recent times?" His answer was predictable: not many but enough to rescue the realm. How would they rescue it? "Imperial authority," Umeda wrote, "exists in the bright, heavenly descendant. We must strive ardently day by day in order to know how to restore antiquity. After a thousand autumns, how should the patriotic and courageous warriors (*yūshi*) endeavor to do this?"[10] There is a hope here, but no clear program. Umeda has been compared with both

[8] See Haga Noboru, *Bakumatsu shishi no seikatsu* (Tokyo, 1965), p. 264ff.

[9] Shibahara Takuji, "Hanbaku shosei ryoku no seikaku," in Iwanami kōza, *Nihon Rekishi* (Kindai I), p. 191.

[10] Aoki Kaizō and Sabaku Chūzō, eds., *Umeda Unpin ikō narabi den* (Tokyo, 1928), p. 16.

Fujita Tōko and Yoshida Shōin, and some writers have seen him
as a spiritual leader.[11] Certainly the letters of Kusaka Genzui or
Takasugi Shinsaku reveal admiration for Umeda. In the company of *shishi* he was a pillar of strength; in the eyes of shogunal
authorities he was an attendant to the ruling family. Together
with the poet Yanagawa, Rai, and Ikeuchi Tōshō, Umeda in the
oshitsu shōsei-ha established political connections with courtiers
and was condemned for its activity, allegedly subversive, in the
wake of the Ansei purge.

Unlike others who were to follow (Maki, Ōhashi, Kusaka),
Umeda was an imperial loyalist, but not one of the restorationists
committed to political action. But like others in 1859 he was the
victim of a purge which made no effort to discriminate between
sedition and nonsedition. The *bakufu* cut a wide swath in a desperate attempt to restore authority in the face of rebellion, confidence in the face of doubt, and order in the face of social
failure. The times confirmed doubters that things were not correct. The autumn of 1859 was rainless, following a hot and dry
late summer; crops were threatened with ruin. In May cholera
had struck Nagasaki, then spread throughout the west and advanced upon Osaka and Kyoto. By August cases were being reported in Edo and the epidemic had increased in virulence. All
these events were viewed as portents of a great calamity. Japan
then was, of course, helpless in face of cholera. Panic and rumor
were rampant, and the "public spirit," we are told, was unstable.
The foreigner was already in the land, and in the countryside
there appeared hysterical chiliastic cults. These cults are marked
by their rejection of corrupt times (*ee ja nai ka*), by their inspiration from popular Buddhism and nativism (*shintō*), and by their
frenzied "dance to correct the world" (*yo naoshi odori*). Their
persistence in the countryside was a constant reminder of the
new uncertainty.

Reflecting this new psychology of mass hysteria, the *bakufu*
held the ceremony of inspection tours by *yin-yang* specialists.[12]
What had been only a ritual observance was taken very seriously

[11] Haga, p. 249; *Ishinshi*, II, 373–379.
[12] *Ishinshi*, II, 558.

in 1859, from fear of calamity and of free movement of foreigners. Social and political unrest reached a new level, which heightened the accepted natural portents. A society reared on the auguries of the *I Ching* could not overlook this evidence. By the end of autumn, purges were sweeping through Edo and Kyoto, designed to arrest political and social unrest and to pacify, by extension, nature itself. During more than a month the *bakufu,* under the strong leadership of Ii Naosuke, sought, by rounding up its real and imagined enemies, to assert its challenged and shabby authority.

It is evident that the purges, regardless of their original intent, were extended because of the mass hysteria. The *bakufu* by imprisoning and executing loyalists like Umeda, provided self-definition to the *shishi* in Kyoto. Umeda and his group shared a common interest and hence congregated in Kyoto; though they no doubt privately entertained radical notions, their loyalism was not political or explicit. But the prosecutor Nagano Shūzen decided that it was essential to arrest Umeda and Yanagawa. Toward the end of August 1859 he met with the Kyoto *shoshidai* Sakai Tadayoshi, who was en route back to Kyoto, and stressed to this shogunal representative the importance of stamping out incipient loyalism to the emperor. A month later Nagano persuaded Sakai's chief retainer (Mitsuura Shichizaemon) of the need to imprison Umeda, the acknowledged leader of the Kyoto loyalists. At approximately the same time, Nagano, whose behavior is familiar to all students of witch-hunts, berated the Kyoto magistrate (*Kyoto machi-bugyō*) Ōkabe Toyomune for hesitating to act against Umeda in deference to the court, and attacked the general laxness in Kyoto. Nagano accused Ōkabe of not seeing "the great disturbance" confronting the realm, singled out Umeda as the most important cause of this disturbance, and demanded his arrest. "If, by any chance, the opportunity is missed," Nagano added, "then we must hunt down the wicked traitors so as not to lose the basic principles of the realm." [13] Umeda's defense, like his manner and writing in general, was el-

[13] *Ibid.,* p. 559.

oquent but unemotional. He pictured himself as a man who had merely served the interests of the "divine land." His fate was that of "a lamp in the wind."

The controversy over *jōi* was to Umeda and Yanagawa simply the most recent reminder that the shogunate had failed to serve the emperor. The implications of this position were far-reaching. Umeda's seemingly pallid loyalism was less a reaction to the specific policy of explusion than a challenge to the shogunal arrangement of power. After all, he and his colleagues were, by choice, attendants to the imperial house. Even though he was not openly seditious, it was well known that he and Yanagawa had conducted a salon (*dōjō*) in Kyoto for samurai who had left their domains. They already believed what Yoshida, who owed much to them, had come to hold a few years before his death: A thousand autumns had indeed passed; it was time for the emperor to set things right, since none of his representatives could. Opposition to one of its policies could be tolerated by the *bakufu,* but an alternate vision of polity was seditious.[14] Ii's purge had the effect of sharpening the conflict rather than blurring it. In the first place, it got him killed. Death came swiftly and violently to Ii Naosuke in 1860 at the Sakuradamon in Edo. His assailants were disgruntled retainers from Mito who believed that Ii must be punished for his contemptuous treatment of their lord Nariaki and of the Hitotsubashi party, and his disrespect for the emperor's response to the signing of the commercial treaties. Although these Mito extremists did not clothe their deed in the language of restorationism and imperial loyalism, their banding together as a group of activists, held together by an ideology directed against Tokugawa officialdom, provided a method by which restorationism and loyalism might be effectively expressed in action. There was by 1860 a variety of examples and theories available as instruments of opposition to the *bakufu.* Somewhere Yoshida's theory of a rising, Umeda's example of passive loyalism, and the Mito assassination of a counselor merged. The result was the restorationist coups of the Bunkyū era.

[14] Nagae Shinzo, *Ansei no taigoku* (Tokyo, 1966), pp. 126–148.

THE ATTENUATION OF MITO: ŌHASHI TOTSUAN

The assassination of Ii relaxed shogunal policies but quickened the opposition and defined its antipathy. Between 1860 and 1864 incident tumbled after incident, and the so-called *sonnō-joi* movement spread out from several domains to become a countrywide movement. My purpose here is not to describe the movement in the separate domains or to chart its rise and fall; others have already done this.[15] What I am interested in is to show how thought was put into the service of the active movement that Yoshida had called for. The writers of the *sonnō-jōi* persuasion— I call them restorationists—acted out a specific vision of politics. Though their conduct was spectacular, I am concerned with their vision: one that owes more to the loyalism and emperorism of Yoshida Shōin (who in turn learned from men like Umeda) than to the later Mito school. For Yoshida in his later years, and for the wild restorationists of the Bunkyū, emperorism was its own justification. Even after the restorationist attempts of the 1860s, activists continued to invoke *sonnō*—but clearly with a different meaning. None was so committed to restoration as Maki Izumi; the way was prepared for him by Ōhashi Totsuan and Arima Shinshichi.

Like most of his restorationist colleagues, Ōhashi Totsuan held a Neo-Confucian culturalism strained through the Mito restatement; nativism in his thought remained recessive. His obsessions were characteristic of all restorationists; the intensity of his devo-

---

[15] For these aspects I would suggest Shibahara Takuji, *Meiji ishin no kenryoku kiban* (Tokyo, 1965), as the best single analysis of the socioeconomic bases of the *sonjō* movement. Professor Shibahara concentrates on trying to show how the movement enlarged its socioeconomic base in key areas such as Hizen, Mito, and Chōshū from the Tempō era down to the Meiji Restoration. Other works on the *sonjō* movement, too numerous to mention here, are also quite familiar: Tōyama's brilliant *Meiji ishin* and a number of articles he has written on the subject; Sakata's already cited book on the restoration (n. 2 above); but none can match Shibahara for sheer depth of analysis.

tion to the emperor prompted Takasugi Shinsaku to call him a fool.[16] Takasugi had gone up to Edo in the summer of 1859 and enrolled in Ōhashi's school, as was fashionable for retainers from Mito and the lesser *han* Utsunomiya. Takasugi, still in the first flush of the emperorism which he had learned from Yoshida, was an able man. Takasugi, in a letter to Yoshida, recorded his disappointment; the Mito retainers enrolled in Ōhashi's school could not be described as heroes. The school, he felt, was overrated: "True men of loyalty in the realm, the true samurai heroes, I do not believe are to be found in Edo." Takasugi's snobbism reflects the provincial; but his view of Ōhashi's academy was shared by Yoshida, who had previously written that Edo did not possess any great teachers. Takasugi's low estimate of the school sprang from a difference of perspective. The men who came to the school were interested not in theory but in the practical problem of destroying foreign influence in Japan. They were concerned with the "stain" produced by the foreigners, the expansion of Christianity and its deception of the people, the threat that the national product would be snatched away. These were real problems, which could be taken on only by men thrown into direct encounters with the foreigner, not by a young provincial whose intensity was still being fueled by his teacher. It is true that when these activists in Edo did discuss how to deal with the barbarians, they could only call for attacking their residences in the ports, terrorizing them in the streets, and beheading their leaders the consuls. To Takasugi, trained in Yoshida's school, this naïve plan probably appeared irrelevant, since it reflected expulsionism rather than emperorism. Takasugi, as I will show later, took on the larger problem of elevating the realm, in which he was eminently successful.

But in fact, the school of Ōhashi Totsuan disseminated information and inspired action. It would have approved of Takasugi's first attempt at direct action which, on closer inspection, would

[16] The incident is reported in Naramoto Tatsuya, *Takasugi Shinsaku* (Toyko, 1965), pp. 51ff., and Ikeda Sutosu, *Takasugi Shinsaku to Kusaka Genzui* (Tokyo, 1966), p. 61ff.

have been found to differ little from the program promoted by its own members. Takasugi, together with fellow retainers from Chōshū, planned to assassinate all the foreigners in Yokohama in November 1862; failing in this enterprise, they set fire to the British legation a month later. Only after this disappointment and the death of his friend Kusaka Genzui did Takasugi turn from what Yoshida denounced as (merely) "meritorious deeds" to a comprehensive program of domainal reform.

Takasugi has left us no observation about Ōhashi's own person; little is known about his personal career until he entered the restorationist stream in the later 1850s.[17] At the time of his arrest for involvement in a plot, many of his personal records were destroyed by his wife on his orders. Ōhashi was born in 1816 in Edo, the fourth son of Kiyomizu Akasaka, a military instructor of the Naganuma school. (A further reason for Yoshida's low estimate of Ōhashi is that they represented competing schools of military instruction.) His education was normal for the son of a samurai; when he turned twenty in 1836 he entered the school of Satō Issai, a path followed also by Sakuma Shōzan a few years later. Ōhashi found that Satō had little to offer him, for he soon left the school and turned to more orthodox Neo-Confucianism.[18] Like most contemporaries, he fell under the spell of Rai Sanyō's patriotism and responded to Ōshio's rebellion with outrage. Hence also his rapid defection from the school of Satō Issai. For reasons that are not entirely clear, Ōhashi resigned from the house of

[17] Naramoto, *Takasugi. . .*, p. 52.

[18] There is, as far as I can determine, one "biography" of Ōhashi which must serve as a standard account. This is Terada Gō's *Ōhashi Totsuan Senseiden* (Tokyo, 1936). The same author is also responsible for compiling and "editing" Ōhashi's extant writings. The work is *Ōhashi Totsuan Sensei zenshū*, 3 vols. (Tokyo, 1938–1943), cited hereafter as *OTSz. OTSz.*, I, 48–57.

There is also a long section on Ōhashi in the exasperatingly jingoistic work by Tamagawa Haruzō, *Sonnō ron* (Tokyo, 1943); *Ishinshi* (n. 3 above), III, 817–843; and Carmen Blacker has written a useful essay on Ōhashi in the *Transactions of the Asiatic Society of Japan* (November, 1959), Third Series, vol. 7.

Sakai, which had raised him; he was adopted by a wealthy merchant named Ōhashi Tanga (Awamiya) as his heir, and was ranked in the domainal roster (*shiseki*) of Utsunomiya *han*.[19] He was then twenty-six years old. Under the patronage of his new father he went on to study several subjects, especially nativist poetics under Ōkuni Takamasa (then called Nonoguchi Masayuki). Also in 1842 he established a school near the Nihonbashi residence of his stepfather. His biographer suggests that his life up to that point had not been particularly happy; he was the fourth son, shunted off at an early age to the province of Shinshū. But experience steeled him, and by the time he opened up his school he was ready to demonstrate (as his biographer records) "commendable acts." The school, which he named Shiseijuku, gave him independence.[20] At first he taught his students the philosophy of Wang Yang-ming, and then later turned to the Chu Hsi persuasion. This switch to a more orthodox position coincided with his growing fascination at the Mito rhetoric and involvement in the theory of emperorism. During the 1850s he wrote his two most distinctive essays, the *Hekija shōgen* and the *Genkōkiryaku* (*Record of the Mongol Invasion*). In this expulsionist phase he wrote a memorial to the *bakufu* on the necessity of naval defense, and also the *Rinsen okugi,* an exhortation to Tokugawa Nariaki to take decisive action on the foreign problem.[21]

In the autumn of 1855 Ōhashi moved his school to the suburbs of Edo. This apparent retirement to academic seclusion in fact marks a more active involvement in anti-Tokugawa activity; the speculative expulsionism of his earlier writings gave way to an abusive assault on the *bakufu* for incompetence. Also in these years Ōhashi took on uncompromising loyalism to the emperor and began to plan, with others, a return of imperial authority. Rumors of his impending arrest circulated throughout Edo, without foundation. After the Sakuradamon incident he acquired a reputation as an underground leader of patriotic samurai; cer-

[19] *OTSz.,* I, 58–59.
[20] Terada, *Ōhashi,* p. 78.
[21] *OTSz.,* I, 107–110.

tainly he turned his energies to the first of several restorationist
coups intended simply to remove incompetents in high shogunal
offices.[22] This effort to rob the *bakufu* of its top leadership
showed later restorationists how to dramatize the issue of able
leadership and also how actually to paralyze the *bakufu*. Ōhashi's
plan was one of the two favored methods of restoration. The
other was to raise an army for an imperial campaign against the
bakufu, suggested first by the Satsuma retainer Arima Shinshichi
at the time of the Teradaya incident (April 1862), and dramatized by Maki Izumi in 1863. Ōhashi's restorationist program
differed from the arbitrary Sakuradamon incident. The Mito
retainers who planned the assassination of Ii Naosuke had an extremely limited objective: to slay an official, not to destroy the
political system. Iwakura Tomomi, a keen observer and an active
participant in politics, reported that Ii's assassins were not "hostile to public affairs." Rather, they acted out of appreciation "for
the favor of two hundred and fifty years [of peace] which the
military families had granted"; and they pursued a course, "correct and good," that might restore to public affairs the right way
based on the emperor.[23] The Sakuradamon conspirators waged
personal war against "corrupt officials," not against the Tokugawa structure of authority. Ōhashi Totsuan revealed somewhat
the same fanaticism but with a new twist. He approved action to
remove corrupt or inept officials, but only as a technique to
achieve a larger purpose: to lay the groundwork for a new arrangement of political authority.[24]

Ōhashi's earlier writings, especially the *Hekija shōgen,* display
an enormous debt to the Mito school. These works were written
in the early 1850s, immediately after *kaikoku,* and it is not surprising that they concentrate on restating the classic requirements

[22] *OTSz.,* I, 149–160.

[23] Iwakura Kō Kyūsei Hozonkai (comp.), *Iwakura Kō jikki* (Tokyo,
1906), I, 342, 351. Also see Shibahara, "Hanbaku shosei . . ." (n. 9 above),
pp. 192ff.

[24] Ikeda Yoshimasa, "Sonnō jōi," in *Nihon rekishi kōza* (Tokyo, 1961),
p. 179.

of expulsionism in the new situation. At this date his thought represents an attenuation of the Mito rhetoric; Ōhashi appears, even more than Fujita Tōko and Aizawa, to be a man who is trying to ignore completely the authority of immediate experience. As we saw, the Mito school made a great point of defining culture by a normative and nonexperiential method. Neither with Aizawa nor with Ōhashi, his most loyal supporter, does theory have anything to do with events and their consequences as they unfolded in the late 1840s and early 1850s. Aizawa at least had the excuse of operating still within a Neo-Confucian world of *sakoku* (seclusion) in which the principle of nature could still be authenticated. Ōhashi's turn to active restorationism in the late 1850s marked a modification of this world view by the datum of contemporary experience.

Ōhashi's expulsionism had two different sources: the classic example of the Hōjō repulsion of superior Mongol forces in the thirteenth century; and the belief that the claims of Western science and technology had to be refuted before pressure to accept them became overwhelming. Expulsionism is the purpose of the *Genkō kiryaku,* which is little more than a chronological account of the coming of the envoys, their subsequent beheading, and the following two invasions. Inspired by the account found in Rai Sanyō's *Nihon gaishi (An Unofficial History of Japan)*, and written in stiff Chinese, its real point lies in its preface, where Ōhashi explains that Japan's repulsion of the Mongols stands unparalleled among the nations of the world.[25] The reasons for its success are obvious but remote. "The realm of our ancestral deities is founded on an unshakable imperial principle. We have collected the essence of these origins, and established pure and hard customs. Our way has been that of loyalty and the military arts. Moreover, the relation of lord to vassal is like the parent's relation to the child; by virtue of this principle, the imperial line has been continuous and its foundation unmoved. Searching for this procedure in other countries, I have discovered that they do not yet possess either correctness or beauty. How will they become el-

[25] *OTSz.,* III: Preface to "Genkō kiryaku."

egant and prosperous?"[26] For Ōhashi, the possession of an ethic
did not by itself promise cultural superiority and protection;
China, after all, had such a morality during the Sui and T'ang
periods, but was overcome.

But an ethic combined with *kokutai,* the idea of a continuous
sacral imperial line, was an even greater guarantee of the eternity
of Japan and the discrimination between civilization and barbarism. Thus in the *Hekija shōgen* Ōhashi found it no accident
that since the beginning of "our great Eastern land, there has not
been a revolution (*kakumei*) throughout the ages."[27] The reason for this was a "divinely appointed imperial line" and, of
course, the benevolence of the national deities. Both the ethic of
status relationships (which made civilized life possible) and the
magic of *kokutai* (which guaranteed the continuation of civilized life) provided Japan with the power to deal with the Mongol emissaries and any other intruders.

This appeal to the historical precedent of expulsionism was
linked to Ōhashi's condemnation of Western science. If the ethics
of discrimination had in the past rescued Japan from outside invaders and removed the specter of revolution, it would surely
overcome the most recent threat also. Ōhashi, unlike Aizawa,
saw enough about Western science and technology to know that
it was powerful and attractive. The West, he argued, possessed
great stores of cunning; and even the slightest adoption of its
skills would result in disaster. "It must be said," he warned, "that
they [the Westerners] are like old foxes who are skilled in bewitching charms."[28] They lie in wait, ready to spin their charms
in order to weaken "the national pulse." By contrast, at the same
time Sakuma Shōzan was trying to show the rationality of Western science, how it too was informed by a universal *ri.* But for
Ōhashi, only the language of superstition adequately described
the barbarian danger. The barbarian possesses "bewitching
charms" and "an evil religion"; contact with either would lead

[26] *Ibid.*
[27] *OTSz.,* I, 1–2 (Preface); II, pp. 2–3.
[28] *OTSz.,* II, 13.

only to corruption. Civilization was in peril simply because the Westerner was a barbarian, despite his "magic," "cunning," and his tantalizing trickery. The barbarian did not know anything about the discrimination of duties and the great principles of nature and the universe.

Into his classic denunciation of the West Ōhashi distilled an entire tradition: "The people of the Divine Land are men among men, while it must be said that the barbarians are like the bird and the beast. . . . They believe in an evil religion which puts into disorder the ethic of the Five Relationships. They act bravely only for profit, and they are never surfeited." [29] Revulsion, hatred, and fear generated Ōhashi's assessment of the West. What could be worse than human beings who place profit above discrimination? Elsewhere, in his exhortation to Tokugawa Nariaki, he sternly advised against any contact with the West, scientific or commercial, because (in the language of Shintō) such contact "stained" and "polluted." "The officials who trade with Holland are fools," he declared, and the great powers are thrifty and cunning. Japan had stood by weakly and done nothing to suppress the ambitions of the West. "The students of Dutch learning (*rangakusha*), who are our equivalents to birds and beasts, and the Western currents that damage the national pulse" must be prohibited.[30] Here in particular he berated Nariaki, who, upon taking the Office of Naval Defense in the shogunate, had done nothing to execute an active expulsionist policy. These grave exhortations were later interpreted by Takasugi Shinsaku as expressions "equal to foolishness."

Ōhashi was inconsolable after the opening of the country. The presence of aliens was an even greater evil than a foreign invasion, for they contributed to moral decline, which (he observed) was a greater danger to social survival than the appearance of barbarians in Japanese waters.[31] Ōhashi's expulsionism no doubt grew out of the Mito belief that *naiyū* was the essential problem

[29] *OTSz.,* II, 18–19.
[30] *OTSz.,* II, 244, "Rinsen okugi."
[31] *OTSz.,* II, 248.

of society. If moral decay characterized Japanese society, then its
arrest required a moral solution. Just as foreigners, especially
traders, showed in their conduct no distinction between high and
low, neither did social groups in Japan. Westerners had failed to
discern the great principles of life and civilization. They lived in
lands, he reported, where only the spirit of *yin* prevails.[32] "Our
country," he added, "is located in East Asia, and because it is a
realm rich and prosperous in the spirit of *yang* we have become
confirmed in the benevolence of the human heart." Western over-
emphasis on *yin* as against *yang* is shown in the importance accorded to women and in various vile habits: Westerners "dissect
the viscera and entrails of men and eat the flesh of humans,"
sometimes to advance medical knowledge.[33] One feels acutely
the loathing which overcame Ōhashi when he talked about such
things.

In short, Western learning was constructed not on principle
but on form. It lacked substance and it precluded true perception
of the natural world. Despite its claim to carry out investigation,
Western learning had produced only mechanisms, not understanding of the principles of the universe or of the human condition. Technology, Ōhashi believed, showed how far the West had
failed to grasp the true intent of principle, the nature of things.
Unlike Sakuma and Yokoi, Ōhashi made no effort to find a possible congruence between the Neo-Confucian emphasis on
"searching out things" and the Western emphasis on inductive
reasoning. The absence of morality (the Five Relationships)
clinched the argument that Westerners could not have understood the meaning of *kakubutsu kyūri*. Yokoi Shōnan argued a
few years later that the concept of *kakubutsu kyūri,* as it had
been originally applied by Sung theorists, did not result in any actual investigation of things or experimentation. Sung writers only
saw in the concept a speculative device, they "pinched principle"
but never explored the concrete possibilities in such an idea. The
West, Yokoi argued by contrast, had shown how *kakubutsu*
might be used in an investigative and experimental technique,

[32] *OTSz.,* II, 106–107.
[33] *OTSz.,* II, 111–112.

and the kind of results it might be expected to yield. Ōhashi simply rejected the argument that the West understood the meaning of *kakubutsu kyūri*.[34] In fact, he reasoned, science and technology showed how wrong the West had been. Ōhashi suggests that, because the West misunderstood the nature of reality, it was hindered from discovering the great principle of human conduct. "Investigation of things" and "exhaustion of principles" required not manipulation but meditation.[35]

The sages showed that investigation leads to a penetration of the Way. "If we inquire today about the Way, we would have to answer that it is called benevolence and loyalty. How do we differentiate between these values? Between all things? It is accomplished by investigating things and their principles. All things will be known: why a horse will try to escape his reins, why a ship will obey the wind, why states prosper and decline, the reasons behind order and disorder."[36] "If one hopes to investigate principle," he continued, "he must first clear his mind and separate principle (*ri*) from substance (*ki*). The universe is one *ki*; but it is divided into *yin* and *yang*, heaven and stars, the five elements, ten thousand things, sun and moon, the zodiacal signs, mountains, rivers, and seas, man and the animal kingdom."[37] Names are given to properties and shapes, but investigation promises understanding that goes beneath the surface; it enters the heart of things, or, as Neo-Confucianists were fond of putting it, it goes "beyond shapes." Such investigation was "within things" and led to personal cultivation, to realization of one's good nature. In the end this process came back to morality and order. "Between the parent and the child there is the principle of fidelity; between friends there is the principle of honesty."[38]

Ōhashi saw Western learning as both useless and dangerous. With its inordinate stress on profit, it obscured the true meaning

[34] *OTSz.*, II, 49–74. This is, in fact, the gist of the second volume of the "Hekija shōgen." The subtitle declares: "The West does not know *kyūri*."

[35] *OTSz.*, II, 50. See, in this connection, C. Blacker, "Ōhashi Totsuan," pp. 158–159 (n. 18 above).

[36] *OTSz.*, II, 52.

[37] *OTSz.*, II, 53.

[38] *OTSz.*, II, 67–68.

of *kakubutsu kyūri*. As a technique it destroyed principle: "Parents are murdered, lords are disobeyed."[39] The basis of Western learning lay in its disrespect for the natural order and its repudiation of discrimination. The barbarian was driven only by utility and self-interest, which led to virulent individualism and competition. Ōhashi confessed that he feared the Westerner in himself, and even more the impact of his principle of self-interest and utility upon the masses. He tried not to imagine the turbulence which these concepts would surely unleash in Japan.[40] Competition between lord and retainer, for example, would introduce into the country the melancholy features of Western history: disorder and revolution. Christianity loosened moral fiber and promoted a love that disregarded the differentiation between lord and retainer, parent and child. It destroyed the natural distinction between civilization (*ka*) and barbarism; it encouraged self-interest and individualism; it promoted parties and factions; and it elevated the masses by denying the Way of Loyalty.[41] The threat to the subservience of the lower classes was what really frightened Ōhashi, and this explains why he rejected any rapprochement between "Eastern morality" and "Western skills." Technique, he argued, could not be a substitute for the life force (*kakki*); it was not even helpful in military defense, since it merely dulled bravery.[42] The correct and only morality endowed its holder with a life energy or force superior to all technologies.

Ōhashi's attempt to revive Neo-Confucian culturalism, at the moment when men such as Sakuma were trying to politicize it, is very plainly an exhausted echo of the Mito statement. His pompous advice to Nariaki discloses the irony of his positions; he was reminding the acknowledged patron of expulsionism of his duties as an expulsionist, at a time when the policy was no longer possible. Yet it was also in this exhortation (*Rinsen okugi*) that

[39] *OTSz.*, II, 69.

[40] Maruyama Masao, "Kaikoku" in *Gendai Nihon shisō taikei*, *Kindai shugi*, ed. Hidaka Rokurō (Tokyo, 1961), p. 287.

[41] *OTSz.*, I, 1–2.

[42] *OTSz.*, I, 180–181.

he proposed for the first time to "restore the spirit of Japan." [43] After his move to the suburbs of Edo, he turned away from broad theorizing about expulsion, toward the problem of revitalizing Japan. Expulsionism receded as emperorism began to suggest a new program. It would be wrong to say that Ōhashi jettisoned the Mito solution. While *kaikoku* was, for the moment, an incontrovertible fact even for someone as obdurate as Ōhashi, he still believed that if *naiyū* were overcome, the problem of foreign invasion would take care of itself. Ōhashi's restorationism hints at a new political consciousness; despite his commitment to the domain-centered vision of Mito, he was willing to drop the *bakufu*. It also hints at social consciousness, in that he tried to recruit non-samurai under the imperial banner. It has been argued that his own recently acquired merchant affiliation inspired this move to gather nonfeudal classes under a symbol lacking feudal associations.[44] Actually, Ōhashi shared a conviction with most restorationists: once they gave up on the lords and their retainers, they turned to the non-samurai classes for recruitment. Extremists like Maki and Kusaka announced a new kind of authority representing all groups.

Ōhashi's biographer suggests that his move outside Edo was made to escape surveillance and to mark time for the right restorationist moment.[45] This may credit Ōhashi with too much prescience, but his major restorationist tract does date from this period of waiting. His new residence at Shoume village, as it was then called, was affected by the prospect of restoration; and in 1861 he completed his *Seiken kaifuku hisaku* (*Secret Policy for a Restoration of Political Authority*) to express his new enthusiasm. The work was probably written in response to the *bakufu*'s attempt in 1860 to unite court and shogunate through the Kazunomiya marriage. This "secret plan" extends the culturalism of the *Hekija shōgen*: "Since the coming of the foreign barbarian and

[43] *OTSz.*, I, 244.

[44] Ikeda, "Sonnō jōi" (n. 24 above), p. 179.

[45] Terada (n. 18 above), p. 126. Closer to the truth is the fact that Ōhashi's home in Nihonbashi was wrecked by an earthquake in 1855.

the expansion of commerce, the *bakufu's* position has not been good; it has carried temporizing to extremes, and the arrogance of the barbarians has become rampant. . . . *Bakufu* officials are frightened by them. . . . Even though only one barbarian was permitted to enter in the beginning, now several have pushed their way in. . . . Although trade is not yet three years old, the rising prices in commodities, the exhaustion of domainal resources, and the impoverishment of the mean people must be viewed as if they were near-disasters." [46] Moreover the *bakufu* has sought to undermine "the brave and loyal samurai" of "courageous domains." Among the largest domains there were none willing "to raise the imperial banner" against the barbarian. "Looking at the *bakufu's* failure of policy is like waiting for the decline and destruction of the imperial land." The *bakufu*, he charged, was in the grips of paralysis, and the domainal lords stood by, fearful that any independent action would be termed treasonable rebellion. What had not yet been tried, Ōhashi stated, was a call to arms under the "banner of an imperial decree." Venal officials had ignored imperial edicts, but if the loyal retainers were aroused to take action under such a sanction, was it not possible to arrest the threat facing the country? [47]

Ōhashi knew that the *bakufu* had ignored the "imperial will." But he was confident in the psychological value of a sudden imperial edict enjoining all "sincerely loyal men to drive out the barbarians. The grief and anger over barbarian violence . . . has brought constant pain to the emperor's heart, and it will ultimately reach down and be felt by people at the grass-roots (*sōmō*) level. All, upon feeling this, will gush tears because of the misfortune [confronting the country]." Taking Japan out of the hands of the barbarian was an imperial decision; hence all people, out of their love of the emperor, lay waiting for "the august movement of the court." "As with the booming clap of a thunderous voice," Ōhashi wrote, "if an imperial decree is promulgated, all men must act, since all will be inspired. It will be

[46] *OTSz.*, I, 281–282.
[47] *OTSz.*, I, 283.

like the collapse of a dam holding back a lake." [48] Such a decree must be based upon a detailed observation of the state of the realm and the condition of the people.

It would be misleading to suggest that Ōhashi was erecting an elaborate restorationist structure merely to emphasize expulsion. He saw that the foreign intrusion exposed above all the corruption and inefficiency of officials. Ōhashi singled the *bakufu* out as responsible for corruption and incompetence. Decisions such as expulsion were avoided, finances were in chaos, and officials had glossed over the emergencies of the day. The Tokugawa, he lamented, had become estranged from the public spirit of the realm.[49] The answer did not lie in the proposed *kōbugattai* arrangement. The *bakufu* had lost its opportunity, decision-making had reverted to the court. The court had been reluctant to issue an imperial decree because of its fear of Tokugawa military power, dating back to the establishment of the Kamakura shogunate; since that time the military families had "driven the realm like a horse." Their power had been so great that they acquired contempt for the court. The military families had become "audacious in a number of ways, so that they no longer know those things which are called *meibun*." Power warps, according to Ōhashi, and a corrective to the insolence and audacity of the Tokugawa would be to take into account "the imperial pleasure." Eight or nine men of every ten were alienated from the Tokugawa exercise of power. "The people of the realm must abandon the Tokugawa before it is too late, deepen their devotion to the imperial court, and move toward a revival of the emperor's power. The time must not be lost." [50]

Ōhashi was keenly aware of decline and decay. The moral categories of Chinese history suggested to him that the original strength of the Tokugawa rested on their strict observance of the principle of nature (*shizen no dōri*). Decline was caused by usurpation; the Hōjō had already shown the price exacted of usur-

[48] *OTSz.*, I, 284.
[49] *OTSz.*, I, 286, 288.
[50] *OTSz.*, I, 286.

pers. The Tokugawa *bakufu's* indifference toward the "imperial will" in its refusal to prosecute an expulsionist policy was the most recent sign of decay. Drained of its moral strength, the *bakufu* was forced to behave weakly. "The city warehouses," Ōhashi wrote, "and the rice granaries are empty, and they [the Tokugawa] have lost the authority to rule the realm. Relying on the merits of their ancestors [who had virtue], and directing the several lords likewise, they are scorned because of their response to the barbarians. They are immersed in this poison, and daily their health gets worse." And, reminding his countrymen of the past warning of Aizawa Seishisai, Ōhashi stated that a restoration was seen once in ten thousand years; the opportunity was as clear as a mirror, and the fall of the Tokugawa was not more than ten years away. Ōhashi was only a few years off in his reckoning; with remarkable prophetic insight, he called for both the imperial court and the *bakufu* to be overturned, because "the time for a restoration is now."

The effort of the *bakufu* to solve its political problems by striking a *kōbugattai* settlement was an example of Tokugawa ineptness and a sure sign of collapse. The unification of court and *bakufu* was little more, Ōhashi charged, than "a view held by a foreigner or a Chinese," "a mediocre opinion." His acute sense of timing in face of crisis prompted him to drop conventional past methods of "rectifying boundaries." He was critical of the feeble effort of the Tokugawa "to depend upon their ancestors" for answers. "Does it not speak eloquently of our seriousness that we leave the *bakufu* out of consideration when planning for the future perfection of the imperial realm? Thus the great solution today is for the imperial court unmistakably to abandon the *bakufu*. It is also understood that an august revival of the imperial court must accompany this action." [51] Ōhashi was not entirely convinced that revival would be useful. The barbarian poison, he noted, had spread throughout the country (*udai*) and even the imperial court had been infected. Before an imperial revival, the court must first be rid of this affliction; this is what he meant by

[51] *OTSz.*, I, 290, 302; *Ishinshi* (n. 3 above), 822.

"overturning the imperial court." But the court, unlike the *ba-kufu*, could be saved. Expulsion offered more than the simple opportunity to throw the foreigners out of the country. "Promulgating an imperial rescript," he advised, "that dealt with expulsion would not only disclose the real strength possessed by the emperor, but also represent the first move in the general restoration of the divine land." [52]

Ōhashi is constantly concerned with the "enemies of the throne" (*chōteki*) who might "shoot an arrow at the court." He had in mind both the "wicked officials of the *bakufu*" and their supporters among the associated (*fudai*) and related (*kamon*) lords. Together they had spun a conspiracy resulting in total estrangement of the people from the realm. "These disloyal lords who honor wicked decrees (*bōrei*) of wicked officials of the *bakufu* and bend an arrow toward the throne will provoke, by their acts, the hearts of the loyal retainers who have been biding their time among the humble and lower orders. Then there will be an explosion of action, and all those lords who are the enemies of the court will be punished." Here Ōhashi, like Yoshida, is calling for a grass-roots loyalist movement and specifically inviting non-samurai to join it. In particular he suggests that "the followers of wealthy merchants and peasants" spearhead an army of some fifty to a hundred men, and that each in turn recruits five or six of his friends. "Within the length and breadth of the realm," he noted confidently, "we could count on the recruitment of numerous heroes." [53] This was the strength available to the court, even though it appeared weak compared to the *bakufu*. While the *bakufu* appeared to be powerful, in reality it was powerless because "it is separated from human nature."

The people, Ōhashi believed, could be roused to revive the health of Japan. The ruinous impact of foreign trade, he wrote, was incalculable, and all people had a stake in stemming the "corrosion" which it was causing. Ōhashi knew that the danger

[52] *OTSz.*, I, 250, "Rinsen okugi." Ōhashi's earlier metaphor for restoration was "preserving the health of *shinshū*." Also p. 296.

[53] *OTSz.*, I, 294.

of an estranged populace, whose personal economic collapse could be linked to the new foreign trade, was even worse than the corruption of shogunal officials. His concept of a restoration of the fortunes of the imperial court represented a "return to human nature" (*jinshin*). The prosperity of the court was synonymous with the prosperity of antiquity, and presupposed a social order secure in status and livelihood. In his petition to the *bakufu* of 1853 written in response to Perry's coming, Ōhashi made "unifying human nature" prior to military preparations.[54] We recall that Aizawa before then had argued that a unified people could withstand any threat. Ōhashi's sentiment was similar, though twenty years after the circumstances which had originally generated it. "If human nature is unified," he announced, "and military preparations are insufficient and cannon are scarce, victory is still a certainty." An "estrangement from human nature" would constitute "a greater anxiety and worry" than "inadequacy of military equipment."

Estrangement meant "exhaustion of national strength" and of "the strength of the people" through trade, and the importation of "useless items in exchange for precious metals and grains."[55] When he composed his Secret Proposal for a restoration, events were confirming these fears, and the idea of an estranged populace possessed more than an ethical meaning. The effects of trade convinced him that the future held only further dislocation. Ōhashi held the shogunate responsible for these conditions and hence advised the throne to abandon the *bakufu*. Yet he was still a good Confucianist who believed in the possibility of a well-ordered and prosperous *jinsei*. Revering the imperial court was linked to reviving the economic "strength of the people." The fortunes of the throne in turn rested on retrieval of a benevolent polity. Ōhashi's restorationism was, to the end, inspired by the Chinese model, which called for a simple reordering of society. His call for an imperial edict arose from hope both of expulsion and of accomplishing a genuine *ōsei fukko* under the new cir-

[54] *OTSz.*, I, 208–210, "Kaei jōshō."
[55] *OTSz.*, I, 217, 224.

cumstances. And this double policy bore with it the economic improvement of the people.[56] "In promulgating an imperial expulsionist edict to the realm, how will we achieve the happiness (*sawai*) of the people?" Down to his own time the imperial court had become increasingly weaker. "Restoring the court to its antique position, owing to its divine eternity, is as clear a proposal as the sight of fire. Is it not in truth a pleasant thing? If there is time . . . it is my hope to promote a policy of offering our bodies to the emperor."[57] Peace and prosperity had soured into poverty because of the *bakufu*'s indifference to *taigi* and *kokutai*.

Ōhashi's only concession to nativism was his demand that restoration serve "as a reply to the heavenly ancestors." He never defined the power of the emperor or the kind of personality he should acquire; he never differentiated the emperor from the imperial court. He was too good a Confucianist to do these things. He pursued a Confucian revival of ethical imperatives, political well-being, and economic prosperity. The last item is important. Prosperity of the people meant overcoming estrangement by straightening the status relationships and reestablishing *taigi* as the measure of conduct. This required only the removal of officials whose actions had brought Japan to its present plight. Ōhashi was unclear about the arrangement that should fill the vacuum created by an "abandonment of the *bakufu*." Unlike others, he did not hint at the kind of imperial polity that must follow a restoration. Since he rarely mentioned the possibility of an actual return of imperial power, the retrieval of antiquity was for him more an ethical sentiment than a historical expectation. Ōhashi's emperorism was more the return of a principle of authentication than the revival of a personality divinely charged to

[56] *Ishinshi*, III, 822. See also Masanao Kano, "Kindai shisō no hōga," *Iwanami kōza, Nihon rekishi*, 316. Kano argues that the ideal of *fukko* for one such as Ninomiya Sontoku had the same meaning. A similar description could be made of late Tokugawa nativists (*kokugakuronsha*). See, by all means, Haga Noboru, *Bakumatsu no kokugaku* (Tokyo, 1962), pp. 71ff., and Matsumoto Sannosuke, *Kokugaku seijishisō no kenkyu* (Osaka, 1957), pp. 65ff.

[57] *OTSz.*, I, 298.

lead the country. Thus his constant concern about "wicked officials," and his emphasis on a moral polity and the economic well-being of the people. His restorationist plea owes much to the Mito program, yet time and experience produce interesting differences. There is no advice to abandon the *bakufu* in any of the writing of Aizawa or Fujita Tōkō, nor a call for a grass-roots movement of samurai and commoners to execute a great cause. Ōhashi, despite his obvious debt to Mito writers, is important because he saw that *naiyū* was at least as critical as *gaikan*. This shift from the Mito position prompted, as the title of his tract *On Restoration* suggests, the reconstruction of political authority to deal both with the foreign threat and with domestic decay. Still his emperorism and his theory of restoration kept his activity limited to Edo, while at the same time men like Arima Shinshichi, Kusaka Genzui, Hirano Kuniomi, Kiyokawa Hachirō, Maki Izumi, and Ogō Kazutoshi were flocking to Kyoto. The difference of locale is important, as we shall see later.

During the early months of 1861, Ōhashi Totsuan became involved in a plot calling for the assassination of a shogunal counselor Andō Nobumasa, that produced the Sakashitamon incident of January 1862.[58] Behind the plot was a mixed group of retainers from Mito and Utsunomiya domains who agreed on little else. Ōhashi, seeing the chance to call for a rising of retainers loyal to the emperor, dispatched a student, Kojima Kirosuke, to Mito to raise support for the enterprise. During negotiations, the Mito group convinced the Utsunomiya group that it was more useful to assassinate Andō than some foreigner. Ōhashi was more interested in raising an army of loyalist patriots and forcing through an imperial decree against the *bakufu*—the major planks of his restorationist platform. Since the Mito wing saw the assassination of Andō as a step merely to reform the *bakufu*, while Ōhashi looked for a genuine restoration, he decided to pull out of the conspiracy. He played no direct role in the attempted murder at

[58] Detailed descriptions of the plot and Ōhashi's dubious participation are found in Terada (n. 18 above), pp. 161–248, and *Ishinshi*, III, 823–843. The following account is an abbreviation of these two sources.

Sakashitamon. Yet his reluctance to participate grew also out of frustration. His Secret Proposal had been submitted secretly for inspection by the emperor. Not long afterwards, shogunal officials got wind of the plan and investigated the Chōshū retainer who had carried it to Kyoto. Ōhashi also suffered harassment, and the policy (which depended on secrecy) was brought into the open. It came to nothing, and Ōhashi turned temporarily to the alternative of the Mito retainers, purposeless murder and violence. But, as I said, before long he rejected it again.

Agreement on the assassination of Andō still brought together Ōhashi's faction (which called for an imperial decree and restoration), and the Mito firebrands, led by Hirayama Hyotsuke, who envisaged only reform. Ōhashi, whose reputation ran before him, was unexpectedly arrested a month before the plot was to come off. He was charged vaguely with participation in activities aiming at assassination and expulsion. This was true enough; and before he had pulled out, Ōhashi confessed that he was willing to carry it out even in view of the possibility that the authorities had uncovered the scheme. He wrote to one of his closest associates: "To the extent that I am the main actor, a part is expected of me. And if I do not go through with it, this will look bad for later action [literally, later action will result in a *kyōgen,* a farce]." This sentiment, a bursting confidence in the sanctity of personal action and responsibility, clearly goes beyond the Confucian ideal of an ethical manager.[59] Andō escaped death luckily, only because the *bakufu,* aware of the possibility of assassinations, was on guard for a sequel to the assassination of Ii Naosuke. Nevertheless Hirayama's group succeeded in breaking through Andō's bodyguards to inflict a wound on the counselor. Although the wound was slight, it proved fatal for his political life. Ōhashi's fate was no better. Prison treatment weakened him, although he and a few others were released through the courtier Ōhara Shigenori, court patron to many an activist, who was sent to Edo as an imperial messenger to call upon the *bakufu* to end

[59] Quoted in Kano, p. 312. Also *OTSz.,* I, 338. The same sentiment is expressed on pp. 340–341.

interrogation of prisoners who had contracted illnesses in prison. Ōhashi's luck ran out; he died from exposure less than a week after his release at the age of forty-seven.

Yet Ōhashi was able to express a last testament before death. His few surviving letters do not go down to the time of his death in July 1862. But a vindication statement (*zankan shuisho*) carried by the six assailants discloses some of his last thoughts, since it is certain that he either wrote the document or dictated it to one of his students. Ōhashi's concern for "wicked and immoral officials" remained with him to the death. The importance of the statement, beyond stock sentiments, lies in the claim that the assassination was the first stage in what he planned as a restoration. In a sense he was right, even though the route from the abortive incident at the Sakashitamon to the Meiji Restoration was not as straight as Ōhashi expected. Publicity ran high in favor of the assassins, and the deed was immortalized in a *senryu:* "When the lamp (*andō*) is extinguished, dawn will break." Ōhashi couldn't have put it better.

THE POLITICIZATION OF THE NATIVIST VISION:
MAKI IZUMI

Confucian restorationism like that of Ōhashi failed to take into account change and the new expectations of what the emperor should be; moreover, it was still rooted in the *bakuhan* system. Although Ōhashi recommended dismantling the *bakufu* in order to dignify the court, he could not make any specific proposal for a new arrangement of power; we can assume that he envisaged a domainal system more or less intact. Maki Izumi, who on the whole was no more precise, went beyond his "imperial campaign" to suggest a new feudalism modeled on that of the Chou period. The restorers of 1868 were not better equipped to come up with a political blueprint once the *bakufu* had been eliminated. Restoration meant for them, as for Ōhashi, simply the recruitment of officials on standards of talent, ability, and youth, rather than on age, social standing, and heredity. Ōhashi at least was interested in removing venal officials; he was still propping up the flagging Tokugawa order. His commitment to the Mito program meant that he called for the elimination of the *bakufu* only to strengthen the domain. His "restoration" was none other than the received system, supported by unconventional devices. As long as the system in general could be made to function smoothly, it was not too great a sacrifice to eliminate elements. Ōhashi, like his Mito forerunners, was still working to retain a particular social order under the theory of seclusion; by the 1860s this was no longer possible.

Just as Ōhashi's theory of restoration rested on an attenuated Mito rhetoric, so the plot to assassinate Andō was the last political effort of Mito retainers, in continuation of their earlier assassination of Ii Naosuke. The failure of the plot coincided with the removal of Tokugawa Nariaki (and hence of Mito also) from center stage of Japanese politics. The plotters, including Ōhashi, assumed that decisions were made in Edo and the east. Yet at the very same time, activists were congregating at Kyoto in the west, for they saw that Japan's dilemma would be solved there, not in Edo. The failure of Ōhashi and the Mito activists to see this explains why the attack at the Sakashitamon, even if it had succeeded, would have been an ineffective stratagem. They concentrated their efforts in Edo out of the central (but by then threadbare) Mito concern to prop up the whole Tokugawa order. And their whole program, since the assassination of Ii, was simply to remove from the *bakufu* officials responsible for its weaknesses. They thereby pared down even Ōhashi's vision of restoration. Those who came out of the west from Chōshū and southern Kyūshū to Kyoto had, like Yoshida, discarded this program as obsolete. But even the restorationists of Kyoto were to be misled. Only a few like Ōkubo Toshimichi, Takasugi Shinsaku, and Kidō Koin knew that power and the future lay not in Kyoto but in the large domains.

The activists in Kyoto under the nominal leadership of Maki Izumi dreamed of a real imperial restoration. Already at Tosa *han* in 1861 a Loyalist Party (*Kinnōtō*) led by Takechi Zuisan announced a plan to raise the "Japanese spirit" (*Yamato dama-shii*) and seize "the opportunity to restore the prosperity of the realm." [60] At Satsuma in 1859 the Seichūshi (a similar loyalist group) was organized around forty members including Saigō Takamori, Ōkubo Toshimichi, and Arima Shinshichi. This group, at least in part, continued Shimazu Hisamitsu's reform wing in the domain, but with the motive (in Ōkubo's words) of "punishing the traitorous *bakufu* officials" and "leading the *han* in a united effort to perform a heroic deed." Hizen domain had a comparable society, the Gisai dōmei, formed in 1850 out of young loyalists including Soejima Taneomi, Nakano Seiko, Ōgi Taka-fusa, Etō Shimpei, and Ōkuma Shigenobu. And Yoshida Shōin's own personal apparatus, the Shōka sonjuku, was transformed into an activist group under the leadership of Kusaka Genzui. These *shishi* of the west left their domains deliberately in the early 1860s and joined Maki Izumi and the Chikuzen floating sa-murai (*rōnin*) Hirano Kuniomi to form a loosely organized ag-gregate of activists. Their activities exploded in a number of plots to rouse Maki's "imperial campaign" against the *bakufu*. It was a season for coups, and between 1861 and 1864 one followed an-other with drum-roll regularity: Teradaya, the risings of the Ten-chūgumi, the disturbances in Ikuno and Yamato, the explosion at the Forbidden Gate, all represent a direct effort to impose emper-orism and expulsionism. Although these actions lacked coordina-tion, they shared a common purpose prepared by the Kurume priest Maki Izumi, who in fact was a participant in many of them. Every major restorationist brought out his program. A reading of key works such as Arima's *Miyako nikki* and his peti-tions to Shimazu Hisamitsu, Kusaka's *Kairan jōgi* and *Kaiwan shirigoto,* Hirano's *Kaiten sansaku* and *Jimmu hitsukatsu,* Ogō's *Ōsei fukko gikyōrodu,* and Kiyokawa's *Senchu shimatsu* dis-closes a wide range of interest, but a common mixture of mythol-ogizing with programs for restoration. Yet all these writer-activ-

[60] Zuizankai (comp.), *Ishin Tosa kinnōshi* (Tokyo, 1911), pp. 70–71. See Marius Jansen, *Sakamoto Ryōma and the Meiji Restoration* (Princeton, 1961), ch. 3.

ists shared a debt to Maki Izumi, the most indefatigable and original restorationist of all. Most things said in these writings were said first by Maki, who above them all dramatized restorationism in thought and practice.

Among the Kyoto restorationists, Maki was not only the ideologue to whom all looked for advice and leadership, but also the oldest by nearly thirty years. Maki was fifty at the time he began to involve his energies, while his associates in restoration were all around twenty. Ever since Yoshida Shōin, the process of change, which took the form of radical reform and restoration, was associated with youth, right down to the Restoration of 1868 and the reorganization of 1873. Maki was deferred to because of his age; also his conduct was often more aberrantly youthful than that of his colleagues. He could be trusted; his several imprisonments authenticated his authority. Maki, despite his age, was an integral part of a movement which attacked the supremacy both of age and of heredity. Sakuma Shōzan of his generation, and Aizawa Seishisai of an even older one, evoked veneration from the young, but none of these men was ever a leader in the nervous years of the Bunkyū era. The young respected their intellectual achievements but identified them with the hopes of another generation. Maki escaped this judgment and, although over thirty, won the trust of a younger generation. (Yokoi Shōnan also enjoyed the admiration of younger activists, even though he appealed less to the problems of youth than to the new possibilities the times were offering.)

Maki Izumi Yasuomi no kami was born in March 1813 into a family of Shinto priests *(shinkan, shinshoku)*.[61] His father was hereditary priest of the Suitengū shrine in Kurume *han* of Kyūshū. Maki himself was trained in this tradition, and in later years he confessed on a number of occasions that the weight of the Suitengū was on his shoulders. The Suitengū was consecrated during the Gempei wars of the thirteenth century as a memorial to

[61] I have drawn biographical information from the "standard" panegyric, Udaka Kō, *Maki Izumi no kami den* (Tokyo, 1913), and Arakawa Kusuo, *Ishin zenya* (Tokyo, 1965), pp. 186–208.

the emperor Antoku, who perished in the sea battle of Dan-
noura. It was the duty of the Maki family to serve the departed
spirit of Antoku. This alone might explain Maki's fiery loyalism,
which few of his contemporaries could match for consistency. In
a sense his career was simply an expansion of his hereditary position and his early training—which also explain the new thing in
his concept of emperorship. Despite his early veneration of Aizawa and the Mito program, Maki's emperorism went far beyond the pallid Confucian views most recently revived by Ōhashi
Totsuan. Maki saw the emperor as a personality who by virtue of
his divinity possessed superior virtue and authority. In his close
association with Shinto ritual, Maki was probably persuaded that
a "restoration of ancient imperial rule" (*ōsei fukko*) was preferable to the Mito notion of a regeneration of the domestic order
(*chūkō*).[62]

Another factor behind Maki's emperorism is the fact that Kurume was also where in 1799 Takayama Hikokurō disemboweled
himself in the home of Mori Kogen, a retainer of the *han*. Takayama was famous for his criticism of the disrepair of imperial
graves and monuments; his devotion was transformed into folk-
lore, especially in Kurume *han*. Maki grew up on such stories
and put great stock in them. He romanticized Takayama in po-

[62] See Inoue Kiyoshi, *Meiji Ishin* (Tokyo, 1954), pp. 107–153. Professor
Inoue argues along similar lines when he pinpoints the merger of *sonnō
ron* and *jōi ron*. Where he fails to make a persuasive case is in his
assumption that *sonnō ron* did not undergo profound transformations
and modifications in response to political changes in the *bakumatsu*. Inoue
and Tōyama, in this sense, assume the notion that restorationism was
potentially inherent in the Mito program. It was, but as I have suggested,
it meant simply restoration of the *bakuhansei*. A restoration of direct
imperial authority was an entirely different concept which had little to do
with the Mito position. Modification of emperorism to make possible an
ōsei fukko required a heavy injection of nativism which writers from
Yoshida to Maki promoted with increasing enthusiasm. The difference
between the Mito "restoration" and the later restorationist efforts is found
in the difference between concepts: *chūkō* and *ōsei fukko*. The former
called for a shoring-up of the *bakuhan* order; the latter was a license for
its destruction.

etry, and made this example of untarnished loyalty a model for himself. Maki also learned when he was young that he was born in the year when another loyalist, Gamō Kunpei, died in Edo. At some point Maki determined to succeed to Takayama and Gamō and carry on their work. He chose early in life a career of heroism, and in preparation he built up his physique and disciplined his mind. This determination was reinforced by a classic Shinto education in Yamazaki Ansai's school of philosophic syncretism (*kimon-ha*); and his teacher's father, Miyabura Nanriku, was a colleague of Asami Keisai. But Japanese biographers pay too much attention to the school of Chinese thought to which men were exposed, and too little to the real psychological reasons behind a man's commitment. Maki's Shinto environment, with its mixture of mytho-history and pure Confucian moralism, his duties at the Suitengū, are far more important in explaining his obsessions. Exposure to the nativist school, from simplistic prayers (*norito*) to the sophisticated political adaptation of Shinto by Hirata Atsutane, did much more to form his vision of the world than the abstract subtleties of *kimon*—after all, these were part of a living tradition.

Finally, Maki's youth was absorbed in a compulsive worship of Kusunoki Masashige in which he resembled Yoshida and a whole generation of samurai. He read the popular *Illustrated Record of Lord Kusunoki* (*Ehon Kusonoki-ki*), and writes how moved he was in body and spirit by this example of pure loyalty and sincerity; it marked an awakening which changed his life.[63] Legend had transformed the fourteenth-century patriot into a figure of great nobility. Like Yoshida Shōin, he vowed early to follow "the traces of Kusunoki's life and career." This meant more than taking the pilgrim road to Minatogawa; it meant, as Maki wrote when he was older, taking the road to an imperial restoration.[64] His emperorism, which early implied restoration, was decided on in his youth, long before expulsionism was an

[63] Arima Hideo, ed., *Maki Izumi no kami ibun* (Tokyo, 1913), pp. 642–643, 711–713, cited hereafter as *MInki*.

[64] Arakawa, pp. 186ff.

issue. In contrast to Ōhashi, Maki made no intellectual or emotional commitment to expulsionism.

Maki saw Kusunoki's suicide as the crowning achievement of the patriot's life. Maki observed that Kusunoki died well to dramatize an unbending loyalty to the court. Maki yearly marked the anniversary of Kusunoki's death (May 25, 1336) by a solemn observance and a vow to receive the heroic spirit into his body. Not even illness prevented him from renewing his vows. In 1859, when Maki was under domainal punishment and house arrest, on the morning of the anniversary he had some kind of hemorrhage; in spite of this he cleansed his body by afternoon, put on his clothes, and renewed his observances. Even when Maki was plunged into national politics after his release, he was never too engaged to remember his obligations to Kusunoki and the purpose of his own life. In the midst of the Teradaya incident, in which Maki was a principal participant, he took time out to make his pledge. Yoshida Shōin possessed a similar but less extreme disciplined zeal; so did other restorationists of the Bunkyū era. Such devotion was for each of these men a constantly renewed reinforcement of personal commitment. In Maki we see a typical revolutionary personality who has removed all obstacles to the carrying out of his purpose. This single-minded "madness" can be found also in Lenin, Gandhi, and Ho Chi-Minh.

Maki's identification with Kusunoki through ritual observance raises the question of his personal motivation for political action. In his most important tactical essay, the *Three Proposals on Dispatching Troops* (*Suishi sansaku*), written in autumn 1863, he outlined steps which could lead to a liberation of the emperor (Kōmei) from his "imprisonment" in the imperial palace. Maki was driven to this plan, which in 1864 he played out at the Forbidden Gate, because he believed the emperor was issuing decrees that did not reflect his real will. He believed that the emperor had to be delivered from shogunal and courtly influence to express his true intention. This would mark the first step toward an imperial campaign against the *bakufu*. What prompted him to act so independently in defiance of conventions? Maki could in some measure claim the retainer's right to "outspoken remonstrance" (*kansō*) in defense of principle. How much margin was allowed by his time? Custom, legal precedent, and moral restraint limited the samurai's right to public protest, and nothing in this tradition of dissent could justify Maki's choice of action. Maki himself acknowledged the limitations of *kansō* and decided to go beyond tradition. He described his actions, even before he took them, as "unprincipled steps"; he justified them by the authority and justice of his personal feelings which, he believed, informed all his judgments. Maki further witnesses to the strong sense of personal responsibility which *bakumatsu* intellectuals revealed in the field of action, and to the new expression of self which we observed first in Yoshida and Ōhashi.

Maki also knew that his decision to carry out a military coup was unprecedented and irregular; the tradition of loyal vassalage would never have confirmed it. But he believed that in his time the alternatives were no longer war or peace (as Aizawa had seen them), but victory or defeat. Maki further related his personal feelings to the example of Kusunoki. Among the Kyoto firebrands he was known as "the Lord Kusunoki of our times." The late Meiji writer Tokutomi Sōho saw in Maki a reminder also of Ashikaga Takauji, the fourteenth-century general who established a new shogunate: "His actions were inspired by Ashikaga Takauji and his feelings by Kusunoki Masashige." Maki acted in coups with a desire to win the approval of the gods only. There is much of the religious revolutionary in Maki, trained as he was to serve in a religious capacity; Maki was satisfied in the self-knowledge that "if these steps [culminating in unprecedented action] are inspired by the spirit (*kokoro*) of Kusunoki and Ashikaga Takauji, one need not hesitate to act." Thus he validated his "unprincipled steps" not by the tradition of *kansō* ("when there are no remonstrating retainers, the realm will collapse"), but rather by his sense of religious vocation.

Maki, like many contemporaries, fell temporarily under the sway of the Mito rhetoric, which provided him permanently

with a ready-made philosophic vocabulary.[65] In the 1830s, early
in the Tempō reforms, political activists (as we have seen)
turned to Aizawa, Fujita Tōko, or Tokugawa Nariaki to resolve
domestic domainal problems. Maki himself made a pilgrimage
from Kurume, talked with Aizawa, reread the *Shinron,* and returned to his *han* full of ideas for domainal reform. One result of
this contact was the *Tempōgaku* of Kurume, a widened educational curriculum in the *han,* which included subjects with practical content (*jitsugaku*).[66] Maki's biographers and interpreters
believe that his involvement in the Mito program was the central
principle of his thought. Hence it is concluded that the main
lines of his thinking were laid between 1830 and 1844, the period
in which he took on the Mito rhetoric and was engaged in domainal reform.[67] But his major writings date from the late 1850s
and early 1860s, when he was involved in interdomainal activities. Certainly Maki's trip to Mito and his devotion to its program is well documented; [68] his adoration for Aizawa, his diary
reveals, was as great as that for the departed heroes of his
childhood.[69] But, as with his sensitive contemporaries, his acceptance of Mito presupposed seclusion (*sakoku*) and was no longer
possible after the opening of the country. After *kaikoku,* Maki,
while retaining his respect for the Mito school, abandoned it as
an ideology and transferred his allegiance to the pieties of his
youth.

During Maki's reformist years in the 1840s with the Kurume
Tempōgakuha, he wrote little and nothing memorable: a few let-

[65] *Ibid.,* ch. 1.

[66] Minamoto Ryōen, "Meiji Ishin to jitsugaku," in *Meiji ishinshi no
mondaiten,* ed. Sakata Yoshio (Tokyo, 1962), pp. 67–68.

[67] Matsumoto Sannosuke, "Sonjō undō ni kindaiteki seiji ishiki no
keisei," in *Meiji ishinshi no mondaiten,* ed. Sakata Yoshio (Tokyo, 1962),
p. 132.

[68] *MInki.,* "Tempō kanshin nikki," pp. 332–333. This account is enlarged
in Arakawa, pp. 192–194, who argues that Maki is the great transmitter of
the *Shinron* in the late Tokugawa period.

[69] Maki recorded his relationship with Aizawa, though brief, as teacher-
pupil. *Ibid.*

ters, poetry in Chinese and Japanese of no lasting value, and some imitative essays. Maki wrote only when he was prevented from acting; he was an ideologue who resorted to the brush only to announce the action he had decided on. Only reluctantly would he accept the role of a thinker; even then he declared he was only restating Aizawa's *Shinron*.

Maki's affiliation with the reformist *Tempōgakuha* when he was thirty-two or thirty-three years old earned him swift reprisals from conservative elements in the domain's administration. The local Confucianist Honjō Ichirō drafted a petition in 1845 calling upon the lord to eradicate the reformers and their "evil ways." The group countered with a proposal for military, administrative, and moral reforms. They justified their recommendations in terms of the countrywide crisis: the *bakufu's* conduct resembled that of the Fujiwara regents. The true master–vassal relationship should exist (they wrote) not between the shogun and the lords, but rather between the emperor and his subjects. In order to restore this relationship, it was necessary to carry out broad administrative reforms based on the selection of talented and able men.[70] Maki's hand was clearly in this proposal, and his affiliation thereby identified. In the following year this allegiance was reinforced by a trip to Kyoto to observe the enthronement of the emperor Kōmei. His awe and wonder are recorded in his diary, *Koka teimi nikki;* he was struck by the splendor of the imperial throne and the beauty of the regalia placed on the rostrum. Seeing these things, he remarked to himself: "The virtue of the *Sen-o* [archetypal sages] has not yet been lost in the land." [71] His expectations were high, and he appeared to be in a frenzy throughout the ceremony; the ceremony was for him a religious experience which transported him back to the age of the gods. Also in Kyoto at this time he struck up a close relationship with both father and son of the court family Nonoyama; some of his most revealing ideological pronouncements are found in his letters to them.

[70] Higo Kazuo, *Kinsei shisōshi kenkyū* (Tokyo, 1944), pp. 232–233.
[71] *MInki.,* pp. 360ff.

Because of his attempt to carry out the domainal reformist program which he had learned from Mito, he was imprisoned in Mitsuta for ten years, a long time in Tokugawa Japan for such an offense. (Yokoi Shōnan, as we shall see, traveled the same route in Kumamoto when he became involved in the reformist program of the newly formed Practical Studies Group, Jitsugaku-tō.) Although removed from national politics during years when calamitous changes and critical decisions were being made, Maki was well informed (as his writings show) and worked out a program that he pursued single-mindedly after his release. In prison this man of practical action became the ideologist of restoration. His preparation is impressive.[72] Not only did he read and reread the *Tso Ch'uan,* the *Ming shih* (filled with examples of loyalty), the history of Ssu Ma-kuang, the *National Histories,* the *Shinron* (three times), and many other works, he also wrote and edited prodigiously. With his talent for finding a historical personality to match his current predicament, he took solace in the life of the Heian courtier Sugawara Michizane who, he believed, was exiled to Kyūshū for his loyalism (actually as the result of a power struggle at court with Fujiwara Tokihira). His devotion to Sugawara sustained him through copying thirteen volumes of his writings (the *Kanke bunsō*), which he offered to the Tenmangū shrine of Mitsuta. Maki's imprisonment rounded out his intellectual development and moved him from the narrow world of domainal reform to the broader world of an imperial restoration. He was released in 1862 and immediately went to Kagoshima—the beginning of his road to Kyoto, momentary triumph, and glorious death.

While Maki's prison education enlarged his views, down to the

---

[72] The complete account of his imprisonment is in the diary "Nansen nichiroku (Diary of a southern hermit)," in *MInki,* pp. 369–553. It is here that we learn of the range of his reading in these years, his sentimental, indeed self-pitying, remarks about how Aizawa, under house arrest in Mito, and the student, Maki, represent the separation of east and west. Here also we are offered a glimpse of his illusion which identified the circumstances of the Heian nobleman Suguwara Michizane with his own.

1860s he believed that he was merely modifying Aizawa's great plan in the changing situation. As late as 1863 he was still promoting the *Shinron* as the most essential guide to restoration, even though he was talking about other things. He retained to the end residual Mito views, which one writer (expressing a majority view) sees as motivating his activity.[73] One Mito legacy was his concern for "practicality" (*jitsugaku*). Central to his *Rules of the Tempō Learning,* in its effort to reform Kurume, was the Mito idea that education had become removed from real needs. Established learning, Maki and his colleagues charged, neglected "the great principles of filial piety and loyalty, and the rules of samurai status." It had fallen into a concern with "poetic and literary styles and currents," "an emulation of principles" and nothing more.[74] Their petition of 1845 to the Kurume *han* administration advised discipline and spiritual rigor: "The education of samurai is chiefly based on the great ethical principle which discriminates lord from vassal, parent from child. It celebrates the great rules of loyalty, and advocates as its foundation that which solidifies the goal of selfless patriotism (*kiseihōkoku*)." Only if this toughness of spirit was known would the Great Plan be revealed. Study was useful when the samurai were steeled by "the will of selfless patriotism." Neo-Confucianism was an ethic, Maki charged with Yoshida, which transformed the samurai class into bureaucrats of the Chinese variety. The values of this ethic were passive, administrative-clerical, civilian, and literary. As an alternative to the bureaucratization of the warrior, Maki offered a spiritual discipline (*kisetsu*) which through "selfless patriotism" would establish a new morality of political action. "The two hundred years of peace have been shattered," the Kurume petition read, "and we cannot allow the martial spirit and nature to weaken and decay. Life cannot be thought of lightly, as mere

[73] See Matsumoto, "Sonjō undō . . . ," pp. 132ff. Needless to say, I am indebted to Professor Matsumoto for the suggestiveness of his short essay on Maki.

[74] Udaka, *op. cit.* (n. 61 above), 150–151; Matsumoto, "Sonjō undō . . . ," p. 132; and Minamoto, p. 68.

rubbish. We cannot forget for a moment the idea of undivided patriotism. It is also associated with spreading a spiritual discipline, and indeed the achievement of such a discipline is our essential destination. We must make loyalty, filial piety, and *taigi* a real thing." [75]

This practicality and morality of political action expressed in patriotism marks a condemnation of Neo-Confucianism and an acceptance of what Sakuma called "extraordinary times." Maki knew that Tokugawa Neo-Confucianism employed *ri* to impersonalize social relationships and establish unchanging rules of behavior. He recognized the transformation of a nonrational ethic, in which men were bound to each other by friendship, into rational rules which demanded unswerving loyalty to status. He knew that this arrangement was justified as a reflection of a perfect moral order—in concrete terms, of a peaceful and tranquil government. But contemporary perceptions had already thrown this premise into doubt, and Maki, armed with Aizawa's *Shinron,* was awakened to the possibility that human order could no longer promise eternal tranquillity. Despite the failure of leading figures to perceive the troubles of Japan, Maki knew that it was facing a crisis of unprecedented dimensions. He therefore reasoned that samurai required an ethic permitting decisions appropriate to the times without fear of violating fixed codes of conduct. Even more than Yoshida Shōin, Maki tried to revive the ethos of the *sengoku bushi,* who acted on his own perceptions and entered or dissolved relationships without fixed rational norms.[76] Maki was attacking the bureaucratic ethic which stifled creative action, and also Neo-Confucianism itself; he was affirming that his society could no longer be served by the assumptions of a received tradition.

In his *Kashōroku* of 1861 he wrote that Neo-Confucianism possessed little sense of practicality:

As for studying such things as the internal existence of principles in things, I would be apt to say that it resembles the empty discussions of

[75] Udaka, pp. 150–151.
[76] Matsumoto, p. 133.

Zen teachers. The more one becomes involved in high-level discussion, the less he learns about daily life. . . . If we do not cleanse ourselves thoroughly . . . to know and clarify things, to lecture on the Way endlessly, and to penetrate and investigate principles quietly, the country will in no time fall to the barbarians. If we do not learn at the same time to pay attention to the unexpected, which is the unknown world, we will not be able to restore [the realm] and raise an army. No matter how heroically one dies, he will not realize his destiny.[77]

Maki found Neo-Confucianism too abstract, every bit as quietistic as Zen, and equally useless in understanding the new stiuation. Proof of this contention, he argued further, was found in Neo-Confucianism's "reverence for the investigation of principles" and its "special esteem for meditation." Yokoi Shōnan, who possessed a stronger intellect than Maki, made the same complaints, but for different reasons. Maki's denunciation of Neo-Confucianism as a quietistic moralism grew out of impatience with high theorizing though he himself denied that he was not bothered by the fineness or coarseness of theory. All he desired was action, and what was useful and not useful to a specific decision to act. Here, he had learned during the Tempō reforms, was the whole meaning of the learning enterprise. In alerting his contemporaries to the danger of Neo-Confucian quietism, Maki still invoked traditional arguments. Learning, he wrote in the *Kashōroku*, should be concerned with knowing the Way of man, not with some abstraction called virtue: "Ascertaining the way of men means knowing how to perform man's enterprise." [78] Learning consists of three basic elements: purpose, ability, and spirit. Samurai were obliged first "to elevate purpose," which would reveal ability; and ability promised the achievement of study in the proper spirit. These three elements were the guarantee of practicality. "From beginning to end," he said, "there is nothing outside the enterprise of learning." [79]

Maki hoped to replace the passivity, meditation, and self-cultivation of Neo-Confucianism with political action. He valued tal-

[77] *MInki.*, pp. 728–729.
[78] *MInki.*, pp. 727–728.
[79] *MInki.*, p. 727.

ent above mere possession of virtue. "However good and virtuous a man is," he wrote in words recalling Fujita Tōko, "if he is without talent (*sai*) to perform certain kinds of duties, he is of no use to society or to the times. He possesses a useless commodity. For example, men who have ability for office, even though they are unschooled (*mugaku*), will be able to make accommodations and succeed in everything they do." Confucianists were without talent, yet served in the schools; the same could be said of those who held important offices, magistrates and *daikan*.[80] Maki's device was to show how his new perspective directed toward action was related to personality. The Confucian ideal of the amateur qualified to hold administrative posts because of his virtue was inoperative "in a time of social and political turbulence." In place of this model Maki called for recruitment of men of talent and ability whose wisdom was "unfixed like a river." Just as he replaces virtue with genuine ability, so he replaces a mastery of principles (*kyūri*) with the immediately useful. Maki believed he was merely releasing a dormant tradition within Neo-Confucianism, which had been imprisoned by the idea of a natural order. But who was to say? After 1854 there was no agreement on acceptable boundaries of tradition, even though men operated on the assumption that some such agreement existed.

When Maki was released from prison in 1861, the national crisis had eclipsed domainal affairs, and he had no alternative to involvement in national politics. The same impulse which drove him earlier into domainal reform led him to assume leadership of the *sonnō jōi* movement. He also enjoyed the right credentials; for despite his domainal allegiance, Maki was a priest easily identified with the imperial realm, "an imperial retainer." Throughout his imprisonment he had remained silent, keeping a copious diary and reading. He quietly observed the signing of the commerical treaties and the growing "oppressiveness" of shogunal policy. But in the spring of 1858 he ended his silence and wrote a long letter to the courtier Sanjō Sanetomi, which marks

[80] *MInki.*, p. 732.

his first involvement in national affairs.[81] It reveals profound resentment toward the "unceremonial" (*mutei*) behavior of the barbarians and the "effeminacy" of the *bakufu*'s wavering attitude. Hence it was the duty of the court to seize the initiative and act; this was the moment, he wrote, to encourage the emperor to promulgate an expulsionist policy which, in itself, would announce the restoration of imperial authority. Maki was not rehearsing familiar expulsionist gestures; he looked upon repudiation of the treaties as an occasion for restoration, because it was "the most important opportunity to return to the heavenly ordinances and the public spirit." This letter demands restoration for the sake of restoration, as a radical solution to corrosive *bakuhan* sectionalism. To achieve restoration, Maki set out three requirements: (1) To select talented and able men for positions of political responsibility, because "if there are such men in court, then the court can be respected without relying on all the people of the realm." (At this time Maki had in mind Tokugawa Nariaki as a spokesman for the court, but later changed his mind as sectionalism receded in his thinking.) This position was expressed unequivocally by Kusaka Genzui to Takechi Zuisan on the eve of the restorationist coups. (2) To make status available to men if they are to act for the imperial court. (3) To preserve "the great polity of the realm" by "returning to the prosperity of antiquity." Here Maki brought together two themes—*kokutai* and the heavenly ordinances—which were to serve him in formulating a new theory of the emperor. To see the emperor as armed with the moral authority of heaven and with the divinity of the national ancestors, and personalized by history, was the condition of Maki's call for restoration.

The ingredients of this formulation had been available throughout the Tokugawa period; but (as Maki himself noted) they had not been previously rendered usable. The Tokugawa writer who came closest to a notion of the emperor as both possess-

[81] This letter does not appear in *MInki.*, which makes no claim of completeness. Part of it, however, is reproduced in Higo (n. 70 above), pp. 236–237.

ing the principle of authority and being an authoritative principal was Motoori Norinaga. The Mito writers, despite their syncretism, held that the only function of the emperor was to authenticate the political and social order. They believed that this view would reinforce domainal autonomy. This Confucian concept of the emperor, at most ornamented or reinforced by native mytho-history, was the accepted view throughout the Tokugawa period. The nativist claim of a divine emperorship both virtuous and powerful was buried because of its embarrassing historical associations. Only nativists like Motoori and Hirata Atsutane ever seriously considered the relation of the emperor's divinity to the question of political authority—and then only to authenticate further the Tokugawa order. Yet by raising this problem to make society even more nonpolitical, they were also raising serious political questions which later writers like Maki Izumi would take up.

Of course, since the Kamakura period, all writers considered emperorship essential, since it provided the ligaments that held political society together. Tokugawa respect for the emperor was simply a continuation of this conviction. However fictitious his role, the emperor, by offering the symbols of legitimation, made social order possible. Even the Mito writers knew this and made it a basis of their political program. But Tokugawa writers also knew that if any power greater than the Tokugawa family appeared in the land it would throw the ethical position of the shogun into question. This is why early writers tried, at times desperately, to empty kingship of any real authority and to make the emperor into a mere ethical principle, seeking, as Maki observed, "to elevate the emperor to an existence above the clouds." This fact also explains why the Tokugawa used every means to weaken the power of the nobility and simultaneously monopolized the channels of communication between lord and emperor.[82] Confucian respect for the emperor never went beyond praising the emperors of antiquity. Since they lived before the military regimes, they were thought of as morally superior men

[82] Sakata, *Meiji Ishinshi*, pp. 9–28.

(*yūtokusha*) who personified the principle of heaven (*tenri*). Confucianists had no other choice. Power and rationalism together obliged them to distinguish between an emperor who *has* absolute authority and one who *is* absolute authority. This distinction, previously discussed, radically altered the concept of restoration by freeing it from the responsibility of salvaging any specific institutional structure. It was later an essential element in Maki Izumi's idea of restoring an emperor in whom virtue and power would be brought together.

Maki thus showed how far he had departed from the Mito persuasion. Mito writers saw in restoration (*chūkō*) simply an affirmation of this Neo-Confucian ideal of kingship and the hope for a regeneration of the domestic order. Tokugawa Nariaki explicitly professed a Confucian theory of kingship to distinguish himself from the Kyoto loyalists (*oshitsuke*)—Umeda, Yanagawa, Ōkuni Takamasa, Rai Mikisaburō—who were arguing that the imperial house had suffered decline.[83] For Nariaki and his supporting ideologues, the decline of direct imperial rule did not matter: Mito writers proposed, and Nariaki promoted, the realignment of relationships. True *ōdō* was possible only when respect (*meibun*) of the lower lords (shogun and daimyo) for the upper orders (the imperial court) was being observed. These writers were concerned only with preserving a tradition. By established procedure the *bakuhan* system functioned to manage the Way; the *bakufu* and the domainal lords succeeded to the Great Way as handed down by "the heavenly ancestors." Mito writers could argue that this arrangement corresponded to *kokutai*, the "national essence," because, after all, the ordinances were passed through the emperor to shogun and lords. Their complaint was against the shogun-first policy which weakened the domains and, in the face of disorder, imperiled the existence of the realm. This policy was clearly a departure from the past, since the *bakufu*, by undermining the *han*, was in two ways breaking the trust which the emperor had placed in it: By dimin-

[83] Tōyama Shigeki, "Bakumatsu seiji kado ni okeru tenshitsu," *Rekishi Hyōron* (1946), I, 32.

ishing domainal military and financial strength, it weakened the realm; by tampering with the integrity of the domains, it violated the requirements of *meibun* and thus showed disrespect to the emperor. Mito writers called for a straightening of "duties and designations," arguing that if the ethical problem were resolved, everything else would take care of itself.

Tokugawa Nariaki appealed to the emperor when the treaties were up for ratification because he knew that criticism of the shogunate could come only from a higher authority. He involved the throne in poltical affairs without permission from the *bakufu* and for this act of disrespect he was punished. Irrespective of his mixed motives, Nariaki was asking *the emperor to make an ethical judgment only,* to remind the shogun of his position and moral responsibilities. Yet the emperor Kōmei's public denunciation of *kaikoku* was loaded with vast political possibilities. His direct participation in politics overthrew the Mito theory of emperorship in which the virtue of the emperor was not action but passivity. When Kōmei sought to exercise his virtue, the emperor became a political principal. Now the idea of direct imperial rule was available and had its own life. The notion of the emperor as an ethical principle was replaced by the notion of an emperor who acted directly, either in his own person or through the device of what came to be known in the 1860s as an "imperial decree." [84] The nativist concept of an emperor who by virtue of his divine descent ruled directly, immune from historical censure, was unleashed by Kōmei's reluctant exercise of direct ethical authority.

Maki's theory of restoration was to call back the historical per-

[84] Reality was always somewhat unmanageable for *bakumatsu* thinkers, and in the case of the Bunkyū restorationists they discovered, much to their surprise, that the emperor, Kōmei, was not interested in playing the kind of role they were envisaging. Kōmei seems to have shared the sentiment of antirestorationist nativists such as Ōkuni Takamasa, and to have aligned himself with the *kōbugattai* faction. Radicals like Maki, Hirano, and even Sanjō were ultimately less concerned with obtaining the consent of Kōmei than they were in acquiring an Imperial Decree. See Tōyama, *op. cit.,* pp. 33–35.

sonality characteristic of ancient emperors who were the highest statesmen in the realm. To do this he had to rescue the emperor from his seat beyond the clouds—to liberate him from court concealment and put him into the world of politics. Only a personality could engage himself in political reality and make meaningful political decisions. This notion of an active emperor in part reflected his earlier commitment to dynamic political action. In part it was inspired by Tokugawa nativism (*kokugakuron*), especially by the writers who located political authority in the personality of the emperor in order to create greater subservience among the ruled. Early writers like Motoori intended only a reminder that the emperor was the highest authority in the land by virtue of his divine appointment. Later nativist writers, notably Ōkuni Takamasa, who lived to see the Meiji Restoration, intended further to make the emperor into a new political object. Maki Izumi, operating within this nativist framework, proposed to restore direct imperial authority, both by calling attention to the vigorous emperors of Japan's antiquity and by offering the new image of an emperor revered as a human personality. Ōkuni, the most original of late Tokugawa nativists and one of the few *oshitsuke* who survived the purges of 1859, made a strong case for a living emperor in his *Hongaku kiyo* by singling out specific historical figures and their achievements: Ōjin, Tenchi, Temmu, Uda, Go Daigo. But Ōkuni failed to link these historical examples to the contemporary problem—probably because he rejected a politically oriented restoration. Many of his colleagues in Kyoto agreed with this view and were actively antirestorationist. But Maki, committed to relevant action rather than contemplation, had no such reservations as he worked out his concept of emperorship against the backdrop of *kaikoku*. His final view was vastly different from the Confucian concept of the emperor, recently tried out by Mito writers and their lord Nariaki and found wanting. Maki's concept of the emperor, embracing hard, irrational elements, fitted the requirements of contemporary political reality more closely than the Confucian concept.[85]

[85] Haga Noboru, *Bakumatsu kokugaku* . . . , pp. 82–115.

His first purpose, as stated in his long letter to Nonoyama in 1858, was to draw out the emperor from his cloudy seclusion and place him in the contemporary world. "Most respectfully," he wrote, "the imperial court has directed the affairs of the country for the past seven hundred years. [The emperor] was condemned to inaction and was seen by the people as only a deity. We have done little in our effort to drive off the barbarian ships, and because there are many important things that require attention today, people should revere the emperor wholeheartedly. Still more, the people together with the imperial court can make the necessary preparations." [86] Maki urged a revival of direct imperial rule as under Go Daigo and Tenchi (two of his favorites), and believed that such a program could be executed at this time. A few years later he put his conviction in stronger language in a letter to Sanjō: "The treatment of the imperial sovereign originates from losing personal authority to his retainers. Among the number of long-standing abuses, this is the most obvious." [87] How had the individual authority of the emperor been neglected? When did the sovereigns actually lose political control over the realm to their retainers? Even though there had been few examples since the Heian period of emperors involving themselves directly in political decision, he noted that before the Nara period emperors conducted their own affairs and military campaigns. Maki suggested that it was unnatural and unhistorical for the emperor to have been removed from the earthly realm like some deity. He held, of course, that the emperor's uniqueness depended upon his divine descent; but divinity itself required him to act in the political world.

Maki's view of the character of the Japanese emperor recalls the European concept of the two bodies of a king who was both physical presence and spiritual authority. By virtue of this spiritual authority, although he loses his body, he never dies. Maki's conception of an emperor who must rule directly but whose authority is transcendent suggests such a duality between the king's

[86] *MInki.*, p. 46.
[87] *MInki.*, p. 39.

physical body and his spiritual presence; that is, between the institutional charisma of the kingly office and the spiritual charisma of his association with the national deities. The difference is that the Japanese emperor did not have a spiritual competitor such as the pope to worry about. Hence Maki wrote that the "Sun goddess, Jimmu Tennō, all the deities of heaven and earth, have not yet abandoned the divine land." [88] A return to the prosperity of antiquity meant reinstating direct imperial authority. Here also, he argued, lay the meaning of the ancient unity of politics and religion; as he put it in his most strongly restorationist essay, *Kei-i gusetsu,* the emperor mediates between heaven and earth because he is both deity and sage ruler.[89]

With Maki, for the emperor to initiate meant to confront the people; he saw the emperor as filled with vitality because he lived in the same world as his subjects yet still had the responsibility of ruling them directly. Maki had high hopes for Kōmei as personalized emperor until he learned that the emperor was unalterably opposed to restoration. He saw the emperor's personality as analogous to practicality in learning. Just as in learning, "if theory is elevated, less of real value is retained daily," so if the emperor was elevated to a transcendental existence, the idea of selfless patriotism among the masses would be weakened.[90] The distance of the emperor from his people is important, but it must have Nietzsche's aristocratic pathos. The emperor must have visibility as a shining emblem of his divine authority. What good was it to talk about the emperor's divine nature and expect abject devotion, if he was never seen? Ancient Japanese texts, notably the *Nihongi,* often spoke of the emperor as a "manifest deity." Maki, despite the sacerdotal functions of the emperor, stressed his role as *manifest*—a characteristic later incorporated into the role played by the Meiji emperor. His manifest ubiquity, traveling throughout the country in an endless series of one-night appearances, arose from a systematic policy of continuing epiphanies,

[88] *MInki.,* p. 55 (Letter to Nonoyama Sadaisa).
[89] *MInki.,* p. 7.
[90] Matsumoto (n. 67 above), p. 135.

which Maki was already promoting in the early 1860s. Such a flash appearance of the emperor in a remote area, as recorded by a Meiji socialist (Yamakawa Hitoshi) at Okayama in 1885, was electrifying. "Numerous people from my village traveled by foot and jinrikisha a long distance to go to Okayama to see the emperor personally as if it were a religious observance in an adjoining village. . . . Because the emperor never got out of his carriage in which he was riding, many never really saw him, but they paid religious devotion to the carriage." [91] The social democrat Kinoshita Naoe records a similar effect of the emperor's tour through Shinshū.

Maki also looked for an emperor who reigned among the living to insure wisdom—at least by recruiting able men to serve in his behalf. The court's indiscretion had forced the emperor to forfeit personal power and allowed its recipients to abuse it. "Generally speaking," Maki wrote to Sanjō, "statesmen have not taken the opportunity of attending to urgent matters. They have not been informed of the living conditions among the higher and lower orders of society." This neglect would surely paralyze "the public spirit" with a "numbing torpor." [92] But social and political vitality could be restored by an active emperor.

We may recall that Sakuma Shōzan, inspired by the example of Peter the Great, associated massive changes with a decisive leader. The Russian experience had ideal relevance, and hence Sakuma called for an emperor who "changed laws to make laws." Sakuma failed to work out his vision of leadership in detail; not so Maki. Maki hoped to show that the Japanese emperor always acted in extraordinary times, dealing with problems by extraordinary measures. What else was an emperor for? Maki, in the *Kei-i gusetsu,* cited also the example of Peter: "His wife, even though a woman, continued his work after his death and achieved great prosperity." [93] The imperial post, irrespective of its holder, was obliged to act by virtue of its authority.

[91] Kano Masanao, *Meiji no shisō* (Tokyo, 1963), pp. 104–126.
[92] *MInki.,* p. 40.
[93] *MInki.,* p. 6.

Separate from the problem of an authority was the question whether the emperor was a decisive personality who participated in decisions, or simply one to whom "conditions are communicated" and decisions of officials are put to review. Maki was indifferent to how decisions were made and authority transmitted to the lower levels of society: "The great principles of state exist at the top [emperor] where power resides; they are never transferred to the lower levels." In any case, decisions are never made by the masses; no realm could survive a day with such an arrangement. Elsewhere he wrote: "It is a fact that emperors possess power, and that it is not given to the lower orders." [94] He fully represents Rai Sanyō's formula: he has name (*mei*) and power (*ken*), and his name corresponds to reality (*jitsu*). He is free to act and must act. Since his role finds its authority not in morality (the Way or social consensus) but in transcendent national deities, he need not fear the ethical judgment of history. Although involved in the making of history, he is above it and not subject to its requirements. Under this arrangement, history itself is liberated from its moral function and becomes simply the account of political ups and downs. There is considerably nativist thought here, and also much that is new.

Politics for Maki was not swallowed up into ethics, because leadership was not identical with virtuous conduct. Since politics was therefore no longer regarded as a subordinate activity, it was no longer necessary to equate political authority with virtuous sages known, not by their capacity to act creatively under changing conditions, but by their placid contemplation. Maki argued that such an ideal had never really existed in the Tokugawa period, even though officials thought of themselves and justified their policies in such terms. The ancient Chinese had taught (he wrote) that virtuous rule lay in following past practices; but while they produced much that was splendid, their political legacy caused stagnation. It failed to provide later leaders with a method of coming to terms with their own times. The archetypal sages of China's remote antiquity, Yao and Shun, were good

[94] *MInki.*, pp. 8, 10.

statesmen (Maki held), but their rule, which resulted in "prosperity and virtue," was not "a great enterprise" because it did not achieve permanence. Almost immediately after it ended, China fell into civil war. The early Chinese believed that virtue was prior to practice. If later lords had observed the formula "self-cultivation, worldly tranquillity" they might have achieved success. But the Sung period showed that self-cultivation never led to the pacification of men. If they had realized this, Maki said, they would have known how to govern "at any time in their long history." [95] (Maki did not share Yokoi's view of the exemplary perfection of the Three Dynasties or the leadership of Yao and Shun).

To understand the "limits of the times," their assumptions and acknowledged needs, was for Maki knowing how to serve the times. Maki translated the "great enterprise" for his times into an "imperial campaign" against the *bakufu*. He saw a "great enterprise" as a departure from tradition in response to contemporary need. Maki is most explicit in his rejection of Neo-Confucian ethical politics. As with many among his contemporaries, his disposition toward practicality produced genuine political realism. Just as Maki's emperor acted politically instead of making ethical judgments, so politics must be free to meet unexpected contingencies.[96] Maki was suggesting that *politics is the unexpected.* How can men rule (he asked Sanjō) if they fail to take into account their times? "What we call 'conditions' are generated neither by men of noble rank nor by wicked dwarves. Conditions are born from the unexpected will of heaven. And if we are to grasp and understand them, we must have men available who will be able to expand authority, despite the perversity of others who do not participate in heaven." [97] Maki, in a letter of March 1863, established three conditions of proper leadership: circumstances, judgment, and action. As for *circumstances,* Maki invoked Aizawa's familiar discussions of *jisei* and argued that the

[95] *MInki.,* pp. 728–729 ("Nanshōroku").

[96] *MInki.,* pp. 615–618 (Letter to Kōmei).

[97] *MInki.,* pp. 16–17 (Letter to Kōmei); also p. 34 (Letter to Sanjō).

first task of men in positions of responsibility was to know the changing conditions of their times. *Judgment,* he said, "is like the cutting edge of the sword among the three items of the imperial regalia." Maki's choice of words was deliberate; "judgment," which he expressed by the character *dan,* also carries the sense "cutting." It was literally a weapon with which leaders are armed as they go out to meet contemporary conditions. Maki wished to show that judgment was the moral equipment of leaders in the face of unexpected change. His third point is heaven's injunction to *act* and to carry out the ordinances which make civilized life possible.[98] Maki went on to invoke past emperors who had satisfied heavenly requirements. "Jimmu Tennō erected the great feudal (*hōken*) system, established the teachings of Shinto, and unified the public spirit." No mean accomplishment, he remarked. "Temmu exhausted skills in an hundred ways; he planned the central administration, swept away abuses in court, established the prefectural system. . . ." Maki's point in this rehearsal of ancient history is that present conditions have to be met likewise by what he called the "labor of the august Imperial Body."

Maki's examples suggested that past needs constantly varied. The achievements of Tenchi, Go Daigo, and the others had in common only the conviction that the times required specific solutions. Maki's call for an imperial restoration of antiquity was made in the same vein. Despite his celebration of an imperial past, he only sought to restore its spirit in his present—the spirit of examining one's circumstances to know how to act. Virtue was not enough; contrary to the theory of "praise and blame," history rewarded only those who understood their times.[99] His varying experience of conditions suggested to Maki that politics was not a rational order, as Neo-Confucians conceived it. If the course of politics has nonrational elements, the political leader must expect the unexpected. "Men who do not skillfully discriminate contemporary circumstances," he wrote in 1846, *"will not be*

[98] *MInki.,* p. 21.

[99] *MInki.,* pp. 20, 22–36 (Letter to Sanjō). Maki here makes the familiar distinction between name and reality.

able to act despite the best of intentions." [100] (Italics mine.)
Later, in a letter to the emperor Kōmei, he insisted how necessary it was for statesmen to keep an eye on events, and stressed
the link between knowing circumstances and making "cutting"
decisions toward a "labor of the august Imperial Body." [101]

For Maki, the motivation to act in a nonnormative way was
provided by the belief that politics is really separate from ethics,
and that each sphere requires its own mode of conduct. Hence he
contrasted his active political concept with the "moral prosperity" of Yao, Shun, and the Three Dynasties. Central to his theory
was an emperor who, as a living personality in the contemporary
world, released the energy of a political movement. Many of
these ideas he borrowed from the nativist school, where they
were used to salvage the existing *bakuhan* order, not to undermine it. But nativism also contained hints of a different political
order which could be used to justify an anti-*bakufu* movement.
When Maki said that discrimination should always be the most
important factor in decision making, he was expressing anew
Motoori's political sentiment in the context of foreign crisis and
domestic failure. Through the language of nativism Maki gave
meaning to contemporary events. His assessment gave priority to
the international situation, and to meet it he decided on a campaign, led directly by the emperor, against the *bakufu* and the
barbarian. Domestic unity would follow from resolution of the
foreign problem. Maki saw the foreign crisis as more demanding
than either Sakuma or Yoshida had seen it; hence his call for the
"labor of the august Imperial Body." [102]

For Maki and many of his contemporaries, the call for a restoration of ancient political authority was little more than a call for
a direct imperial campaign against the *bakufu*. To realize this
campaign, Maki advised, "it is necessary to excel, in military
prowess. We must with suddenness suppress the lavish prosperity
of the several lords and all thoughts of leisure, in order to protect

[100] *MInki.*, p. 84.
[101] *MInki.*, pp. 17–23 ("Seidanrō sanjo").
[102] *MInki.*, pp. 22–23.

the realm resolutely while promoting financial reforms at the lowest level. We must face circumstances with the flame of heroism, since there is a strong breeze which is converging upon us from the sea in all four directions." [103] He hoped by this plan to hit two birds—the incompetence of the *bakufu* and the foreign threat—with one stone. He complained to the courtier Nonoyama Sadaisa that the *bakufu* had shamelessly disregarded the court's opinions, flattered the barbarians, and neglected the domestic situation by its oppressive policies. In 1860 and 1861 Maki began to hope for an imperial campaign. While he was still in prison, he wrote an essay called *The Record of the Great Dream* (*Taiyumeki*), which worked out in detail a plan to overthrow the *bakufu* behind the screen of an imperial campaign. The dream was of course a shield for sedition. Maki wrote that the occasion had arrived for the emperor to issue an imperial edict and overthrow the *bakufu*. He must personally lead the lords; take up residence in the east (the Hakone mountains) and assemble the shogunal officials for punishment; summon the young shogun Iemochi and demand the return of his former possessions; then take up residence in Edo castle, which would become the imperial capital, and "issue an edict announcing a great new beginning" (*kōshi*).[104] This was also the scheme of his later "Secret Draft Proposal," which was the basis for the later restorationist uprising in Yamato.

The case for a direct imperial campaign was put more eloquently in the *Kei-i gusetsu*, completed in March 1861, just before the attempted restorationist coups. In this remarkable essay, Maki gave the restorers of the Bunkyū years both a plan and a cosmological justification. "We name warp (*kei*)," he explained, "that which is informed by the Great Principle." The woof (*i*) includes the conditions that conform to the warp. The concept of *kei* embraces the whole world under one virtuous principle; it includes rewards and punishments in the judgment of human behavior, the requirements of a frugal life, observance of the rules

[103] *MInki.*, pp. 58–59 (Letter to Nonoyama Sadaisa).
[104] *MInki.*, pp. 619–620 (*Taiyumeki*).

established by the founders of the state, and the achievement of a hundred victories during the emperor's personal campaign against the *bakufu* and the barbarian. The woof represents the execution of action leading to victory. It involves "opening discussions" among the politically important groups in the realm; abolishing antiquated practices and long-standing abuses; making political affairs correct in accordance with the true meaning of *hōken* (feudalism); sanctifying the loyal and filial warriors of the past so that their children might be properly rewarded; observing the rank system of nine grades; restoring the order of merit; correcting emblems of dress and garb; establishing a great school for the children of civilian and military families; "wrapping up in a silk net the able and talented men of the country"; removing the sacred regalia from Ise and placing them under guard; recruiting Buddhist priests as guards and making temples into garrisons; lightening the tax burden and reforming the bureaucracy.[105] In analyzing the "warp and woof," which was his ideal of society, Maki announced a series of reforms which he considered an indispensable condition for a properly functioning political order. Maki included in this "basic plan" practically everything that was later incorporated into the original restorationist government of 1868; both the Restoration Edict and the Charter Oath are pale abbreviations of Maki's earlier proposal. The program for an imperial campaign and reconstruction, both with Maki and with later restorers, was guided by the achievements of antiquity, in particular the pre-Taika past. "It is my intention to be guided by the precedents of the age of the gods, from Jimmu to Tenchi." [106]

Maki chose the remotest antiquity, when the warrior families had not yet appeared and Chinese civilization had not come to Japan. It was mythical rather than historical, nativist rather than Confucian, allowing Maki to stress permanent elements of a national personality without fear of restrictive historical associations. As I have suggested, the nativists wished to revive a pre-

[105] *MInki.*, pp. 5–16.
[106] *MInki.*, p. 12.

Chinese past because they recognized a discontinuity in life, which they saw first in the psychological sector. In their poetic studies they discovered pure Japanese sentiments which antedated the coming of Chinese civilization. Maki knew this, and so did the restorers of 1868. Both he and they, by their retrieval of a mythic past (historicized for credibility), sought to emphasize the power of myth, promising identity and a fresh start unhampered by history. Maki had no idea of literally recovering every detail of a pre-Taika past; restoration was simply a euphemism for a campaign led personally by the emperor. In a letter to a friend of Sendai *han* he pointed out that a restoration was merely "an adornment of the contemporary feudal system with an ancient label such as 'Realm of the Imperial Court' (*kyojō no kuni*)." He repeated this belief in a letter to Saigō Takamori in 1863.

A complementary sentiment is expressed in a poem he wrote on the occasion of scaling Mt. Kōra: "Today is the beginning of eternity (*senzai*). How will we be able to restrain ourselves in setting out to work?" Maki meant that the unique moment of his present represented the starting point for future history inaugurated by the reconstruction of Japan. The same historical consciousness appears in the writings of Maki's confederate Kusaka Genzui who, echoing the sound and fury of his teacher Yoshida, declared his hope to make history anew by directing the future course of humanity. An intellectual condition of any revolutionary movement must be a decision to discard the immediate past. Japanese restorers, regardless of their alleged reliance on traditional values, were no less eager to repudiate history than French revolutionaries in 1789. The values they espoused were traditional in name only. They used the only vocabulary they had at their disposal, but the content was new. And Maki knew that the dynamic inherent in his emperor was not enough by itself to animate a movement. First by a spirituality doomed to failure, then by an imperial campaign, Maki hoped to protect human nature from "bestiality" and "triviality." But he knew that the divinity of the realm and the sacerdotal powers of the emperor were inad-

equate. Hence he came to believe that the *ōsei fukko* must be realized, if at all, as a great political enterprise.

Maki's critics are wrong in condemning his scheme as "feudal," "quixotic," and "romantic." [107] Most revolutionaries have
been romantic; without romanticism chances for revolution are
diminished. If Maki's plan for a return was nostalgic, so was the
later Meiji Restoration which succeeded despite the absence of a
blueprint. The difference between Maki's plan and the Meiji coup
lay not in the goals but in the means. While Maki saw great possibilities in a coup,[108] where restoration was reduced to an imperial campaign, it was not until 1861 that he worked this insight
into a theory of action. The *Gikyō sansaku* (*Three Points of a
Worthy Undertaking*), drafted in the latter part of 1861, shows
an astonishing concern for detail for one supposed to be a vague
romantic. This proposal lays down the principle that before expulsion there must first be an expression of *sonnō:* an elaborate
series of coordinated coups to overcome shogunal control. Maki's
plan resembles, in its essential aspects, the course of the Meiji activists. In an earlier essay, *Dōben* (*Discriminating the Way*), he
urged that "to expel the barbarian it is best to begin by revering
the emperor." [109] Emperorism meant domestic reorganization—
the replacement of the *bakufu*. Then the realm, now united,
could turn to *jōi*. Maki failed to look beyond this point; even the

[107] See, for example, Tōyama Shigeki, *Meiji Ishinshi kenkyū kōza,* ed.
Rekishigaku kenkyūkai (Tokyo, 1961), III, 39ff.

[108] In the "Nanshōroku," Maki discloses another reason for action, given
his strong bent toward active loyalty and practicality. He points out that
he has been in prison for 10 years or some 3,000 days in which time he has
only read and thought about things. Maki, like Yoshida, admits that imprisonment has only inhibited him from acting, but, it is surely true, his
tenure sharpened his anxiety about acting. Perhaps this anxious state
explains why he was so committed to a course of action so speedily after
his release. The years between 1861 and 1864 are crammed full of activity,
and Maki seems to be everywhere doing everything. He was a man who
appeared, even to contemporaries, to be making up for lost time. *MInki.,*
p. 739.

[109] *MInki.,* p. 633.

Meiji restorers hedged on expulsion after their successful imperial campaign, despite having promised a similar schedule.

Since for Maki the purpose of an imperial campaign was to destroy the *bakufu,* like the earlier nativists he asked for return to an antiquity in which the *bakufu* did not yet exist.[110] But he was far from calling for the dissolution of the *hōken* order. The *Gikyō sansaku* has as its first point that the loyal lords must be recruited against the *bakufu.*[111] In letters to his own lord Maki seeks to involve in the undertaking as many lords as possible. He looked first for leadership to the Satsuma daimyo Shimazu Hisamitsu, and then to Mori Chikafusa. "If there are less than nine thousand men, we will in all probability not carry out the worthy undertaking today . . . and if we do not have the assistance of several of the great lords, we will fail altogether. If we have both the support of several lords and nine thousand or more troops, we will of course achieve our goal, and the circumstances of the times will begin to prosper." [112] Maki changed his mind on the best use of the greater lords. His part in the Teradaya incident of April 1862, and in the lightning-like events of 1863, prompted him to shift among domains, and finally to settle on a few lords led by patriotic samurai.[113]

The Teradaya incident shows best how personal involvement changed Maki's mind on tactics and refined his revolutionary theory. The incident happened because Maki, Hirano, Ogō, and Arima expected too much of Shimazu Hisamitsu's armed trip to Kyoto in spring 1862. When Shimazu marched a thousand retainers to the capital, he told the emperor that he planned to reinstate Matsudaira Yoshinaga, Hitotsubashi Keiki, and other casualties of the Ansei purge to positions where they might accomplish a *kōbugattai* settlement. But many of the *shishi* from Kyūshū operating out of Kyoto were unaware of this purpose. While Shimazu's real intention was to clear activists off the streets

---

[110] See *MInki.,* p. 276; also Higo (n. 70 above), p. 266.

[111] *MInki.,* p. 193.

[112] *Ibid.*

[113] See *MInki.,* pp. 61–66, 189–192.

of Kyoto and pacify the city, Maki and Hirano saw his coming as an opportunity to topple the *bakufu,* and expected him to cooperate by putting his troops at their disposal. Hirano Kuniomi expressed their excitement in his *Kaiten sansaku (Three Stupendous Proposals),* written apparently in expectation of Shimazu's arrival. First, Hirano believed that Shimazu would be armed with an imperial decree, and that the court itself would be removed to Osaka. Shimazu would attack the shogunal strongholds in the Kansai area, absolve victims of recent purges, and imprison guilty officials. Then the emperor would enter upon a campaign, leading troops eastward to Hakone. Second, Shimazu would remove supporters of the *bakufu* from the Kansai. Third, once the "commanding heights" had been seized, the imperial forces would implement a policy of *sonnō jōi.*[114] Upon hearing that Shimazu had indeed received an imperial charge, but only to carry out reforms leading to *kōbugattai,* the activists gathered at the Teradaya inn to execute a "plan of direct action." The group was largely made up of extremists from Satsuma, though Maki was included, and led by Arima Shinshichi, who no doubt had raised hopes about Shimazu's intentions. When news of the proposed direct action reached Shimazu, he dispatched an emis-

---

[114] Inoue Tetsujirō, Ueda Mannen, and Inobe Shigeo (comp.), *Kinnō shishi ibunshū,* 4 vols. (Tokyo, 1936), II, 115–119 ("Kaiten sansaku"). Hirano went on to become the chief organizer of the Ikuno Rising (1863) in Tajima. Like other restorationist uprisings of these years it proved to be an annoyance to the *bakufu* but failed to achieve its central purpose. Hirano was imprisoned in Rōkaku where, it is reported, he lectured on the *Jinnō Shōtōki.* (Yoshida Shōin lectured his guards on Mencius.) Later Hirano was transferred to a prison in Fukuoka and deprived of brush and inkstone. Undaunted, his zeal proved to be the source of invention: he made Chinese characters by twisting into shape a Japanese string made of paper (*koyori*), pasted them on paper (which apparently was provided) with boiled grains of rice. This is how he wrote. Moreover, to amuse himself he constructed a makeshift *koto* by stringing out his own hair over a wooden lunch box (*bentōbako*). This example shows, we are told, how Hirano, despite being an activist, never forgot elegance, which in this case meant the triumph of character possessed only by samurai. He died in prison at the age of thirty-seven.

sary (Narahara Kihachirō) to dissuade the activists. Arima chose to ignore the warning. Fighting then broke out with Satsuma troops in which the extremists were overcome. In the midst of dying comrades (Arima was already dead) Maki and the remaining conspirators decided to stop fighting and submit to persuasion. Abandonment of "direct action" by Maki and his supporters won them their lives.[115]

The incident removed Satsuma from the restorationist domains, among which Arima had enlisted it. Retainers of Satsuma such as Ōkubo Toshimichi, Komatsu Tatewaki, and Saigō Takamori turned away from extreme restorationism. Maki's disappointment with the Teradaya fiasco led him to consider Chōshū as the base for a "worthy undertaking." Still, he admitted how "grievously inadequate it is to rely on the several lords," and how important to recruit real "followers of righteousness." "Five hundred men, of whom a certain number are peasants, can be utilized as a strong force." [116] The use of a small cohesive group of "righteous followers" as the vanguard of a restorationist coup was repeated in the attack on the *bakufu,* as part of a larger scheme employing trusted daimyo as well. After Teradaya, Maki was never again sure about using lords, even though in his realism he knew it would be difficult to carry out a restoration without them. Perhaps he also retained a belief in sectionalism as the best arrangement of power after a "worthy undertaking." If all other plans failed, he proposed to bypass the daimyo and recruit a smaller group of handpicked "followers of righteousness" using guerrilla tactics of arson, assassination, and small-scale raids.[117] Maki confessed that of all methods this was the most difficult, because it required expert planning and coordination and committed men. Yet it was the course which excited Maki most, just because it was dangerous and expressed his ideal of devotion. And this tactic in fact marked the restorationist outbursts of 1863 (the

[115] See Ikeda Kiyōmasa, "Satsuma han to Teradaya no hen," *Nihonshi kenkyū* (1966), 87: 1–18.

[116] *MInki.,* pp. 193–194. See also "Gojikensaku," pp. 23–24.

[117] *MInki.,* p. 194.

Tenchūgumi and the Ikuno rebellion) and the Kimon incident which claimed Maki's life. All these uprisings, inspired by Maki's third proposal in the *Gikyō sansaku,* sought to seize power for the throne with a small band of "loyal patriots" by lightning violence. Maki can claim credit for all even though he participated in only one.

Recruitment for the ranks of the "righteous followers" was extended by Maki to non-samurai classes. Maki went beyond Ōhashi in calling for nonfeudal social classes to share his "worthy undertaking." Actually the uprisings were always led by samurai, even though of theoretically low rank, who in turn recruited wealthy peasants, village officials, and rural samurai (*gōshi*) to rise up against the social order for their own reasons. Maki wrote to the Chōshū daimyo in late summer of 1863: "As to how we can flourish at this moment, it is through the establishment of a military system. The base of this military system is the peasantry. The peasantry can be strengthened by a land survey and an equitable distribution of fields. . . . Even though this is difficult to do today, it must be carried out." However, if a peasant army was organized but not integrated into the political system of pre-Chou feudalism, it would grow independent. Maki feared that such an independent organization would eventually constitute a challenge to social order and "brew," as he characteristically put it, "great events in and around society." [118] And the brew would spill over into disorder and domestic turbulence.

Broadening the base of recruitment reflects less a quickened social consciousness than a willingness to accept all help available. Still Maki and his associates did look to those classes with least to lose and most to gain from such a "worthy undertaking." And Maki, like Yoshida, without abandoning the domainal structure, held that a direct relationship between "loyal followers" and the emperor was the only way to remove the *bakufu.* In spite of his concern for domainal reform, he believed it possible only after the *bakufu* had been eliminated and when the emperor ruled directly. His petitions to his lord, like the *Ishin hisaku (Secret Plan*

[118] *MInki.,* pp. 64–65.

for a Renovation of the Domain), testify to his continuing interest in domainal reform. But these anachronistic proposals are not associated with a restorationist plan for the country. Maki invokes pre-Chou feudalism in contrast to the more centralized *gunken* arrangement to show domainal leaders how the system should really operate. In astonishing detail he considers all aspects of *han* life to reconsecrate the domain under the new dispensation of imperial power.[119] Yet in the end it is the power of the emperor which he saw as the basis of a countrywide restoration. "How must we interpret the position of the bright son of heaven who appears to us [in the figure of Kōmei] today? Of course Jimmu Tennō did not abandon the divine land. Today is a time of emergency events which require the restoration of this kind of ancient prosperity." [120] This language expresses not just reverence toward Kōmei (who in any case was unresponsive) but a conviction that Kōmei contained the spark of divinity from the sun goddess transmitted throughout the ages. Maki constantly invited all to give themselves to a "naked, self-abandoning patriotism," which no doubt was one of the sources of emperor worship in modern Japan. In all this Maki was not indifferent to the uses of Western military technology. But he was less interested in the effectiveness of "instrument" than in the power of the spirit to gather loyalty. Here he came down strongly for the "naked" spirit of an honorable death and "the national custom of bravery." As he wrote in a letter of 1858, "Bravery is of great importance to military affairs. There are special means employed in military affairs, but they do not depend upon the sharpness or bluntness of a technical instrument. Today I am offended by the insults and contempt shown by people of all levels toward

[119] *MInki.*, pp. 127–182. This *han* discussion reveals that Maki had some idea of how power should be arranged. It was, in fact, a baby step to the kind of sectionalism promoted by Yokoi Shōnan and Takasugi Shinsaku. Maki differed in his belief that the emperor should be more than a symbol and that foreigners ought to be expelled. His bitter experience at the Teradaya Inn soured him on the actual usefulness of the domain in the emerging arrangement of power after a restoration.

[120] *MInki.*, p. 55 (Letter to Nonoyama Sadaisa).

such affairs. If we do not lose our inclination to be proud of our tradition of bravery, the country will not turn to desert." [121]

Maki made good his words. With Sanjō Sanetomi and dissident extremists from Chōshū, and assisted by Kusaka Genzui, he planned a desperate uprising in 1864. The plan never came off, since violence struck Kyoto with lightning intensity in August 1864, when extremists (mostly retainers from Chōshū led by Maki) faced combined forces from Satsuma and Aizu at the Forbidden Gate of the Imperial Palace.[122] Kusaka was killed, the Chōshū forces were defeated, and Maki, with seventeen close followers, fled the city to Yamazaki where they climbed Mount Tennō to commit suicide. A poem summarized Maki's last thought on his achievements: "I have ended by being interred in the rocky crags of a large mountain peak; the Japanese spirit [is summed up] in the months and years of my life."

RESTORATION AS UTOPIA: KUSAKA GENZUI

Maki Izumi never really decided how the emperor could be related to the growing autonomy of the *han*. Like many of his confederates, he hedged on the continuance of domainal integrity. On the one hand, he needed domainal power and approved a "pre-Chou" feudalism; on the other hand, he was never enthusiastic about relying on the daimyo or sharing power with them. Three men, each in his own way, subordinated the domain to the omnipotent emperor. Sakuma wrote about a new and enlarged political community. Yoshida recognized dual loyalty to emperor and lord, but finally settled on the "imperial retainer" serving in an imperial space. Maki returned always to emperorism as the indispensable condition of any reorganization, in the belief that all else would take care of itself. But in their shifts of position none ever advised total abandonment of the domainal system. This vacillation between *sonnō* and *jōi*—that is between the poles of a

[121] *MInki.,* p. 245.

[122] Full details of this incident are available in *Ishinshi* (n. 1 above, IV, 71–92.

unified realm and autonomous domains—spawned extremists on both sides. Drifts toward both emperorism and sectionalism (*kakkyōron*) were intensified by the failure of the restorationist coups.

Extreme emperorism was represented by the restorationists who perished in the violence of the Bunkyū years. Yet restoration as a political method did not die. Others who followed a more sectionalist course (what Matsumoto Sannosuke has called greater political realism) to security made possible the Meiji Restoration. But that achievement, carried out by the strength of large domains, would have been different without the energy of the restorationists. The best among them, Hirano and Kusaka, differed in small but significant ways from Maki Izumi. Where Maki always kept the door open to some kind of sectionalism, Kusaka, the leader of the Chōshū firebrands, was willing to close it. Kusaka best represents the youthful aspirations finally built into the restorationist settlement. By his close association with Chōshū and with the leaders-to-be of the Restoration, Kusaka commanded respect. It was his failure which turned Takasugi and Kido toward restoration through sectionalism.

Yoshida Shōin singled out Kusaka Genzui as the most promising of his disciples. He came under Yoshida's influence when he was very young, and followed what might well have been Yoshida's chastisement of Takasugi and himself for not performing "loyal deeds." Kusaka failed to understand that Yoshida's personal charisma was intended to inspire his students to follow their leader, not to pursue independent action. Yoshida's break with all but a few of his most devoted followers shows how he pressed this point. Kusaka declared to Yoshida's brother Sugi Umetarō that he wanted to shape history: "I told Takasugi that we must reform the national administration by strengthening finances and the economy . . . it is my hope to clarify the Way humanity should advance." [123] Kusaka saw the solution to this problem in the purity and sincerity which Yoshida was always talking about but never made clear.

[123] Quoted in Ikeda, *Takasugi Shinsaku to Kusaka Genzui* (n. 16 above), p. 92.

Kusaka chose direct action because he saw the effects of the
foreign menace upon the domestic economy. His two best-known
writings, the *Kairan jōgi* and the *Kaiwan shirigoto,* were both
written in 1862 in response to this threat. He was convinced that
the financial troubles of the *bakufu* had been caused by the treaties and the trade they produced. Kusaka's sense of the necessity
to expel the foreigner was so extreme that his restorationism excluded all but the most loyal men. He had already noted in 1858
that nothing could be expected from the authorities: "In the conditions of the realm, both the top and the bottom are flourishing.
Only the middle levels are not flourishing, and since they are not,
I hope that the realm will be invigorated by the top and by the
bottom." [124] By the "top" he meant the court to which all devotion was due; by the "bottom" he meant the unattached patriots
and loyalists to the emperor. The middle level, of which he despaired, included the *bakufu* and the domainal lords, who he believed deserved only distrust, contempt, and opposition. This
view of the social order lay behind his action in the desperate adventures of the Bunkyū years. When Kusaka joined Maki Izumi
in a restorationist coup, he had different reasons. Because he was
unyielding in his methods, he was more extreme than Maki—
also more unrealistic. He tended toward a grandiose elimination
of all "evils" (*jaku*) especially the domains, which were in league
with the *bakufu* to prevent a coalition between "red-hearted patriots" and "the pleasure of the emperor." Only such a coalition
could provide an answer to the foreigner in Japan and to the
treaties that were destroying the national economy.[125] Kusaka
used the language of Neo-Confucianism, misleading phrases like
"the opening of public discussions" (*dōkai*), "mass deliberation"
(*shūgi*), "the public opinion of the realm" (*tenka no kōron*).
These traditional phrases—all he had available—express neither a
traditional political theory nor a modern political vision. Nothing
suggests that he was using Neo-Confucianism to convey the no-

[124] Quoted in Matsumoto, p. 163.
[125] *Kinnō shishi ibunshū* (n. 114 above), II, 213–219 ("Bunkyū ninen
. . . Kairan jōgi").

tion of a unified state based on consent of all elements. Kusaka was merely reminding his contemporaries how the *bakufu* had failed in its duty by ignoring the domains.

The language he used can be decoded. Because *taigi* and "red-hearted patriotism" are characteristics of the "imperial retainers," "opening public discussion" is not a statement of egalitarianism but a call for the *shishi* to reject the "indecision of the *bakufu*." [126] His usage of *shūgi* is decoded thus: "The several red-hearted lords have been informed of important decisions but they are never consulted beforehand. The usefulness or uselessness of opening the ports, the pros and cons of war and peace, must be a matter of public discussion throughout the country. If these red-hearted patriots are consulted, they will certainly announce the fact that they will speak against the blunders of *bakufu* officials." [127] The "red heart" of loyalism is Kusaka's criterion of organization and action; despite lip service to the domains, he can bypass them in the interest of *sonnō* and *jōi*. Hence his later declaration to abandon even the lords—the "middle." Kusaka retained some hold on the central assumptions of Neo-Confucianism until the end, adapting its debris to his perception of reality. Yet his retention of optimism about the possibility of an ethicosocial order shows that he had not heard the teaching of Yoshida Shōin; the "red-hearted patriot" took precedence over experience and utility.

In his artificial view of the social order, the "bottom" would naturally join with the "top" if the obstacles were removed. Kusaka, like Maki and the nativists, saw direct relations between emperor and retainer as sacred. This was Yoshida's last position on loyalty; Kusaka saw it from the first as the proper basis of society and of action. It was the task of the bottom to remove the obstacles. Kusaka viewed this relationship as basically moral but spoke of it in sacerdotal metaphors to give men inspiration to leave their domains. His call arose in large part from his disapproval of Nagai Uta's "Maritime Policy," and of his party's policy

[126] *Ibid.*, p. 216.
[127] *Ibid.*, p. 218.

to align Chōshū with the *bakufu*.[128] Despite Nagai's rhetorical criticism of shogunal policies, his proposals in reality gave complete support to the *bakufu*—and thus spurred on loyalists like Kusaka and Takasugi. Kusaka's renunciation of Nagai and the "uninvigorated middle" drew him and his associates into direct action to "fulfill the imperial pleasure." They hoped to "harmonize high and low" by linking "the imperial pleasure" to the "red-hearted patriots." Those in the middle who stood between activists and emperor had to be removed. Kusaka's catalogue included lords, courtiers, shogunal officials, and of course foreigners. As he wrote to his fellow loyalist Takechi Zuisan: "It is not enough to depend upon the several lords; nor is it sufficient to depend upon the courtiers. There is no possibility other than assembling the unattached patriots. Forgive me, but even if your domain or mine is destroyed because of this, it is nothing if we conduct a righteous and loyal cause. If our two domains exist or survive, if we do not realize the equality of the people (*manminheitō*) and the peace which is at the heart of the emperor, then living in this country is not worth a thing." [129] On the same date he drafted a similar letter to a retainer in Satsuma, and called for an assemblage of "retainers from the several domains to accomplish a great enterprise of *sonnō jōi*."

In his anger and indignation Kusaka developed from Maki Izumi the idea of the "august imperial deed," for which he saw abundant opportunity.[130] The deed he hoped for was rectification of the financial and economic malaise caused by the treaties and trade; but he was doing more than responding to public events. In the *Kaiwan shirigoto*, his last major essay, there are vague elements of a utopian scheme. Its language is derived from

---

[128] The details of Nagai's policies are found in Seki Junya, *Hansei kaikaku to Meiji ishin* (Tokyo, 1955), pp. 110ff; and Shibahara, *Meiji ishin no kenryoku kiban*, pp. 241–252.

[129] Quoted in Ikeda, *Takasugi Shinsaku to Kusaka Genzui* (n. 16 above), p. 108.

[130] *Kinnō shishi ibunshū*, II, 229–242. (This is the gist of the *Kaiwan shirigoto*.)

the Kyoto loyalist Umeda Unpin, to whom Kusaka owed as much
as to Yoshida. His political radicalism, devised to meet the contemporary situation, yielded a dim vision of things to come. Kusaka promises an eternal age if the conditions of *sonnō jōi* are
met: to seize the opportunity and achieve a great enterprise, restoring a policy of expulsion. "Entrust the country to the august
Son of Amaterasu Ōmikami to govern for ten thousand autumns." [131] "An eternal emperor" (*miyomiyo no tennō*) had
governed the imperial land tranquilly, so that it had been the
"peaceful and tranquil country" (*yasukuni*). Now that the barbarian has come and brought destruction, even though the realm
is eternal, "it has become polluted" (*kegasare*). "Even the people
(*tamikusa*), who are the august treasure, have been abused by
the barbarian"; they had sought to spread "an evil religion"
which was "resented by the gods." Again and again he returns to
a basic sentiment of Shinto: pollution by the barbarian required a
massive purification.

The result of purification would be "the promulgation of an
imperial decree." All would submit to it, and the "august enterprise" would be accomplished. "An imperial decree to the realm
will illuminate, straighten, and purify" (*akiraki jikiriyoki*).
Kusaka uses nativist religious notions filled with antique associations about ritual purification and conduct.[132] He could have used
a more familiar Neo-Confucian exhortation to correct behavior;
the reason for his choice is clear. Kusaka has the vision of a "prosperous antiquity"; and while he never suggests an actual return to
archaic conditions, he is writing about an Arcadia whose spirit
must be recaptured. In his time Japan had been granted the blessing of the gods. His belief that the opportunity for *sonnō* and *jōi*
is "experienced in every thousand years" suggests also a genuine
recognition of his present as unique and of the need to meet the
crisis with unique measures. His invocation of "return" and "antiquity" meant either a romantic flight from the present or a mad-
cap scheme to solve the problems of the present by use of the

[131] *Ibid.*, p. 235.
[132] *Ibid.*, p. 239.

past. Like most restorationists he was ahistorical in his proposals. When he called for return to an anterior time, it was to a time that never existed in Japan's historical past; it was a call to return to the gods in a prehistoric mythic past. But a return to the gods meant both the destruction of history and the belief that a fresh start must be made without historically binding associations. Kusaka envisaged a return to Arcadia, but appeal to a utopia is always the attempt to find a new beginning. His use of religious values wavers between political expediency and genuine commitment; the ambivalence is a real part of his thought. Kusaka, like many contemporaries, was committed to action without ever knowing which course to take. But he was firmly devoted to "recruiting talented and able men to administer the realm" and "the necessity to know about useful things." The rest, he believed, could be played by ear so long as the emperor was reinstated and an imperial decree issued. He was confident that "if we move with the imperial banners, the heroic and brave will rush everywhere to destroy the crafty traitors and annihilate the cunning barbarians." The lesson of antiquity was clear. If the imperial majesty was illuminated far and wide, "the Eight-Island Country [Japan] can truly be called brave." For ancient man had already said that "if decisive action is taken, even monsters can be overcome."

Kusaka Genzui died at the age of twenty-five, fighting troops who represented a greater reality than any monsters.

VI *Sectionalism and National Unity: Yokoi Shōnan*

FROM RESTORATION TO REORGANIZATION:
A NEW POLITICAL SOLUTION

The restorationists of the early 1860s failed, not from lack of idealism (Kusaka carried the ideal of restoration as far as it could go), but from a lack of method, which drove activists "back to the drawing boards." They were not trying to blueprint a new society; rather they sought to ensure the success of a restorationist coup, and thereby to restore direct imperial authority and establish talent and ability as the criteria for leadership in the emerging political order. By "talent and ability" late Tokugawa writers meant practical knowledge in daily affairs, and in the 1860s this included Western military technology and economics. The *bakumatsu* debate had produced no more concrete political solution than this. It was believed that the details of a new political order and of policy must be subordinated to the necessity of finding the ablest men; that done, the political future would take care of itself.[1]

Political writers after the abortive coups presupposed restora-

---

[1] B. Silberman and H. D. Harootunian, *Modern Japanese Leadership* (Tucson, 1966), pp. 83–119.

tion and saw talent and practicality as the best mode for reorganization of Japanese society to meet internal and external problems.[2] They had to overcome the *bakufu* and set up a new
arrangement of power from what was left—the emperor and the
several domains. Despite various invitations that men should
leave their domains, it was recognized by summer 1864 that activism had to be supported by the domain. Until the *kōbugattai*
coup of August 1863, the end of domainal sectionalism was seen
as a prerequisite of restoration. Writers like Sakuma, Yoshida,
Maki, and Kusaka failed to reconcile imperial authority with the
persistence of the domains because they believed the foreign crisis
required immediate attention. However, out of their failure arose
a new theory of sectionalism (*kakkyōron*) with new possibilities.
The notion of powerful autonomous domains was new, since
originally domainal integrity had meant only "preserving the
good name of the *han*." Yet even this modest aim, it was discovered within the unstable late Tokugawa environment, could be
realized only through augmenting domainal power. It was first
in Chōshū around 1862 that domainal theorists began to think
about destroying the *bakufu*. By 1864 it was recognized that only
strong domains could overcome the *bakufu* and unify the country.

Although restorationists preferred to gather around the unifying symbol of the emperor and dissolve sectionalism, they had to
admit that the most powerful force was the *han*. This is very
clear after the failure of the coups, on the eve of the *bakufu*'s first
punitive expedition to Chōshū. Yokoi Shōnan, Takasugi Shinsaku, and Ōkubo Toshimichi turned to sectionalism as an alternative to "the breach of conduct of the expulsionist policy"—that is,
the recognition that expulsionism led to adventures like Maki's
attempted coups and dangers like the bombardment of Shimonoseki by foreign ships. Chōshū in particular was forced to reorgan-
ize by the *bakufu*'s invasion and by its plan to absorb the domains in a reorganized shogunal centralism. Sectionalism was or-

[2] Shibahara Takuji, "Hanbaku shosei ryoku no seikaku," in Iwanami
kōza, *Nihon Rekishi* (Kindai I), pp. 200ff.

ganized by strengthening domainal budget and army (*fukoku kyōhei*)—the Mito program enlarged to demand the removal of the *bakufu*. Sectionalism made the Restoration of 1868 possible by balancing the demands of a unitary structure (the emperor) with domainal interests. The theory was most fully worked out by Yokoi Shōnan, and dramatized by Takasugi Shinsaku in Chō-shū and Ōkubo Toshimichi in Satsuma. It assumed that the newly emerging community of the entire realm depended upon the strength of the individual domains. Kido Kōin at the time of the first campaign against Chōshū stated that "Chōshū is the best utensil (*dōgu*) for curing the illness of the imperial country." [3] Chōshū was not merely serving itself, but also playing a larger role to establish "the basis of eternity" through "enriching the imperial country and strengthening its army (*tenkoku fukoku kyōhei*)." Of course, as a member of a *han* threatened with extinction, Kido had no choice but to adorn Chōshū's defense with a larger purpose. Yet it is significant that he linked the domain with the new political space headed by the emperor, making sectionalism a condition of unity in power and wealth. We will see that the same sentiment marks much of Yokoi's and Takasugi's writings between 1863 and 1868.

To reconcile emperorism with domainal interests, loyalists like Yoshida, Maki, and Kusaka had sought simply to suppress sectionalism for a higher principle of authority (*sonnō-ron*), without calculating the tenacity of domainal claims. They and even Sakuma were concerned with the foreign menace. Their responses are a dialectical antithesis to the Mito conviction about the priority of the inner problem. But *their* successors in turn—the theorist Yokoi, activists like Ōkubo and Takasugi—viewing domestic circumstances and foreign affairs as separate, tried to satisfy the requirements of each. They saw *naiyū* and *gaikan* as equally important, each demanding its own resolution; this recognition was the key to success, since it brought together past policies in different spheres into a comprehensive plan. The Mito

[3] In *ibid.*, p. 202; also Tsumaki Chūta, ed., *Kido Kōin bunsho* (Tokyo, 1929–1931), I, 90–91, for comparable expressions of sectionalist sentiment.

school wished to treat the external problem through domestic moral reform. Sakuma, Yoshida, and Maki, reversing priorities in response to *kaikoku* and the treaties, promoted elaborate defense programs under the direction of the emperor, which they believed were better than anything the *bakufu* might offer. Hence their proposals for domestic reorganization, from Sakuma's moderate reform through the call for restoration by Yoshida and Maki, have so little substance. Their stress on expulsion, however modified, blurred the distinction between domestic and foreign needs. But sectionalists believed that the foreign problem could be met through domainal military preparedness based on Western technology and organization; while the domestic problem required the strengthening of local authority (which meant fiscal autonomy), so that the *han* could help form national policy (*kokuze*). Sectional insights explain Yokoi's identification of national policy with *fukoku kyōhei,* and his concern for "public discussions within the realm" and broader representation of power; more generally they lie behind the new political consciousness of men like Ōkubo and Takasugi that accounts for much of the Meiji achievement.

Of all the late Tokugawa ideologues, none was more insistent on rational political procedure than Yokoi Shōnan, and none did more to work out a realistic political vision based on utility and practicality. His program helped domainal activists such as Takasugi and Ōkubo shake loose from normative Neo-Confucian morality (*meibun*), without the hesitancy of their predecessors, and take on a new basis of accountability: an understanding of contemporary reality without recourse to precedent. Paradoxically, Yokoi also tried to revive Confucianism under the changing conditions of the *bakumatsu.* Nothing was more real to Yokoi and domainal activists, after the failure of *kōbugattai* and the coups of the early 1860s, than the position of the *han* in a new political environment—especially as evidence of shogunal paralysis mounted. Yokoi, who never threw off Mito influence, had long worked for domainal integrity, first in Kumamoto and then later in Fukui (Echizen *han*); as an adviser to Matsudaira Shungaku he was involved in the politics behind *kōbugattai*. From his experience in domain reform since the Tempō years, Yokoi settled on a simple formula which Ōkubo and Takasugi applied each in his *han:* the strength of the whole realm depended on the strength of its individual parts, the domains. If an imperial restoration was to succeed, it must be accommodated to the virtual federalism represented by the several *han;* and any subsequent imperial administration would have to reflect sectional autonomy. But (as Yokoi argued eloquently in the *Kokuze sanron*) domainal integrity never precluded a unified realm under the nominal authority of an emperor.

TEMPŌ: THE CHALLENGE TO CONFUCIAN REFORM

Unlike most of his early associates, Yokoi Shōnan (1809–1869) lived to see a partial realization of his hopes before the Restoration. Unlike others who died along the way, he spent his energies in less spectacular and more durable exploits: exploring the possibilities of a new political order; preparing leadership for the crucial time when the crisis was overcome and a new stage of development was inaugurated. More than any other ideologue, Yokoi accepted a new reality as a datum in the resolution of political and social problems. He was at once the most realistic and the most visionary of late Tokugawa thinkers, the most original and imaginative, and also the most consistent and persuasive. Yokoi Shōnan was a man of many seasons who saw everything there was to see. The publicist and gadfly Fukuzawa Yūkichi later in life attributed such a prescience to his early self. But Yokoi's vision is documented, and his assassination is testimony to its disturbing originality; Fukuzawa has left us a contrived autobiography of his wondrous thoughts composed decades afterwards. Fukuzawa's consciousness that a historical drama had already taken place prompted him to find a place for himself in it; Yokoi knew only that his times were out of joint and only guessed what drama might take place.

Yokoi's talents in the *bakumatsu* as scholar, swordsman, and political reformer, were widely known. So were his monumental drinking bouts, which more than once earned him domainal censure. But his reputation was dimmed in the early Meiji period for at least two reasons. For one thing, the few men who could be called for his students—for example, Yuri Kimimasa (a drafter of the Charter Oath) and Motoda Eifu—either died or slipped into obscurity themselves. Yokoi really never had a school either in Kumamoto or in Fukui. His best known student, Motoda Eifu, who recorded his recollections of Shōnan and was tutor to the young emperor Meiji, revered Yokoi as a teacher but not as an original thinker. Motoda's abrasive and anachronistic moralism prevented him from really understanding Yokoi. Shōnan's son Yokoi Tokio and the Kumamoto group of young samurai Christians (Kanamori Tsurin, Kozaki Hiromichi, Tokutomi Ichirō [Sōho], and Ebina Danjō) remembered his "progressive spirit" and pursued a course which no doubt would have been approved by him, but meant a break with the *bakumatsu* tradition. And Yokoi is compared with Sakuma Shōzan or even Yoshida Shōin he invariably appears to lose in stature. Sakuma's pupils became the vanguard of "civilization and enlightenment." They included prominent members of the Meirokusha, the early Meiji establishment's captive group of intellectuals who justified changes in the name of material progress: Tsuda Mamichi, Nishimura Shigeki, and Kato Hiroyuki. Sakuma's simplistic and universally misunderstood formula, *Tōyō dōtoku, seiyō gei,* was used to rationalize early Meiji society, whereas Yokoi's more comprehensive criticism of social organization and his complex proposals failed to animate the leaders of Meiji Japan. Yokoi's impact was felt (I suspect) in the Charter Oath, but thereafter his political solutions were ignored and his memory neglected. The comparison with Yoshida, made early by Tokutomi Sōho, is even more invidious. Yoshida, despite his friction with his followers, was elevated at death to national martyr. Since the most influential Meiji statesmen had been his students, his legend was sealed in the mytho-history of modern Japan. Yokoi had nothing like the apparatus of the Meiji state to fuel the fire of his memory.

Until recently Yokoi Shōnan was remembered only by a few adherents of minority political traditions who sought a genealogy for their own positions. Thus Yoshino Sakuzō found in Yokoi a "progressive" political thinker whose voice was drowned out by greater volume. Yoshino believed that Yokoi was a precursor of social democracy.[4] Since 1945 there has been a stampede among Japanese historians to find roots of a democratic tradition before fascism, and Yokoi like Yoshino has been elevated to a position of unparalleled esteem. By writers as different as Sir George Sansom and Kōsaka Masaaki, Yokoi is seen as a farsighted progressive who envisaged a truly modern political community, when those around him were satisfied with less-than-revolutionary schemes.[5] Both historians make Yokoi a precursor of modernity with foresight which transcended his own age. Recently the first full-length biography of Yokoi since before the war has appeared in the popular *Jinbutsu sōsho* (Biographical Series) by Tamamuro Taijō, a well-known historian of Kyūshū—but it is little more than an abbreviation of the work (*denki*) published by Yamazaki Masashige in 1938.

Whatever the truth in seeing him as a precursor of modernization, Yokoi Shōnan's own purpose was far more modest. He sought to resuscitate Confucianism as a relevant political ethic and to establish on this foundation a new kind of political order. Sakuma Shōzan by contrast was an orthodox Neo-Confucianist who tried to fit scientific knowledge into the tradition because of his concern for defense; in the end he concluded that science complemented the "spiritualism" of Neo-Confucian moralism. Yokoi did not possess Sakuma's flair for scientific knowledge; his priorities were different, because he perceived that Japan faced more than a question of defense. Yokoi was a political theoreti-

---

[4] See Yoshino Sakuzō, *Meiji bunka kenkyū* (Tokyo, 1946), Vol. 8 of *Yoshino Sakuzō Hakushi Minshu shugi Ronshū* pp. 11–101.

[5] Sir George Sansom, *The Western World and Japan* (London, 1950), pp. 280–284. Kōsaka Masaaki, *Japanese Thought in the Meiji Era*, trans. D. Abosch (Tokyo, 1958), pp. 27–38. There is a dissertation on Yokoi by Dixon Miyauchi, completed at Harvard in 1957.

cian, unlike Sakuma, less concerned with the compatibility of their two cultures than with the ethical problems raised by the new knowledge. Yokoi (unlike Sakuma, who saw no need even to modify the Neo-Confucian ethic) came to believe that Japanese society was not prepared for navigation, industry, science, and technology.

Yokoi's proposal to "return to the Three Dynasties" contrasts with Sakuma even more sharply. Sakuma tried to adapt Neo-Confucianism to natural science by an interpretation of universal principle (*ri*); Yokoi found in a pure tradition prior to Sung thought a transcendent Way valid in all times and places. In contrast with the particularism of Sung thought (which Sakuma had tried to salvage) Yokoi saw the Three Dynasties as pointing to the universality of experience; Yao and Shun were innovators who constructed a political and social order adequate to their times; they had no intention of bequeathing it to different times and places. The particularity of their achievement corresponded to the universality of their method. Hence Yokoi, unlike Sakuma, was liberated from the obligation to defend a specific social and political order, and was able to entertain the possibilities offered by the West. In a letter of 1859 to a friend in Echizen *han* he explained that "the Way is found through heaven and earth. It is not something possessed either by us or by foreigners. Wherever the Way is possessed, there you will find the central kingdom even among barbarians; where there is an absence of the Way, there you will find barbarians, even though they are the Chinese or the Japanese." This discovery of the Way in countries other than Japan and China is Yokoi's most striking contribution to late Tokugawa thought. This universal criterion enabled him to abandon the Sinocentric conceit behind much of the traditional East Asian thought. Sakuma compared the West and Japan from the level of technology and power; Yokoi could judge the social and political organization of countries by their appropriateness to contemporary conditions. Late Meiji intellectuals agonized to find an ethic appropriate to industrialization; Yokoi much earlier had both formulated the problem and tried to solve it. He began by trying to purify Confucianism; in his zeal he transcended the philosophical tradition.

Born into the family of a Kumamoto samurai, Yokoi was early enrolled in the *han* school to receive a traditional education in military arts and Chinese classics.[6] We can only guess at his education from the curriculum and from practice elsewhere, since Yokoi did not leave a record of these early years.[7] We do know that Yokoi performed well enough in the established course. Like Sakuma, Yokoi first showed his proficiency in literary studies, especially Chinese. He was known as an outstanding Chinese scholar much earlier than as a practical reformer or a political theoretician. His earliest writings are in literary Chinese of classical genres. These poems, essays, and moral pieces show more interest in style than in intellectual content. Yokoi's later pieces, written in the thick of political affairs, show a shift to easy Japanese. His principal theme in his early years was expulsionism (*jōi*), which up to 1853 was proper for young samurai intellectuals. Yokoi took cognizance of the growing foreign menace in classical Chinese; but his rhetoric belonged to Mito, little more than echoing expulsionists like Aizawa Seishisai and Fujita Tōko.[8] Yokoi studied Chinese philosophy in domainal schools until he was thirty-one years old (1839) when he was rewarded for his ability and persistence and sent to Edo for further educa-

[6] See Minamoto Ryōen, "Yokoi Shōnan: Kindai kokka e mezame," in *Nihon no gendai shisōka*, 3 vols. (Tokyo, 1961), I, 40–41. Biographical information on Yokoi I have taken from the massive and exceedingly dull account by Yamazaki Masashige, *Yokoi Shōnan: denkihen*, (Tokyo, 1938), 22–34 (hereafter cited as *YSdk*); and Tamamuro Taijō's shorter *Yokoi Shōnan* (Tokyo, 1966).

[7] See, by all means, Ronald Dore's relevant *Education in Tokugawa Japan* (Berkeley and London, 1964).

[8] *YSdk.*, pp. 43–82; also *Yokoi Shōnan iko*, ed. Yamazaki Masashige (Tokyo, 1943), pp. 672–674, 678–679, 679–680, 692–693, 698, where he records his admiration for Aizawa after reading some of his writings. Hereafter this source will be cited as *YSi*.

It is interesting to note, in this connection, that Yokoi wrote in Chinese only in his "youthful" period, his loyalist phase, after which he turned to Japanese styles—no doubt to put important ideas into accessible language?

tion. This long exposure to Chinese philosophy explains why Yokoi to the end of his life sought to adapt Confucian rationalism to new circumstances. While it was established practice in Tokugawa Japan to send the most able retainer-students of each *han* to Edo for further study in military and civilian arts, most went at a much earlier age. Yokoi was already holding official positions within the domain while his contemporary *shi* were in Edo completing their training.[9]

Yokoi was excited by his first introduction to national politics.[10] He seized every occasion to talk and listen in the fencing academies and lecture halls. In the *Tōyū Shōnan,* a work constructed around Chinese poems, written while in Edo, Yokoi announced that he wished to "practice the Way of tranquilizing the realm" rather than study more in Confucian texts.[11] To this end he sought out men who promised results: the gunnery expert Egawa Tarōzaemon; Satō Issai, Sakuma's teacher in Wang Yang-ming philosophy at the Matsuzakidō, now an aged recluse; Fujita Tōko, who became his firm friend until his death in the earthquake of 1853 in Edo. A poem describes their first meeting: "I met with Fujita Toranosuke/kept up with the night's talk/ equalled Toranosuke's elegance." He went on to describe an evening of revelry in which "I warmed myself with saké in a winter garden, and through frank discussion completely forgot about myself and where I was. While the heat of the argument failed to melt the ice around us, the excitement of words reminded me of my experience in reading the *Shūgi naigai* of Kumazawa Banzan."[12] (Probably the heat of argument was fueled as much by saké as by brilliance.) Yokoi and Fujita Tōko met a number of times to "eat, drink and talk frankly." Tōko, we recall,

[9] *YSdk.,* pp. 41ff.

[10] *YSi.,* pp. 789–822. "Yūgaku zasshi," written in the style of a poetic essay.

[11] *YSi.,* p. 855.

[12] *YSi.,* p. 863. Actually Kumazawa's *Shūgi washo* had been an eye opener for Yokoi since youth. He turned to this text on a number of occasions in the course of his life for guidance and revelation. See *YSdk.,* p. 58.

was becoming the type of the activist samurai (*shishi*), distinguished both as scholar and reformer. Yokoi saw Tōko as repeating the role of Kumazawa Banzan, remembered as the model samurai reformer of the early Tokugawa period. Yokoi's conversations with Tōko reinforced his expulsionism and introduced him to domainal reform. All this was on the eve of the Tempō reforms in which Tōko and his lord Nariaki made their mark on the world. Tōko was recalled to Mito in December 1839 while Yokoi was still in Edo; Yōkoi wrote a parting poem filled with moral pieties from the Chinese.[13] Tōko was no doubt pleased at hearing the sentiments he had held so long. Even more important, Yokoi learned from Tōko the distinction between "original standards, old precedent" (*senkaku korei*) and "longstanding customs, old abuses" (*ryūzoku kyūhei*), a formula which helped him evaluate the social and political tradition. For Tōko it provided reforms to restrengthen the *bakuhan* order; by identifying contemporary conditions with *ryūzoku kyūhei* he could appeal to *senkaku korei* as framework for the reconstituted order. Yokoi's separation of the contemporary social and political order from the Way reveals how he had transformed this inheritance into a justification for reform which promised to alter the basis of the structure itself.

In February 1840 Yokoi planned to leave Edo for a study trip (*yūgaku*) to Mito; though it never came off, he received an invitation from Nariaki to teach in the *han* school. (Nariaki had heard about Yokoi's talents through Fujita Tōko's enthusiastic reports.) Yokoi declined the offer because he was recalled to Kumamoto for domainal discipline on a charge of improper language after a banquet. In all probability his recall had less to do with drinking than with political criticism.[14] Kido Kōin later commented that Yokoi possessed a "blade-like tongue." Yokoi upon his return wrote a massive paean of praise for Mito. This was the *Nanchōshi, The History of the Southern Court,* which summarized the legitimist argument of the loyalists. In the fol-

[13] *YSi.*, p. 864.

[14] For full details of Yokoi's problems at this time, see *YSdk.*, pp. 63–76.

lowing years Yokoi established a domainal party, the Jitsugakutō, that worked out in Kumamoto the general tenor of the
Tempō reforms of 1843. His Practical Study Party promoted
"learning useful in daily life" and discouraged textual studies. It
tried to introduce financial and administrative reforms to apply
Western skills. To do so it had to wrest political control from the
faction dominant in *han* politics since the late eighteenth century, the Shuryutō (Chief Stream Party). Although the Practical
Study Party included high-ranking retainers such as Nagaoka
Kenmotsu and Shimotsu Kyūya, ideological direction was provided by Yokoi, an extremely low ranking retainer. Yokoi's contact with Fujita Tōko had revealed to him new possibilities for
reform in the *han;* the example of Mito guided a number of domains in reform during the 1840s. Many members of the Jitsugakutō had earlier formed a reading group which went over
classical philosophic texts to find ideas that might serve the present; Yokoi and the group settled on "practicality." Of course it
was found in any number of earlier texts. The immediate source
of the idea was Kumazawa Banzan, who wrote in the *Shūgi
washo:* "In learning the literature of antiquity, it is best to begin
with poetry. Poetry talks about intent and goals, and it reflects
the real facts about human feeling and sentiment, good and bad,
evil and correct. Therefore men who study poetry are really studying practical things. It makes men conscious of the good heart
in the real facts of daily life and human behavior, arouses in men
good conduct, and helps them to protect themselves against evil."
Yokoi also noted that the rationalist Satō Naokata (1650–1719)
wrote approvingly of practical studies in his *Onzōroku.* The most
helpful guide of all was Fujita Tōko, who in the *Kōdōkanki
jutsugi* counted "the abandonment of practicality" as one of "the
four great abuses" of his time, and identified practical studies
with *han* reform. But *jitsugaku* as Yokoi came to use it was quite
different than its meaning for classical writers or even Fujita
Tōko.

The principles of the Jitsugakutō, drawn up by Yokoi in 1844, attacked economic problems through domainal politics.[15] The proposal called for economy in government and relief for impoverished samurai. Yokoi emphasized the change in rural economy produced by the steady alienation of peasants from the land; unable even to produce their own subsistence, they had "become as a grove of trees in a swamp, idle people forced to leave the countryside in search of new occupations." [16] By the new affluence of merchants and townsmen, usually acquired at the expense of the *shi, "han* power and strength have been undermined." Yokoi and his colleagues (who, like Fujita Yūkoku, really failed to understand the problem) saw the only solution as greater administrative control over the merchants (*chōnin*) and town life. This would include rehabilitation projects to relieve samurai poverty and unemployment; sumptuary legislation to check the extravagances of the domain's upper classes; forcing the peasantry to return to the land; measures to exclude businessmen from positions of authority; and a comprehensive reform of the domain's finances. There are echoes of the *Kannō wakumon* and of Mito experience in this reform manifesto. There is also a call for Confucian restoration of the "benevolent government" (*jinsei*) which is supposed to have previously existed in Kumamoto. Despite the peculiar problems agitating Higo (Kumamoto) and Mito, this summons was a pledge of a common purpose between the two *han* and indeed the entire reform movement during the Tempō period. Both Yokoi and Fujita Tōko constantly read Kumazawa Banzan, finding in him not only the clearest exposition of Confucian political thought (*ōdōron*), but also guidelines for economic reform (*nōhonshugi*).

In spite of Yokoi's interest in *han* finances and his detailed recommendations for reform, he was less interested in economy per se than in a better political administration. His economic proposals presupposed the correction of government through the responsibility of officials "to establish the Way of the sages." Yokoi's

[15] *YSi.*, pp. 65–79, "Jimusaku."
[16] *YSi.*, p. 72.

procedure had been used earlier by Fujita Yūkoku in his work
on agricultural reform. Neither was really concerned with the details of domainal finance or administration. But by raising the
issue of financial administration, they could dramatize again the
importance of moral leadership among *han* officials. Yokoi was
most concerned with the method of collecting taxes (*shūren*).
Failure to provide "nourishment" to the people was "bad administration of the first order, because it has forfeited the spirit of the
people (*shinmin*). Generally, when we observe hard times and rebellions in both China and Japan, they are usually caused by the
administration of tax collecting. There is nothing more important." [17] Hence the sages sought to maintain an equilibrium
between upper and lower orders and avoided serving "the convenience of one high man." There was always abundant wealth
in the land; but when only the government profits from it,
"there can be no prosperity, and disturbances will brew and
explode everywhere." To prevent this, able men must rigorously
reform "the means and administration of the Way, and enrich
the realm (*fukoku*)" through legislation.[18] Yokoi later charged
the *bakufu* with the same autocracy; but in Kumamoto in the
1840s his aims were modest and immediate. He was far from rejecting the *han* as an administrative unit; he simply affirmed that
it was not functioning efficiently in the public interest.

While the Jitsugakutō sought a return to prosperity by enforced economy, it also began to study the smatterings of Western technology available. Yokoi and his students investigated military equipment and techniques, medicine, and even political and
economic conditions of Western nations—as listed in Wei Yüan's
ill-informed *Gazetteer on Maritime Conditions* (*Hai-kuo t'u-
chih*).[19] Yokoi went on with these studies when, after 1843, he
established a private school, the Shōnandō. Even old-fashioned
moralists like Aizawa or Nariaki saw some use in the new military technology, however tainted; Yokoi differed in encouraging

[17] *YSi.*, p. 70.
[18] *YSi.*, pp. 69–73.
[19] Minamoto, "Yokoi Shōnan" (n. 6 above), p. 48.

the study of Western political and economic conditions, and later of Western political and economic ideas. Yokoi welcomed what Sakuma avoided: a serious confrontation with the "spiritual" aspects of Western culture. This concern later led him to identify *jitsugaku* with Western politics and economy; it allowed him to look beyond the political world of the *bakufu* and *han;* and it pushed him in his last years, into a serious consideration of Christianity.[20] Christianity appeared to Yokoi as the *ethic of practicality or rationality* although he did not share Weber's view of the necessity of legal and rational development in politics and economics. Yokoi, more perceptive than much later Japanese writers, in seeing the intimate relationship between Western technological and economic power and Christianity, perceived the relationship between modernity and an adequate ethic.

Yokoi taught in the Shōnandō for twelve or thirteen years, and at the same time worked with the Jitsugakutō. He was still operating within the Mito framework of thought and in 1850 was still affirming his belief in expulsionism. To a retainer of Fukui he wrote: "Because our *shinkoku* has been independent for three thousand years, it is unique among the nations of the world. Even if all the people die and all the land is exhausted, we will never be reconciled to the ugly barbarian." [21] This characteristic sentiment marks an essay of 1853, *Opinions on the Plan to Receive the Barbarians (Iryo ōsetsu tai-i)*, which repeats the familiar Mito arguments for expulsion. But it also shows the beginnings of a change in attitude. He still thinks of the foreigners as barbarians (*iryo*); but it was a present reality, he argued, for Japan to follow the movement of civilization. By this he means a relaxation of seclusion as a national policy. "Those who define *sakoku* as our national policy do not understand the Great Way of our national policy." [22] The world is divided between countries which pursue virtue and those which do not. "Countries

[20] *YSdk.*, p. 139.

[21] *YSi.*, pp. 135–136, "Letter to Mitera Missaku"; also pp. 204–205, "Letter to Fujita Tōko."

[22] *YSi.*, pp. 11-12.

which possess virtue permit communications (*tsūshin*) and promote a national policy with which to manage the barbarians. I
have an objection against those without virtue: by not distinguishing between possession and lack of virtue they have obscured the real principles practiced throughout [civilized] society
and the world." Societies that have virtue include not only Japan
but also others that have not violated the spirit of the universe; the preservation of true principles can really be found
in other countries.[23] The desire to open up communications and
trade with another country is more a sign of virtue than of barbarism. Isolation had nothing to do with the possession of virtue
and civilization or with expulsion. Although designed to keep
foreign countries out of Japan, it also kept Japan out of the
world; and for Yokoi Shōnan this had inflicted inestimable harm
on the country.

Japan had lost true principles through "worrying about national essence (*kokutai*)." Just before the opening (*kaikoku*)
Yokoi called for limited trade and exchange of knowledge to
help the Japanese recover lost virtue. This, he urged, was not a
violation of *jōi* nor a complete departure from seclusion. Japan
should make a policy of maintaining communications with countries that possessed virtue and excluding those which did not.
The spirit of seclusion (*sakoku*) would be retained, together
with the possibility of useful communication and trade. His argument, a classic Confucian theory of foreign relations, concludes
that the choice between expulsion and opening depended not
solely upon the "interest of Japan's rulers, but more on the question whether other countries are governed by virtue." [24] Yokoi
believed in a larger comity of civilized nations, guided by "a clarification of virtue (*taigi*)," and which "will be able to stand up
to the barbarian and force him to submit in fear." He was working under the handicap of inadequate knowledge about world
conditions. But his position, pushed a step further, would ap-

[23] *YSi.*, p. 11. See Tamamuro's analysis of this Confucian foreign policy,
op. cit. (n. 6 above), pp. 144ff.
[24] *YSi.* pp. 13–14.

prove of opening relations between Japan and other "virtuous countries"; and precisely this happened after the opening of the country and the signing of the Treaty of Kanagawa. This change meant that he had abandoned the Mito solution and was searching for a new political ethic consistent with his belief in universal principles. "We must not lose," he is supposed to have said at this time, "justice and the rules of propriety toward the foreigner (*gaijin*). Seclusion is not the true intent of our national ancestors. Today we must decide between seclusion and foreign intercourse by obeying the Way of principle and justice." [25]

Yokoi acknowledged this dramatic departure from the Mito position in a letter to Tachibana Iki, which criticizes the *bakufu* for inaction in a new situation, and also Tokugawa Nariaki. Yokoi complained that, even though the *bakufu* knew that foreign ships had been coming to Japan several years before Perry's appearance, it had done nothing. Nariaki's guilt lay in his willingness to concur with "an artificial policy." The whole affair, Yokoi wrote to Tachibana, revived in his mind the Neo-Confucian ideal of moral lords (*kunshin*) rectifying the realm, and underlined how far this responsibility was being disregarded.

The self-interest of the lord Nariaki results in beautiful words. But without fail it goes nowhere. More important, the learning of Mito degenerates all at once, because it does not view the correct principles of heaven and earth. Rather than lose the great principles of this school, there are a number of things that must be avoided. These will be known well when the events, past and present, in Japan and China are scrutinized. A restoration (*chūkō*) will never be accomplished by enduring shame and inviting reconciliation. . . . It is the personal interest in profit which I have come to deplore.[26]

Lords like Nariaki were not acting consistently; the Mito arguments had not prepared the realm for the foreign crisis. It was not enough to use "a theory of the sages for both past and present, and to do things today with the techniques of yesterday."

---

[25] Quoted in Tamamuro, p. 115, from *Shōnan sensei shoden.*
[26] *YSi.,* p. 221.

Here Yokoi's disposition toward practicality was expressed most radically. Some authors see it as a reflection of intuitionism (*shingei*)—and explain his radicalism by deriving it from the "fugitive" Wang Yang-ming tradition (*ōyōmei-gaku*).[27] But too much is made of the pedigree of *bakumatsu* intellectual positions. All thinkers, and Yokoi in particular, had available the different forms of Confucianism; in the new envionment after 1853 they used whatever worked. *Bakumatsu* ideologues have in common a willingness to experiment with the tradition and to change their minds. Yokoi showed little sign of intuitionism before the coming of Perry. He rejected the Mito school, not because he wished to adopt a new instrumentality like intutitionism, but because the Mito school obscured both the real tradition and present reality. He was a good enough Confucianist to get away with this charge. After 1854 every *bakumatsu* ideologue except Ōhashi also questioned the adequacy of Mito.

In another major move, Yokoi Shōnan ended in 1855 a twenty-year collaboration with his fellow *han* reformer, the domainal elder (*karō*) Nagaoka Kenmotsu.[28] The real difference was Yokoi's new conviction about the need for a line of communication between Japan and the outside world. But the break came in an intellectual argument over a remote text, which compelled Yokoi and Nagaoka to take up opposing positions on current policy. In interpreting a passage from the ambiguous *Great Learning* (*Ta hsüeh*), Yokoi found sanction for extreme change while Nagaoka clung to the orthodox view. Nagaoka interpreted the phrase "the Way of the Great Learning exists in illuminating

[27] Minamoto Ryōen, "Meiji ishin to jitsugaku," in *Meiji ishinshi no mondaiten*, ed. Sakata Yoshio (Tokyo, 1962), p. 72.

[28] The account I have relied on is found in *YSdk.*, pp. 312–319. The original record of the controversy was taken down by Motoda Tōno (Eifu) in his "Kanreki no ki" in *YSdk.*, pp. 313–314. I have not had access to the "Kanreki no ki" which, according to D. Shively, "Motoda Eifu: Confucian Teacher to the Meiji Emperor," in *Confucianism in Action*, ed. D. S. Nivison and A. Wright (Stanford, 1959), p. 370, exists in manuscript in the possession of the Motoda family. The portions relating to Yokoi have been reproduced in *YSdk*.

and illustrating virtue; it exists in renovating the people" to say that before renovation is possible, one must first clarify the meaning of virtue. Conversely, Yokoi argued that since the exigencies of the times demand renovation, it will of itself illuminate the meaning of virtue.[29] Yokoi's exegesis marked his liberation from an inflexible moralism (already being discredited) and opened the way for a powerful relativism in behavior and policy. The dispute divided the Jitsugakutō into two factions and gave Yokoi's conservative enemies in the domain opportunity to undermine his work. A few years later, when he went to work for the lord of Echizen, Yokoi wrote a poem about the controversy: "The Way of learning/that is illuminated, changes;/the heart does not/for the lord or for the times."

A few years after the break with Nagaoka, Yokoi was invited to Fukui by Matsudaira Shungaku. Down to the mid-1860s he served Matsudaira on four occasions as adviser, ultimately replacing Hashimoto Sanai (a casualty of the Ansei purge). These were Yokoi's best years, during which he produced his most significant essays and letters; he also had administrative status while Matsudaira served as a new *bakufu* counselor (*seiji sōsaishoku*) (August 1862 to May 1863) and as Kyoto *shugoshoku* (March to May 1864). In the same years politics came to the boiling point, when the restorationist movement (many of whose members like Miyabe Teizō were friends of Yokoi's) agitated in Kyoto for renewal. Yet Yokoi, despite his radical associations, worked for moderate reform to save Japan from the excesses invited by younger firebrands bent on expulsion. Just as he was reaching the pinnacle of his career, in the center of the center as an adviser for national policy in Kyoto, he was removed from the scene. Old habits die hard. In December 1862, Yokoi, with some retainers from Higo, was drinking at the official Edo residence of Yoshida Hyonosuke, the caretaker of Higo *han*. There they were attacked by assassins, members of the radical Loyalist Party (Kinnōtō) of Higo; Yokoi had enemies, as a moderate reformer among extremists. Yokoi escaped with his life, but the domainal government

[29] *YSdk.*, pp. 314–315.

at Kumamoto recalled him to give an account of himself. It
found him guilty of improper conduct and robbed him of what
promised to be his most significant years. He was also stripped of
his stipend (*chigyō*) and his seniority (*shiseki*). This harsh punishment represents the determination of his enemies in the domain, sympathetic to the restorationism and expulsionism of the
Kinnōtō, to put him under wraps. Between the ages of fifty and
fifty-five Yokoi Shōnan was under house arrest, confined in Nuyamatzu outside Kumamoto, and prevented from playing any political role in the Meiji Restoration. During these years he turned
to philosophy. Upon his release he was made a counselor in the
new government, but was struck down for good by an assassin
on Teramachi Street of Kyoto in January 1869.[30]

"SINCERITY": THE FOUNDATION FOR
A NEW THEORY OF ACTION

Yokoi Shōnan's defection from Mito led him to replace nature
as the standard of reality with what he called "world movements." Yet he never lost his sense of crisis, nor the conviction
that he was destined to play a political role. In his mature writings Yokoi saw the problem facing Japan, despite external and
internal threats, as above all one of leadership. And it is to this
question he returned over and over again in his mature writings.
His traditional education identified learning and politics, teaching and leadership. He tried to apply these Confucian associations to a new social and political reality. In a youthful work he
remarked that he expected of himself the same performance
achieved by the sages of the past.[31] Confucianism, especially in
its position toward practical learning, was the governing principle of his thought and conduct. While Mito awoke him to aware-

[30] The assassination of Yokoi and the torment it caused his assassin,
Tsuge Shirōzaemon, was fictionalized by the late Meiji novelist Mori Ōgai
in a story named for the assassin. The story represents Mori's late interest
in historical subjects and the historicity of the Restoration.
[31] *YSi.*, p. 3ff.

ness of a public role, the course of history convinced him that the
ethic of a status order (the major item in the Mito tradition) was
no longer of any help. Instead Yokoi made *makoto,* sincerity and
honesty, his standard of conduct after 1854. "Self-examination is
the route of sincerity and honesty," he wrote to a friend. The
idea was not new, since *makoto* reflected the "good faith" which
was one of the Eight Points of the Great Learning: investigation
of things, penetration of principle (*kakubutsu kyūri*), good
faith, correct mind, moral training, regulation of the family, ordering the Realm, and tranquilizing the world (*tenka*).[32] Traditionally "good faith" was the motive of an interior ethic, the sincerity which governed the conduct expecially of the sage-teacher.
Yokoi adapted this traditional notion for a nontraditional use.

The major changes in Yokoi's thinking at *kaikoku* were directed to maintaining independence under the new dispensation
of power; they are illustrated by his quarrel with Nagaoka and
his abandonment of the Mito program. The idea of *makoto* was
a part of what he called the "Learning of the Three Dynasties,"
marking a disenchantment with Sung Neo-Confucianism (*Li-
hsüeh*). Yokoi discovered that his Confucianism had been filtered
through the Mito rhetoric. But abandonment of one school did not
mean relinquishing the entire tradition; and he sought to work
out a position intellectually satisfactory and preserving the spirit
of Confucianism, which would also help solve Japan's problems.
Just as Yoshida Shōin made the independence of Japan a political condition of resolving his psychological problems, so Yokoi
Shōnan equated the personal intellectual search for a truly modern ethic with finding a way out of the national crisis. Yokoi's
language resembles the much earlier rhetoric of Ogyū Sorai, but
crisis pushed him further. Yokoi gave new meanings to traditional concepts: he transmuted *makoto* into an ethic of action,
the will to act in conformity with reality. Yokoi wrote to Inoue
Kōwashi that, despite living in a universe that is a proper place
for "our thinking, our minds have not investigated the various

[32] I have, in this instance, drawn much from Miyagi Kimiko's brilliant
article, "Yamato damashii yōsai," *Nihonshi kenkyū* (1964), 72: 45.

things or penetrated the principles." Where one puts *makoto* into practice and thus relies on "daily experiences, there you have movement or the exercise of the mind."[33] Existence, for Yokoi, meant the exercise of thought, and the perception and investigation of the universe in which one lives. *Makoto* involved the obligation to investigate the outer world; and where the mind fails to work actively, there is no possibility of *kakubutsu* or *kyūri*. Reading the classics of itself results only in a repetition of past insights. Here Yokoi distinguished between "knowing" (*shiru*) and "understanding" (*gaten*). Only exercise of the mind promises "true understanding of the governing principles which we bring out from thought."[34] His adaptation of *makoto* represents a crude but significant attempt to equip Confucianism with a psychology and to liberate the individual from "meditation" and the quest for "inner harmony." Yokoi, more careful than Yoshida, bent over backwards to preserve the philosophic integrity of Confucianism. He saw Zen Buddhism as maiming Neo-Confucianism with its quietism:

You must strive to master the learning of the ancients; that is, to penetrate and understand the principles found in the *Great Learning*. To penetrate and understand these principles you must investigate all things under heaven; that is, you must exercise thought. Even though the followers of Buddhism practice similar methods to attain personal purity and disinterestedness, by not employing thought they are forever prevented from understanding the principles of nature.[35]

Yokoi's stress on the "individual's true (*makoto*) thought" involved subjective value judgments and experience, but moved away from personal cultivation.

Neo-Confucianism sees no disparity between the external world and the mind's purpose (as expressed in the classics). If a man's original nature is related to the wider universe, as the Ch'eng brothers and also Chu Hsi believed, then a turn to one's original nature is an act of sincerity (*makoto*). Thus the essence

[33] *YSi.*, pp. 899-900.
[34] *YSi.*, p. 898.
[35] *Ibid.*

of *makoto* for Yokoi is an active operation of mind: the faculty which regulates intellectual inquiry. All inquiry, for Yokoi, especially the "investigation of things" which leads to "great wisdom," must be sustained by an internal ethic called "good faith" or "sincere intent." In a letter to Tachibana Iki he complained that the "good faith" of Mito thought was not really good faith at all but rather profit which always showed itself in the activities of men.[36] Mito writers, as we saw earlier, paid lip service to the notion of an investigative method, but ultimately rejected active search for both knowledge and principles unless they were related to the ethic of *chūkō no michi* and the authority of immediate experience. Rather than encourage understanding of the external world they closed off all avenues to it, since it was what they were seeking to overcome. By invoking this critical faculty of *makoto*, Yokoi hoped to liberate empirical inquiry into the external world from the dogma that the only function of intellectual activity was rectifying the status order into conformity with the hierarchy of nature. Yokoi, like his predecessor at Fukui, Hashimoto Sanai, expressed this conviction in his rejection of history as a mirror.

Yokoi argued that Sung theorists, especially the Ch'eng brothers and Chu Hsi, though generally correct in their assessment of the past, did not go far enough: they only wrote about principles but never saw in them a means to "improve the welfare of the people." [37] In their hands the method of *kakubutsu kyūri* was only a speculative instrument that never realized its promise—namely, the understanding of the external world, not as a manifestation of a natural order, but as a reality that is constantly changing and forcing men to make new responses. Yokoi criticized the original Sung writers for not using this method to understand changes in contemporary conditions; as for the Sung commentators, instead of trying "to understand with their minds" they merely aped the masters. "Even though we are equipped with copious commentators from the Sung period, if

[36] *YSi.*, p. 227.
[37] *YSi.*, p. 922.

you seek to understand the meaning of learning with the aid of these commentators, you will not know the true meaning of learning, since they [the commentators] are slaves of Chu Hsi." [38]

Yokoi believed that the perimeter of human experience could be expanded if society were relieved of its reliance on the normative Way, what one writer calls "transcendental propriety." [39] In his conversations with Inoue Kōwashi, Yokoi was asked: "Is the learning of antiquity different than the learning of later times?" He responded: "The perceptions of human nature are in truth without limitaton; if these perceptions are expanded, all things in the realm will be bequeathed to our hearts. The perception of the heart exists in thinking, and if this logic is understood, we can develop a law of physics with our own resources." [40] He was opening up the "heart" to the varieties of experience in the external world and capturing them within the individual. Only through actual contact with the material world can we learn the true principles behind "mountains, rivers, trees, grass." The Three Dynasties knew the meaning of learning, but later generations did no more than read books in their search for principles. Hence Yokoi advised Inoue "to pursue the principle of things with a true heart"; then "your consciousness is expanded instinctively on a daily basis, and you will greatly increase the spirit of knowledge." [41]

Yokoi's elaborate expansion of the possibilities in an internalized ethic witnesses the tenacity of the Mito vision of Neo-Confucianism in general. His use of *makoto* was not new, as we have seen, but was drawn from "the Way of loyalty and filial piety" central in the Mito scheme. But Yokoi went beyond his contemporaries in lifting *makoto* out of its traditional moral context and using it to judge whether the *bakuhan* social structure was suitable to contemporary existence. He discovered that what men consciously experience in their encounters did not conform to what

[38] *YSi.*, p. 931.
[39] See Miyagi, pp. 46ff.
[40] *YSi.*, p. 898.
[41] *YSi.*, p. 899.

they had been taught to expect by the notion of society as an extension of the natural order. By his transformation of *makoto* into an active principle of inquiry, Yokoi parted company with Mito writers, freed from a vain attempt to reconstitute the status order, " the Way of loyalty and filial piety," as if nothing had happened. Yokoi's celebration of critical purpose (*makoto*) and experience was not, as it was with Sakuma Shōzan (who in many ways fits Yokoi's description of Sung thinkers), an effort to round out the Neo-Confucian world view. Rather it was a perilous attempt to make an established ethic serve unanticipated demands, taking seriously the political and social claims of the new Western experience. Although it was not his primary purpose to save Neo-Confucianism, he could not help breathing some new life into it along the way.

Yokoi adapted a public rhetoric for the use of a public not yet existent. He used accessible language, all he had, to express ideas it had never been designed to convey. Hence he utilized nearly all the concepts the tradition had to offer—including the remote Three Dynasties. Precedents not burdened by specific historical associations were the most useful to him. Yokoi had a sense of emerging social and political realities and tried to deal with them. In contrast, Yoshida, who also sensed new realities, was concerned with the future only out of the self-centered fear that his work could not be continued by worthy hands. Yokoi, with the assistance of Western political and social concepts, tried to envisage what shape the new reality might take when fully established. He invoked *makoto* as motive and "the investigation of things" as an ethic of action, to guide experiment in the new situation.

Thought, not blind obedience to fixed precedents and morally irrelevant pieties, was the essential condition of that learning which alone led to the mastery of principle. This was the lesson of antiquity—its only real lesson for the present. Yokoi was very clear that change was the only basis of accountability.[42] Comprehension (*gaten*) was really a new method of historical analysis,

[42] See my introduction in B. Silberman and H. D. Harootunian, *Modern Japanese Leadership* (Tucson, 1966).

for Yokoi believed that history (like the rest of reality) changed
and had to be understood fully so as to make action in any present possible. The antitheses of "longstanding customs, old abuses"
(*ryūzoku kyuhei*) and "original standards, old precedent" (*senkaku korei*), gave him a method of abandoning portions of the
past no longer applicable to his present. He was saying that the
historical process has to be known if it is to be excluded in part
or in whole as a present alternative.[43] In contrast to the unhistorical character of Neo-Confucianism, Yokoi, through his appeal to
the Three Dynasties, insisted on the necessity of historical study
in forming policy. Neo-Confucianists engaged in large-scale historiographical collections precisely out of their firm belief that investigation would show that "the Way of heaven and earth" does
not change. In contrast, Yokoi, in his discussions with Inoue Kōwashi at Nuyamatzu, argued that "the conditions of past and present are different, and although today and yesterday correspond to
principle, they are not the same." Here Yokoi stressed the need to
distinguish between principle (*ri*) and conditions (*sei*) in understanding the conduct of affairs. Principle served as a guide in
human affairs, but excessive reliance on it made men meditative;
its true use lay in impelling men to investigate conditions before
making decisions. In transforming *ri* into an active principle,
Yokoi was arguing that the condition of history is constant
change. This sensitivity to change, the specific conditions of the
present, is basic in Yokoi's understanding of "pacifying the people, tranquilizing the realm." If history teaches any lesson, Yokoi
argued, it is the fact that conditions change; hence just as knowledge of things is useless if there is no way of applying it, so historical knowledge is unimportant unless men in the present can
derive practicable precepts from past experience.[44] In the end
Yokoi admitted to Inoue that the past is so vastly different from
the present that its principal lesson is the importance of practicality and innovation.

In his reexamination of the function of history, Yokoi knew

[43] Minamoto, "Meiji ishin to jitsugaku" (n. 27 above), p. 76.
[44] *YSi.*, p. 899.

there is no guarantee that a study of the past will yield usable knowledge for contemporary action. But the effort is essential. In particular he condemned contemporaries for relying on later traditions to the exclusion of a "return to Three Dynasties." Yokoi makes the point thus: "When studying and thinking about Chu Hsi today, one should think about what Chu Hsi studied. If he does not, he will become a complete slave to Chu's writings. Moreover when he thinks about composing a poem by studying Tu Fu, he should consider what Tu Fu studied, which goes back to the Han, the Wei, and the Six Dynasties." [45] More generally, "from one principle, it is possible to understand many things; from many things, it is possible to return to one principle." [46]

Yokoi agreed with the "great Confucianists of the Sung who explained the principles of heaven and man"; but he felt that their explanation of principles was too abstract, not grounded in daily experiences. If the "shape of contemporary relations between man and heaven" is viewed from the standpoint of a transcendent principle (*dōri*), it has no more authority than "idle speculation." When the Sung writers recommended the "investigation of things," they appeared, in contrast to men in the Three Dynasties, to be following Yao and Shun. (So men had been led to believe.) "But even though men in the Sung had heard about the basic principle behind all things . . . they did not think actually to investigate the world around them in such a manner as to create new things for use by the people. Although Sung writers had heard about the investigation of things they never went beyond looking at principles or 'pricking' them." [47] Yao and Shun used the technique of experiment to achieve practical gains for the people's interest. Yokoi was approaching the modern technological view that nature is merely an inert mass for man to control when he argued that Yao and Shun (and thus all men) must resort to *kakubutsu kyūri* to assist the work of nature.[48] In-

---

[45] *YSi.,* p. 932.
[46] *YSi.,* p. 4, "Gakkō mongaisho."
[47] *YSi.,* pp. 922, 923.
[48] *YSi.,* p. 898.

vestigation of things led to productivity, it "expanded the work of nature." The Three Dynasties showed clearly that *kakubutsu kyūri* helped achieve a useful life; and Yokoi found its expression in his times in the policy of *fukoku kyōhei*. Besides motivating Confucianism with a new psychology, he gave it a new purpose, which he deduced, not (as he claimed) from its original texts, but from Japan's contact with Western capitalism. In contrast, Sakuma Shōzan put *kakubutsu kyūri* into the service of the technical problem of defense, and experimentation generally in the world of material things; he never saw the "investigation of things" as a means of forging a new ethic. Yokoi, on the other hand, rarely involved himself in technological experiment; since he was less concerned with defense than with the totality of external and internal problems, he turned to the world of social and political affairs. In this he had "sincerity" as his guide; "the work of investigation comes from the individual's sincere thought." [49]

Yokoi complained that Sung thinkers failed in "the extension of knowledge." They heard and talked about principles, but never acted to assist "nature's work." The promise of *makoto* was that an inner ethic would oblige the individual to overcome the temptations of inactive subjectivism and pure meditation. The sincerity of individuals led outward to judging the administration of the realm. "Where the extension of knowledge is measured in terms of importance and unimportance, there you have real practice." Real sincerity is what the *Great Learning* referred to as "outward pacification," which meant ruling the country in peace and prosperity; Yokoi believed this to be the true content of ethical politics.[50] Yokoi, like Kusaka Genzui, concluded that the end of practical action must be benevolence. However, men had to be careful that their action was in the public interest. Profit (*ri*) should exist only in behalf of all the people. "The usefulness of benevolence . . . reaches men in the form of

[49] *Ibid.*
[50] *YSi.*, p. 906.

profit. . . . To abandon the self is to profit the people. For when profit is possessed by the individual, there is the name of disloyalty. When all men are profited, there is the name of benevolence." [51] Yokoi makes a clear distinction between the private and public realms, between self-interest and public interest. Yokoi probably owed this distinction to Ogyū Sorai, who had previously rejected any identification of the leader's private interest with the public interest. Ogyū and Yokoi agreed that profit to all was simply the fulfillment of one of the cardinal precepts of a benevolent realm (*jinsei*). Yokoi, writing in a more troubled time than Ogyū, had to be both moralist and pragmatist; the right inner morality, he argued, would surely lead to proper political conduct serving the public interest.

A comparison with Sakuma Shōzan is instructive here. Sakuma confined the "extension of knowledge" to the physical world and satisfied his sense of intellectual integrity by arguing that Sung writers had opened the way to scientific inquiry for later ages. In this realm the West had done what China had not. The two kinds of knowledge informed by *ri* were not incompatible; on the contrary, they were two halves of a complete circle, representing a total achievement. Sakuma's line, while a justification of interest in science and technology, was also a barrier against any serious concern with Western social and political ideas. On the question of political reform Sakuma was resistant to new impulses. Unlike Yokoi, he saw the contrast between Japan and the West purely in terms of power as defined by scientific and technological knowledge. Hence Sakuma promoted only limited political reforms, designed to establish a technologial discipline in Japan. The fact that Sakuma said so little about political and social reorganization suggests that he approved of the system in essential aspects and saw a need to reform only those sections relating to actual defense of the realm. Even though he saw Japan as a member of a comity of nations, he did not see in Japan the political culture of European states. Down to the end

[51] *Ibid.*

of his life (as his last letters to his mistress show) he was convinced that the problem was the technology of defense, not politics or ethics.[52]

Yokoi, on the other hand, saw both Western technology and
Western political institutions as equally available if the judgment
of conditions called for them. Whereas Sakuma gave *kakubutsu
kyūri* a specific fixed content, Yokoi saw it as simply an instrument.

If, as in the time of the Three Dynasties, there had been the study of
principles of nature in order to assist the work of Heaven, then there
should have been a way of administration corresponding to the opening of the sea lanes by Western ships in recent history and international trade. . . . What has there been? . . . If we can give birth in
our times to what Yao and Shun did in theirs—that is, if we can accomplish meritorious deeds, which in our case requires technology,
industry, and the manufacturing of cannons—in short, by ministering
to our times, then we will not only expand the work of nature but
also equal the strength of the West.[53]

He rejected political solutions of the past with equal firmness, as
not being the way to satisfy "daily human needs."

A more traditional reason prompted Yokoi to concentrate on
politico-ethical problems. Reform in Kumamoto showed him
early that the failure was less economic than administrative.
After the opening of the country, and its disturbing impact on
the "syntax of events," [54] Yokoi concluded again that the problem was essentially political. Moreover, he was also early persuaded of an intimate relation between learning and political affairs; he presumed that an inner morality must be united with
the political and social values.[55] He knew of course that in actual
political society no such internal morality was being heeded. He
established *makoto* as inner morality precisely to serve as guide

[52] *Shōzan zenshū*, II, 1322–1323.

[53] *YSi.*, pp. 922–923.

[54] I am indebted to my colleague R. J. Kaufmann for this phrase.

[55] *YSi.*, pp. 4ff.

to outward political conduct. Yokoi was very serious about the role of inner morality in the administration of the political realm. The content of *makoto* was not bound by external rules but projected from inside. Behind this concept lies the assumption that men are naturally good. Politics must be conducted spontaneously according to the "sincerity of our heart and mind." [56]

For Yokoi, the final results of a decision or of action are more important than personal motive; here he stood in contrast to Yoshida, who prized purity of intent over all other considerations. Despite his seeming pragmatism, Yokoi added that political skills should never be separated from inner morality; he saw a man's actions in the Confucian way as an extension of his inner goodness and possession of ethical knowledge. Still, for Yokoi political results were a guarantee that the sage-ruler had liberated himself from private meditation, the personal cultivation of knowledge, inaction. In this new set of priorities morality, for Yokoi, was taken up into politics; just as a man's outer conduct was now prior to his inner perfection, so political activity was more important than the personal cultivation of ethical knowledge. He still believed that proper inner morality produced the maximum political good. But, unlike Neo-Confucianists, he was unwilling to see politics as a lower form of activity. Rather, Yokoi attributed prior importance to political activity; the leader's inner goodness is disclosed in the results of successful political action. Thus he could preserve the integrity of the traditional relationship between Neo-Confucian "inner moral perfection" and "pacification of the outer world." But Yokoi's formulation destroyed the last vestiges of the Neo-Confucian scheme whereby the private morality of the sage becomes the public morality of the masses, and the masses, who have no real inner life, live only in a public realm where they submit to the leadership through "reverence and respect" (*kei*). In this subtle separation of politics from ethics, Yokoi did not abandon morality as a requirement for leadership; but he made it secondary to political skill and technical

<hr>

[56] See Sakata Ikuko, "Bakumatsu ni okeru kindaiteki tōitsu kokkaron seiritsu no zentei," *Nihonshi Kenkyū* (1966), 85: 76ff.

expertise. Hence he advised leaders "to exhaust their good faith to illustrate virtuous principles." [57] If the motive is pure, then the results will surely be beneficial for all; for a pure motive would always take specific times into account before formulating a plan. "In coming to terms with our times, we see that some things occur and other things do not. Yet if we are to establish the correct Way [in dealing with our circumstances], we must rely on an understanding of the conditions of the times." [58]

What Yokoi called "political affairs" was the realization that the public interest, whatever it might be, changed as times changed. Mismanagement reflects the private interest of the administrator and makes proper political procedure an impossibility because it inhibits an investigation of needs in conformity with the public interest. In a letter to Yajima Josuke (January 1860), Yokoi cited Mencius to illustrate what is expected of the leader's heart and mind in the public interest. "Abuses are born in the heart of men. . . . The rules of nobility are not enough to direct the lower orders, and that is why they will not submit. Owing to the private heart of the nobility [upper-ranking samurai officials], those in the lower orders who refuse to submit [to rules] come to envy this selfishness." Those who lead, if they are to achieve success, must conduct "a government with hearts open to the people, concealing nothing." [59] The administrator must pursue the most disinterested course if he is to win support. This program had recently been described by Fujita Yūkoku in traditional language as "benevolent polity"; Yokoi was trying in 1860 to make it the framework for the acceptance of new knowledge and new events. Again he was using a traditional metaphor for a nontraditional purpose: Japan could be advanced only if there were able and talented administrators to discover and serve the public interest.

Leadership required men equipped to investigate social reality. But such an investigation was worthless (Yokoi warned) unless

[57] *YSi.*, p. 728.
[58] *YSi.*, p. 727.
[59] *YSi.*, p. 322.

it was accompanied by benevolence in the administrator. Hence he insisted in traditional language that there was an indivisible relationship between inner and outer conduct. "The Way," he instructed Inoue in the dialogue at Nuyamatzu, "which is the way of the universe and nature is lodged in our bosom, and it is the ideograph for benevolence. When people attach intention to this character of benevolence, then there is the way of nature." [60] An administrator needs benevolence, because it disposes him to action with love and to feeling toward others. If sincerity guarantees action and devotion to public interest, then benevolence promises a human political society and the conquest of self-interest. Yokoi's elaborate exposure of self-interest and insincerity was more than a concealed attack on shogunal policies. While Yoshida screamed at the heavens denouncing incompetents, Yokoi delivered a measured but comprehensive attack which also suggested remedies. A benevolent regime, for Yokoi, was simply the goal which all societies must work toward. Its content—the public interest—involved no fixed associations, but leaders were, in all times and places, required to determine those needs before they acted. Yokoi referred to his administrator as a *yūtokusha* in the hope of preserving the traditional ideal of the Confucian ethical manager; yet his leader was very different from the classical one. Yokoi's leaders were to be active men, not meditative teachers; they were to be inspired by concrete historical personalities, many of whom had lived beyond the frontiers of civilization (*t'ien hsia*) as he knew it. But wherever they were found, so was civilization. His Hall of Fame was inhabited by a mixed bag of politicians from Yao and Shun to George Washington.[61] The fact that Yokoi chose Washington as ideal, Yoshida, Napoleon, and Sakuma, Peter the Great, suggests interesting differences among the three ideologues. Yokoi was more interested in dramatizing the need for talent and ability than in defining the contours of his benevolent polity specifically, even though he explored the possibility of a federal and republican system on the

[60] *YSi.,* p. 910.
[61] *YSi.,* p. 29–56. "Kokuze sanron." Sakata Ikuko, p. 77.

eve of the Restoration. He was certain that ability brought sound government. Just before the Restoration he summarized his position: "The philosopher has ended by illuminating ability; his thought serves completely the conditions of nature."

FUKOKU KYŌHEI: THE SHAPE OF POLITICAL REORGANIZATION

Yokoi's complaint about Mito was that it had failed to work out a realistic politics, open to the new knowledge revealed in contact with Western nations. He also found it necessary to jettison the narrow view which saw civilization only where *meibun* is found. He believed that Western nations conformed to the "principle (*ri*) of the universe," and reflected in their impressive achievements his notion of sincerity. Yokoi equated the heavenly way (*tendō*) or heavenly principles (*tenri*) of Confucian moralists with the international law and natural law which, he observed, guided the conduct of Western nations with each other. Thus he argued in the *Kokuze sanron* of 1860, his major work, that Western nations provided in his time the complete model of the benevolent government which Yao and Shun had worked for in another time and place.[62] The essence of Western strength (he argued implicitly with Sakuma) lay less in military technology than in trade and economy, which reflected a different political arrangement. In spite of claims for Honda Toshiaki (an unread early nineteenth-century writer) and the nativist Satō Nobuhirō, Yokoi was the first Japanese proponent of mercantilism and "national" capitalism. He acknowledged that *jinsei* required an increase in national wealth; he also concluded from the example of the West that expansion of capital required a specific political organization. In the *Kokuze sanron* he remarked that even the sages in the Three Dynasties worked to increase wealth through commerce. Yokoi also urged how "imperative it is to achieve wealth [in our times] anew." [63] This also is the meaning of his earlier distinction between "countries with vir-

[62] *YSi.*, p. 29.
[63] *YSi.*, p. 36.

tue" and those without; a mercantile policy is an expression of virtue. The consequences of opening the country were clear; Japan must enter the international comity of nations and participate in trade and friendship. Yokoi believed naïvely that only a desire for free trade and amity brought Western ships to Eastern Asia to open closed doors, and that Japan should show the same "benevolence." To Motoda, who listened to Yokoi at great length, he revealed a vision of Japan's future after responding to *kaikoku:* "The way of the universal reason calls for opening the country. . . . If administrative measures are adopted, the decline of the realm will be reversed, and Japan will forge to the front of the states of the world as a rich country with a strong army. To establish this practically, we ought to start first of all by friendly relations with America. . . . By consultations with America the destructiveness of war can be avoided." [64] Japan would win capitalist success and play the benevolent role of mediator among the maritime nations.

But Yokoi was more interested in the *bakuhan* system as decision-making than in international trade and amity. In his thinking, economic activity followed political organization. He despaired at the failure of the cumbersome machinery set up by Abe Masahiro to act decisively in response to Perry's demands.[65] In the deliberation of the lords, he observed, indecision was heightened by fear and ignorance. The arguments for isolation had been discredited by recent events; yet the lords clung aimlessly to the tattered threads of the old romance of *sakoku.* In this event Yokoi discovered the real need for government to be administered by men of talent and ability—as judged by their capacity to decide swiftly on the basis of new information. Yokoi was reacting against established procedure in the making of decision—namely, consensus with the framework of custom, law, and precedent Abe's creation of a broader base of opinion by appealing to more lords expressed this pattern of consensus by committee. As long as foreign ships did no more than probe, the arguments for *jōi*

[64] "Kanreki no ki," quoted in Kōsaka (n. 5 above), pp. 33–34.
[65] *YSi.,* p. 29.

had a reasonable ring; after 1854 they became meaningless. Exponents of seclusion argued that for the past two hundred years "the land, because it was productive in all things, did not know insufficiency. . . . If we open up our locked doors, useful items will leave our country and unnecessary things will enter." [66] But Yokoi made the radical claim that seclusion (*sakoku*) had inflicted real harm on national life.

Further, in Yokoi's mind repudiation of *sakoku* really involved an attack on something much bigger: the *bakuhansei* itself. For seclusion by the 1850s had become identified with the basic values that the Tokugawa were pledged to uphold. Yokoi's criticism of the policy of isolation, after demolishing the classic arguments for it, ended in a full-scale critique of the political order on the grounds that it was not increasing "national wealth and power." His sense of practicality kept the specific content of a benevolent polity open; investigation of social reality by itself was a guarantee that the "public interest" was being served and the "principles of heaven and earth" followed. Yokoi saw unwillingness to accept *kaikoku* as an abdication of responsibility, a violation of the universal principles of civilization.[67] When the opponents of *kaikoku* quaked before its possible calamities, Yokoi retorted that isolation itself had brought untold disasters to Japan. It was impossible to "return to old habits of plainness." It was also foolish to believe, like many officials, that opening the country would gain time for Japan to build up its defenses and strengthen the military. The logic behind this kind of thinking, Yokoi wrote, was that, once the country became strong enough, it would drive out the foreigners and return to a policy of isolation. Isolation had cut Japan off from "world movements" and "the conditions of foreign nations"; it had also created distress within the country. Writers have argued that when Yokoi condemned seclusion he was also denouncing the sectional system (*hōkensei*).[68] The

[66] *Ibid.*

[67] *YSi.*, p. 40; also p. 32.

[68] Miyagi (n. 32 above), pp. 50–51. Naramoto Tatsuya, *Senkakusha no shisō*, 10 vols. (Tokyo, 1966), II, 66.

truth is, his complaint came from the belief that *sakoku* interfered with the workings of the sectional system by setting up barriers among domains, so that each had to look after itself; when "one profits it does not worry much about harming others." [69] Elsewhere he included among "the troubles created by seclusion" the arbitrary distinction between "large and small domains." His policy of *fukoku kyōhei* was designed to sustain domainal economy while some feudal arrangement was providing political unity. The *Kokuze sanron* argues consistently that an alleviation of problems in the individual domains will resolve national problems. His reformist activity in Echizen during the late 1850s and earlier in Kumamoto—in particular his work to abolish restrictive policies like the "alternate hostages system" (*sankin kōtai*)—shows his determination to retain the *han* and the Mito elaboration of it as an integral part of any revised politico-economic system.

Echoing the *Great Learning,* Yokoi argued that Japan could be administered effectively if a way could be found for even one domain to be administered effectively. "It would be a mistake to separate the realm as a whole (*tenka*) from the estates (*kokka*); and if we realize the public way in one domain (*kuni*), we could enlarge the scope of our discussion to the country as a whole." [70] Isolation blocked recovery of the domain as a healthy political and economic unit; the restraints on contact and cooperation were an advanced form of tyranny. Yokoi knew that *kaikoku* could be beneficial; if it was guided in the public interest, "we need not worry about foreign obstruction." The oppressive *hōken* system had turned the elements of society against each other; "to tyrannize over the lower classes is like cutting one's thigh to fill his mouth and stomach thus bringing personal injury to the whole body." [71] These are the words of a good Confucianist who

[69] *YSi.*, p. 31.

[70] *YSi.*, p. 32; also in a letter to his office staff in Kumamoto in 1863, p. 412; letter to Katsu Kaishū (1864), pp. 450–451; and as late as 1866 in a letter to Mōjū Kanosuke, p. 495.

[71] *YSi.*, pp. 32–33.

still fears mass disorder and chaos, even while he realizes that the problem is less simple than Mito writers had thought. Yet it was the folly of deliberate divisiveness that lay behind the policies of "unenlightened" lords and the *bakufu,* and ultimately invited the "mockery of the foreigner." Yokoi Shōnan was less concerned with the process of decision-making than with the institution which had gathered up all the reins of power. The shogunal clique had resorted to repression of the lower orders to conceal its own incompetence. The Tokugawa administration was at odds with "public government." "This is not the time," he urged, "to stand by coldly while . . . blunders go on before our eyes. It is my hope that we will model ourselves after the principles of heaven, rely on the teachings of the sages, examine the conditions of foreign nations, and open the way for an administration that will promote the people's interest and alter political doctrine." [72] He was calling for an administration that would augment "the people's wealth." Until recently, the country had been governed as a "private management" to satisfy the "convenience of the Toku-gawa family." [73] But this "is not the political doctrine with which to tranquilize the realm and make the masses into dutiful sons." To dramatize the consequences of "private management" Yokoi recalled China's recent history. Though generous in praise of the "virtuous reigns" of early Ch'ing sovereigns such as K'ang Hsi and Ch'ien Lung, he was critical of the course of affairs since that time:

Ever since ancient times, the Chinese have slighted the barbarians and accorded them the status of birds and beasts. At the end of Tao Kuang's reign, the Chinese were badly defeated by the British during the Opium War and thus, unavoidably, forced to sign a peace treaty. But the Chinese did not keep their promises and continued in their ways, showing at all times their contempt toward the English. . . . They committed additional insolence by assassinating an English consul, and this merely angered the British all the more. Four months later the [British] were joined by the French and struck out against

[72] *YSi.,* p. 41.
[73] *YSi.,* p. 39.

these wrongs and faithlessness. The allies, in the end, occupied Peking. . . . and China became an empire in name only.[74]

The shortsighted self-interest which produced isolation and To-kugawa management and led Perry to see Japan as a disunited realm, threatened, if persisted in, to lead to the same ruin as China.

The escape from self-interest was provided by the ideal of "be-nevolent polity" (*jinsei*) and the example of the Three Dynasties as Yokoi understood it. To accomplish the people's interest he ad-vised "altering (or renovating) political doctrine." The fact that *bakufu* officialdom acted tyrannically over the masses was further evidence that the public interest was not being satisfied. Yokoi was taught that the "realm belonged to the realm" not only by Yao and Shun but also by contemporary Anglo-American politi-cal experience. Yokoi to the end expressed admiration for the American experiment (on which he was unusually well informed), and transmitted it to his son, his nephews (who studied in the United States), and a host of young retainers in Kumamoto. George Washington symbolized for him the principles that had made the United States the power it was. For him the United States represented the most successful example of "public admin-istration," in its service to the people a worthy reminder of the Three Dynasties. Yokoi was particularly impressed by the fact that the United States, alone among modern nations, had re-moved the threat of "rebellion and massacre" by declaring itself free of all foreign entanglements. Washington's Farewell Address conformed with Yokoi's strongly revised version of seclusion. The United States had not cut off all ties with the outside world, like Tokugawa Japan, but engaged in friendly relations on a selective basis with those nations which (as he wrote earlier) "possessed virtue."

In December 1862 Yokoi Shōnan drafted a "Three-Point Policy on Expulsion" (*Jōi sansaku*) just before the shogun received an expulsionist decree from the emperor. In this curious document,

[74] *YSi.*, p. 40.

Yokoi appears to have shed his earlier enthusiasm for selective contact with "virtuous nations" in favor of a return to Tokugawa seclusion. He makes three points. (1) Japan has bent under pressure of foreign nations and concluded a treaty with them. In so doing, the country has gone against an imperial ordinance and opened the ports. At the top level this has tormented the emperor's heart (*shinkin*); at the bottom, the behavior of shogunal officials shows that they have incurred the resentment of the masses. The shogun, who is proceeding to Kyoto to explain his true intent, must show the reality of *sonnō*. (2) To show the reality of revering the emperor, after the culpable officials have been punished for their disobedience to him, the retainers from different parts of the realm must be summoned to the castle in Edo and ranked in proper order under the shogun. It must then be explained to them, especially to the officials of the *bakufu,* why the treaties ought to be abandoned. Officials at the various ports must be advised that they do not have imperial permission to open their ports to foreigners; nor are they to take it upon themselves to evacuate the ports in the event of a foreign arrival. Rather, the most able men must be selected and dispatched as special envoys to the countries of the world, to explain the limited conditions under which Japan might enter into relations with other nations. (3) Japan must prepare for war on the coast.[75]

Yokoi's apparent *volte-face* is not really a return to the archaic political organization which he had denounced in the *Kokuze sanron* two years earlier, but rather an attack on political leadership which, since the coming of Perry, had turned to inappropriate precedents and shown fear and indecision. He supported able moderates like Hitotsubashi Keiki (a candidate in the struggle for shogunal succession) and the acknowledged leaders of a party advocating immediate shogunal reform. Yokoi reasoned that it was wrong for Japan either to adopt a blind expulsionist policy or to open the country indiscriminately to all foreigners; both policies would lead to the same result, colonization. Rather,

[75] Tamamuro *op. cit.* (n. 6 above), pp. 196–198; *YSi.*, pp. 949–950.

Japan should enter into relations with other countries on a selective basis: from a position of relative strength, willingly and only after deciding whether such intercourse would benefit both parties. But Japan could not throw itself into foreign relations out of fear and intimidation. The Meiji writer Tokutomi Sōho explained:

Yokoi really went against the so-called expulsionists of the times. He was an advocate of *kaikoku,* but he also believed in the universal way of heaven and earth. The opening of Japan was done not voluntarily but forcibly; the country was opened by threats, not on a basis of equality. It was caused by foreigners and it was imposed by them. He saw the great diminishment of our national authority and acknowledged that we must correct this in a basic way. Utilizing prosperously the whole nation and the opportunity of expulsion, riding on this spirit, we have to change this disgrace since 1854 and 1855. It is this reason that gave vent to this discourse.[76]

This exaggerated opinion runs counter to a contemporary assessment of Yokoi's motivation by Katsu Kaishū, who records in his diary that Yokoi was asked in conversation why he promoted an apparently expulsionist policy at this time. He answered that decision between "*kaikoku* and *sakoku* resembles a decision on war or peace." One cannot live in the country and assassinate foreigners, yet still support *kaikoku.* This first concern must be to transform the realm speedily into a prosperous and powerful state; only then should it "be decided whether Japan should open its doors or remain secluded." The expulsionists wished foolishly to enflame the entire country; still this was understandable and inevitable, since they were grieving for the future of Japan. To conciliate them, Yokoi offered his notion of a "national reconstruction" (*kōkoku*) as solution to the continuing debate, and won the support of both Hitotsubashi and Matsudaira Shungaku. It was simply a method to check an incendiary course and get the state of affairs under control.[77] When Japan became a power-

[76] Tamamuro, pp. 196-197.
[77] *Ibid.*

ful nation it could make its own choice about commercial intercourse on the criterion of virtue; the American experience was
available as a guideline.

Even more impressive than Western power and commerce to
Yokoi, after he decided to reconstruct the *bakuhan* system and
Japan, was American political theory. This theory, he wrote, was
based on "world knowledge" since it combined the best elements
in the modern experience. In its search for a workable political
doctrine (*seikyō*), the United States had freely availed itself of
what European civilization offered, taking what served its interests
and rejecting the rest. Yokoi saw the success of this doctrine in
its avoidance of "private management" of the realm by delegat-
ing power to an elected president; thus the country has "succeeded in becoming an egalitarian republic (*kōkyō wahei*)." [78]
The American political system was remarkably free of such
weaknesses as the "principle of lord and vassal" and the problem
of succession. As an example of a true *jinsei*, it also showed the
working of a system of political recruitment based (as he believed) on merit and pledged to the pursuit of virtue in the public interest. Yokoi believed from his reading of the "times of the
Three Dynasties" that a benevolent polity must always be in the
hands of "enlightened despots" who have acquired political responsibility through the possession of "talent and ability." The
Three Dynasties should not be slavishly imitated, but the principle of rewarding ability is valid in all times.

The Three Dynasties had men of unusual ability at the top and many
wise men at the bottom. The establishment of schools also contributed
to rulership and produced sufficient men of talent and ability (*jinzai*).
Even if the rulers today do not possess talent and virtue equal to that
of the Three Dynasties, there is no choice but to set up these dynasties
as models. Rulers and ministers have to realize that they must not separate themselves from the Way of civilian and military arts. The sovereign who is at the top nourishes affection, modesty, fairness, and an upright mind; he guides his retainers, according to morality based on the
teachings of the sages, to rule the masses with sincere feeling and intent.

[78] Y*Si.*, p. 39; also "Shinsei ni tsukete Shungaku ni kengen," (1866),
pp. 93–96.

The lower-level managers "who assist in government" and "spread teachings," complying with the heart of the ruler, must not be given to personal extravagances and "must practice the virtue of frugal economies." [79]

Bureaucratic management for Yokoi involves both talent and consensus. In bureaucracy, where officials "follow the traces of the sages" and serve as an example to the people, listen to others and "teach the unskilled," obey the wishes of the lord without thought of personal gain, the great object is to serve the people's needs as they change from time to time. But while his able administrators control the people completely by a managed economy, they must cooperate harmoniously in politics. Where Neo-Confucianism was plainly a theory of rulership designed to keep the ruled in subjection, Yokoi tried to secure the voluntary cooperation of the ruled. The Neo-Confucian sentiment about the need to "bestow affection on the masses" was born from contempt and from fear of public disorder, and was expressed only in repressive measures. Yokoi hoped by commerce and industry to improve the lot of the masses and to enlist their active support for the government, based on personal loyalty between manager and people. In an interesting letter (January 4, 1861) to Ogi Kakubei, a confederate during the Tempō reforms, Yokoi called for the familiar "unification of high and low." This, he explained, could be done when "the benevolence of those who are beneath and the conscience (*ryōshin*) of the lower orders is made known to the upper levels. . . . Those at the top are pleased and overjoyed with lower-class wealth, and grieved when the masses are impoverished." [80] In return, Yokoi hoped the people would cooperate with the leaders.

Yokoi Shōnan promoted all this as an antidote to shogunal incompetence. In Echizen in the early 1860s he shared in domainal reform and also in decisions at the "national" level as Matsudaira Shungaku's adviser. During this time he sought to define his political views more sharply, while reluctant to entertain the extremist solutions then fashionable. Deliberate, purposeful, com-

[79] *YSi.*, p. 56; "Letter to Tachibana Iki" (1856), pp. 234–237.
[80] *YSi.*, p. 349.

prehensive, Yokoi's proposals grew naturally out of his consistent effort to modernize his ethical tradition—and to show how the *bakufu,* by tying its flag to seclusion, was responsible for "great ples; on the other hand, he proposed concrete measures which calamities." On the one hand, he spoke of great universal princi-changed from time to time out of expedience. "If you speak only of clarifying the principles of the Way and do not do anything about strengthening the army, you will surely fail to control insub-ordination"; and conversely, "if you speak only of strengthening the army and do not clarify ethical principles (*dōri*), you will not be able to serve the public spirit." [81] This double concern, he observed, was the proper method both to deal with the foreign barbarian (*gai-teki*) and "to govern our domestic order." Yokoi altered Confucian political theory to support the measures he later proposed in Echizen. Externally the country should be opened to communications and trade with virtuous nations, fol-lowing a "standard principle inherent throughout heaven and earth"; at the same time internally it should move toward a "populist" political ideal inspired by the ideas of *jinsei* and the "principle in which people are the base" (*minpon-shugi*).[82] In Echizen domain Yokoi proposed a detailed reform which worked toward a benevolent realm in the concrete form of *fukoku kyōhei.* He chose the *han* as the testing place of reform because he be-lieved that "the proper administration of one realm could be ex-panded to the whole country." On the national level he sup-ported the *kōbugattai* program, to salvage not the *bakufu* but the domain. It was his belief that retaining the shogunate was a slight price to pay if it would strengthen the *han* economically and militarily and free the *han* to play a larger role in the public interest.

[81] *YSi.,* p. 23.

[82] *Minpon shugi:* A Mencian term, wrongly used to denote "democracy" later on. Its real meaning suggests care for the people, educational and economic, in return for which they will offer the leadership their coopera-tion. Yoshino Sakuzō later employed it as a possible alternative to *minshū shugi,* which carried with it the sense of mass democracy.

Yokoi operated, especially at Fukui in Echizen, as a theorist of sectionalism convinced that the domainal system could work in a new political arrangement. But he also had broader hopes. Thus, while he wrote his *Kokuze sanron* explicitly for domainal reform, its underlying mercantilism in later writings is applied to the national scene.[83] Takasugi Shinsaku, who spoke to Yokoi in 1860 on a visit to Fukui, later called his program a "true start." In Echizen (like his brilliant predecessor Hashimoto Sanai) Yokoi worked closely with the daimyo Matsudaira Shungaku. He saw in the new conditions, above all, an opportunity to increase the power of the domain, and he believed that if all the domains were revived, the nation would achieve "national reconstruction" (*kōkoku*).

It is characteristic of late Tokugawa thought that ideologues like Yokoi altered received political doctrines, but rarely envisaged an entirely new polity. Reformers like Yokoi, Ōkubo, and Takasugi saw in the domain, liberated from shogunal despotism, the key to a revision of the *bakuhan* system in the face of new problems. Yokoi's economic plans for Echizen were intended to increase its power; and his proposal for a conciliar arrangement expressed the hope that the domains might play a larger role in national policy. Yet Yokoi and his more active contemporaries Ōkubo and Takasugi were also realistic enough to accept the elimination of the domains as administrative units if necessity required.

Yokoi's domainal reform proposals represented an implicit critique of the Tokugawa system, in contrast with the pallid reformism of the Mito school, which called for realignment of ethical relations to achieve a tranquil and prosperous order. The echoes of the Tempō reform were still audible to him; and while he stopped short of calling for an abandonment of the "feudal system," he knew that more was needed than a mere "adjustment"

---

[83] See Yokoi's "Letter to Katsu Kaishū (November 1864)" when, on the eve of the *bakufu's* first punitive expedition against Chōshū, he saw this as an opportunity and a principal reason for unification of Satsuma, Higo, and Echizen. *YSi.*, pp. 450–451.

of the techniques of moral suasion. Yokoi also knew that it was not enough to call for "economies" and frugality; in fact, it was unrealistic to ask people to give up "habits" which were no longer luxurious but essential to daily living.[84] In a letter of 1858 to Shimotsu, Ogi, and Motoda he condemned the Mito policy of regulating existing industries more strictly while refusing to initiate new industries, arguing that "military and civilian arts rely too heavily on economy and thrift." [85] By failure to establish a legal system throughout Japan to regulate communications and trade, "the country today has become an impoverished nation." [86] To cope with the crisis of Japan, in the face of which traditional remedies were merely "meddlesome" (i.e., palliative), it was necessary to gain the wealth and power already achieved by the West. The object of his "mercantilist" reforms in Echizen was to secure "the independence of the country," which he listed first among twelve goals of national policy in 1866.[87]

The *bakufu,* which had wagered its existence on strict economies and agrarianism, had failed to guarantee security from without and to meet the growing needs from within. Its policies were inappropriate and out of touch with contemporary conditions, because they served only the (misconceived) interests of the Tokugawa house. "When Perry came to Japan and reported it was a country without political affairs, it could be said that he was perceptive, since the entire realm was divided into sections [against each other] and there was no unified system (*tōitsu no sei*)." [88] The country in his time existed as a loose amalgam of political units, all "emulating the conventions of their ancestral founders," including the domains directly controlled by the Tokugawa family. (While the Tokugawa represented a national authority in certain affairs, it drew its strength from its own base, consisting of land it owned directly and domains held by more or less dis-

---

[84] *YSi.,* p. 31.
[85] *YSi.,* p. 262.
[86] *YSi.,* p. 904.
[87] *YSi.,* p. 89.
[88] *YSi.,* p. 39.

tant branches of the family. The Tokugawa at any time was simply a lord among lords—but first among equals.) The Tokugawa as an instrument of policy had forced the domainal lords to "isolate their own provinces, not considering the harm to others so long as there was gain for themselves," working at cross-purposes, each in a "valley" cut off from its neighbor. "Neither the *bakufu* nor the several lords have escaped the narrow limits imposed by isolation." This impasse, as well as his own frustrating experiences in Kumamoto, motivated Yokoi to work out a better-unified scheme of administration. If, as he wrote to Tachibana Iki in 1856, there is "a common morality between lord and retainer," then there will be "agreement on national policy." [89] Of course, the policy must be formulated by the lord, who was surrounded with "talented advisers." The arrangement of authority was fixed, and must be observed to preserve order. "If there is no agreement between the lord and his ministers, the political affairs of the realm will be at cross-purposes." Neither shogunate nor domains had yet achieved the mechanism for a united effort. At the domainal level, Yokoi observed how progressives were censured by the daimyo for going against his will. He was looking for a way to admit talented retainers into important positions within existing administrative structures, both in the domain and on the shogunal (or national) level. This concern was embodied both in his support for *kōbugattai* and in his proposals for domainal reform.

Yokoi Shōnan observed at Fukui in Echizen that when a lord and retainer share one purpose, a consistent policy can be carried out. He was fortunate to be in the employ there of an able, and at times progressive, daimyo.[90] Together they hammered out domainal reforms which they believed to be generally applicable; further, they proposed a rearrangement of political elements at the national level consisting of broader participation among the lords to realize unified control. To increase the domain's fiscal

and military autonomy, Yokoi settled on the formula *fukoku
kyōhei,* a traditional metaphor with fixed associations, inspired
by his part in the Tempō experiment and his dealings with Mito
ideologues. Whereas Fujita Yūkoku had employed the formula
earlier to express the ideals of agrarianism (*nōhonshugi*), Yokoi
saw it as pointing to mercantilism. He had already to his own
satisfaction refuted the economic arguments for seclusion and an
exclusively agrarian "natural" economic order. It was essential to
promote traditional agriculture and well-established native industries; their products could be sold under official management to
avoid the venality of "deceitful merchants." (Yokoi never reconciled his enthusiasm for commerce and mercantilism with his
built-in class contempt for merchants.) This meant a systematic
countryside trade arrangement. They should begin by "investigating the monthly market prices of products at Nagasaki, Yokohama, and other places, so that we can determine prices and
costs." This survey would also indicate which items were selling
well. After the cost of freight was calculated, a price for the
product could be established. In this way (he reasoned) products
from Echizen could be sold, or traded, throughout Japan in the
most remote places.[91]

Such a trade policy was the first point of Yokoi's proposal for
economic development within the domain. The total volume of
the trade which he believed might result from expansion and development in Echizen alone would amount to 100,000 gold pieces
(*kin*) per annum. The new program for trade and its eventual
expansion throughout the domain would also require a commercial manager (*daitonya*) at each of Echizen's three ports, to
control excesses resulting from private practices of wealthy merchants and peasants. Such a procedure of control could be dupli-
cated by the *bakufu* in every domain throughout the country.
Second, it was important to increase productivity capacity within
the domain. He was aware of the "insufficiency of productive
strength" among many of the *han*'s producers, and believed that
official loans in money or grain would help overcome it. Here he

[91] *YSi.,* p. 33ff.

also urged, reflecting traditional prejudices, the avoidance of "useless expenses of debt in silver and gold specie." The government, at the same time, should make overseas loans at interest. "Government profit should come from foreign countries." Furthermore, "domainal administration should teach the people the methods of manufacturing." He cited textiles, especially silk, as an area where technology could increase production and "save human ability." [92] Yokoi, in his conviction that industry and commerce were inseparable, also sugested that new forms of livelihood would increase employment. He was confident that if all these measures were carried out, the basic capacity of the land would increase and the "emergencies of the day" be met.

Yokoi Shōnan's crude theory of economic development, amplified later by the early Meiji government, also took on the problem of samurai livelihood. By the 1850s the stipends of samurai in most domains had been reduced to subsistence level. The functions of the majority unable to find paying bureaucratic jobs were questionable, their social superiority a mockery. The Meiji government in the 1870s promulgated measures to use this pool of manpower without antagonizing the samurai class. The *shizoku jusan* ("samurai rehabilitation policy") was integrated into the government's overall program of economic development.[93] Yokoi much earlier had felt the samurai discontent and waste in human talent. In the 1860s in Echizen he proposed the employment of impoverished samurai in new ventures as part of his policy of domainal economic development. As with the planners in the Meiji Finance Ministry, Yokoi's attitude toward the samurai was one part sentiment and nine parts economic logic. His "Essay on the Warrior's Way" (*Shidōron*) in the *Kokuze sanron* shows the same faith in the natural superiority of the samurai that Iwakura Tomomi disclosed later in pleading their case.[94] Both men also recognize in the samurai as a class a key to the

[92] *YSi.*, p. 34.

[93] See my article, "The Meiji Government and Samurai Rehabilitation," in *Journal of Asian Studies* (August 1960), 19: 4.

[94] *YSi.*, p. 49–56.

general expansion of the economy. Yokoi argued that the policy of *fukoku kyōhei* must also take on the job of alleviating the distress of the class. Since industry and mercantilism opened new opportunities for mass employment, "these companions (*shi*) can be collected and placed wherever they desire to work." Samurai interested in maritime trade would be removed to coastal areas and given the proper equipment; those desiring work in sericulture would be provided silkworms and other supplies. In general, samurai families would be encouraged to pull up roots and transplant themselves wherever they were needed. This program involved dropping prohibitions on the samurai from working with their hands; it would relieve certain domains of overpopulation and unemployment; and it would diminish the sociogeographical ties of samurai. When the later Meiji government sought to encourage this migration, one of the aims was to break up the social cohesion of the class by removing it from centers of sentiment and memory. Forcing them into nonmilitary and nonadministrative tasks would also help destroy managerial exclusiveness. Yokoi had the same thoughts in mind when he suggested such an occupational regrouping in Fukui. Moreover, he saw in the relocated samurai what the later planners hoped for in Hokkaido: laborers who might double as sailors or soldiers in times of national emergency.

Yokoi showed concern at times over the need for capital accumulation. It had not been a problem in earlier times when few products were available. But today if "we are to elevate the people's wealth, capital is needed." His solution, along mercantilist lines, was to export products "which are being manufactured in great proportions" to foreign countries. And Yokoi was sufficiently acute to realize that profit from domainally controlled trade could come only from open ports, where domestic and foreign traders would meet. He believed that if open ports were established in Echizen as an inducement to foreigners, then trade would change character; local barter would be replaced by foreign purchase of local products from western Japan with hard money—which could be used to expand local business and rural industry.[95]

Beside the plan just outlined for the "wealth of the realm" (*fu-koku*), the second part of Yokoi's plan of domainal development was for the "strength of the army" (*kyōhei*). His devotion to a "rich realm" grew in part out of his recognition that only wealth could secure military power. Like others who abandoned *jōi*, Yokoi learned that a modern military establishment cost more than Japan could afford. He remarked that the encounter between Japan and Western powers had so far produced among the Japanese neither a slavish reliance on Western military techniques nor a powerful army able to defend the realm. "The defense of the Japanese archipelago is not to be found in the creation of a strong army that is more powerful than a navy." Yet, he lamented, a navy had never been part of the Japanese military tradition. Mercantilism, colonization, and large navies went hand in hand.[96] Japan possessed the natural advantage of being an island nation "alone amidst the eastern seas." Its relationship to the Asian continent was the same as England's to Europe. Its being an island discouraged invaders, who, in any case, could easily be kept off with a navy. Also, because Japan is an island, it must depend on the seas for trade with other nations. The best naval defense, he argued, citing the example of England, "is strutting about the adjacent seas, forcibly seizing lands with our navy, and cutting off this or that passage to our country." [97] In fact Japan could surpass the English by its tradition of iron discipline and heroic bravery, if only the *bakufu* would act.

Despite such grand flights Yokoi always returned to the immediate problem of *han* reform. Since the creation of a modern

---

[95] In the "Shojihengi (1863)," he suggests that in antiquity money was the property of the government, and in his day it belongs to the people. *YSi.*, p. 60.

[96] *YSi.*, pp. 42, 62–64; "Kaigun mondōsho," p. 19.

[97] *YSi.*, p. 46; also pp. 20–22, where the same argument is made in terms of progress and profit, retreat and loss.

navy exceeded the capacity of a single domain, defense proposals pointed to a larger common political purpose. A navy, he knew, was a national institution, yet beginnings could be laid at the domainal level. Yokoi viewed the larger political scene, *tenka,* as an amalgam of powerful semiautonomous units, exactly as powerful as its several parts. In the *Kokuze sanron* he asked how a law of state leading to the creation of a navy might be implemented under the present administrative arrangement. In a later petition on naval affairs (*Kaigun mondōshō*) addressed to Katsu Kaishū, he indicated that a balance must be maintained between the claims of the several domains and those of the larger realm (*tenka*). "The present anxiety which occupies both the realm and the several domains has been very important in unifying the people's spirit (*jinshin*). . . . How can the realm be elevated in unifying the domain?" Yokoi argued that a navy built up from the bottom was the answer. If the several domains agreed to construct ships in order to put together a navy, this would establish the base of something larger, the "navy of the realm which is the aim of unity." [98] If the base did not prosper, there was no chance of a national navy.

Yokoi's defense of a sound sectionalism was even more forceful in his political proposals for shogunal reform. These proposals were inspired by the emergence of a few powerful domains, and by his belief that this development toward domainal autonomy and participation in national policy should be encouraged. In 1862, a year after working out the military aspects of reform, he petitioned Matsudaira Shungaku in Kyoto on the political status of the reconstituted *han.* Matsudaira was then *seiji sōsaishoku,* a new office created in August 1862 as part of the *kōbugattai* mediation; it was nearly equivalent to shogunal regent (*tairō*) except that it was open to lords not from "related families." Yokoi's petition was ultimately directed at the *bakufu* and reveals, I think, a theory of countrywide political unification. It called for (1) abolition of the alternate hostage system (*sankin kōtai*), the proposal which shocked Sakuma Shōzan into resistance; (2) a

[98] *YSi.,* pp. 21–23.

return to their homes of all the families and retainers in the retinue of the daimyo; (3) appointment of men of ability to high shogunal offices, and removal of traditional prohibitions restricting these offices to retainers of families that were loyal or related to the Tokugawa; (4) opening of public discussions (*genro*) among various groups in the country to broaden political participation in national decision-making. Here (Yokoi argued) was a way of creating a realm that is "public" (*ōyake*), as against the private practices (*watakushi*) of the Tokugawa house. In such an arrangement, "politics," Yokoi wrote cryptically, "is really politics."

In these reform proposals Yokoi intended, not an alternative to established political rule, but a method to unify contending groups. He also hoped to give the *bakufu,* in revised form, a new lease on life at least during the political emergency. His most extreme proposal was abolition of the *sankin kōtai* system, since it revealed his belief in the need to change the actual principles behind political organization. The alternate hostage system had been designed as a shogunal stratagem to remove the lords from political participation and to keep the domains dependent and weak. Yokoi reasoned that the system was only an elaborate defense of shogunal authority against all possible alternatives. The abolition of the policy and the return of daimyo wives and children permanently to their homes was a humane gesture. But the reform of the system itself to let the lords spend their time in their own domains rather than in Edo would (as Yokoi wrote in countless letters during 1862) promote their participation in the political affairs of the *bakufu.* He hoped to change completely the established relationship between the lords and the shogun, and urged that actual political partnership was the surest guarantee to political unity and to sound decision-making at the national level. In the mutual participation of shogun and lord to determine national policy, Yokoi sketched out a new political structure for Japan. In 1861 he was simply concerned with returning to the relationship of lord and retainer that existed before the twelfth century, in order to prevent civil disturbance. But the call for the abolition of the alternate hostage system went beyond fear of civil war to clarify the relationship of lord and vassal between emperor and shogun, and to envisage a governing body in which the shogun was no longer dominant. Yokoi's later "Seven Points on National Policy" (*Kokuze shichijō*) connected the "abolition of the alternate hostage system" with "the establishment of a system in which people work for the throne (*chōkin*)."

In this attack upon the existing shogunal system and in his revision of the relationship between lord and vassal, Yokoi was calling for abandonment of the private policies of the *bakufu*. In their place he urged his contemporaries (especially lords in high offices) to establish a governmental system, authenticated by the emperor, to work for "unification and a republic (*kyōwa*) within Japan." The chief ingredient in this republic would be the large domains; its chief purpose, to relieve Japan of shogunal despotism. Yokoi again cited with approval George Washington, who "abolished the principle of lord-vassal relationships and earnestly worked for a public republic (*kokyōwa*)." Writing to Matsudaira Shungaku in 1862, he urged "the abandonment of the selfishness (*owatakushi*) which the Tokugawa *bakufu* has pursued since it acquired countrywide authority." It was time to "reform the nonpolitics (*ohisei*)" of the Tokugawa and to "govern the realm" in the public interest. There was no way to save the *bakufu* but "returning the realm to the public" (i.e., to the lords of the larger domains). Recalling one of the most problematic issues in Chinese and Japanese political thought, Yokoi in criticizing shogunal "privatism" implied that the real question for Japan was "a conflict between private and public interests (*kōshi*)." He warned that the continuation of "private politics" would interfere with the establishment of a government pursuing the "public spirit" (*minshin*). "Because we have been obliged to express loyalty to the *bakufu*, we have lost the will to respond to [the needs of] the realm." The time to "tranquilize the public spirit" was upon Japan, not by strengthening "the private interests of the *bakufu*" but rather by "following the public interests of the realm." At about the same time, in 1862, Yokoi expressed the same sentiment to his student Motoda Eifu, later tutor to the

Meiji emperor. To Motoda he equated private politics with oppression and argued that establishing a realm governed in the public interest would result in "a renovation of the country" (*tenka ishin*). The clarification of the two realms of private and public "must be the aim of reform today."

Yokoi's reform policies and the political theory behind them accused the Tokugawa *bakufu* of guilt for monopolizing the channels of political power. Rather than serve the realm, the Tokugawa pressed it and its resources into their private interests. This policy had undermined the strength of the domains, destroyed the life of the people, and left Japan unprepared to meet the crisis of *kaikoku*. The *bakufu* must "seek repentance for its selfishness and apologize for the past." He wrote to the *bakufu* in a petition of 1862 that if the conditions of the times were made to correspond to heavenly ordinances and the human spirit, if the great principle (*taigi*) of the lord-vassal relationship were reinstated and affairs so conducted that the lord (emperor) commands (*kummei*) and the retainer obeys, then "the human spirit and the imperial country will surely become unified." Despite the vagueness and generality of these charges, Yokoi tried to give them concrete shape. His republican political arrangement was expressed in what later Meiji politicians called "public discussions" (*kōgi yoron*), which meant, in the early 1860s, permanently retaining *kōbugattai* and consulting the lords on questions of national import. But Yokoi, in contrast to the restorationists, saw in "the consultation of public opinion" (*kōgi yoron*) not simply the power of imperial sanction but an expression of the will of the state. The shogun was limited to being chief lord among the lords.

Yokoi was making these recommendations over against restorationist clamor for an expedition against the *bakufu* and the barbarian. He rejected restorationist violence and the demand (as with Maki and Kusaka) for a dismantling of the *bakufu;* these things defied "the principle of heaven and earth," and Japan was too weak to face the consequences of an action against the foreigner.[99] Yokoi's sectionalism meant working to diminish sho-

[99] *YSi.*, pp. 97–98, "Kokuze shichijō."

gunal authority but not to destroy it. Even though he expressed these views during the brief years of *kōbugattai* fervor, there is every reason to believe he continued to hold them right down to the Restoration. Yokoi respected the court, but did not exalt its claims, since he was a Confucian rationalist who believed in the "Kingly Way" (*ōdō-ron*). He also respected the *bakufu*, which he believed should continue to play a role in national affairs; its complete removal, he feared, would lead to political disorganization. But since recent history had showed the shogunate to be incapable of exercising supreme powers or speaking for the realm as a whole, Yokoi concluded that it should be demoted in the coming rearrangement of power. He agreed with extremists in Chōshū that the *bakufu's* dealings with the foreigner and unwillingness to obey an imperial command called for a new political arrangement. His commitment to the "independence of the country" (*kokka*) prompted him to avoid recurrence of internal disturbances. Hence his constant admonition "to secure the basis of independence," and his equation of the assemblage of strong domains to a unified realm. He told Katsu that contemporary conditions were forcing a unification of the public spirit, and he was concerned about the relation between a unified domain and the prosperity of the broader realm. This concern expressed his public position as Matsudaira Shungaku's adviser and his firm belief in sectionalism, which remained with him even after the failure of *kōbugattai*. In the reorganization he envisaged, the *bakufu* was slated to play only the role of one among the domains.

How strongly Yokoi retained this sectionalism after restoration is hard to say; probably he saw it as a necessary step to a more permanent arrangement. Since he had already rejected the status ethic in the *han,* he was no doubt willing to let the domain wither away if conditions required it. For his day he sought to promote a federated grouping of the large domains under the nominal authority of the emperor. When he called for "efficient government" and the "opening of public discussions" in the *Kokuze junijō*, he was stressing the importance of a broader base of political participation. Still, this federalism was supposed to operate within a modified *bakuhan* framework. Yokoi was not clear about the precise role of the *bakufu;* and while he viewed the Tokugawa as the largest domain among the domains, he was uncertain about the administrative functions to be exercised by the shogunate. The question was answered for him by extreme sectionalist like Ōkubo and Takasugi when they turned to destroying the *bakufu.* In one of his last political petitions, written to Matsudaira Shungaku while under house arrest (1867), Yokoi still affirmed his belief in a federation of larger domains. Conditions had changed, he noted, and even though the *bakufu* had not been abolished, its powers had been greatly reduced. The four domains of Satsuma, Chōshū, Tosa, and Hizen had thrown in their lot with the imperial court. "Since it is a time of great change, a deliberative assembly (*gijiin*) has to be established. The upper house will seat courtiers and lords; the lower house will be composed of the most able men in the country, selected on the basis of talent and ability." The four domains would be obliged to establish some sort of administrative system if it was found necessary to remove the *bakufu.* Yokoi repeats to Matsudaira here the same concern he conveyed to Tachibana years earlier: because the times were unique, decisions should be preceded by "public discussions" among the political principals.[100] Yokoi promoted "sectionalism" as a step toward broader political participation, and further toward a new political arena offering unification of purpose. His sectionalism was less extreme than that of Ōkubo and Takasugi; but Yokoi did not have to make the decision before them—destruction of the *bakufu* or of their own domain. His moderate proposals, careful and deliberate, did not have the backing of either a large domain or the *bakufu.* He was interested not in aggrandizement for any particular domain, but in broader political participation adequate to national needs. In the opening stages of political reorganization Yokoi used institutions at hand; this did not preclude future evolution of a truly federal system free from the onerous task of representing domainal autonomy. He hoped for what Sakamoto Ryōma wished to avoid:

[100] *YSi.,* pp. 232–233.

the monopolization of power by a few large domains, paying lip service to the ideal of "public discussions."

Among his contemporaries, none came closer to modernizing a traditional ethic for contemporary action, or to shaping a unified state supported by broad consensus and participation. No doubt Yokoi's domainal affiliations spared him excessive concern to preserve the *han* at all cost. He saw it as a convenient unit of organization which could eventually be superseded in the continuing process of unification. This view was shared by Ōkubo and Kido in their late attempts to divest decision-making of its sectional ties. But Yokoi did see the domain, transformed by *fukoku kyōhei,* as an essential part of the political development in Japanese society. His proposals were later utilized by the early Meiji government, as in the Five Charter Oath and in the creation of deliberative assemblies composed of lords and upper-ranking samurai.

It is perhaps significant that Yokoi Shōnan, the most moderate among later Tokugawa political reformers, was the first casualty of the Restoration. He had worked hard to smooth the transition into a political order that would represent the important elements in Japanese society. It was his lifelong purpose to shape the splintered fragments of late Tokugawa political life into a unified order able to meet pressures from without and problems from within. In the tumultuous *bakumatsu* generation of activists and ideologues, he was one of the few who lived to see the Restoration and a partial realization of his political proposals. That he was singled out by malcontents, who saw in him and in the Restoration the destruction of a way of life which they blindly sought to preserve, is a tribute to Yokoi's intelligence and to the vision informing his political consciousness. What better epitaph for Yokoi Shōnan than the vindication statement (*zankanjo*) of his assassins? "He intended to make our splendid divine land a vassal state of the ugly barbarian who are like sheep and dogs." Or in his own words, an early sentiment of 1860, expressed in Chinese, which served as navigational guide for his course: "In clarifying the Way of Yao and Shun and Confucius, we must exhaust the skills of Western technology. Why stop with enriching the nation? Why stop with strengthening the army? Our task will be in spreading the great principles of the sages to the four seas." [101]

[101] *YSi.*, p. 728.

VII *Epilogue*

SECTIONALISM INTO NATIONAL UNITY

The only reason that Yokoi Shōnan's vision of broader political participation could include even the *bakufu* is that he was debarred from active politics at the time. It is also true that throughout his career he favored reform based on existing elements. Yet he was flexible enough that he did not have to rely on the *bakufu* once history required new adjustments; all along he had been looking ahead to the resolution of crisis when a more effective structure might be erected. His reevaluation of "sincerity" or "truth" (*makoto*) paved the way for a better theory of leadership by elevating experience and perception over received norms. Through the exercise of *makoto,* Yokoi believed, men could always understand the needs of their times, free of irrelevant precedents. In his admiration for George Washington and in scattered opinions about representative institutions we have a glimpse of the future order he had in mind for Japan. And it is important for Yokoi, as for many contemporaries, that it was a future order. Restoration liberated men from the immediate past to entertain the shape of things to come, without being utopian. In the meantime, Yokoi could wait and adapt his thinking to changes in the political and social environment. Inspired by the example of the semimythic age of the Three Dynasties, he wrote in an early letter to Tachibana Iki: "Everything will turn out well without the slightest meddling, either this year, or the year after that, or in a lifetime, or even after death. I believe that to serve with sincerity (*makoto*) is the moral way." [1]

The "meddling" Yokoi spoke about was the wild activity of loyalists promising revolutionary changes; yet it ultimately made all the difference between his moderate views and the Meiji Restoration. Yokoi to the end believed in moderate reform based on rationality; not a full-scale reorganization, but one which used existing political elements. He saw the solution to Japan's political problems as a realignment of elements such as the shogunate and domains, not their abandonment. He saw this realignment as taking the form of a conciliar arrangment, consisting of an upper and lower house presided over by the emperor; this was his way of satisfying the *kōbugattai* movement. Such a council, he believed, would accurately reflect the strength of its constituents which recently had gained power—the emperor and the large domains. It would also provide proper representation to the reduced authority of the shogunate. But just as the restorationists dissolved as a coherent group in the summer of 1864, so the supporters of *kōbugattai*, among whom Yokoi was the acknowledged theoretician, also failed at about the same time.

It is not my purpose to detail the failure of this movement to bring about a "unification of court and military." [2] This moderate formula, devised by the Satsuma lord Shimazu Nariakira in the 1850s and later adopted by Yokoi, was launched during the frenzied days of restoration, expulsionism, and terror. The *kōbugattai* party consisted of daimyo of large domains who were unwilling to support exclusively either imperial loyalists or the *bakufu*. Many of the lords of this group had sided with Mito Na-

---

[1] Quoted in Kōsaka Masaaki, *Japanese Thought in the Meiji Era*, trans. David Abosch (Tokyo, 1958), p. 28.

[2] The most exhaustive treatment of this subject is in *Ishinshi* (Tokyo, 1942), III, 639–712; a shorter and more convenient account is Sakata Yoshio, *Meiji Ishinshi* (Tokyo, 1960), pp. 151–186, and Tōyama Shigeki, *Meiji Ishin* (Tokyo, 1954), pp. 116–169.

riaki's son Hitotsubashi Keiki in his bid to become heir to the shogun Iesada during the succession struggle in 1857–58. They included Matsudaira Keiei, Yamauchi Toyoshige, Date Muneki, and Shimazu Hisamitsu; in the years after 1858 they continued to operate as a coherent group, seeking to mediate between an emerging radicalism gathered around the imperial symbol and a shogunal administration growing rapidly inept. In the end they favored reform of the *bakufu* through broadening of participation in the determination of policy. Their aspiration, documented in the writings of Yokoi Shōnan, was to induce the *bakufu* to share power with them. The group gained some political prominence in 1862–1863 when, after successfully pressuring the *bakufu*, they won appointments for some of their members in Edo and in Kyoto.

The *kōbugattai* movement failed initially because the new offices created to bring about conciliation between "court and *bakufu*" possessed no real authority either in Edo or Kyoto. Also, both *bakufu* and anti-*bakufu* partisans were reluctant to give up power to a group of great lords; and the factionalism among members of the group prevented unity of purpose. But beyond all these reasons, the formula itself was destined to failure owing to its essential vagueness, reflected also in Yokoi's thinking. Yokoi recommended a two-house assembly that would represent the various interests. He was uncertain about the status of the *bakufu* and the Tokugawa family. It is certain that in the 1860s he did not stand with those who called for the demolition of both. We can assume that he viewed the shogunal bureaucracy as a possible element in the new structure. There is evidence in his writings to suggest that he saw in the *bakufu* a structure that might be used purely for the administration of policy, not its determination. Yokoi also saw the Tokugawa, now relieved of its autocratic control (as exercised through the shogunate over the past two hundred years), as simply a large domainal house occupying a seat in the upper assembly of lords. He was certain that because the Tokugawa owned so much land, they would play a powerful role in this new assembly.

Yokoi's idea of a two-house assembly was similar to the plan promoted by the *bakufu* official Katsu Kaishū at the time of the second punitive expedition to Chōshū in 1866. Katsu offered his plan to counter the program of Oguri Kōzuke (another shogunal official), which aimed at reconstituting shogunal absolutism by expanding its financial and military capability. This could be achieved only by confiscating the domains. Over against his program, which had support in shogunal councils, Katsu proposed return of the shogun's power to the emperor and establishment in Kyoto of a representative assembly consisting of two houses composed of lords deliberating under imperial sanction. Katsu's proposal diverged from Yokoi's in the direction of preserving the *bakufu*. But there were weaknesses in these programs which neither Katsu nor Yokoi was able to overcome. A deliberative assembly under the nominal direction of the emperor could serve the lords in their effort to reduce the authority of the *bakufu;* it could also provide the *bakufu* a base from which to recruit wider support for its policies. Yokoi saw a representative institution as a reflection of the *han*'s military and financial strength; Katsu saw it as a way to prevent political anarchy, civil war, and the displacement of the Tokugawa by a realignment of large domains. But neither was able to work out a way to resolve disagreements between constitutents—great lords, outer lords, Tokugawa interests, imperial supporters—or clarify the relationship between the two houses. In fact, there was little agreement among supporters of this plan on the composition of the two houses. In any case Katsu's plan, inspired by Yokoi's earlier formula of a "republic" serving "the public interest," was virtually the plan outlined in the Tosa memorial to which the last shogun, Hitotsubashi Keiki, acquiesced in 1867.[3] By that time a representative arrangement was seen as a guarantee by weaker domains such as Tosa and

[3] The relationship between Katsu Kaishū and Sakamoto Ryōma is fully described in Marius Jansen, *Sakamoto Ryōma and the Meiji Restoration* (Princeton, 1961), especially chapter 4. Through Katsu and service to him Sakamoto met Yokoi, who had long been associated with Katsu, and was given the opportunity to talk with him on several occasions.

Echizen that the new order would not be dominated by Satsuma and *Chōshū,* whose members had already taken the lead against the *bakufu.*

The failure of Katsu's proposal coincided with the *bakufu's* plan to reconstitute itself as a centralized power. The plan presupposed the dissolution of large domains, especially Satsuma and Chōshū. Both extremists (Arima, Kusaka, Takasugi) and supporters of *kōbugattai* (Nagai Uta, Shimazu Hisamitsu) from Satsuma and Chōshū were either killed for their beliefs or shaken out of their convictions. And both domains had already been forced into a naked confrontation with foreign military power. The bombardment of Kagoshima in 1863 by the British (over the Namamugi incident), and of Shimonoseki in 1864 by an allied fleet (in retaliation for damages inflicted by Chōshū against foreign ships in the straits of Shimonoseki), convinced even the extremists in Chōshū and Satsuma that expulsion could not be carried out with resources then available. To deal with the domestic problem, now dominated by the *bakufu's* threat to destroy the large domains, and the external problem, made very real by the foreign bombardments, activists found in past solutions, such as the domain-centered *kōbugattai* movement and restorationism, building blocks of a new political organization and action. Faced with a struggle for domainal survival, former activists of the restorationist movement—together with supporters of *kōbugattai* like Takasugi Shinsaku and Kido Kōin of Chōshū, and Ōkubo Toshimichi of Satsuma—grasped clearly that overthrow of the *bakufu* was the indispensable condition of any solution to both external and internal problems. To their theory of "sectionalism" (*kakkyōron*) they applied the formula *fukoku kyōhei,* which had grown out of *han* reformism in the 1850s and had recently been elaborated by Yokoi Shōnan. From the *sonnō jōi* extremists (Yoshida Shōin and Maki Izumi) they took the idea of a restoration of direct imperial authority. The big novelty of putting sectionalism under a higher principal of authority, the emperor, was elicited by a new purpose: destruction of the *bakufu* and construction of a new political unity. The Restoration of 1868, and the subsequent creation of a unified polity, grew directly out of the sectionalist program to destroy the *bakufu*. The initial motivation of the sectionalists was provided by the *bakufu*'s decision to destroy the major domains; but behind this immediate threat lay the more profound conviction, shared by most activists, that the recruitment of men of talent and ability for positions of political responsibility was the basic condition for an independent Japan. The advance planning of the activists in 1867 and 1868 went no further than overthrowing the *bakufu* to insure the survival of the domains and the recruitment of what Iwakura Tomomi called a "government of talent and ability." This sectionalist route to restoration was marked out by Takasugi Shinsaku of Chōshū and Ōkubo Toshimichi of Satsuma through the resources of their great domains. These two men, major political actors in bringing the *bakufu* down, converged on sectionalism from different directions: Takasugi from a vague culturalism, based on the Mito discrimination of duties and designations (*meibun*), and from expulsionist extremism; Ōkubo from his involvement in *kōbugattai* in the late 1850s and early 1860s.

In a long letter of 1866 to his nephews in the United States, Yokoi Shōnan described the military situation: the conflict between Chōshū and the *bakufu,* and the recent battle at Kokura. After reporting appeals for help in Kumamoto by emissaries from Chōshū, Yokoi turned to events in Satsuma in the midst of an emerging civil war.

Satsuma has decided as a domainal proposal to harden its independence (*jikaku*), and it is all the more relying on enriching the *han* and strengthening its army (*fukoku kyōhei*). In general it has acquired Western military equipment, and summoned four to five Westerners as well, in order to assure prosperity of military exercises. The younger retainers wear Western clothes [uniforms] with their hair bobbed. Travelers within the domain are subject to strict prohibitions at certain places. But inside Kagoshima merchants of various areas and countries, where it is permitted, have been allowed to enter for business. The area around the castle has prospered daily, and the domainal programs understand how to carry out a wise policy that has great returns.[4]

[4] *YSi.* (chap. 6, n. 8), p. 489; see also Nakaoka Shintarō's remarks on Takasugi and Chōshū in his "Jiseiron," in Inoue Tetsujiro et al., *Kinnō shishi ibunshū*, 4 vols. (Tokyo, 1936), II, 438–439.

Yokoi applauded the program as an expression of "sincerity" (*makoto*) and "justice" (*kōhei*); he could as well have been speaking about Chōshū and other domains which were promoting "restorations" within their own boundaries before becoming involved in a national restoration.[5]

The temporary withdrawal of Chōshū to sectional reform in preparation for return was best expressed in the political thought of Takasugi Shinsaku (1839–1867) in the years after the destruction of the *sonnō jōi* movement.[6] Takasugi was one of Yoshida's closest followers, a fellow extremist with Kusaka Genzui and Irie Sugizō, and later a domainal reformer with Kido Kōin. While Yoshida viewed Kusaka as his ablest student, it was Takasugi who could free himself from a slavish devotion to *meibun* and oppose his teacher. Takasugi passed judgment on Yoshida's recklessness in action, which he described as "jumping to his feet" without purpose. Takasugi rejected spontaneous and unrestrained loyalty, brilliantly and tragically portrayed by his teacher, for a more restrained theory of action based on "calculation"—according to Yoshida, on "self-interest." And his independence earned Yoshida's scorn, recorded in a letter where the teacher berated the student for seeking meritorious deeds. Their reconciliation before Yoshida's execution did not affect Takasugi's growing independence.

Doubt whether Yoshida's methods were correct crept over Takasugi early. In a letter (November 1858) to Sufu Masanosuke, a leader in Chōshū, he complained that Yoshida's exploits were bringing shame to the *han*. "It is foolish of men today to

[5] Ikeda Kiyōmasa, "Bakufu no tōkai to Boshin sensō," in Iwanami kōza, *Nihon rekishi*, pp. 261–298.

[6] Information on Takasugi is sparse. Albert Craig in *Chōshū in the Meiji Restoration* (Cambridge, 1961), throws some light on Takasugi's activities during the civil war. I have relied on Naramoto Tatsuya's recent biography, *Takasugi Shinsaku* (Tokyo, 1965), and the sections on Chōshū politics in Shibahara Takuji, *Meiji ishin no kenryoku kiban*. For Takasugi's political ideas I have used the basic collection, Tōgyō Sensei Gojunensai Kinenkai (comp.), *Tōgyō sensei ibun* (Tokyo, 1916).

ask if embellishing vocabulary, practicing sword playing in the morning, reading books at night, refining sincerity, and striving to be filial and loyal to the lord will be enough to destroy our enemies." Despite Yoshida's intent, Takasugi explained, he thought that his actions would bring only further criticism from Chōshū's enemies. While he criticized Yoshida's tactics and craving for followers, Takasugi shared his sense of crisis. He learned from Yoshida who his enemies were, but turned away from him when he discovered he was not learning how to deal with them. He wrote Kusaka in 1859 that he had changed his mind about the nature and purpose of learning. "Until recently I have been extremely foolish. In considering my positions . . . I realize I have made mistakes. I do not wish to be like those known in the world for their erudition. Nor do I desire to be like those who deceive people with empty theories. . . . It is my purpose to study nothing but economics, in order to serve such people as you. What little I can do, will be to put my thought night and day into the service of the chiefs. I will endeavor to strengthen the millitary system within the august realm." By the "realm" Takasugi was referring to the country as a whole. Takasugi also records in this letter his abandonment of a literary career, in exchange for practical learning useful to the domain; in particular, a knowledge of economics and military affairs. Where he differed from others who exprsssed this sentiment was in being serious about it, as proved by his subsequent political career, dominated by action. Unlike Kusaka, who agreed with this declaration but wished to replace doctrinaire Neo-Confucianism with "intuitionism" (*ōyōmei-gaku*), Takasugi was not interested in a simple exchange of masters. Takasugi's commitment to practicality (*jitsugaku*) in the shape of technological support for the *han* did indeed limit his political vision; he saw the domain as imperiled only by "outside" forces.

Takasugi's insight into the Japanese problem was deepened by a trip to China in spring 1862. He was serving as attendant to a *bakufu* official on the ship *Senzaimaru* bound for Shanghai, on a mission to investigate trade in China; its personnel was made up of retainers from several *han*. Others on board played roles in the Restoration era: the Saga retainer Nakamuda Kuranosuke, one of the founders of the Meiji navy; Godai Saisuke (later Tomoatsu) of Satsuma. Takasugi kept a detailed diary (*Yūshu nikki*) of the trip and his two-months' stay in Shanghai, in which he was witness to the virtual collapse of the Ch'ing state. Upon entering the estuary of the Yangtze River he noted how closely the coastal scenery and color resembled Japan. In Shanghai he saw Chinese, who should have held positions of authority in their own land, impoverished and working in the most menial jobs. "In viewing earnestly the conditions in Shanghai, I have observed Chinese serving foreigners, and Englishmen strutting along the streets of the city. The Chinese are avoided in the streets and their ways have been replaced. In reality, though the territory of Shanghai is part of China, it should be said to belong to the English and the French." Takasugi expressed his fears in a short poem addressed to himself: "Will it not be like this in our country?" What was worse (he noted further in his diary) was Chinese dependence on Western powers. The Chinese possessed the *Gazetteer of Maritime Nations* (*Hai-kuo t'u-chih*) of Wei Yüan, but it had not equipped them with a defense plan or an understanding of armament. Two wars with the foreigner had been fought and lost. Owing to obstinacy and idleness "they did not know enough to absorb the new foreign studies." The Chinese around the Shanghai area, faced with a large-scale rebellion which threatened to topple the empire, had to rely on British and French arms to put it down—further proof to Takasugi of the complete reduction of the Chinese people to colonial status. Takasugi and his companions spent their time in part talking with foreigners and Chinese, but more (owing to language problems) in observing the new commercial and technological environment of the treaty port. He concluded, just before returning to Nagasaki in July, that it was unwise of the Japanese to attack foreign culture; rather, they should take it seriously, establish industries, and embark upon a program of foreign trade.

He rightly concluded that the decline of the Ch'ing state resulted from the Chinese "not knowing ways to resist the foreigner." But he also expressed enthusiasm for the practicality of Shanghai in a remarkable poem: "To begin to follow Western words, one must pledge himself to abstain from reading books in Chinese and Japanese." The powerful attraction of Western commercial establishments in Shanghai profoundly affected Takasugi's political consciousness. A year earlier he had made a special trip to the east to visit Yokoi Shōnan, who explained to him the need for practicality in daily affairs.[7] While in Nagasaki he noted in his diary the idea of "inquiring among the foreigners how trade and commerce arise from mountains, rivers, fields, and wilderness." Earlier he had stated that he never really opposed *kaikoku* but only the way it was forced upon Japan (also the view of Yokoi). Like many contemporaries, he feared that opening the country under such conditions would result in the seizing of control by the foreigner; Shanghai taught him that the possibility was real. Takasugi complained that *kaikoku* was devised by the shogunate to avoid embarrassment, and failed to bring the benefits of Western technology. In opposition to the *bakufu,* Takasugi and his associates resorted after his return to the most blatant xenophobia. He became one of the leaders of the *jōi* party in late 1862 and plunged into intimidation of foreigners, with plots of assassination and destruction of consular residences. His group sought to liquidate the foreigners by attacking them in Yokohama; failing in this, they set fire to the British legation at Go Tenmaya in December of 1862. How can this line be squared with his Shanghai experience?

Takasugi had long advocated foreign trade; his convictions were no doubt reinforced by what he saw in Shanghai and his conversations with Yokoi Shōnan. In spring 1862, at about the time of his trip, he wrote the essay *Nagasaki goshi no saku* (*A Policy for Nagasaki Trade*) discussing the defects of existing trade arrangements in the city. In particular, Takasugi was concerned with Chōshū's representation in the port city. The domain

---

[7] Ikeda Sutosu, *Takasugi Shinsaku to Kusaka Genzui* (Tokyo, 1966), pp. 116–117.

had negotiated the sale of local products in Nagasaki; but (he noted) improper methods resulted in the flow of profit into the hands of foreign merchants and Nagasaki businessmen. Rather than rely on established facilities, he urged, the domain should construct its own warehouse in the city and involve itself directly in the exchange of goods. Takasugi had become acquainted with Yokoi's scheme for economic development during their visit in 1861; in line with it, he called for studying the market in hope of times when the *han* could sell its products directly to foreigners. Under such an arrangement Chōshū would increase its share of profit and be thrown via Nagasaki into direct commercial relations with London and Washington. Takasugi's earlier rejection of Nagai Uta's "Maritime Policy" was consistent with his later mercantilism, since Nagai was promoting a commercial scheme which, Takasugi believed, would benefit the *bakufu*. He viewed the policy as a total capitulation of domainal integrity to the *bakufu* and even entertained the possibility of assassinating Nagai. (Nagai was forced by domainal authorities to commit suicide a little later because of this policy.) Takasugi's terrorism against foreigners and legations was merely an extension of this earlier view. He was not against trade or relevant foreign knowledge; but he was a sworn enemy of shogunal acquiescence to foreign demands. He was pledged throughout to the hope that commerce and technology would strengthen Chōshū—but not the *bakufu,* the foreigner, or the Nagasaki merchant. "It is not my intention," he wrote to Kido Kōin, "to contest the rights or wrongs of foreigners. My true intention is to contest the merits of the *bakufu.*"

Takasugi concluded by 1862 that continued existence of the *bakufu* was detrimental to the *han.* His language about "endeavoring in behalf of the imperial country" and "the way of the sages" was simply a policy of *fukoku kyōhei* in the service of Chōshū. "In reality, what we call working for the country is expressed in *fukoku kyōhei;* that is, strengthening the army will lead to an enriched realm. Even the sages meant this when they cited the popular belief that a realm must always have sufficient food and an adequate army. Today has brought out sages who also cry out loudly 'serve the country, serve the country,' but it has ended only in resentment." Yoshida had made "principle" and "loyalty" superior to a "meritorious (*ko*) act," without ever specifying what he meant; Takasugi elevated the notion of a meritorious deed to the level of principled loyalty (*gi*). He seems to have had second thoughts about his extremism, and to have reassessed his attack on the British legation and his "mad action" (*kyōko*) in Yoshida's categories. He decided that he had been performing meritorious deeds in order to call himself a loyalist, rather than in order to serve the realm and the people. He differentiated between the "true loyalists" (*makoto no kinnō*) and "great-achievement loyalists" (*kōmyō kinnō*). Despite this distinction, Takasugi's action, which he described in Kyoto as "true loyalty" was (I believe) reckless and vague and resembled what Yoshida had earlier described as "meritorious and selfish." Only after Takasugi became involved in domainal reorganization in Chōshū was he able to escape the charge of "merit" (*kō*) and assert a claim to loyalty (*gi*). Kusaka Genzui, as I have suggested, swung forever between the two poles of merit and loyalty without knowing the meaning of either. Only the full strengthening of domainal power, Takasugi argued in 1864, could produce the "realization of true imperial loyalty."[8] Those who engaged

---

[8] It is interesting to note here that just as Takasugi learned the meaning of true loyalty in the performance of service to Chōshū after his extremist experience, so his character changed. He acquired a discipline he never possessed. Takasugi was well known for his addiction to wine and women, and while he seemed to be anguished by this personal weakness, especially before the withering exhortations of Yoshida and the unyielding claims of loyal service, it wasn't until he returned to Chōshū in the spring of 1863 and his subsequent involvement in *han* affairs that he was able to mend his ways. Even on his return trip Takasugi was apparently drunk most of the way, having borrowed money for this spree from Sufu Masanosuke, which he blew by the time he got to Osaka. In Osaka he borrowed more money (his talents for borrowing were unprecedented), this time from the domain's offices in the city, and continued on what became a monumental bender. By the time he and his friend Hori Shingorō boarded a ship for Shimonoseki he was nearly penniless. Yet all this was to change in a very short period of time.

in quarrels in Kyoto, who criticized *bakufu* officials and the endless stratagems of the lords, were all guilty of "empty gestures" and "the loyalty of meritorious achievements." They were just talking and not performing acts of "true loyalty." Action in the domain, he later observed, was more important to him than the "loyalty" of a flamboyant desperation, even though he had once seen it as true loyalty. Hence Takasugi supported a commercial program directed by the *han* for its own benefit, while Yoshida and Kusaka could only lament the horrors of trade and commerce and reaffirm the external correctness of agrarianism (*nō-honshugi*). (Kusaka's *Kaiwan chigen,* written during the heat of loyalism and restorationism, was a blistering attack on the economic consequences of *kaikoku*.)

Yoshida shared the dread of Mito writers that the introduction by trade of new but useless products into Japan would destroy the natural order. Despite his radicalism, Yoshida in this respect still clung precariously to the authority of *meibun*. Yokoi and Takasugi had already gone beyond established order, since commerce by itself represented an assault on normative standards and a denial of the universalism of the Neo-Confucian ethical order. For Takasugi, trade and commerce, serving the needs of the *han,* represented both a response of the moment and a willingness to entertain a new kind of order. His "Policy of Trade for Nagasaki," little more than a restatement of Yokoi's *Kokuze sanron,* was a concrete program of "wealth and power" for Chōshū. The strengthening of Chōshū led him to the larger vision of sectionalism.

Takasugi's theory of sectionalism sought to overcome the selfishness of "loyal meritorious service" in which the individual "sold himself" instead of contributing to "the destiny of the realm." [9] Takasugi was able to act differently than *sonnō jōi* activists because he had shaken loose from the Neo-Confucian optimism which had hamstrung restorationism up to this time. Takasugi stated that the radicalism of recent years, which had become

[9] Naramoto, *Takasugi Shinsaku,* pp. 120–122. This is, apparently, the conclusion he reached before returning to Chōshū.

"bewitched" by the ethical and sacerdotal authority of the emperor, was an "empty gesture" (*kyodo*). "If we make Chōshū into a first-rate military and economic power (*kyō fukoku*) among the five continents," he wrote in 1866, the loyalists would look foolish and "their good name will become discredited." In what appeared to be a *volte-face*, Takasugi showed, as did Ōkubo at the same time, a real understanding of power: he gave teeth to emperorism by investing it with the real authority of a powerful domain.

Takasugi's sectionalism dates back at least to 1861, and perhaps to 1858, when he expressed a germinal version of the idea. From autumn 1862 to 1864 he worked it out in a series of letters.[10] They first denounced Nagai Uta's "Maritime Policy" and the *kō-bugattai* compromise (his one major disagreement with Yokoi); then they turn toward a constructive policy of *fukoku kyōhei* in Chōshū. He decided that the "imperial realm" which Yoshida hoped for was impossible without wealthy and powerful domains. Even during the years in which Takasugi participated in the extremist cause and acted on the stage of national affairs, his belief in the possibility of reconstituting domainal power stayed with him as a strong, but recessive, intellectual impulse. His writings show, even when he was most involved in "mad action," an ambivalence over priorities between the realm and the domain. The reason for this is difficult to find. It may have something to do with the fact that he occupied a higher status in the samurai ranking system than most of his colleagues, and that his stake in the domain was greater. It also may reflect a belief he revealed in many letters to Kusaka Genzui that the real meaning of "loyal action" was found only in a concrete plan relating to domainal affairs—that a program of action outside the *han* was a meaningless gesture. His involvement with Kusaka in Edo and Kyoto required his leaving the domain. But Takasugi, unlike Kusaka (or Yoshida), always showed a certain reluctance to commit himself fully to act at the national level. Takasugi's decision to plunge

[10] Naramoto Tatsuya, *Senkakusha no shisō* (Tokyo, 1966), pp. 137–141; also Naramoto, *Takasugi Shinsaku*, pp. 148–157.

into "mad action" was prompted by his associations in Yoshida's academy with people like Kusaka, Irie and Kido; but he never believed fully in the capacity of men to act meaningfully at the national level. Hence Takasugi ultimately left the restorationist movement at the height of its intensity.

In the end older beliefs surfaced, and the doubts he entertained about the correct course of action vanished. "Chōshū today," he complained in one of his letters, "and its four classes of people have been abandoned because of [higher] loyalties; it is the season to decide upon the life or death [of our domain]." "The *kōbu* mediation is completely useless . . . even though they [officials, lords, and retainers] have not yet decided one way or another today, they call this [indecision] loyalty. This empty and meritorious achievement is not true loyalty." Here and elsewhere Takasugi rejected, over and over again, as merely "meritorious" and selfish any conduct not rooted in a concrete plan. Something in Takasugi's psychological makeup drove him ceaselessly into refining his understanding of "true loyalty," as if the ghost of Yoshida Shōin tormented him to pursue the path of true righteousness. Through a painful and dangerous odyssey, Takasugi experimented with the range of possibilities open to him; along the way he plunged into the depths of personal dissipation as a condition of his final deliverance. In the end, Yoshida won out, and Takasugi found the meaning of true loyalty in a program to build up Chōshū *han.*

After the restorationist coups, at the time of the *bakufu's* first campaign against Chōshū (November 1864), Takasugi called for a "true sectionalism" and "a true start." "I believe that sectionalism (*kakkyō*) has to be a true sectionalism; that a start has to be a true start. A hasty sectionalism is not profitable. 'The heart that exhausts itself for the lord is a jewel, our broken bodies are like tiles.' A hasty start is credence to rumor." A "true start" and a "true sectionalism" could lead to a "great sectionalism" (*dai kakkyō*), which he never really clarified. Some writers have attributed to Takasugi a vision of national unity based on his theory of a sound sectionalism. It is difficult to say what he had in mind, since his commitment to the domain at this time eclipsed all

other considerations. Even if Takasugi was not consciously aiming at national unification, it was precisely the strength of domainal sectionalism that made political restoration possible. He
did envisage a larger unity, even though shapeless, when he
wrote: "If we do not push the prosperity of Chōshū and support
a mercantilist program, a great sectionalism will never be
realized." [11] Elsewhere he wrote more clearly: "If we resort to
trickery in promoting the purpose of Chōshū among the nations
of the five continents, the *dai kakkyō* will not be realized." If Takasugi's *dai kakkyō* meant a unified realm (as seems likely), it is
also true that his concern to strengthen the *han,* a sectionalist
stage in the development of a larger political organization, revealed that he was still operating under traditional political assumptions. His unified realm probably meant only centralization
of power in the feudal managerial class, against the defeudaliza-
tion represented by the *bakufu,* as in its recent policies against
Chōshū.

Down to the end of his life Takasugi helped organize the
Kiheitai, a domainal militia, to swing the domain away from con-
servatism to face the shogunal forces; hence it is natural that his
sentiments clung to the domain rather than to any vision of a
unified state. Unlike Yokoi, Takasugi believed he was fighting
for the survival of the domain and for his own life. He insisted
that all men should endeavor mightily for the Mori house; none
should ever forget he was a member of Chōshū, owing the *han*
loyalty and sincerity. If saving the *han* meant the destruction of
the *bakufu* and a rearrangement of political authority, so much
the better.[12] He wrote Yamagata Aritomo that "affairs today,
apart from being entrusted to the conditions of heaven, earth,
and nature, are not being guided by a good plan." If the destruc-

[11] *Tōgyō sensei ibun,* p. 184.

[12] It is well to point out that Takasugi's attachment to the domain did
not mean an attachment to the daimyo. His activities in the *shotai,* the
attack on Shimonoseki operating as a renegade and generally disregarding
the government in Chōshū (Hagi) is eloquent testimony to this sharp
distinction. It was the season for this kind of defection, and Takasugi had
before him the burning example of Yoshida Shōin who insisted on making
this distinction between *han* and lord.

tion of the various principalities were in some way averted, it would be done without any planning, by accident. His concern was the present and Chōshū, not the future salvation of other provinces; but had he lived beyond 1867, it is conceivable that he would have moved beyond domainal sectionalism to an idea of political unity.

Those like Ōkubo Toshimichi, Saigō Takamori, and Kido Kōin, who were most intimately involved in restoration and the destruction of shogunal power, also went on record for a sectionalism marked by wealth and power. Only an imperial restoration could provide the umbrella of political unification covering the real driving force of essential sectionalism. But the idea of a unifying imperial restoration was really a political illusion to which few men subscribed. Despite the religious claims in a restoration of imperial authority, and the unity it promised, most political participants saw little beyond some sort of sectional arrangement. This kind of thinking prompted Matsudaira Yoshinaga (Shungaku, lord of Echizen) to remark, echoing the words of his adviser Yokoi Shōnan, that "the public spirit of the realm is tending toward a breakup (*shibun hachiretsu*)." So also the lord of Tosa, Yamauchi Yōdō, proposed to a retainer that it was time "to erect the foundation of an august return of imperial authority and to encourage the cooperation of the several lords." Yamauchi Yōdō urged this program because, he believed, there were no principles left with which to unify the realm; everywhere he saw "the rise of sectionalism among the domainal lords, contempt of the foreigners in the land, and the decline of imperial authority." [13] In these circumstances, Yamauchi called for a "return to imperial authority" linked to "the cooperation of the several lords." But he also suggested that any effort to achieve a termination of the contemporary "disruption" and to realize an amicable political arrangement would depend on the good will of large domains—which, as with Chōshū and Satsuma, were preparing for autonomous existence.

Yamauchi Yōdō's sentiment was best expressed and realized by

[13] Ikeda Kiyōmasa, "Bakufu to tōkai . . ." (n. 5 above), p. 265.

Ōkubo Toshimichi (1830–1878).[14] Much of Ōkubo's commitment to sectionalism grew out of his contact with the Satsuma daimyo Shimazu Hisamitsu and his promotion of the *kōbugattai* compromise. Like other activists in the 1860s, Ōkubo saw sectionalism as continuous with earlier domainal reforms. His own disenchantment with *kōbugattai* came in April 1865 when the shogunate announced the second Chōshū expedition. Ōkubo made this issue the basis of a general assault on the capacity of the shogunate to act in the general interest. He saw the *bakufu* as acting against "popular feeling" and consigning Japan to the fate of Ch'ing China.[15] During the heyday of restorationism he was still an active proponent of moderation; when all eyes were fastened on Kyoto in 1862–1863 and a *kōbugattai* settlement there, he saw the possibilities of sectionalism. In a letter he wrote: "In a few days there will be published an imperial decree, stressing the importance of defending the country from the standpoint of *jōi*, and urging the several domains diligently to prepare themselves militarily." [16] A year later he was explaining to Matsudaira Shungaku and Yamauchi Yōdō in great detail a sectionalist theory of military preparations. From sectionalism he went on to a vision of new political unity. At this period Ōkubo accepted the policy of wealth and power already being promoted by Takasugi in Chōshū. In 1864 he was still arguing that "assistance to the

---

[14] On Ōkubo there is also a paucity of reliable writings. I have relied on his writings, Ōkubo Toshiaki, ed., *Ōkubo Toshimichi monjo*, 8 vols. (Tokyo, 1965–1966); Kano Masanao, *Nihon Kindai shisō no seiritsiu*, especially the sections dealing with the transmutation of *kōbugattai ron* into *tōbaku ron*, pp. 118–163; Matsumoto Sannosuke, "Sonjō undō ni kindaiteki seiji ishiki no keisei," in *Meiji ishinshi no mondaiten*, ed. Sakata Yoshio (Tokyo, 1962), pp. 166–167, and his brilliant article, "Tennōsei hōshisō," in *Nihon kindai hō hattatsushi* (Tokyo, 1961), 10: 3-40; and Tōyama Shigeki, "Ōkubo Toshimichi," in Tōyama Shigeki, ed., *Kindai Nihon no seijika* (Tokyo, 1964), pp. 16–78. Masakazu Iwata has written a biography in English, *Ōkubo Toshimichi, The Bismarck of Japan* (Berkeley and Los Angeles, 1965).

[15] In Tōyama, "Ōkubo Toshimichi," p. 18.

[16] *Ibid.*

bakufu will prosper the imperial court"; but a year later, faced with the domainal destruction threatened by the punitive expeditions to Chōshū, he threw in his lot with sectionalism. "The trend toward sectionalism among the various domains should not be taken lightly. There is nothing today except this great policy which promotes the power and wealth of one domain and the sudden illumination everywhere of the imperial authority." [17] Ōkubo helped topple the *bakufu* by advancing domainal sectionalism in Satsuma; everything else he said had been said before by Takasugi.

But Ōkubo went beyond Takasugi's domainal limitations. He lived to see events move the way he had wished through the Restoration and the destruction of the *bakufu*. His responses during the last five or six years of the Tokugawa era determined his decisions after the *bakufu* had been removed. He had as great concern for the *han* as spokesmen of lesser domains—Yokoi Shōnan, Nakaoka Shintarō, Sakamoto Ryōma—who, fearing loss of power after the removal of the *bakufu,* worked for a political arrangement preserving the integrity of all the domains. Ōkubo agreed with this formula provisionally but not permanently. Underlying "people's attitudes toward the state of affairs," he wrote his lord in 1862, "is an urgency of the times and the first principle of the public spirit." [18] If such attitudes are known, he argued, "all measures will correspond to the times." His letters from 1865 to 1868 refer increasingly to a "responsive humanity" in the country (lords eager to participate in national decisions), and the basic "disposition of human nature" to explain "all things" and to relate "all measures to the times."

Ōkubo also took on a problem never found in the writings of Takasugi (except for conventional sentiments on *kokutai*): the actual function of the emperor as a matter of practical politics. This problem was no doubt raised at the time of the second *bakufu* expedition against Chōshū, when Ōkubo felt obliged to weigh the

---

[17] *Ōkubo Toshimichi monjo*, I, 293.
[18] *Ibid.,* pp. 294ff.

imperial decree in terms of its possible consequences for Satsuma. He concluded like many in Chōshū that the decree did not represent the true will of the emperor.

Maki Izumi believed that an imperial decree, as in the case of expulsionism, should be obeyed, and that the *bakufu's* unwillingness to do so was justification for direct action. Ōkubo was more critical of the imperial decree as a device for policy. He measured the decree in terms of "the needs of the times" and the contemporary "public spirit"; and he saw, when the emperor sanctioned the second *bakufu* expedition against Chōshū, political ruin and an expression of sentiment that in no way corresponded to reality.

But Ōkubo surely believed that the emperor could serve as an effective symbol in the countrywide unification of sectionalism. Though he clung to domainal autonomy as base, this never precluded a broader structure under the nominal authority of the emperor. His concept of the emperor was closest to that of the nativists and (more recently) of the restorationists of the Bunkyū era. Like both, he conceived of this emperor as one who would not actually rule the realm, but rather would submit voluntarily to "an imperial administration" composed of representatives of the domains. Where he differed from his predecessors was in specifying the kind of political arrangement that might constitute an "imperial administration."

He also incorporated the conciliarist sentiment of *kōbugattai* that the authority of the emperor was merely another way of describing "the public opinion of the realm" (*tenka no kōron*). Hence Ōkubu insisted, when the *bakufu* announced its plan to destroy Chōshū, that decrees must always reflect the consensus of the realm; anything less was unworthy. "If a decree is an unprincipled decree," he wrote Saigō, "it is not an imperial decree and it ought not to be obeyed." [19] Here Ōkubo is clearly saying that the emperor does not personally execute power; rather, power must be mediated by the decisions of "the realm's peoples," as he

[19] In Kano, p. 147.

says in another letter to Saigō in 1865. The decree must reflect "the will of the people," a consensus among the domains and daimyo. Emperorism, in Ōkubo's pragmatic view, came to include a theory of broadening the base of political participation (*kōronshugi*). He politicized Maki's emperor. He transformed the idea of an imperial campaign, which Maki saw only as a means of destroying the *bakufu,* into a permanent arrangement by giving it institutional expression. Hence Ōkubo's concept of an "imperial administration," combining emperorism (as symbolized by the power of an imperial campaign) with the idea of *kōronshugi* was the way he tried to put into practice Maki's restorationist vision.

In the years after 1866, Ōkubo elaborated upon this notion of an emperor served by an imperial administration. It served him both to sanctify the "will of the people" and to move against the *bakufu*. For if there was such a thing as an unprincipled decree, then there was also the reverse, a principled decree requiring obedience. By such a decree the *bakufu* could be branded an enemy of the emperor, and the emperor could provide the political and human symbol of the countrywide unification of the domains against the *bakufu*. This is what Maki Izumi had urged a few years earlier. This vision could fulfill the hope of Takasugi's "great sectionalism," reformulated to satisfy the demands of political order. Here too is the meaning of Ōkubo's desire "to steal the jewel"—that is, the emperor, whom *bakumatsu* ideologues referred to in terms of the jewel, one of the three items of the divine imperial regalia. This phrase reflects the power of imperial symbolism, loaded with rich associations, even though it is certain Ōkubo never believed in personal imperial authority. He felt it necessary to liberate the emperor from shogunal control—and later, from courtiers, as in his effort to have the capital moved to Osaka. For Ōkubo actual imperial authority promoted two interrelated ideas: that "the country belonged to the emperor," and that proper political procedure depended on "the public opinion of the country." The emperor was limited but not without use. Ōkubo was quick to realize the importance of planned epiphanies in which the emperor would appear to the masses in all his humanity. His human presence served to reinforce the ethical associations of loyalty and obedience. "Seizing the jewel" promised what the nativists and Maki Izumi had long believed: voluntary submission of the ruled to the emperor was both an ethical and a sacred duty. In his thinking about the character of the emperor —"seizing the jewel," and the establishment of an imperial administration—Ōkubo showed his understanding of the idea that the "realm belonged to the emperor," even though it was "publicly administered." Yet at the same time, Ōkubo never expected this emperor to exceed the consensus of the domains, which was to become the "imperial administration" after the restoration. In a certain sense, Yoshida's "imperial retainers" were realized after 1868 when restorers constructed a centralized political order. The only difference is that Yoshida viewed his "imperial retainers" as swaggering loyalists, and those who acquired this status after the Meiji transformation were governmental functionaries.

Actual involvement in restoration changed Ōkubo's mind about the idea of broad political participation in decision-making which late Tokugawa sectionalism demanded. In the years immediately after the Restoration, Ōkubo seemed to abandon his earlier advocacy of a representative system, consisting of domains, as the imperial administration, for an arrangement of power that once more narrowed the base of participation. The removal of the *bakufu* from the arena of politics dashed the hopes of remaining conciliarists: Yokoi Shōnan, and Yuri Kimimasa who drafted the Five Charter Oath. Activists then jettisoned their domainal status to become imperial bureaucrats in a new national structure. Perhaps the new Meiji arrangement was described best some years earlier by the nativist writer Katsura Homeshige in his *Keisei yōroku:* "Even though the whole nation is the august treasure of the emperor, the countless number of people is today . . . entrusted to the shogun's house and to the several lords who hold down a variety of administrative offices and posts. All ordinances are transmitted as imperial messages. Because the

various lords serve the imperial court, should we not make it a
law of the people today to defend prudently and tenaciously the
august system of the imperial court and the imperial message?"

The Meiji Restoration was a realization of Katsura's plea: a
preservation of direct imperial authority. This concept provided
restorers such as Ōkubo in 1867 maximum political authority and
ironclad guarantees against possible political opposition among
the ruled. In the eyes of the ruled, as Motoori had seen much earlier, the emperor's intimate identification with the political and
public world ruled out for them any share in politics or legislation. Meiji leaders, in hoisting up the figure of an all-powerful
emperor, had no idea of actually broadening the base of political
participation. In the nervous years after 1867, they intended to
convert the personnel of the domainal system, the lords and their
retainers, into imperial administrators, who would now convey
the will of the emperor to the masses. The Meiji emperor merely
validated the new political arrangement; nothing seemed to have
changed except nomenclature. Yet everything had changed, since
it was a world, as the nativists had suspected, where only those
could engage in politics who managed, in Ōkubo's words, "to
steal the jewel," that is, the imperial symbol. The rest of humanity was obliged, as a religious and ethical imperative, to accept an
unpolitical role, cut off forever from the real world of decision.
Meiji leaders like Ōkubo Toshimichi found the nativist theory of
"direct imperial rule" the most flexible of ideologies. Revisions of
detail would not alter the permanent fact—spelled out by the
later constitution, the imperial rescript on education, and civil
code—of an absolute separation of public and private spheres,
which Motoori and succeeding nativists had established as an indispensable condition for political order. In this arrangement, as
Ōkubo knew, there was no middle ground between public and
private, between political and unpolitical, those who possessed authority and those who were required to submit voluntarily. Yet it
was precisely this political arrangement in Meiji Japan and beyond which made possible the dazzling successes of modernity in
the twentieth century.

THE RESTORATION RECONSIDERED

The inevitable question raised by our study is the relationship between the late Tokugawa discourse and the Meiji Restoration. Since most intellectuals in the late Tokugawa period were also activists, what is the importance of their thinking and writing? I have sought throughout simply to stress their perceptions of changing events and their responses to these perceptions. *Bakumatsu* ideologue-activists responded to immediate problems posed by a discontinuity between an inherited tradition and the course of contemporary history. Each in his own way, following the lead of the Mito program, sought to overcome the present by denying either it or the immediate past responsible for the present predicament. A synthesis of the tradition was provided by Mito writers, and throughout the Tempō years down to the coming of Perry there was widespread agreement among intellectuals on its elements. Agreement collapsed in the years after the opening of the country, and thereafter only isolated fragments of the Mito program appear. The quest to retrace steps and to rebuild splinters into a new unity under conditions which Karl Mannheim has described as "dynamic destabilization" was roundabout and involved in uncertainties and dangers. The ideas we have analyzed here were the product of a trial-and-error experimentation in the laboratory of late Tokugawa political society. Failure meant subjection or extinction; success, independence and survival.

Yet despite the vagueness in which men often expressed their ideas, there was intensity and meaning in them. In trying to come to terms with a collapsing intellectual tradition, writers chose not to abandon it completely but to reconsecrate it in a more attractive way. But while their efforts were a reconsecration of the inherited tradition, they were also something more. The most recent and fashionable description of the Meiji Restoration has been a change prompted by the tenacity of old values: under the propelling force of inherited tradition, activists sought, not to remake society in a revolutionary way, but rather to establish conditions that would satisfy traditional goals. Because the men who engineered this change possessed no detailed blueprint of things to come, it has been called, as one writer put it, "an unwitting act." [20] Implicit in this argument is the notion that revolutions by their nature must bring, in the wake of destruction, a new vision of society. Even so far as this is true, we have ample evidence that the vision behind the revolution is usually abandoned in the early days of reorganization.

More important to revolutionary events is the decision, on the part of activists, to abandon history before the pressure of the future. In this sense, it would seem that the Meiji Restoration, rather than being simply a political change powered by traditional values, was a revolutionary event. Despite its appeal to history and its reliance on a mythical past, there was a revolutionary impulse informing the Restoration even before it realized the social and economic ambitions of its makers. It should be remembered that one of the declared aims of the Restoration was to destroy the immediate past. In their promise to establish an order "based on the beginning of state foundation at the time of Jimmu Tennō" and "to wash away old abuses," restorers were saying something very revolutionary. While they appealed widely to "tradition," by 1867 there was no agreement at all on what constituted the inherited tradition. I would argue that the appeal to tradition was simply a device to promote schemes that were not traditional at all. This technique is clearest in the metaphor of restoration itself. Because men had long been calling for a repudiation of the past to ensure a proper commitment to the present, the restorers resorted to native mytho-history to express the newness of their effort. Just as they believed that the foundation of the state by the emperor Jimmu was a genuinely unique and revolutionary event, so they believed that what they were doing was the beginning of a new history. Uniqueness was the condition for starting out anew, and a liberation from old historical associations allowed them to act without the need to accommodate the past to their present or to the future.

[20] Albert Craig, *Chōshū in the Meiji Restoration* (Cambridge, 1961), p. 360.

On the face of it, the Meiji Restoration summoned traditional values. But we know that the men who dreamed of change and realized it were not tradition-bound. Although they experimented with traditional ideas and values, their experiments show they thought they were working with genuine historical possibilities. Yet such devices as a "benevolent polity," "practical studies," or "the public interest" were historically possible in name only, since, as I have tried to show, there was no agreement on their content. Ultimately these "traditional" values were sanctified under the names of "truth," "fidelity," "loyal action," and "sincerity." Rather than commit themselves to the traditionally agreed content of these concepts, activists and ideologues found security only in honesty of intent. Yet correct intent allowed them to interpret these traditional notions as freely as they desired, and such reinterpretation provided them the motivation to act on their newly formed judgments. In the end men called for the dissolution of history and for the reinstatement of a distant mythic past whose contours were never clear. But this call disclosed mostly the psychological need for a source of identity that would provide the uninhabited revolutionary energy required for the creation of a new order. A repudiation of history really meant the dissolution of public roles and the criteria of bureaucratic recruitment. It is for this reason that activists ultimately turned to dismantling the shogunate itself.

Writers and activists agreed on one thing: the offices of decision-making were being occupied by incompetents who did not deserve responsibility. They were right in charging that leadership of inherited institutions had failed precisely when the realm stood to lose its independence, and that this failure was the fault of the recruitment system. When they were unable to dent that system, they blamed not only the system of recruitment but also the institutions of decision-making itself. Late Tokugawa rhetoric is monotonously predictable on this point. The writers I select, and many others I omit, all express concerns for competence in office, for talent and ability as criteria of enlistment. Invocation of *jinzai* was of course itself drawn from the arsenal of traditional ideas; but its usage was not traditional. The Tokugawa political system had not absolutely precluded recruitment along the lines of talent and ability, but it had favored heredity. Writers first resuscitated *jinzai* as a critical device to expose the incompetence of the leadership; but once they saw its possibilities for change, the idea quickly underwent transformations which no Confucian would have recognized. This was especially true after it was combined with the notion of "practicality" (*jitsugaku*), which itself was undergoing profound changes to include new knowledge and methods. Armed with the slogan of "practicality," these men sought to express their belief in *jinzai* as the surest cure for Japan's political maladies. There is much personal motivation here. Men often had themselves in mind as candidates for responsible offices which had been denied them in the past, owing to their domainal membership or rank within the class structure. Whether they desired political power or economic wealth is irrelevant; political power provided an easy path to economic wealth. Men also often identified the resolution of their own psychological problems (including being out of office) with the resolution of national political problems. Even though Yoshida Shōin was the most insistent about his own indispensability, I have found few activists who did not share his conviction that the safety of the state hung in large part on themselves.

In 1856 Etō Shimpei, working as a scribe recording the trade of his domain (Hizen) with foreigners (*kawarishinakata*), wrote in his *Zukaisaku* about the promises of trade and renewed military power. But he saw beyond the sparkle of technique and money. Etō's experiences in foreign trade suggested to him the combination of *ōsei fukko* ("washing away old abuses") with "talent and ability" as informing principle in the social formula. "First we ought to enter into treaty relations with the powerful nations of today; then we will have to summon the ablest men in the realm and use them. Then we should buy warships and prepare ourselves in naval warfare. The prosperity of trade relations exists in enriching the country." [21] This sentiment was later repeated by

[21] Shibahara, "Hanbaku shosei ryoku no seikaku," in Iwanami kōza, *Nihon Rekishi*, I, 203. See also Kano Masanao, "Kindai shisō no hōga," p. 311.

the author of the *Hanron* and confirmed by Iwakura Tomomi when, in the most intense days of the Restoration, he wrote that *Ōsei fukko* was little more than the establishment of a government of talent and ability—a political upheaval motivated by men in search of public roles and responsibility. The demand for *jinzai* and *jitsugaku* in decision-making did not just mean universal standards of recruitment and performance, if indeed it meant that at all; it also implied a new elitism. By 1866 and 1867 Takasugi, Kido, and Ōkubo were really writing and acting for a different arrangement of political power. After the sound and fury of Yoshida Shōin and the fires of the Bunkyū restorationists, these two "traditional" values, which had become the possession of youth searching for public roles, were increasingly associated with the destruction of the *bakufu* and the hierarchy of inherited roles. What was initially expressed as a psychological protest of youth was changed into a major principle of political motivation. Young men grew older, if they lived, and those who lived were no less committed to this ideal in 1868 than in their youth. Moreover, it had been a fixed program of talented youths committed to "practicality" to change the roles themselves—to make history anew as a number of them said in chorus—if contemporary reality required it. The creation of new roles was the meaning of Yoshida's vague call for a restoration of ancient imperial prosperity, and the informing vision behind the Meiji Restoration; it satisfied the dual quest for identity and for public usefulness. While the Restoration appears to many to be a triumph of traditional values, it was still a young man's movement, like most revolutions, and its announced purpose was to break with old customs by observing the principle of talent and ability. Yoshida, Maki, Kusaka, and even Yokoi created the possibility of several new roles but played only one well: the revolutionary. Yet without the revolutionary there would not have been other roles to play.

What this "transvaluation of values" disclosed is a radical break with accepted usage. Writers and activists showed, in their various efforts, an enormous disposition to transfer the standard of value and judgment from institution, system, or class to the individual. This bursting new confidence in the individual's capac-

ity to make decisions apart from the group also marked the dissolution of inherited norms of behavior, conventions of taste, and
guidelines of thought. While its invitation was not extended to
the whole people (still only samurai were allowed to move
heaven and earth) its purpose was to demolish the privileged position of feudal values.

Much of this personalism stemmed from experience in horizon-
tally organized groups and academies. Many late Tokugawa activists and writers in their formative years experienced relationships which bypassed the established vertical moral hierarchy of
superiors and inferiors. Through domainal academies and less
formal educational groups, as well as the experience of leaving
the domain for further study in Edo, they formed horizontal relationships with like-minded samurai of other domains. The
peer-group ties were further reinforced by the fact that activists
belonged to the same generation.

Through exercise of personal judgment activists exchanged
laws and norms which had been emptied of meaning and relevance by *kaikoku* for practicality and usage in daily affairs. Thus,
while Sakuma flirted with *jitsugaku* as a means of establishing a
secure defense network, Yokoi Shōnan saw in it a transforming
principle in daily life. Tokugawa ideologues never went so far as
the later writer Nishi Amane in exploring how utility might be
translated into objective laws; but the transition from cultural ex-
clusivism to *kaikoku,* from an ethical Confucianism to adoption
of new technology, would not have been possible without commitment to practicality. Of course the consciousness of utility disposed activists to spectacular but purposeless acts which Yoshida
denounced as merely "meritorious deeds." And this often led either to premature compromise or to alliance with established authority. The cynical manipulation of the emperor, expressed in
Ōkubo's famous phrase "stealing the jewel," was one result of the
activist tendency to practicality.

If *jinzai, jitsugaku,* and the search for public roles served as the
forms of revolt in the late Tokugawa period, the sustaining motives were resentment and rage. Current historical writing has

made an inordinate effort to minimize the revolutionary dimensions of the Meiji Restoration; it has also underplayed the element of extremism in favor of moderation and good sense. Historians are quick to point out that the Restoration was a relatively bloodless affair, a smooth and orderly transition to a new concept of political order. If the revolution in fact never occurred (so the assumption runs), and if the change was carried out in the name of traditional values, then the events of 1867 and 1868 could not have been attended by wide-scale violence and bloodshed. For some curious reason we feel obliged to equate terror, bloodshed, and physical destruction with revolution. Revolutions have happened this way, but often the violence and terror are unessential spillovers. In the Japanese case, the apparent absence of sustained violence has prompted historians to argue that society was in a better position to promote limited reforms than to take on the totality of its problems. This is absurd in view of the ramifying reforms of the Meiji period; by the end of the century Japan had been virtually transformed into a new order. A further contention is that for all the sound and fury of *bakumatsu* extremists, it was the more moderate elements that had more in common with Japan's later modernity. But the precondition of a bloodless transition from restoration (*ōsei fukko*) to renovation (*ishin*) was in fact the extremism that had scarred the preceding decade and removed from the field of activity an inestimable amount of real talent and energy. In this sense the Meiji Restoration is no less a revolutionary event than better known and "classical" revolutions. The later achievements of "moderates" such as Kido and Ōkubo oblige biographers and historians to try and show that they were equally important before the event. Likewise, the later accomplishments of the Meiji state, for which these two can take a large measure of credit, force liberal historians to search out early roots of this "modernity" as if there were visible early in the *bakumatsu* a rational process of modernization.

Historians invest the "winners" with a prescience they never possessed, on the grounds that the "losers," owing to their extremism, could not possibly have generated the vision confirmed by later achievements. Despite controversy, it can be categorically stated that the Restoration as a discrete political event simply would not have been possible without the extremists, many of whom never lived to see the results of their convictions. Most principals in the *bakumatsu* drama were extremists of one sort or another. It is foolish to suppose that moderation, temporarily extinguished by hotheads brandishing swords at anything that moved, could possibly have provided motivation or energy for a political event such as the Meiji Restoration. The Restoration was propelled above all else by the rage of young men: rage at the coming of the foreigner; rage at the monumental incompetence of the shogunate, carefully concealed until it was exposed by the opening of the country; rage at the prospect of continuing incompetence and national deterioration; and finally, rage because they were being denied any opportunity to resolve the problems of the day. If the Restoration was not a revolution in the conventional sense, it was still the result of revolutionary rage which had been nearly dissipated in the struggles of the decade preceding the event; and while later Meiji politicians tried (for obvious reasons) to minimize the revolutionary character of their earlier work, there was no way to conceal an event that had destroyed history and wrenched life from its moorings to give the Japanese a new lease on the future.

Index